CALCULATED RISK

CALCULATED RISK

A GUIDE TO ENTREPRENEURSHIP

W. M Greenfield

W. M Greenfield Associates

D. C. Heath and Company

Lexington, Massachusetts   Toronto

DEDICATION

For my dad, who would have been pleased,
and my mom, who is.

PREFACE

There is a resurgence of activity in new ventures in the United States today. Even large companies are getting into the act, trying to figure out how to encourage the innovation and commitment that entrepreneurial activity seems to engender. There is even a new term for this activity within large corporations—"intrapreneurship." Yet, not unlike the pattern in earlier waves of entrepreneurial activity, the vast majority of new small companies is the result of the effort of just plain people.

For such individual entrepreneurs, there has generally been little formal assistance. Now, however, courses in entrepreneurial activity are springing up on college campuses and in business schools everywhere. As these courses proliferate and grow, a major problem has been the acquisition of adequate material—material that makes sense in the altered and increasingly frenetic atmosphere of the small business development field.

THE DILEMMA—AND MY SOLUTION

Most books about small businesses tell you how to run them or how to manage them. If what you want to know is how to start a small business of your own, there are two general sets of options, neither of them very practical or particularly appealing. On the one hand, there are popular books about how to make thousands of dollars at home in your spare time. On the other hand, there are scholarly studies of the kinds of people who start companies, what they start, and why they succeed. Until *Calculated Risk: A Guide to Entrepreneurship,* there was little between these two extremes. Now there is—and you have it in your hands.

This book was written, in fact, to fill that gap. I began developing the material that eventually became *Calculated Risk* because I could not find materials for my own course at Boston University that were adequate to help students work through the development of a practical business plan for a small company. Thus, *Calculated Risk* responds to the concrete, highly practical needs of people with ideas and dreams about (but no experience in) starting and operating their own businesses. It is intended to be useful to those who have never studied business before as well as to those who have had prior management courses.

Calculated Risk offers a step-by-step guide to what you have to do to put together a practical, workable business plan for a prospective business. Unfortunately, it will not guarantee business success. I have not yet found anything that will do that for you. (If I ever do come up with such a gold mine, my consulting company will rapidly develop a lucrative and unique sideline in guaranteed startups.) What this book *will* do is to show you why and how many business startups fail and offer help in working and planning around these critical problem areas.

In addition to the structured understanding of how a business is begun and the elements that must be developed to start a successful company, *Calculated Risk* provides a survey of basic small business principles and practices. It takes you through marketing, organizational design and development, accounting, and planning and control as they apply to small companies. Most important, perhaps, is the fact that it does so in an easy-to-read, easy-to-understand style and format. I do not believe that it is necessary to make your work harder in order to make your business life easier. I want *Calculated Risk* to be a book you can read, understand, enjoy, and most of all, use.

THE CASE CYCLES

To this end, I have provided opportunities to apply the principles and techniques described in the text to the business development processes of four separate hypothetical entrepreneurs. These entrepreneurs are involved in building a restaurant (Sally Jones), a financial services consulting company (Rob King), a pottery-making company (Danielle Mackie), and a retail bookstore (Ed James). Each case cycle lets you see the difficulties and choices facing each entrepreneur as he or she attempts to make the dream become an operational reality. The cases at the end of each section of this book let you exercise your knowledge, skill, and common sense in assisting them with their problems and answering their questions.

While many textbooks offer cases to demonstrate the application of one or another principle or technique, the continuity of our cases is emphasized throughout the book. This case-cycle approach is useful in seeing the many ways in which standard pieces of businesses, for example, location, product choices, personal objectives, and so forth, can fit together to form very different kinds of working companies. The development of these four hypothetical companies also lets you examine (at some distance) the pitfalls into which many entrepreneurs may fall enroute to building their companies. It is always easier to see what is going on in somebody else's company than it is to really see your own. In short, the approach shows business planning as a process, rather than as a single explosive act.

The case-cycle approach also highlights the unified nature of any business—how the effects of one choice limit and alter later options and choices. All the entrepreneur's choices must eventually come together to form a single coherent whole at the end of the business planning process. Only the process of following the development of another business, from idea and desire to finished, detailed business plan, can provide a real sense of the need to integrate new choices into an already-existing body of plans. In this regard, isolated cases simply cannot fill the bill.

REALITY

Calculated Risk goes even beyond the case-cycle approach in bringing reality into the business development process. Throughout the book, in both text and features, the *real* difficulties and solutions of *real* entrepreneurs are presented for your examination. I not only tell you about the problems of cash flow in small companies, for example, I show you one temporary help service that almost went under before it learned to manage its cash flows better. I also show you a Christmas tree company that spends money for years to grow a tree that can be wiped out in a thunderstorm—and can be sold during one three-week period if it survives.

Material chosen for Features or Profiles is generally drawn from the national business press. The in-text examples come either from press reports or from my own experiences as a consultant to smaller companies. In either case, the people and situations that illustrate *Calculated Risk* are largely real. Thus, in addition to meeting interesting entrepreneurs, you get to see how they handled some of the more common difficulties faced by smaller companies. More to the point, you get to see the results of their actions so that you can adopt (or adapt) what worked and avoid (or adapt) what did not work. I believe that this kind of reality is absolutely essential in building a company that is likely to work and to move you toward your personal goals.

TOPIC ARRANGEMENT

The arrangement of topics in *Calculated Risk* also enhances the practical nature of the book. I have created a phased approach—the kind that an entrepreneur follows when evaluating the probable success of a business idea and developing a business plan to test it, describe it, and get it funded. For example, marketing issues are broken into two main sections separated by a number of other topics. The first marketing-related section deals with an issue that has to be decided early—whether there is enough of a market for whatever it is you are selling to justify spending more time on planning the business. The second marketing-related segment addresses the very nitty-gritty details of pricing and designing advertising and promotional activity for your new company.

A similar split is made in the accounting and finance areas. It is important for an entrepreneur to know early in the planning process approximately how much money the business is going to require and how much it is likely to produce. The former is needed to make initial financing decisions and decisions about the company's legal structure. The latter is needed to determine whether the return is likely to justify the expenditure of further effort and time on the planning process for this particular venture. Because it recognizes these early needs, *Calculated Risk* offers an approach to developing ballpark figures as an aid to early decision making. In later chapters, the text offers the more standard methods of developing and refining cost and revenue estimates for inclusion in the final business plan.

The section outline clearly reflects this bias toward practical planning.

Part 1: "Starting a Business," provides a brief overview of the small business arena, including who begins companies and why, the major economic sectors in which small companies operate, and the reasons for casting wary eyes on surveys and quizzes that purport to identify the "entrepreneurial types."

Part 2, "Who Will Buy What You're Selling?," develops an approach to initial assessment of the market for the products or services of the proposed company, including objective-setting, initial market research techniques, broad marketing strategies, and initial decision making.

Part 3, "Foundations of Your Business," describes the basic structural issues facing a prospective entrepreneur, pointing out tradeoffs, highlighting key considerations, and discussing areas that often create difficulties for the entrepreneur or the business but that may go unnoticed in the initial planning processes.

Part 4, "Structuring Operations," discusses the resources, both physical and human, that an entrepreneur has to provide for and organize in order to open the doors of the business. This section includes approaches to staffing and to assuring supplies of needed goods and services.

Part 5, "Getting Into the Market—And Staying In," discusses direct contact with the market for the new business, including the kinds of advertising, promotion, and marketing approaches that might be used and various methods of pricing products and services for the market. The pricing chapter also considers basic costing and breakeven analysis.

Part 6, "Setting Up the Scorecard," explains accounting, cash flow, and projecting results of operations for a new company. Its focus, however, is on *using* numbers to enhance entrepreneurial understanding of how the business really works. It presents accounting data and results as tools for management, rather than as annoyances visited on an entrepreneur by forces outside the business.

Part 7, "If You'd Rather Not Start From Scratch...," addresses alternative approaches to owning a business: buying a going concern or a franchise. This section is placed late in the text to emphasize that most of the same planning, research, and organization procedures are required to succeed using these approaches as are necessary for a startup. It notes that, rather than less work, buying or franchising will require the additional tasks of researching the franchisors or the sellers and their companies.

Part 8, "Keeping Score," considers the issue of controlling and directing what the entrepreneur has built, stressing that control and planning processes work best and most easily when integrated, from the beginning, into the normal life and flows of a company.

Appendixes

Appendix A is a simple business plan outline. It is not intended as *the* only outline to use, but rather as a checklist of the items that will have to be included in the final plan. As is usual in building a business, the form and specific order are less critical than whether the entire plan fits together well and makes sense given the business purpose. I have added two sections, one on personal objectives and one on contingency planning, that you might not want to offer a banker initially. But they will be needed in written form for your own planning processes.

Appendix B is a practical overview of the potential for using microcomputers in your business. While it discusses the possible benefits to be derived from using them, it also presents some of the difficulties and dangers that they can create in a new, small company.

ADDITIONAL MATERIAL IN CALCULATED RISK

Questions

To provide additional emphasis and consideration, questions are offered at the end of each chapter and each case segment. While these questions are sometimes review opportunities, many require application of the material in the chapter or part to hypothetical business situations. These, in particular, call for consideration and decision making—both of which should be emphasized in any practical course in entrepreneurship.

Boxed Features

While the Features and Profiles in Calculated Risk introduce you to real people and real business situations, they also serve other purposes. They provide examples of material discussed in the text, hypothetical caselets that illustrate underlying principles, or outlines and question lists for use in planning. Blank forms or formats for planning also appear in the Feature format. In short, even though they are not, strictly speaking, "text," you will find them useful and fun to read.

ACKNOWLEDGMENTS

"Acknowledgments" is barely an adequate word for recognizing the levels of support and assistance I have received from a large number of people. In the order in which events occurred, I would like, particularly, to thank:

- John Mahon and Patti Andrews, colleagues at Boston University, for reading and commenting on early drafts of some of this material in its "for use with my classes" phase.
- My former students at Boston University who offered (at my request) very candid assessments of much of this material in its initial and first-draft stages.
- Harry Briggs, Acquisitions Editor at D. C. Heath, for offering his encouragement and, especially, for sharing his insight and experience about how a good textbook is developed and constructed.
- Cathy Labresh, Production Editor, and Sue Gleason, Developmental Editor, at Heath. Cathy was invaluable in synthesizing the very useful comments of reviewers and in offering suggestions of her own, as well as guiding the manuscript through the stages of production. Sue was instrumental in developing the format of the book.
- The numerous reviewers of this text in its various stages of development:
    In its initial stage:
        Albert V. Bruno, University of Santa Clara
        Jeffrey C. Susbauer, Cleveland State University
        Mark Weaver, University of Alabama
        William E. Wetzel, Jr., University of New Hampshire
        Rudolph Winston, Jr., University of Lowell
    In its full first draft stage:
        Marc J. Dollinger, University of Kentucky
        Charles H. Matthews, University of Cincinnati
        Douglas W. Schell, Wichita State University
        Vern Sumner, Portland State University
        Barry L. Van Hook, Arizona State University

Their comments and suggestions were extremely helpful in clarifying my thinking about what was important in this effort and in helping me to pinpoint areas where improvements could be made.
- My closest friends, particularly Joe, who listened patiently through the entire process and who are still my friends, despite all that.

Needless to say, despite these acknowledgments of assistance, any lack of clarity, differences regarding emphasis, or outright errors that may be found in this text are solely my own responsibility. In fact, should you find any, or have any comments or questions, I would appreciate hearing from you (at W. M Greenfield Associates, 37 Lawrence Street, Boston, Massachusetts 02116).

W. M Greenfield

CONTENTS

✳ **PART 4 STRUCTURING OPERATIONS**

CASES FOR PART 5

PART 6   SETTING UP THE SCORECARD

Chapter 13   Accounting and Financial Ratios: Using Numbers to Tell You Things

Chapter 14   Cash Flow: You Can't Pay 'Em With Promises

Chapter 15   Projections: Will This Business Really Fly?   338

CASES FOR PART 6

PART 7 IF YOU'D RATHER NOT START FROM SCRATCH...

CASES FOR PART 8

APPENDIXES

PART 1
STARTING A BUSINESS

1. Is Small Business Small?

Winston Churchill once referred to Britain as "a nation of shopkeepers." To the extent that a nation can be characterized in such a fashion, the United States could be seen as "a nation of small business owners". Given this statement, it is particularly odd that so little is really known and published about small companies and their operations and finances. As you will see, there is not even a standard definition for what constitutes a small business in the United States.

The fact that there are no generally accepted definitions, of course, does not prevent small businesses from existing, succeeding, or failing. It merely makes it more difficult to describe the process. What we have tried to do in this chapter is to avoid as much of the definitional debate as possible and to delineate, in broad terms, what is happening in the world of smaller companies. Our purpose in doing so is to give you some sense of the landscape you are proposing to enter and of the triumphs and/or pitfalls that are clearly out there. As such, though better definitions would be nice, they are not absolutely necessary.

THE DATA: WHAT IS SMALL? AND OTHER ISSUES

As usual in the field of business, the most reliable broad-based statistics about small businesses come from agencies of the federal government. Quite naturally, the Internal Revenue Service takes some interest in business, as does the Department of Commerce (of which the Census Bureau is a part). Also as usual, the government's publishing schedule lags far behind evolving reality. While in mature, stable fields this lag is a minor difficulty, in a field that moves as rapidly as small business, such lags can foster major problems. Since reliance on government statistics is essential, however, we caution against using the data presented in this chapter as anything but broad background data. General direction derived from trends in the data may be particularly useful.

Despite these difficulties, there is a great deal to be gleaned from a statistical view of the state of small business in the United States. One of the more interesting issues is the one with which we began—the issue of definition. The issue has two dimensions. First, what are the relevant size indicators? Second, given a choice of indicator, what is the cutoff point for "small"?

Size Indicators

Depending on the purposes of the viewer, virtually any statistic can be used as a size indicator. Within the federal government, at least four are used.

Numbers of employees.   The number of people employed by a company is a widely used indicator. Federal, state, and local governments often track employment for insurance as well as tax purposes. The level of job creation or job loss has become a political issue often in recent years. Numbers of employees is also a useful indicator if the issue under consideration is productivity—another hot topic in recent times.

Sales.   An obvious way to define the size of a company is by how much money it brings in as revenue. States and localities that levy sales taxes are likely to keep their data by sales category for companies that are subject to such taxes.

Assets.   The size of a company can also be defined by the amount the company owns—its assets. This is often a key consideration in corporation organization fees and in state and local taxation. Interestingly, because of tax laws, governments cannot show all businesses by asset size. Sole pro-prietorships, about 75 percent of all business enterprises according to Internal Revenue Service (IRS) statistics (1981), do not have to file balance sheets showing business assets.

Numbers of shareholders.   This approach to size would, clearly, be of greatest interest to the Securities and Exchange authorities at all levels. It is also, as you will see in Chapter 6, a key factor in determining whether a corporation is eligible for taxation as a "small business corporation".

Size Cutoffs

The most interesting indicator in the debate over "what is small" is employment statistics. Three cutoff points are often seen. The main question seems to be whether fewer than 100 employees makes you "small" or fewer than 500 employees should be deemed "small." Some statistics, notably the government's various business censuses, generally show "establishments" with fewer than 20 employees as separate from all others. From this structure, one might assume that "fewer than 20" should be considered "small."

Please note that "establishments" are not the same as "enterprises." One enterprise can have more than one establishment or location. I found this out the hard way when I bought a mailing list of small businesses in a particular city. "Small" was supposed to be under 100 employees, but I found IBM and Price Waterhouse, among other giants, on my list. In fact, each did have fewer than 100 employees at the relevant location—which was not of much help to me.

There are two real points of note about size cutoffs. First, as I learned, you need to be careful about how "small" is being defined before you use any small business information. Because of the multiplicity of definitions and cutoffs, it is very easy to compare or combine apples and oranges, arriving at useless and/or misleading conclusions in the process.

Second, any definition of "small" should be viewed in relation to the characteristics of the specific industry you are considering. Some industries—retailing, for example—are people-intensive, while others, like chemical processing, rely more heavily on equipment. To compare a retail business with a chemical plant in terms of numbers of employees, then, would give a false sense of which was "larger." While the retailer might well have more employees, the sales, assets, and ownership group of the chemical processor would probably be significantly larger.

We expect, however, that this discussion of "what is small" will be largely academic for you for the first few years. Most businesses can, should, and do start small—by any definition. It is quite likely, though, that you will want to use some of the available statistics to help you shape and define your enterprise. Only there will the "what is small" issue touch your planning process.

SMALL COMPANIES ARE BIG BUSINESS

By any definition, small companies in the United States constitute a significant part of the economic fabric of the nation. As you can see in Table 1.1, small businesses are the bulk of all businesses in terms of numbers of firms. In addition, several interesting things are occurring in the smaller company share of total business. First, firms are getting smaller. At the same time, a greater proportion of sales dollars are going to larger firms. This may well be a reflection of the trends in new business starts, which will be discussed later, coupled with the tendency of new businesses to start small.

Table 1.1 Small company share of total U.S. industry, 1978–1982

	1978		1980		1982	
NUMBER OF ENTERPRISES						
All enterprises	3,736,594	100.0%	3,971,068	100.0%	4,369,726	100.0%
< 100 employees	3,663,614	98.0	3,890,875	98.0	4,285,558	98.1
100–500						
employees	59,357	1.6	65,463	1.6	68,743	1.6
> 500 employees	13,623	0.4	14,730	0.4	14,813	0.3
FEWER THAN 100 EMPLOYEES						
Percent of						
employment	33.2%		32.5%		34.1%	
Percent of sales	34.1		33.3		31.6	
SIZE OF AVERAGE ENTERPRISE						
Number of						
employees	26.2	(1976)			21.7	
Average sales	$1,374,000				$1,935,200	

Source: *The State of Small Business: A Report of the President* (Washington, D.C.: U.S. Government Printing Office, 1982): 65, 67, 73.

From a societal perspective, small businesses may be providing the economy with a great deal more than sheer numbers. Two of every three workers get their starts in the working world in small businesses. Moreover, according to recent studies, small businesses account for more than 80 percent of the job creation that has been going on in the United States over the last decade. Between 1980 and 1982, for example, firms with fewer than 100 employees provided the economy with an additional 2,648,000 jobs, while firms with 100 or more employees showed a loss of jobs of 1,666,000. No matter how you define small businesses, then, the job creation potential and performance record of small business has been impressive.

As you can see, while definitions of "small" vary, the impact of smaller companies on the United States economy is significant. The main point remains. However you choose to define "small companies," there are lots of them in the United States, and they are a major force in the economy. This *is* basically a nation of small businesses.

The key point for you to remember is that it is clearly not terribly offbeat to open your own company. According to 1981 statistics of the IRS, there were 17.3 million taxpaying business units in the country. While the precise number of these that were "small" may be open to debate, the fact remains that the vast majority of them were small. And somebody started each of them.

SMALL BUSINESS CONCENTRATIONS

To the extent that you have already considered what type of business you are planning to enter, it's likely that you have chosen one in the wholesale, retail, or services field. We make this prediction with confidence because the odds on your business being in one of these fields are high. These are the areas in which smaller companies tend to concentrate. The Small Business Administration (SBA) speculates that this concentration occurs because these business sectors are essentially easy to enter. While building nuclear reactors, say, demands a great deal of money, manpower, and technological expertise, opening a small retail establishment does not. Therefore, most entrepreneurs tend toward the small retail establishment. Service establishments generally appear to be even easier to enter, although that may not always be the case.

In Table 1.2 you can see the concentrations of smaller companies across all economic sectors, but you can also see that the concentrations of sales and employees in smaller companies exist in relatively few sectors: agriculture, construction, and wholesale and retail trade.

You can also see the reasons for these patterns, if you consider the industries in question. Agriculture, these days, consists of two groups of owners: the giant corporate farms and the traditional family farms. There is little in between these two extremes. The construction business tends to be similar in industry structure. Existing next to the national and international giants are the small, local construction companies that build the local housing and government and business structures down the street.

The wholesale and retail business sectors generally have more "middle" and fewer "giant sized" units. This structure also leaves a great deal of room for the smaller company to have a significant share of the sector. Moreover, in this field in particular, people and other small companies tend to like dealing with the smaller, local concern.

Table 1.2   Percentages of sectors by firms with fewer than 100 employees

	1978			1982		
Industry Division	*Firms*	*Sales*	*Employm.*	*Firms*	*Sales*	*Employm.*
All industries	98.1	32.1	33.2	98.1	31.6	34.1
Agriculture, forestry, fisheries	95.1	62.0	69.8	99.4	75.2	73.7
Mining	97.2	4.1	23.9	96.9	4.3	27.9
Construction	99.3	68.9	65.4	99.3	62.3	67.3
Manufacturing	94.0	12.3	14.7	94.2	12.1	15.3
Transportation, communication, utilities	97.9	15.5	20.9	97.6	15.2	19.4
Wholesale trade	98.9	59.1	69.3	98.9	56.2	69.8
Retail trade	99.3	56.5	54.5	99.2	51.1	52.5
Finance, insurance, real estate	97.9	22.2	33.3	98.1	33.6	36.4
Services	97.2	44.8	31.0	97.1	42.2	31.9

Source: *The State of Small Business: A Report of the President* (Washington, D.C.: U.S. Government Printing Office, 1984): 73.

It is equally clear why other sectors have relatively few smaller companies. In manufacturing, for example, in addition to the often heavy initial investments in plant and equipment mentioned earlier, there may be economies of scale in the manufacturing process. That is, the more units of something you produce, the less expensive it becomes to produce each unit. This phenomenon may result from the simple economics of buying in bulk, or from the more esoteric operation of the learning curve. The point is that it would be inherently difficult for a smaller firm to compete in such a business. Hence, relatively few smaller firms exist in that sector.

Another interesting piece of information that can be gleaned from the federal data is that smaller companies have disproportionately small shares of sales in all sectors. This observation is borne out in data assembled by the Internal Revenue Service for 1980:

	Business receipts/business
All businesses	$ 524,497
Large corporations	$1,801,000
Small corporations	$ 864,455
Non-corporate units (small)	$ 61,183

Department of Commerce (1977) data concurs. Although there are many more small firms than there are large ones, the small ones take in less money.

Share of sales receipts by size class

Number of Employees:	0	1–19	20–99	100–499	500+
All businesses	2.47%	20.21%	18.13%	11.77%	47.42%
Minerals	0.39	9.75	14.05	12.74	63.07
Manufacturing	0.05	3.63	8.31	10.50	77.51
Construction	8.61	35.50	25.14	13.56	17.19
Wholesale	0.98	36.84	30.78	16.36	15.04
Retail	4.73	28.23	22.80	8.86	35.38
Services	10.89	35.33	18.24	12.83	22.71

And lest you believe that it is purely a function of size of each overall firm, the Small Business Administration has collected some data showing that firms with fewer than 100 employees generally make less in profit for each dollar collected in sales than do larger firms in the traditionally small business-dominated sectors (1979 data). Smaller firms have a miniscule edge in wholesale trade.

These statistics should be viewed as informational. You should be aware of them—if only to consider whether the field you intend to enter is likely to be hospitable or hostile to the entry of smaller companies. If your business is going to be in a sector that includes few small companies, or in which small firms have a vastly disproportionate share of sales, it might be wise to consider why this has been true. You might then ask yourself whether and how your particular business is going to be able to overcome or skirt the obstacles to small business success in that field. Do not let the numbers discourage you without further consideration. Remember that even in mining, some small companies exist, are making sales, and keeping employees.

BUSINESS FORMATION

The creation of new companies also follows patterns of industry sector and of geography. Not surprisingly, most starts came in the traditional small business sectors. Changes in business starts by industry for the first nine months of 1982 and 1983 are shown in Table 1.3. The major surprise in these figures is that manufacturing starts are growing so rapidly.

Industries that have recently been deregulated—for example, airlines, telephone services, and certain financial services industries—spawned relatively more new companies than did industries untouched by deregulation. Most of these kinds of businesses, however, require either a large initial investment or a high level of expertise or both. They are thus closed to most of us.

Regional characteristics also appear to affect the propensity to start businesses. New business incorporations were up by the largest percentages in the west north central states and the Mountain states. They grew least in the Pacific states and actually declined in Texas, Oklahoma, and Louisiana.

Table 1.3 Changes in business starts by industry sector, first nine months of 1982 and 1983

Industry Division	Jan–Sept 1983	Jan–Sept 1982
All industries	66,572	58,950
Agriculture, forestry, fisheries	673	637
Mining	624	804
Construction	8,190	5,760
Manufacturing	5,986	5,291
Transportation, communication, utilities	1,996	1,732
Wholesale trade	8,392	7,545
Retail trade	25,323	23,244
Finance, insurance, real estate	2,907	2,185
Services	12,481	11,752

Source: *The State of Small Business: A Report of the President* (Washington, D.C.: U.S. Government Printing Office, 1984): 32.

The other major indicator of business starts is the incorporation rate, tracked by both the Internal Revenue Service and Dun & Bradstreet, the financial services firm. Dun & Bradstreet reported 596,178 new incorporations for 1983—a new record high, breaking the 1981 record of 581,242. The IRS reports that for 1981, the last year for which data is available, new incorporations comprised 3.5 percent of all business income tax returns filed. This can be compared with 3.2 percent for 1980.

The IRS data also shows a trend in the legal forms of the companies being started. This trend is clear in Table 1.4. Fewer sole proprietorships exist as entrepreneurs discover the advantages (and disadvantages) of the more complex forms of legal structure. These differences are discussed at length in Chapter 6.

Table 1.4 Income tax returns filed by legal form of filer, 1974–1981

	1974		1977		1981	
Sole proprietorships	10,874,000	78.2%	11,345,616	77.0%	13,000,420	75.3%
Partnerships	1,062,000	7.6	1,153,398	7.8	1,460,502	8.5
Corporations	1,966,000	14.1	2,241,887	15.2	2,812,987	16.3
Total	13,902,000	100.0%	14,740,901	100.0%	17,273,909	100.0%

Source: *The State of Small Business: A Report of the President* (Washington, D.C.: U.S. Government Printing Office, 1982): 70; (1984): 104.

In short, the period from 1981 to 1983 was, from some points of view, a very good one for small business startups. In prior years, the net business formation rate (new businesses less those that went out of business) ranged from 2.1 percent to 4.2 percent per year. Clearly, the business of starting businesses is booming.

This boom occurred despite the recession that has also been around during this period. Some commentators believe that the high rate of startups is partly the result, in fact, of the recession. Their reasoning goes that as large, existing firms lay off employees, numbers of those employees take the opportunity to strike out on their own. John Eden, at 39, is a case in point. After being laid off from his Department of Energy job, he began making stencilled notepaper with his line drawings and selling them to local retailers.[1] Other entrepreneurs simply think that a recession is a great time to start a business. Such optimists note that, "When the economy is all set to turn up, we'll be all set to expand."

Whatever the reasons, entrepreneurial activity is growing in the United States. It is no longer fashionable to be anti-business. It is fairly common to find a person who owns his or her own company or at least sidelines in such an arrangement after normal working hours. You are definitely not alone in your interest in beginning a company of your own. But, lest your decision be based on only positive input, it is only fair to tell you that the odds on most of these new companies being around in five years are slim indeed.

SMALL BUSINESS FAILURES

Small businesses do fail. They fail at a greater rate than do large businesses. While it may seem strange to be discussing small business failures in the early stages of your potential business development, it is a useful thing to do for two reasons. First, it never makes sense to walk into a major undertaking without evaluating the risks of walking out in one piece. Second, many of the specific causes of small business failure can be minimized through proper planning— if, and only if, you know what they are and that they are there.

It is also true that an explicit consideration of the risks will give you a better sense of how willing and able you are to deal with the realities of small business life. In the end, it may be that recognition and acceptance of the potential for failure are two of the keys to success. This is one of those areas in which ignorance is *not* bliss.

The business formation data just mentioned should be reevaluated in light of the failure data. While the startup information gives glimpses of the American Dream to would-be entrepreneurs, that view is overly rosy. In 1977, for example, although 450,000 new companies were formed, only 135,000 extra tax returns were filed in 1978. Somewhere, more than 300,000 corporations were lost in that year. (Unless you believe that there was wholesale non-compliance with the tax laws.) In that same year, 1978, the IRS reported that, of 1,234,000 partnership returns filed, 126,825 (10.3 percent) were final returns, indicating the dissolution of partnerships.

Since those years the number of failures posted annually has risen. This may be due, in part, to the recession. In times of tight or expensive money, small businesses generally fare worse than their larger counterparts. But even under these circumstances, the statistics are staggering. Dun & Bradstreet also reports on business failures. Their figures for businesses of all sizes show:

1980	11,742 companies failed
1981	17,040 companies failed
1982	23,814 companies failed
1983	31,334 companies failed

It must also be noted that D&B's figures cover only those companies that closed owing creditors money—that is, those with unpaid liabilities. Companies that simply closed their doors with no harm to any outsider are not counted in these statistics. According to the Small Business Administration, 99 percent of failed businesses have fewer than 100 employees and are less than 10 years old.

Bankruptcy courts see yet another side of business failure. In addition to outright collapse, the bankruptcy laws permit businesses to reorganize under the protection of the courts (with the consent of their creditors). Such reorganizations under Chapter 11 of the bankruptcy laws may well be an even better indication of firms in trouble than are the D&B statistics. Bankruptcy court statistics for comparable years show:

1981	47,555 companies were in bankruptcy court
1982	65,807 companies were in bankruptcy court
1983	58,898 companies were in bankruptcy court

The dry statistics cannot describe what a bankruptcy proceeding is really like for an honest entrepreneur. Sal Valente, who recently brought his company through a Chapter 11 and back to health, can describe it far better. His comments are highlighted in Feature 1.1.

In short, what we are seeing is massive and rapid turnover at the small end of the business spectrum. Some argue, as does David Birch of the Massachusetts Institute of Technology, that business failure is simply the economic means of redirecting investment. Others tell stories about how, in the United States, "you're not considered to be a real entrepreneur until you've been through your first bankruptcy." One story in particular demonstrates the value of failure in redirecting effort, energy, and resources. It concerns the principal of Arp Instruments, a maker of music synthesizers. After 12 years of operation, growing to 200 employees and $7 million, Arp was bankrupt. David Friend, the principal in question, went on to use the remains of Arp to build another (successful) company. He then sold out to a larger company and used the proceeds from that sale to underwrite two more startups and operate a venture capital firm.[2]

Short of making the government the bailer-outer of last resort for all companies, there is no way, and no wish, to stop this process. It is the free market in action at its freest. It would be gratifying, however, if yours was not one of the companies in the revolving door. An examination of the factors that appear to influence the chances of a company for success, therefore, seems in order.

Factors That Influence Failures

Two main factors appear to influence the failure rate of small businesses. The first is the size and age of the business. The second is the kind of business you choose to enter. The President's Report on Small Business (1982) reports a 1969–1976 study of business survival. The "survival probabilities" developed appear to be directly tied to the size of the business at inception. The results are shown in Table 1.5.

FEATURE 1.1
Sal Valente Talks About Chapter 11

My lawyer's offices were on the 32nd floor and I kept saying to myself that if I jumped I could hit the hotel across the way.

The first thing I had to do was go back and fire half the people in the company—that was my first project. After that I had to go home and tell my wife what happened. It was not an easy day.

Over and over people told me to throw everything in, but I do believe you have to look at yourself in the mirror each morning. The best way to try to undo what happened was to make the business succeed again. That's what drove me. It took about two and a half years for the business to stabilize.

People don't understand what it means to go through Chapter 11. It means you fail as a person when your company fails. No matter how hard you've worked, everything that you've ever done just disappears. I'm not out of shock yet. But if you pulled a D&B on Bildisco today, you'd see a nice report, and I'm proud of that.

From "Courting Bankruptcy" by Curtis Hartman. Reprinted with permission, *Inc.* magazine, October, 1984. Copyright © 1984 by *Inc.* Publishing Company, 38 Commercial Wharf, Boston, MA 02110.

Table 1.5   Business survival rates by initial employment size

	Probability of Surviving Past		
Initial Employment Level	*4 Years*	*9 Years*	*10 Years*
0–20	37.4%	17.3%	8.6%
21–50	53.6	35.2	26.2
51–100	55.7	36.4	27.4
101–500	56.4	36.8	28.3
More than 500	67.7	42.5	35.7

Source: Harvey Garn and Larry Ledebur, An Urban Institute White Paper, February 22, 1980, reported in *The State of Small Business: A Report of the President* (Washington, D.C.: U.S. Government Printing Office, 1982): 79.

An earlier study focused on retail operations. It considered retail stores by type opened in Illinois in 1974. The researchers rechecked the businesses in 1979. The data is similarly depressing. Only some categories are shown in Table 1.6, but the message is clear: most retail operations do not live to see their fifth birthdays.

Table 1.6   Retail businesses remaining after five years (Illinois), by type

	Of Firms Begun in 1975, Percent Still Active in 1979
Shoe stores	44.3
Book and stationery stores	43.5
Antique stores	42.5
Sporting goods and bicycle	37.7
Eating and drinking places	36.5
Women's ready-to-wear	31.8
Drinking places	30.5
Family clothing	29.4
Gifts, novelties, souvenirs	28.9
Grocery	27.0

Source: Alvin Star and Michael Massel, "Survival Rates for Retailers," *Journal of Retailing* (Summer, 1981): 92.

It should be clear that the odds are stacked against small businesses in general. This is not necessarily a reason for abandoning the field, however. It *is* reason for caution and for further exploration of the failures. Your key questions are why these companies failed and how to prevent such things from bringing your company down.

Why Businesses Fail: Improving the Odds

Dun & Bradstreet collects a full range of data on most startups and failures. It goes beyond a mere head count, however, to develop some data about why the business that failed failed. The set of reasons and the proportional distribution among reasons remains remarkably stable over time. This stability makes it likely that the same reasons will also be the most dangerous for your prospective company.

	1972	*1977*	*1980*
Incompetence/inexperience	93.1%	94.0%	92.1%
Neglect	2.0		0.8
Fraud	1.5	0.4	0.5
Disaster	0.9	0.5	0.8
Unknown	2.5	5.1	5.8

Management is clearly the key factor in this array. Recognizing this, D&B data permits us to follow this exploration to the next layer. Within the "incompetence/inexperience" category, they cite some more specific causes and show distributions of failures due mainly to each cause. (The sum of the percentages may exceed 100 percent because some failures were considered to be the result of more than one cause.)

	1972	*1977*	*1980*
Inadequate sales	45.4%	53.9%	49.9%
Competitive weakness	26.4	24.0	25.3
Heavy operating expenses	8.5	17.0	13.0
Receivables difficulties	9.6	7.7	8.3
Inventory difficulties	5.7	6.3	7.7
Excessive fixed assets	3.8	NA	3.2
Poor location	4.3	1.9	2.7

There is no need, just now, to get into the technicalities of the lists above. That is the purpose of the rest of this book. But do look at the lists. As you can see, the items really stem from one of two root causes. Either the company had money problems or it had management problems. Sometimes, undoubtedly, the failed company had both.

The fact that these have historically been the problem areas is perfectly reasonable when considered in terms of the basic requirements of business survival. At its most basic, success in business involves selling a product or a service at a profit. The two critical factors are the costs and revenues (the money) and the way it is done (how it is managed). In the rush of enthusiasm over a new idea or a new venture, this basic requirement is often lost. Part of the purpose of this book is to not let you lose sight of it. More to the point, this book will help you do it right. Assuming that your basic idea/concept is reasonable and assuming that you do your planning well, both money and management difficulties are avoidable.

SUMMARY

Small business may be the "backbone of America" or what makes the United States a nation of small business owners, but how "small business" should be defined is still an open question. Definitions based on employment size, sales, assets, and numbers of shareholders abound, but the key to definition is the reasonableness of the comparisons you wish to make or the use you intend to make of the data in your own planning.

We contend that the available data should be used only as a rough guide because it is often out of date and because of the problems of conflicting definitions. As a guide, however, the statistical information available to describe "smaller" businesses can be extremely useful. It can point to economic sectors in which small companies may well encounter difficulties with entry and operations. It can flag potential pitfalls in starting and operating a new business. In short, a consideration of the broad outlines of "small business" in the United States can assist you in the very early stages of your planning process—positively, by offering information about sectors hospitable to small companies, and negatively, by flagging areas in which inattention engenders failures.

FOR YOU TO CONSIDER

1. What are three parameters that are often used to define "small" for small business purposes? How would you use a definition by each parameter in your exploration and planning process?
2. Why might the United States be considered a nation of small business owners? What data supports this contention? What factors might lead you to believe that this is an overly facile description of the state of the economy?
3. Business startups often rise in times of high unemployment and a generally poor economy. What factors might account for such a phenomenon?
4. Why is it wise to study business failures before you begin to develop a detailed plan for your own business startup?

NOTES

1. David Gumpert, "Manager's Journal," *Wall Street Journal* (September 9, 1982): 22.
2. David Birch, "What America Needs is a Few Good Failures," *Inc.* magazine (September, 1983): 63 ff.

2. Are You Really Sure You Want to Start a Business?

"Lucky? I'm the luckiest guy in the world," says Charles H. Kaman, builder of Kaman Corp which sells over $400 million a year in helicopters, bearings and guitars. "And the harder I work, the luckier I get."

Sally Jacobs, *New England Business*

Unlike most books, which introduce their topics with great fanfare, this book has already provided some rather downbeat information about how likely you are to win at the new company game. This is because, although everyone knows that entrepreneurs are risk-takers, we know that you are not entirely irrational. Before you become significantly involved in the process of developing your company, you want to know your odds. You want to be able to calculate the level of risk you will be taking. While the information in this book will help you reduce your risk by flagging some of the more common stumbling blocks that entrepreneurs encounter, it cannot guarantee that you will beat the odds. Only you can determine whether you like your particular set of odds well enough to proceed with the serious business planning process outlined in the rest of this book.

Building a working company is hard. It is not for everyone. It is not a simple alternative to the effort of getting a job. You want to be reasonably sure that starting a new business is the right thing for you to do before you invest large amounts of time and energy in building or developing a company. This chapter will raise some very difficult questions for you to consider. It is designed to help you to decide whether you want to begin the building and developing process. It does so by first looking at who seems to succeed at company-building. It continues with a look at how business ideas happen. Finally, it addresses the issue of personal goals and objective-setting, a topic that may seem out of place, but that is, in fact, critical to your ultimate success as an entrepreneur.

WHAT ARE ENTREPRENEURS LIKE?

Everyone seems fascinated by the question of what entrepreneurs are like and whether they are really any different from "regular folks." Virtually everyone who writes in this field seems to have a quiz or checklist designed to tell you definitively whether you are the entrepreneurial type. None of them has proven particularly good at predicting who will make it in entrepreneuring. We have included this section, in fact, solely because people seem to feel better if there is some material in their books about what entrepreneurs are like. In real life, as you will see later, people who start their own companies have very little in common. Entrepreneurial quizzes, then, should be viewed as good, clean fun—and little else.

The bases for the particular questions asked and characteristics highlighted in entrepreneurial quizzes vary widely. Some of them are backed by research, some by surveys, and some, apparently, by nothing at all. The most interesting things about such writings are that they often reach different conclusions, and that they all raise issues you need to consider in deciding whether you want to start your own company.

Writings on Entrepreneurial Characteristics

The simplest approach to categorizing business founders comes from Cooper and Dunkelberg of Purdue University.[1] After studying 890 founders, they concluded that there are three types of people who start companies. There are "craftsmen," who start their own companies largely to do what they like to do. Theirs are generally the slowest growing companies. Second, there are "growth-oriented people seeking to accomplish financial or other personal goals." These founders usually have previous business experience, either in their own or other companies. Finally, there are those who start companies to avoid working for other people. Fully 20 percent of founders in this category had never worked in a profit-making company before they started their own businesses.

Cooper and Dunkelberg also found that the "average" entrepreneur is between 25 and 40 years old. Half of them had parents who owned small companies. A third had partners who worked in the business. They found that these partnerships did better than one-owner companies.

Most attempts to identify entrepreneurial characteristics are more complex in conclusions and somewhat simpler in development. A. David Silver's list of 10 characteristics, for example, requires a strong background in psychology just to interpret, let alone to apply.[2] Silver is a venture capitalist who is relying on his own experience in his characterization of an entrepreneur. This is his list.

Ten Significant Characteristics of Entrepreneurs
1. Outer-directed background
2. Absent father/dynamic mother
3. Optimal childhood deprivation
4. Guilt
5. Ability to focus intensively
6. Courage; no fear of failure
7. Creativity
8. Insight
9. Happiness
10. Communications skills

Numerous surveys of entrepreneurs are also available. Data from two are discussed in the remainder of this section. The first is a recent (1983) survey of the 2,500 members of Joseph Mancuso's Center for Entrepreneurial Management (CEM). The second is a small-sample survey by Daniel Robert Fierro, author of *The New American Entrepreneur: How to Get Off the Fast Track into a Business of Your Own*.[3] Fierro's objective was to test a survey developed in 1980 for *Venture* magazine on his own small group of 30 entrepreneurs. A third item, a quiz offered by the *New York Daily News*, is one of many quizzes not supported, apparently, by anything.[4] It is also noted in passing. Some of the key issues that seem to be significant to these survey-takers and questioners in defining entrepreneurs are noted below.

- Whether your parents or close relatives were self-employed and/or had their own businesses. Some 67 percent of both survey groups has apparently had such close contact with entrepreneurship.
- Whether you have started businesses before (including paper routes, lemonade stands, and the like). Almost 75 percent of the CEM sample had done so. Only 60 percent of Fierro's sample had done so. The *Daily News*, focuses, rather, on the organizing of events as a good indicator of entrepreneurial potential.
- Whether you were ever fired from a job. The CEM sample showed that about half their entrepreneurs had been fired. Fierro's group had only a 33 percent rate of firings. Presumably, all the "true entrepreneurs" were fired because they could not get along in the group or in the hierarchies.

Differences Among Conclusions

It may be more interesting to explore areas in which these writings differ significantly from one another. The *Venture* survey (15 questions) seeks information about involvement in reality. Do you prefer watching sports to playing them? Do you prefer fiction to nonfiction? Do you get involved in community affairs? Do you prefer planning to execution? If you answered at least 12 of the 15 questions in a positive manner, *Venture* claimed that you were already an entrepreneur. Four or more negative answers were presumed to impair the probability of your success. Eighty percent was thus a "passing" score.

The *Daily News* quiz focuses on your organizational abilities and your physical stamina. How long could you sustain a schedule of 12- to 14-hour days, five or six days a week? How good is your health? (And, by the way, can you balance your checkbook?) Their quiz is also 15 questions, multiple choice, with answers scored from 1 to 4 points. With the maximum possible score of 60, the *Daily News* suggests that if you score as low as between 35 and 45, "you might succeed in your own business if you team up with a partner." Below 35 points, forget it.

The CEM questionnaire is broader than the other two, at 26 questions, and has two main foci: working relationships and risk-taking behavior. Its messages are, very basically, that entrepreneurial types tend to emphasize getting the job done, prefer to work with experts rather than friends, and believe that a clear chain of command helps in getting things done quickly.

An interesting finding in the CEM survey is the one upon which this book is based. Entrepreneurs take risks, but they are not outrageous, uncontrollable risks. Forty percent of the sample would choose a 3–1 shot at the track rather than a 2–1 favorite, a 10–1 longshot, or a chance at a real killing. They bet on themselves, 92 percent preferring a 1–3 chance at solving a problem within a given time to a 1–3 chance on a roll of the dice.

Some of the findings of this survey contradict two of Silver's conclusions mentioned earlier. CEM found that more than half their sample termed their relationships with their parents "comfortable." Silver regards early family stress as important in building an entrepreneur.

Finally, on a key issue, money, the writings differ. You win top points (4) from the *Daily News* if money is "extremely" important to you. Mancuso's survey, however, shows that only 34 percent of his sample started their businesses for the primary purpose of making money. Like those studied by Cooper and Dunkelberg, most (56 percent) simply did not like working for someone else.

You figure it out. There are some very clear messages in all this. The first is, obviously, not to believe the results of every survey you read or every quiz you take. Fierro's group of successful entrepreneurs failed the *Venture* quiz, with an overall average score for the group of less than 60 percent of the "right" answers. The second message is that entrepreneurial characteristics vary widely from person to person and from sample to sample.

We can offer one observation, however. Entrepreneurs seem to be able to recognize a good idea and have the tenacity to follow through. A group of friends was talking in a pub one day when someone came up with the idea of packaging lumps of coal as joke Christmas presents. Together, we developed potential sources of supply, a production process, and a distribution program. We decided to package in two ways—as lumps of coal for people who had been "bad" and as "unpressed diamonds" to be given as presents to people who had been very "good" from people who were not yet millionaires. We were going to have the next Pet Rock. We did nothing. Two years later, someone else began selling lumps of coal—with a much less sophisticated marketing approach. While the product did not take the world by storm, storekeepers say that it sold very well that Christmas.

FEATURE 2.1

And a High Tolerance for Frustration . . .

Members of the staff of *New England Business Magazine* wanted to test whether hotcakes really sold "like hotcakes." They approached this earth-shaking issue quite rationally, deciding to try selling hotcakes for one day from a cart in downtown Boston, Massachusetts. Their main story was to be less about hotcakes than about the process of going into business selling hotcakes.

They comment that their difficulties were "doubtless but a fraction of the frustration and red tape that a legitimate effort to start a *real* business would encounter. In fact, we would guess," they add, "that most people who tried the process would have sworn off hotcakes, and perhaps voting, for life."

In the end, they talked with six city agencies about three or four different types of permit, ranging in price from $53 for a city-only Hawker and Peddler permit (they would have had to keep moving continuously) to a vendor's license for public land, which would have cost more than $700 a month. They found that they could not cook the hotcakes in an unlicensed facility (the reporter's kitchen) for sale to the public. They found that they had to have the fire department issue a permit for the cart.

Finally, the reporters revealed who they were and why they wanted the permit. A city insider found the entire notion amusing and proceeded to arrange for the reporter to acquire a one-day permit for the Boston Common—free. "If the world is a closed clam to a not-quite-earnest-looking entrepreneur of flapjacks, it's an open door to a damned fool working on an elaborate joke," they commented.

By the way, they found out within two hours that if your product is "selling like hotcakes," you are probably in deep trouble.

Adapted from Sally Jacobs, "Permit Me," *New England Business* (June 18, 1984):36–38.

By contrast, consider the story of Chris Haney and Scott Abbott. They, too, were sitting in a bar, just talking, when they began to develop a board game. The high school dropout and the sports reporter had difficulties finding investors, difficulties finding distributors, difficulties across the board. But, unlike my group, they perservered to create and market "Trivial Pursuit," a board game that has spawned an industry and that sold to the tune of more than $750 million in the United States alone in 1984.[5] Was this an inherently better idea? Or were follow-through and execution the keys to success? We will never know because my group never actually got it together to do the job properly.

The point here is that entrepreneurs really appear to be "regular people" —but ones who generally want something badly or have something that they need to accomplish. If you fill that bill, do not let the statistical types get to you. You are the only one who can decide whether you have what it takes to make it—and whether it is a game you would care to join.

WHO ARE THE ENTREPRENEURS?

While no one seems to be able to define the qualities of mind and heart that combine to make a successful entrepreneur, it is fairly simple to define the demographic characteristics of people who start their own companies. The profile is changing rapidly, however. It is expected that the trends will have continued and have become more pronounced by the time you read this.

The "average" entrepreneur is the oldest child in the family. Most are married. Most are male. In 1984, the average age of those who start their own businesses was in the thirties. Just two decades before the average was between 40 and 45.[6] The average age is dropping sharply due to two trends. The first is the swing to high-tech businesses. Many of these firms are begun by people in their twenties. Apple Computer, for example, was begun by Steven Jobs and Steven Wozniak when they were in their twenties. Technical innovation is considered to be the province of the young.

The second factor pushing the average age for entrepreneurship downward is the current crowd in the market for employment coupled with the attitudes of younger people toward work. The coming-of-age of the "baby boom" generation is the key to both. This generation is giant, relative to other demographic cohorts. The labor market is having difficulty absorbing their sheer numbers. It certainly cannot provide enough of the fast-track, interesting and challenging jobs that many baby boomers expect and want. One response of this younger generation has been to leave the traditional workplace to set up new companies in which new rules apply. In fact, in 1980, when the National Federation of Independent Business polled its 560,000 members, it found that one of every three new businesses was started by someone aged 30 or less.[7]

Another trend in the new business field has been the entry of new groups. Until recently, almost all entrepreneurial activity has been the province of white males. Now, three times as many businesses are being started by women as by men. As of 1977, however, the last year for which information is available, women owned only 7.1 percent of all small companies, and minority group members owned only 5.7 percent. Moreover, these firms are generally on the small side of "small," generating 6.6 percent and 3.5 percent of receipts, respectively.[8]

Interestingly enough, the women who own companies are as "regular" as the entrepreneurial group as a whole. A 1977 study by the Census Bureau of woman business owners shows conclusively that owners of small companies come in all shapes and sizes. While only 5.3 percent were younger than 25 and 41.7 percent were over 54, the remaining 53 percent were spread evenly over

PROFILE
Debbie Fields—Making a Better Chocolate Chip Cookie

She intends to have six children. She was foul-line ballcatcher for the Oakland Athletics when she was 13. At 16, she bought herself a new Volkswagen with her own savings. She preferred working to dating, and didn't have a date for the prom or the ceremony at which she was crowned Homecoming Queen. She dropped out of a community college at 19 to bake cookies.

Who is the human dynamo? Debbie Fields, of Mrs. Fields' Cookies, a chain of cookie outlets employing more than 1000 (1984) and operating out of more than 140 locations. The chain is still growing and Fields is talking about international operations.

All this began on $50,000, borrowed from Fields' husband, Randy. She did no advertising, but rather offered free samples of her wares. By the end of her first year, she had two stores, had grossed $200,000, and showed a profit of $25,000.

She sees herself as a "survivor, and what I'm going to do when I make a mistake is evaluate exactly what happened and work so it can never happen again. So it's picking up the pieces and always moving on, always, never stopping." She deals with employee error in the same way. While employees can disappoint her in ways she takes personally, she views today's errors as history. "But there's tomorrow," she says. "And tomorrow I want you to be at the winning gate. I want you to learn from today and be better for tomorrow."

the middle age ranges. Except for women who never married (only 18.8% of owners), the group was evenly split among owners of other marital status.

If you do not fit the demographic profile, however, do not lose sleep over it. What is "average" in this field appears to be the result of combining impressive extremes. NBC News reported that a pair of California grandmothers have gone into competition in long-distance phone service with AT&T. They expect their business to thrive. They refer to themselves as "GrandMas Bell." The *New York Times* reported that a high school student, bored, as he put it, by just "hanging out," signed an agreement to act as a broker for the People's Republic of China in the United States bicycle market.

The real point is that entrepreneurs come in all ages, colors, and mindsets. Each, when you get right down to it, has a different, highly specific reason for starting a company and a unique objective for that company. Not fitting almost makes you fit in this field.

WHERE DO THE IDEAS COME FROM?

"Where do the ideas come from? The same place a poem comes from. When in doubt, go with your own experiences and to what you know is the emotional truth." (Ray Welch, founder of an advertising agency)

At base, a new business has to be able to capitalize on one of two things to be highly successful. The entrepreneur must spot an opportunity before most others do, or must have a new and better way of getting something done than others do. It is particularly nice to do both. To have a business that returns you a living, however, it is not absolutely necessary that you do either. Confusing? That's part of the problem. A business is, essentially, anything that works. It need not be fancy to just get by. To make a splash, however, it has to capitalize on opportunity or method.

Seeing Opportunities

Most entrepreneurs have stories about their beginnings that include the opportunity they saw that others did not see. A particularly clear statement of the process comes from Bruce Burdick, owner of a chain of Computerland franchises in Kansas City. When it occurred to him that Kansas City would be a great market for computers, he was growing worms in Sioux City, Iowa. In short order, he left the worms, moved to Kansas City with his family, and bought the franchise.

His mother's comment and his response are typical. She said that he was just lucky, that he was in the right place at the right time. No way, says Burdick, "I was in Sioux City, which was the wrong place. I had to move.

There were millions of people in Kansas City who could have taken advantage of that opportunity, but I recognized it and they didn't. It's not just luck."[9]

A Whole New Idea

For those with a new and different idea, the game may be one of persistence and grit. It is almost never luck. Thomas Edison is credited with noting that luck is nine parts hard work. After trying 2,000 times to make his theory work, an observer is reputed to have asked him how he could continue in the face of 2,000 failures. Edison supposedly said, "They are not failures. I now know 2,000 ways in which electricity will not work."

Charles Kaman, quoted at the opening of this chapter, is another case in point. He came up with a new design for a helicopter propeller and his employer rejected it. He quit his paying job and spent time tinkering with it in his basement. Charlie's Folly, his friends called it. Well, within two years of his quitting date, the new design was deemed a success, and Charlie was on the way to a $450 million company. His comment? "I never envisioned that I wouldn't succeed. There's just no room to be afraid. If you're afraid, then get the hell out."[10]

Doing Something Better

Kaman's is one of the splashy new companies. Most new small companies are variants on old themes. In these cases, the job of the owner is to find something in the market that he or she can do better (or faster or cleaner, whatever) than any other guy on the block. Once you have pinpointed that particular advantage, your job is to sell it to and in your marketplace. Much of this book is designed to help you do just that.

Unless you are looking for that splashy idea, then, getting an idea that you want to build on is usually not a problem. Most people who are seriously considering going into business already have a pretty fair idea of what they want to do. They know the general field. Perhaps a relative was or is in a related field. (Or, perhaps, they have chosen a field as far away from Daddy's as is humanly possible.)

If you are among those who do not have a specific type of business in mind, start with the things that turn you on, make you happy. If you start by considering fields that you know and enjoy, workable business ideas will often simply appear. Buck Metz, for example, began with a love of fishing and a desire to make trout flies for himself and his friends. Metz Hatchery now supplies the fly-tying community with top quality feathers from about 45,000 birds—and he is unable to fill all the orders.[11]

If trout and roosters are not your thing, similar idea-getting processes occur in cities. Doug Sheley, a former fast-food franchisee, is now a franchisor of his own chain, D'Lites. A dieter himself, he saw—and heard about from his customers—a need for a diet/fitness-oriented fast-food operation. His chain sells typical fast-food fare, made with lower calorie ingredients, but it also sells items that have never been considered fast food before. He must have tapped a real desire. His four outlets have average sales of over $1 million each, compared with a national average of $300,000 per fast-food outlet.[12]

The keys are knowing the field you are considering and enjoying being in it and thinking about it. You will be spending the bulk of the next period of your life in the business you choose. You certainly ought to enjoy it. Once you have found a field that interests you, get creative about what that field needs that it does not yet have or that it does not have properly. Target your prospective business to fill that need. You will not have fun all the time, obviously, but, in the main, enjoyment and/or fulfillment is what will keep you through 60- to 80-hour weeks and through the really trying times that go with any business startup.

This ethic is clear among the stellar successes in small businesses. Dennis Hayes, of Hayes Microcomputer Products (the modem people), was asked about what made his company different, successful. He replied, "Fun. It's fun seeing the company grow. It's fun seeing my products shipped all around the country and knowing that people are happy with them."[13] Burdick, the former worm rancher, perhaps summed it up best. He said: "I went to my 25th reunion, and most of the people there acted like their lives were over. I felt I was the only one who still had a dream. . . . Every day I feel like I'm just beginning."[14]

SETTING GOALS AND OBJECTIVES: WHY ARE YOU DOING THIS?

This discussion about enjoying what you do and feeling fulfilled by it raises the question of why you are contemplating starting your own business at all. While this may sound like a silly question, it is really vital to your choice of business and your success (as you define it) in the business you eventually start. The really critical part of your business planning, in fact, starts right here—with what you really want out of the process of starting and running your own company and why you want it.

You will already have noted that successful entrepreneurs seem to be highly targeted people, clear about what they are doing and about the ways of getting there. This section of this chapter will give you an opportunity to consider your personal objectives and reasons. In fact, we will describe, briefly, some potential choices of objectives and show you an approach to defining your own primary objectives.

Physical and Mental Stresses

Even those who run businesses that they love feel the stresses that Ray Welch speaks of in the Profile. Without a clear personal reason for subjecting yourself to those stresses, you are quite likely to throw in the towel. Your daily routine will be long—12 to 16 hours a day, six to seven days a week is not unheard of. You will be called upon to do numerous things, usually all at the same time. You will be the one responsible for everything.

Particularly if you intend to open your business as a one-person business, you will spend a great deal of time alone. Even when you hire employees, it is unlikely that you will be able to share your real concerns with them. You will have no peers in your company. In a small-sample survey by Boyd and Gumpert reported in the *Wall Street Journal*,[15] 60 percent of company owners agreed with the statement: "There is no one with whom I can share my deepest concerns." Of those surveyed, 56 percent actually showed physical symptoms of the level of stress they felt, including back pain, chest pain, headaches, impaired digestion, or insomnia.

PROFILE
Ray Welch—The Business of Doing What You Like

If it is a typical day, Welch will spend seven of nine hours on chores he considers nothing but an unmitigated bore. If it's a Monday, it will be worse.

Running a startup (advertising) agency, with 15 employees and somewhere around $100,000 a month in overhead and expenses in an industry where competition is unabashedly cutthroat, Welch finds that more and more of his time is spent with the details of running a *business*. Hiring and training employees and wooing and worrying about clients, for example, eat up huge chunks of a day. Only about 30% of Welch's work time in a week—in a good week, that is—is left for creating campaigns and writing copy.

For him, the chores that come from owning one's own business are the toughest of all. "I'm like an overwound watch on Mondays. My stomach is in knots. As we navigate toward Friday, I relax more, and I have less fear that the boat's going to overturn. I get looser. But I'm not emotionally cut out for the *business* side. I despise the business part of it. If I don't get ulcers or die of a heart attack in 10 years, I'll be surprised."

From Claudia M. Christie, "The Number One Pencil at an Advertising Agency," *New England Business* (January 7, 1985):70–73.

While the potential for stress-related illness is real in a small company setting, you should also keep in mind that such stresses also occur at the tops of large business operations. They merely stem from different sources. No one has yet done a comparative study of the two situations. The issue for you, then, is from which source you prefer your stress, rather than stress versus non-stress. It should also be noted that some entrepreneurs claim to feel no particular stress. Fully 100 percent of a (small—49 responses) sample of company founders polled by William Delaney in 1984 reported themselves healthy.[16]

The Need for Well-Defined Reasons

The reason you might want to take on the level of responsibility and stress inherent in starting and operating a company is ultimately a highly personal matter. Difficulties in this area generally stem from three factors: failure to consider the matter at all, murky or confusing definitions of personal "success," and what other people tell you should be your objectives or reasons. Once recognized, these difficulties are easy to overcome. Overcoming them will let you understand better what it is you want your prospective business to do for you. This understanding, in turn, will help you to choose an appropriate business and to structure your business to help meet your personal objectives.

This process of considering why you, personally, want to open a business is often difficult, simply because raising the issue requires you to think about what you really want out of your life. This is always hard to do, largely because specifying personal goals involves the (significant) risk of falling short or of failing entirely. Thus, most of us avoid the problem. As you begin to develop a long-term career—your company—however, failure to consider where it will take you in relation to where you want to go can ensure not only personal failure, but also business failure. The key notion is that, particularly in the beginning, you and your company will be virtually interchangeable. If one of the two has no direction, odds are that neither will get there.

It is particularly important that you not let others do your choosing and defining for you. Such influence is often a subtle process that occurs almost by osmosis. People in general, and writers and teachers in the field of business in particular, generally assume that the only reason for a person to open his or her own business is to make bundles of money. While making money is a perfectly legitimate personal objective, you need to understand that it is not the only legitimate personal objective. It may be one of yours. It may be secondary to objectives that are more important to you. It may not even rate on your scale of objectives. These, too, are legitimate positions for you as an entrepreneur, as you will see in the next section.

Potential Purposes

To assist you in the difficult process of defining your personal objectives, this section describes a number of broad areas that might account for your basic desire to start your own business. We also offer some comments on the relationship of some characteristics of businesses that might prevent you from reaching each type of personal objective.

Money.   Because of the outside emphasis on money-making as the primary reason for starting businesses, we have begun our brief discussion of possible priorities with a discussion of money.

Two things must be noted about money as a personal objective for an entrepreneur. First, if making money is *not* a primary objective of yours, you will still need to make enough money to keep your business afloat. No matter what your objectives are, your business must take in at least as much as it pays out in order to remain in business. This is why so much of this book (and other books) spends so much time discussing business profitability.

Second, if making a great deal of money *is* your primary objective, you will need to define how much is "a great deal." If you do not have a number or a level of income defined, you are quite likely to spend time and energy worrying about reaching an ever-receding goal. In short, you will never feel as if you have "gotten there"—"there" being undefined. Also, and more immediately important to the business planning process, you will not know whether the business you propose to enter will permit you to reach the personal goal you have set. In either case, you will feel as if you are floundering, getting nowhere.

Needless to say, few people would turn down large supplies of money. The question that you have to address is whether money is the primary thing that you are after. Is it money, primarily, that is leading you to take this business and personal risk? Or is it really something else that is driving you? To reinforce the idea that money may be neither the main thing nor the only thing, we offer additional comments from entrepreneurs who have been successful in business and who claim to be meeting their personal goals.

Ron Schultz, founder and owner of tea companies, set up one company specifically to generate money for charity. "It's not everything, you know, being rich," he says.[17] The president of Antioch Bookplate, Lee Morgan, agrees. "I don't think that people should go into business to get rich. They do it because they have a product or a concept that they are interested in. If you happen to get rich, that's OK. But that's not why you do it. If you're only in it for the money, and nothing else, it isn't going to work. You do it because it's fun and stimulating."[18]

A professor I know, for example, invested time and money in a company that was designed and developed entirely to provide work for the people in a small village in India. The company provided funds for the making of clothing and then added the expertise and the facilities for importing the products into the United States and marketing them. The products caught on, and the company wound up not only meeting the primary goal of the founders—providing employment for villagers—but also a major financial success.

Please note that we are not pressing the notion that you should *not* be entering your own business with making a great deal of money as your primary objective. We are suggesting only that you may be equally successful in your own terms and in the marketplace if non-monetary objectives are your primary motivations.

Independence.   Another fairly common primary objective for entrepreneurs is the establishment of independence. If this is your personal objective, we recommend that you consider very carefully what you are seeking independence *from*. If it is independence from a "9 to 5" job, we can guarantee that any new business will fill that bill. If it is from people telling you what to do, we doubt that there is any business on earth that will satisfy your need. In fact, it has been pointed out that a business owner usually merely exchanges one boss (the corporate superior) for many bosses (all the customers of the business).

Control.   Entrepreneurs often express the desire to be in complete control of their destinies, succeeding or failing by their own efforts alone. If this is your primary personal objective, your choice of business will be critical. You cannot choose a business in which you will be a captive supplier to some other company or industry.

If, for example, your company made Post Office-approved mailboxes for installation in apartment buildings, you would be entirely dependent upon the policies of the Post Office. If that agency altered its policy about how it chose to deliver mail, you would find yourself in trouble—which would have absolutely nothing to do with how well or poorly you made the product or how well you marketed to building owners.

This problem actually occurred to Auth Electric Company. The Post Office now prefers central mail delivery sites in apartment and condominium complexes. The policy change wiped out any money that the company used to make selling the boxes to builders. The Post Office gives builders the cluster boxes, saving more in more efficient delivery than the cost of the boxes themselves.[19]

Control problems may also exist in situations where your company has one major customer. At least one consulting company almost met disaster by tying its fate too closely to a set of government agencies. When there were cutbacks in Washington, consulting funds were among the first to go. The company very nearly went right along with those funds.

In short, maintaining a reasonable level of control over your own success or failure demands a situation in which your company will have many customers who are not connected with one another. You will have to structure your operation so that no single customer, client, or customer group can wield significant financial power over your total operation.

Authority.   If you are a person to whom the wielding of authority is of prime importance, your company will have to have, or grow rapidly to include, numbers of people over whom you can exercise that authority. A one-man show would not be a good business for you. Similarly, a company peopled with employees who may reject authority in general—a software development company, for example—would probably not be a good idea for you.

Status.   Businesses that require "professional" credentials or advanced degrees are generally those accorded high status in this society (with the exception, oddly enough, of elementary and secondary school teachers). If status is your primary personal goal, then, businesses based on these credentials should be among your top choices. Please note that you may not need to have the credentials yourself. Often experience, coupled with the ability to hire credentialled talent will suffice.

Beyond the professions-based businesses, status is whatever your community says or believes it is. Often entrepreneurs with high status needs will use their businesses as a base for doing charitable and/or community work. Often the businesses of status-oriented people are used as springboards into politics. If the business you want to start is not inherently status-laden, status, recognition, and public approbation can often be built along with the business.

Needless to say, we have not exhausted all the possible personal objectives involved in starting a business. Our intent was, rather, to demonstrate that there are any number of potential personal objectives and that each has a different set of implications for an entrepreneur's choice of business. Most people have a mix of desires in a startup situation. Your first job, then, is sorting through your own unique mix of objectives and coming up with your priorities. Once through that part, you also need to consider your prospective company in light of your defined objectives and priorities.

It will help to remember that, even if you set a number of personal objectives today, they are not engraved in stone. You can change your mind or your outlook or your priorities as it makes sense in your life to do so. To recognize the change explicitly as a change, however, will let you also reevaluate your business operation in light of your new or altered personal objectives.

How to Approach Recognizing Your Personal Objective(s)

A reasonably simple and painless way to begin considering what you really want to get out of your business on a personal level is to dream a bit—and then analyze the dream. Start by sitting in your favorite chair or under your favorite tree and closing your eyes. Then, "see" yourself 10 years from today, a successful person.

What do you see? Where are you (at home or in the office or shop or factory, someplace else entirely)? What kind of clothes are you wearing? Are you married? Children? What is your family like? What does your home look like? How do you get to your place of business? What kind of vehicle did you drive to work in or do you have parked in the garage (driveway?)? Pretend you are going out tonight. Where will you be going? What kinds of people will also be there? When did you take your last vacation? Where did you go? With whom? What did you do?

In short, the idea is to envision your lifestyle in 10 years. Once you have that vision, consider what that lifestyle requires. If you were in a large office, with your Guccis resting on a giant rosewood desk or a thick imported carpet, if your home was filled with authentic objets d'art, your vacation was a ski weekend last month in Switzerland, and your evening out included a formal dress ball in Austria, you can conclude that money and influence are high on your list of personal priorities. If, on the other hand, you saw yourself in a dark suit before a cheering crowd, being whisked off in a limosine to a $1,000 dollar-a-plate fund raiser, you might conclude that public respect and general influence are your priorities.

Now, perform the process over again, this time seeing yourself as the owner of the company you are contemplating beginning. Ask similar questions. Do the images match? Are your images of yourself as successful owner of your prospective business reasonable and realistic? If so, you're in good shape. If not, it might be wise to think a bit more about your lifestyle vision or about the type of business you are considering.

Whatever your visions show you, you must ensure that the business you will build will help you get from wherever you are to that place you know you want to be. Ultimately, your personal visions are unique to you. There is no "right" or "wrong" in this part of your business development process. (We must point out, however, that "legal" and "illegal" do exist and are enforceable regardless of your vision.) Judgments you make in this process of defining your personal objectives are yours alone. You must recognize, however, that your vision of personal success will interact with your business choices. Thus these visions must play a part in your choice of business. Do not neglect this frivolous-sounding, but really vital, part of your business planning process.

SUMMARY

The idea of owning your own business is highly seductive. It often seems an appropriate alternative to working for others. The question that you need to answer is whether building your own business is the best thing for you to do. Part of this question appears to involve the issue of whether you are the "right" type of person—that is, the entrepreneurial type. There are numerous quizzes, questionnaires, and surveys designed to tell you whether you are that type. We believe, however, that 15 or 26 questions hardly constitute a valid test of whether you have what it takes to succeed in a business of your own. Too many different types of people have succeeded to permit reliance on questionnaires, quizzes, or even demographics.

Successful business ideas abound, as a check of business concepts in almost any field will attest. The ideas come in three general categories: seeing an opportunity that nobody else has yet seen, seeing a totally new way to do or make something (or figuring out how to make or do something totally new), and figuring out how to do something better. You stand the best chance of a hit in one of these categories if you seek your ideas in a field you know well and enjoy.

Once you have a business idea, the real key to entrepreneurial success seems to be how badly you want to succeed. This requires that you assess your own tenacity and stamina and that you consider whether there is anything you want badly enough to go through a normal business startup. Part and parcel of this evaluation is the consideration of why you want your own business at all. This involves explicit thought about your personal objectives and how your business can provide you the with the vehicle for achieving those objectives.

Should you decide to go ahead with your business planning process, the remainder of this book is intended to help you with the business of putting together a business.

FOR YOU TO CONSIDER

1. Why do you believe that entrepreneurial quizzes are so interesting to so many people? Do you believe that they are helpful? How?
2. Discuss two major ways in which the profile of the "average" entrepreneur is changing. Why are these changes occurring?
3. What seem to be the main reasons that people start their own companies?
4. Comment on the notion that "the only purpose for going into business is to make money."

5. How and why is the statement in question 4 essentially different from the statement that a business has to take in at least as much money as it pays out in order to stay in operation?
6. Why is it important for a beginning entrepreneur to consider his or her personal objectives explicitly before embarking on the planning for a startup?
7. What is a valid or legitimate personal objective for a new entrepreneur? Give two examples of potential priority objectives and discuss how they might relate to the entrepreneur's choice of a business to begin.

NOTES

1. "Small Business," *Wall Street Journal* (July 25, 1983):13.
2. A. David Silver, *The Entrepreneurial Life: How to Go for It and Get It* (New York: Ronald Press, Wiley, 1983):5.
3. Daniel Robert Fierro, *The New American Entrepreneur: How to Get Off the Fast Track into a Business of Your Own* (New York: Morrow, 1982):28ff.
4. *New York Daily News* (August 7, 1983):5.
5. Bruce Mohl, "Their Pursuit No Trivial Matter," *Boston Globe* (July 8, 1984):A1.
6. Brochure, Center for Entrepreneurial Management, (New York, 1984).
7. National Federation of Independent Business poll, *Venture* (October, 1983):40.
8. *The State of Small Business, A Report of the President* (Washington, D.C.: U.S. Government Printing Office 1982):281ff.
9. Tom Richman, "Going Their Way," *Inc.* magazine (December 1983):70.
10. Sally Jacobs, "New England Business Profile," *New England Business* (February 20, 1984):52.
11. Sanford Jacobs, "Hatchery's Profitable Sideline Taps Long-Neglected Market," *Wall Street Journal* (October 31, 1983):33.
12. John F. Persinos, "Where's the Salt?", *Inc.* magazine (June, 1984):23.
13. Richman, "Going Their Way," 76.
14. Ibid.
15. *Wall Street Journal* (May 7, 1984):35.
16. Jake Simon, "So What Does It Take to Establish a Mark as an Entrepreneur?", *New England Business* (May 17, 1984):47.
17. Susan Buchsbaum, "Tea and Sympathy," *Inc.* magazine (June 1984):97–100.
18. Jerome Goldstein, *In Business For Yourself,* (New York: Scribner's, 1982):11.
19. Sanford Jacobs, "Postal Service Hurts Makers of Multiple-Unit Mail Boxes," *Wall Street Journal* (February 13, 1984):29.

CASES FOR PART 1

SALLY JONES AND "NEIGHBORS"

Sally Jones was 30 years old—a turning point for her. She was married to a corporate fast-tracker. They had two children, Aline, age eight, and Jason, age six. Now that both children were in school, Sally felt she should be doing something more with her life than she was doing. After all, how many soap opera episodes could a human being watch before the characters began getting all mixed up? She also firmly believed that too many of those things could begin to permanently rot the brain.

Not only were the children gone most of the day—school and various kinds of lessons and sports and such—but Don was home less and less these days, too. As he moved up the corporate ladder, more of his time and energy were going into his work. He often stayed late for meetings. He traveled often for the company. In short, he was rarely around to provide aid and moral support. Sally often felt bored and alone. She was convinced that her continual tiredness was the result of sheer boredom.

She needed to get out of the house, expand her life, do something on her own and for herself. She thought first about joining some volunteer organization in her local area. It was nice, respectable stuff—and it might even indirectly help Don in his career. Over the years, though, she had come to believe that work not paid for was work not valued. She just wasn't prepared to give her services away. Moreover, though Don was making good money—and threatened to do even better in the future—both kids would need money for college eventually. An additional income certainly couldn't hurt. And Sally would feel that she was contributing more than tender loving care to the family's goals.

"So I'll go to work," she decided. "After all, I have a college degree. In business, no less. I should have no trouble finding something that would be fun and exciting." But the more she thought about what kind of work she wanted to look for, the more turned off she became. She certainly didn't want jobs like those some of her friends had—secretarial work or research and analysis. She wanted to *do* something. The main problem, she realized after thinking about it for a while, was that the very idea of taking orders from just anyone—particularly from people like the guys Joanne or Ellen worked for—was a real impossibility for her. She had never done well at responding to authority, nor did she particularly respect a person merely because he had attained some lofty position.

The more she thought about it, the more she realized that she wanted to build a career, not to take a job, and that *she* wanted to be the one giving the orders. She suddenly knew that her only real option, then, was to open her own business. That way, she would not be tied to other people's schedules or hindered by their incompetence. In addition, as the kids got even more involved in school and eventually went off to college, she would have the business to work with forever.

Sally knew that Don and her father and her Uncle Harry would lend her money to start a company. Maybe they'd even give it to her. Her main question, then, was what kind of a business she wanted to start.

She began with what she liked to do and did well. Since she and Don had begun to entertain at home, Sally had discovered that she loved to cook. She was, by the accounts of all her friends and assorted guests, very good at it as well. People loved her food and were always telling her that she should open a restaurant. They always asked for her recipes, many of which were her own creations.

The restaurant idea attracted her. She would be able to have a physical space of her own. She would have employees to take care of things she did not particularly want to do. She would be able to be gracious and welcoming, treating her customers as her guests. She just knew that the restaurant business was the right one for her. She would open her own restaurant, then.

1. What do you believe are Sally Jones' objectives in starting her business?
2. What effect, if any, will these objectives have on her business?
3. Given her objectives, has she chosen the right business in your opinion? Why or why not?

ROB KING AND "KING FINANCIAL"

Rob King was 38. He looked around the living room of his small, three-bedroom house outside San Diego. It was a fairly new place—but then almost everything in that area was pretty new. It was O.K., he decided, but not what he had expected to have by the time he was 40.

His wife, Ginny, and his three children (ages 12, 9, and 7) were grouped around the big color television, cheering on the Padres. Rob himself didn't feel much like cheering. There had to be more to life than this. What did he really have to leave his children? What was he really giving to Ginny? When he got right down to it, the answers were "nothing much." He didn't want it to be that way. He hadn't planned his life that way.

And even his "nothing much" was currently in some danger. Since it was Sunday, his thoughts had inevitably drifted to Monday and to work. Rob King really hated his job. The job itself might not have been so bad without John Helm, his boss. The guy was erratic and unpredictable—that is, until he decided he didn't like you. Then you could do nothing right and nothing good or useful. Though Rob really disliked very few people, Helm made the short list of those he hated. Rob feared him, too, because he was so erratic.

He knew that for years Helm had built the paperwork that would allow him to get rid of Rob at virtually any moment. In fact, he enjoyed reminding Rob of its existence. None of it was real, but it was so meticulously done and so extended that nobody would believe it wasn't all true. Since it had not been made public, there was not even anyone Rob could talk to about it without sounding completely paranoid and slightly crazy.

In fact, he felt that if he didn't get out of there soon, he *would* go crazy. Every morning as he left the house, Rob's stomach would knot up. He had grown distant with Ginny and short with the kids. He'd even come close to kicking the dog once or twice. He clearly had to get out of Consolidated National Bank—and he had to do it soon, before he drove everyone crazy.

But what was he to do? He was pushing 40. He had tried to transfer within the bank, but Helm had scotched all moves in that direction. He also knew that there were a lot of guys like Helm running around loose in banks, so he was wary of seeking a similar position in another bank. Also, Helm had seen to it that he remained an assistant vice president—of which every bank had hundreds—so moving would be difficult. He had sent resumes to numerous local companies looking for a spot in their treasury departments. No dice. He suspected that Helm had had a hand in these negatives, too.

He was about at the end of his rope. But during the seventh inning stretch, a small idea slipped into his head. He had seen some of the people who came into the bank asking for—and getting—loans to start their own businesses. Although it was not his department that handled such loans, he had been close enough to watch and, sometimes, to listen. He had followed several of these people as they paid off their loans and become successful. One guy, in particular, Rob remembered. He now had more than 200 employees and was a shoo-in for election to the next City Council. None of these people seemed a great deal smarter than Rob himself.

This, he thought, might be the answer to his dilemma! He could leave Consolidated National, leave Helm (without Helm's approval or rejection), and set up his own consulting business. He was, after all, a C.P.A. with experience in industry and in bank lending. He was somewhat short on specific small business lending knowledge and experience, but he could remedy that, he thought. He knew how banks worked and why loans were or were not made. In short, he had specialized knowledge to sell.

His strength, he thought, would be in advising and assisting new small companies through their initial banking experiences. He knew, from brief stints as a lecturer, that he was a good teacher and good at explaining things. He also knew the banking and financing end. He could help a beginning business through all the paperwork and all the hoops.

The more he thought about this idea, the better it sounded. He would get to tell Helm to take a walk. He would be independent at long last. He would have a chance to give his family something more like what he had envisioned for them—maybe not by the time he was 40 (he knew that these things take time to develop), but reasonably soon. The company wouldn't cost much to start and he was confident that he could do the work.

He smiled, just thinking about beating Helm at his own game. Slowly, he began to relax. He leaned back in his chair, smiled at the backs of his family, and turned his attention to the last innings of the Padres game.

1. What do you believe are Rob King's objectives in starting his business?
2. What effect, if any, will these objectives have on his business?
3. Given his objectives, do you believe he has chosen the right business? Why or why not?

DANIELLE MACKIE AND "DANIELLE DESIGNS IN CERAMICS"

At 23, Danielle Mackie, Danni to her friends, should have been inordinately pleased with herself. She had recently graduated with a degree in arts administration from a rather prestigious university. She had done well in the job sweepstakes, too. She was now a valued member of the staff of the New York State Museum of Fine Arts in Albany. She was pulling down the handsome sum (for arts administration) of $23,000 a year and was exactly where she had wanted to be when she began her studies years ago.

So why, she kept asking herself, was she so unhappy? Her folks kept asking her the same question, too. They had the best of intentions, of course, and they only wanted her to be happy. But they kept telling her over and over again why she should be happy and feel satisfied with her progress. And she knew they were right. So the more often she heard it, the more miserable she felt—first, because she wasn't happy, and second, because she was causing her parents concern and worry.

In fact, these days, the only time she was fully content was when she was lost in a lump of clay, a lump she was shaping into something beautiful, an object that everyone would enjoy just looking at. When she was apartment-hunting in the Albany area, a prime concern had been extra space for the workroom she now had. She was able to immediately set the heated garage aside as her studio consigning her car to a covered breezeway. Luckily, rents in the area had not yet become totally outrageous, so her extravagance of extra space could be managed within her budget. Her studio became her place of escape, her hideout when her job or anything else got to be too much for her.

Danni thought she was pretty good with clays and glazes. And numbers of people liked the results. Throughout her school years, she had been urged by various teachers and assorted other people to study ceramics and pottery seriously. She, on the other hand, never wanted to turn what was, for her, sheer pleasure into something she had to worry about, to submit for grading or criticism. She also knew how impractical it would be to pursue pottery, or any of the arts, as a career option. Had she not already known it herself, her very practical parents would have reminded her. Thus, she came as close to a career in the arts as she safely could—a nice, practical degree in arts administration. She now could push numbers and write grant proposals with the best of them!

Unfortunately, she didn't really want to . . .

As she sat one evening contemplating a not-yet-finished figure, it occurred to her that she might actually be able to have it all. "Why not?" she thought to herself. "Just because I have a good job doesn't mean I can't do anything else with my life. Why shouldn't I take a shot at placing some of my work? Then we'll see what happens and where we go from there. Maybe I can really have the career I want *and* enough security so that neither I nor my parents will have to worry too much."

As she considered the matter further, the inevitable snags began to appear. First, where could she place her pieces for a trial run? Since she had never really tested her work on people who "knew," she was understandably hesitant to test her talent very close to home. Second, what if the results were surprising? Suppose everyone loved her work? What then? Worse, suppose everyone hated her work? Would she still find such enjoyment in it for herself?

The more she thought about it, the more she knew that she would at least have to give it a try. She had been good and had done something practical with her education. Nobody but Danni was aware of how much that effort had cost her. She recognized that if she didn't test her talent now, she might never do it—and then she'd spend her life wondering whether she really should have tried. And being unhappy at whatever work she was doing. Besides, having taken a business-oriented degree could have enormous benefits for her if her work proved salable. "How many artists do you know who can push numbers?!" she thought with a grin.

1. What do you believe to be Danielle Mackie's objectives in considering starting to sell her ceramics pieces?
2. Consider some of the hazards for Mackie in testing the waters as she plans to do. Should she do it anyway?
3. At what point, if ever, is Mackie likely to mention her new venture to her parents? Her employers? Do you think this is a good approach? Why or why not?

ED JAMES AND "OAK TREE BOOKS"

Edgar James heaved a huge sigh of relief when the last student trailed out of his classroom on the last day of the school year. He put his feet up on the desk, tipped his chair back, and contemplated the empty classroom. It seemed so peaceful and quiet without the kids. Now all he had left was the final grading and an appearance at commencement (and maybe a party or two).

He felt satisfied with himself, and he also felt a sense of anticipation. With any kind of luck, it would have been his last class of students ever. He was about to embark on a long-standing dream. He was going to start his bookstore.

Even when he was a kid, books had held great fascination for him. Though he was generally good at sports, and genuinely liked other people, he had usually preferred reading to playing games. He grinned, thinking about his many childhood hours in libraries. His mother used to say that when he was into a book, the house could burn down around him and he'd never notice until the pages started to singe. She claimed that he would even read cereal boxes if nothing else was available! Now, finally, he'd get to buy and sell books, to deal with them all the time—and make money doing it besides. Sheer joy!

It had been a long time coming. His parents had not been wealthy. He had been unlucky enough to have been born too late for GI Bill benefits and too early for the Sputnik-induced scholarship/loan programs of the late fifties and early sixties. So he joined the army and let them help him through a college degree. He stayed in, rising through the ranks, for the 20 years necessary to gain his retirement benefits of 50 percent of his base salary. He was sure, then, that he would never starve.

As a transition from total regimentation to total independence, he chose to teach at The Academy, an exclusive private school for young men. It had been a wise choice, even in retrospect. He had regained contact with the world of books and with the reading tastes of a non-military public. He got to meet a number of influential people. He could live on campus, so he had been able to save a sizable sum of money. This was intended to be used to begin the business.

In short, he was pleased with himself. And he was ready to begin the next phase of his life.

1. What do you believe are Ed James' objectives in starting a bookstore?
2. Assuming that you are right, will these objectives help or hinder him in starting and operating the business?
3. In your opinion, what would make Ed feel successful in this bookstore phase of his life?

PART 2

WHO WILL BUY WHAT YOU'RE SELLING?

3. Building the Framework

"Would you tell me, please, which way I ought to
go from here?'
"That depends a good deal on where you want to
get to," said the Cat.
"I don't much care where—" said Alice.
"Then it doesn't matter which way you go," said
the Cat.
"—so long as I get somewhere," Alice added as
an explanation.
"Oh, you're sure to do that," said the Cat, "if you
only walk long enough."

Lewis Carroll, *Alice's Adventures in Wonderland*

"I have been so taken up with the thoughts of
leaving . . . that I have never even considered the
direction," said Frodo. "For where am I to go?
And by what shall I steer?"

J. R. R. Tolkien, *Fellowship of the Ring*

In the first section of this book, we asked you to begin to examine yourself—
your strengths, your weaknesses, and your objectives—as they relate to
businesses in general. In this chapter, you will begin to focus on the business
you are thinking about starting. You will begin to develop its objectives and
begin to plan for its direction and its strengths.

As you no doubt discovered in the first section of this book, setting useful
objectives for your personal life is difficult business. The difficulty of it turns
many people away from actually doing objective-setting. And while it is
possible for many people to live adequately without defining their objectives—going with the flow—for entrepreneurs and for their businesses, such
behavior can be terminal. Yet, like Frodo, we often get so taken up with the

idea of starting our own businesses that we neglect to consider anything beyond the notion that we will be successful. We fail to consider the ways in which we will bring about our successes.

In this chapter, we consider ways of providing initial direction for your business through development of a *basic business definition* for your proposed new venture. We also begin to pinpoint some of the factors in the environment of your new venture about which you will need to be particularly aware in order to succeed—your *critical success factors*. The basic business definition and the critical success factors that you will develop for your business will provide a framework for later decision making and will ensure that you have started your enterprise with a hefty shove in a well-considered direction. (It may not turn out to be the only "right" direction, but at least you will have decided, rather than drifted.)

SEPARATING YOUR SELF FROM YOUR BUSINESS

There is some controversy regarding whether an entrepreneur should see himself as separate from the business he is creating. Those who insist that such a separation is detrimental cite the enormous energy that must attend a new venture's development and suggest that the only way to achieve that level of energy is to identify the entrepreneur totally with the enterprise. Thus, the person and the business become one, and all energies can flow to the business.

Of course, this means that there is little or no energy left over for yourself, or your spouse, or your friends, or even your dog. One tends to burn out rather rapidly in that sort of environment. Not only could this be detrimental to you personally, but, more to the point, such a personal condition quite often leads to the total loss of objectivity and realistic perspective regarding your venture.

Loss of objectivity is the real danger inherent in a total identification between you and your business. You will need to be able to see both the forest *and* the trees (often at the same time), the long-term as well as the short- and medium-terms in order to make your venture succeed. Total identification between you and your business tends to enable you to see the short-term very clearly—in terms of personal survival—and the longer term very little, if at all.

The ultimate choice about how to live your life and how to integrate your business into it is, of course, yours. (That's probably one of the reasons you wanted to start your own business, in fact.) But consider the potential negative effects of total identification. First, if by some strange chance your current venture fails, do you want to be essentially forced to consider your *self* to have failed? Or merely your current venture?

Figure 3.1   Your relationship to your business

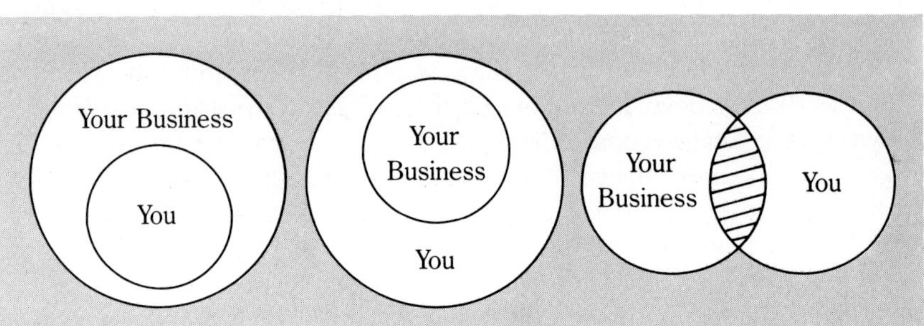

It is quite often the case that successful entrepreneurs have one or more failures or, at least, less-than-howling-successes in their histories. Henry Ford tried out a few before the Ford Motor Company. The man who built Celestial Seasonings had previous experience with a health food store he owned. The man who conceived and built Rent-A-Wreck was not a phenomenal success in the used car sales business. These people, and hundreds of others more or less like them, took something from their prior experiences *because* they could separate themselves from their former businesses and analyze, or at least consider, what went wrong. They did not lose their essential belief in themselves. Their businesses did not do well. *They* were poorer financially, perhaps, but still O.K.

Another factor to consider in terms of total versus sizable commitment to your venture is the effect of each on the other people in your life—your close family and friends. Total identification between yourself and your business essentially shuts them out, unless it sucks them in completely as well. In either case, you tend to lose. Either they resent your total commitment to this non-person, or they resent being drawn into what is essentially *your* dream. Your only real hope is to convince them that it is really their vision as well as yours—a tough job when you have a few other things on your mind.

The case for giant, though not total, commitment is essentially a case for objectivity and perspective. If you think about this process of starting a new venture, you will see that the objective(s) you developed for yourself could theoretically be satisfied by any number of successful ventures—however you defined "successful." This particular venture is the vehicle that you expect to get you there, but if it doesn't, another will present itself eventually. If you absolutely must have a good business rationale for that part of your life that you will keep separate from the business, think of it as a means of giving you perspective on your venture. (Your relatives and friends may also have some useful insights if they are still talking to you.)

Less than total commitment to your fledgling company does not imply a cavalier attitude toward it. It is your current best shot at whatever you have defined as "success". While you can succeed, eventually, without this particular vehicle, it cannot succeed without you. While you may have a life outside this business, it has absolutely no life, at this point, without you. Before you consider reading "minimal" where we have actually said "less than total," ask yourself how much time and energy and money you are prepared to waste on fooling around before you really decide to go after your vision of success.

APPROACHING OBJECTIVE-SETTING FOR YOUR BUSINESS

Wherever you choose to draw the line between you and "it," you must know in very concrete terms what "it" is. If you opt for some separation of your personal life from your business life, defining the business will help you to define the separation. If you opt for total identification, think of defining the business as a means of telling others about what you are doing and why you no longer see them. In either case, unless you have developed objectives for your business and directions for it to pursue, you are unlikely to make a go of it. Even a riverboat gambler knew what the object of the game was and why he was in it.

While the objectives of your business can and probably should be different from your personal objectives, they should mesh. After all, it is your company. And while its success does not necessarily guarantee your own personal success, however you define it, its success should at least contribute to your own.

As was noted earlier, an objective, or a series of objectives, provides both a direction for your efforts and some measure of when you have accomplished whatever it is you set out to do. The initial objective for Celestial Seasonings' herbal teas, for example, was to become the largest purveyor of such items in the United States within three years. (They did it.) For Mo Siegal, founder of Celestial Seasonings, however, this business success was merely a means to his personal goal. What he really wanted to do was to help people in the United States become healthier through the use of herbs.

Whatever personal objective you defined for yourself, you need to know how—precisely how—your business is to contribute to achieving that objective. In order to develop this connection, you will need to know what it is the business is to do and how its success will be defined.

A good place to begin to consider the objectives of the business and how its objectives will mesh with your personal objectives is to define the business in some very basic ways. Sometimes, however, even defining what the business will do is difficult. Sam Goldwyn, of movies fame, is said to have had a sure-fire method of determining whether a would-be entrepreneur had his act together. He grew tired of listening to lengthy and rambling pitches for money to fund new projects and concepts. He reportedly began handing out his business card, saying that if the proposer could not write his concept on the back of the card, he did not have it clear enough in his own mind to discuss it rationally. As Goldwyn recognized, the key is being able to state clearly and succinctly what you are about to do.

BASIC BUSINESS DEFINITION

A basic business definition is such a brief, clear statement. It answers two very simple questions:

- *What* is the business going to do?
- *Who* is it going to do it for?

This simplicity is deceptive, however, because of what you want your basic business definition to do for you. You want it to provide you with a framework within which to make decisions. You want it to provide enough information to permit you to use it as a cornerstone of the business. You want to be able to use it to tell people, particularly people with money to invest or to lend, what you are about.

You also want to be able to use your basic business definition to convey your excitement and your vision to your new employees so that they may share in your goals and help to make your venture a success. According to Peters and Waterman, authors of *In Search of Excellence,* one of the hallmarks of an "excellent" company is its desire and its ability to communicate the goals of management or of the founders to its employees. Goals are matters of seriousness and intensity in such companies. They matter to participants throughout the organization. They should matter to you—if for no reason other than to help focus everyone in the same general direction. Needless to say, in order to communicate your goals and your concepts effectively, you must have defined them reasonably well.

What Will Your Company Do?

The first part of your basic business definition deals with what your company is going to make or sell or distribute or do by way of service. At its simplest level, you could merely describe the general line of business you will be in—a restaurant or a clothing store or a paper bag manufacturer. Consider, however, what would happen if you told 10 different people that you were

PROFILE
Steven B. Belkin—Trans National Inc.

What was once a little travel company, operating out of an "office" in an apartment in Belmont, Massachusetts is now a $57 million company selling travel, insurance, financial service and office furniture by direct mail out of its own eight-story building. The trip took 10 years.

"My parents inspired me," says Belkin. "They made it clear that being a success in business was very important. I just wanted to go into business and become successful. There was never a second thought." He now says that money, his original measure of success, no longer gives him the inspiration it once did. His objective these days is to give back to the community that "provided us with the opportunity to become successful."

He owes his success as an entrepreneur, he claims, to his ability to see things differently from the way others see them. Though trained at the Harvard Business School, he does not believe that his training taught him to be an entrepreneur. He was born with that, he believes. But Harvard did help him learn to define better.

"Defining a business in a broader sense allows you to see opportunity. When I started Trans National, people thought it was a travel agency. But I saw it as a direct mail company that initially sold travel."

Adapted from Douglas M. Bailey, "New England Business Profile," *New England Business* (September 3, 1984):104.

going to open a clothing store. Ten different pictures would form, one in each different mind. The likelihood of any of them matching your image of what you mean to do is practically nil. Clearly, you need a somewhat more informative definition of what you mean your business to do.

Suppose, for example, that you were opening a restaurant, Johnnie's. You could define what the business will do in innumerable ways including, but by no means limited to:

1. Johnnie's will be a restaurant.
2. Johnnie's will be a fast-food restaurant.
3. Johnnie's will sell hamburgers, providing both eat-in space and take-out service.
4. Johnnie's will be a fast-food-type hamburger place, offering eat-in or take-out food and emphasizing low cost with friendly service.

Of these four, clearly the last is the most descriptive definition of your restaurant. It tells people that Johnnie's will sell hamburgers (and probably the standard adjuncts). Its priorities will include low cost and friendliness. This definition also implies that Johnnie's will seek volume business, since high volume is normally required to achieve profit in low-cost operations.

Using your own basic business definition.   But you are not going through all this definition and priority-stating only for the benefit of other people—not even for the money people. One of the classic problems for new venturers is how to keep their own plans on track. While you may know what Johnnie's will be like on the day you start your planning, at the end of a month or two you may have added so many bells and whistles or made so many seemingly minor changes that your current enterprise bears little resemblance to your original concept for Johnnie's. A good basic business definition can serve to remind you, throughout the planning process and the initial phases of operation, of what you were about when you started.

Suppose, for example, that you are developing your restaurant, Johnnie's. As your plans begin to take shape, your cousin Betty goes on a natural foods kick. She attempts to convince you to change hamburgers for bean curd and, failing that, is prepared to settle for the addition of a salad bar to Johnnie's. Thousands of people, she contends, are salad fans and many would be attracted to Johnnie's by the addition. Besides, she adds, it would be good for them and you'd be doing them a service. Now, even if you have been convinced personally to trade steak for spinach, should you, in your rush of enthusiasm, add a salad bar to Johnnie's?

The first and second definitions in the list above, definitions 1 and 2, would pose no barrier to the addition of a salad bar—after all, Johnnie's will be a restaurant. Definition 3 centers on hamburgers—but why not put some lettuce on them? Only the fourth definition of Johnnie's will give you any sense of the basic change you are considering in adding a salad bar to your original concept.

First, it will mean people stay in your place longer and more of them will stay there to eat. Your expected eat-in/take-out ratio will change. You will probably have to provide more seating space for your customers than you had originally planned (remember the seating expansions that occurred at some Burger King outlets when they added salad bars?). This will probably mean that you'll need more space in which to do the same volume of business. More space will cost you more money. Will you still be able to maintain your low cost priority?

And there will be other cost changes required by the addition of a salad bar. Some staff member (probably "additional") will have to chop the vegetables, ensure that the ice on which they will be displayed is adequate and that the supply of fixings is itself adequate at all times. You will need additional refrigerated storage for the vegetables, and you will need additional suppliers and more frequent deliveries simply to ensure that the greens are fresh.

Now obviously some of this cost can be made up in the price of the salads themselves. But some is likely to lap over into the cost of your hamburgers. Now, even if you are onto spinach forever, do you still want Johnnie's, as you see it, to have a salad bar?

If you still think that it will be a great addition, then go ahead and add it, remembering to change your basic business definition in appropriate ways. Your original definition will have served one of its major purposes by alerting you to the magnitude and type of change you were about to make and by asking you to think through the changes that your change is going to require.

As with any objective or statement of purpose, your business definition is not set in concrete. It can change and grow as your business or your life requires. Its main purpose is to provide direction and to serve as a yardstick against which to measure proposed changes. The clearer and more specific your business definition is, the better it can serve that purpose.

Other considerations in defining your business.   As you consider what your business is going to do, you might also think a bit about two major issues that relate to the "what": types of competition and substitution or obsolescence. Types of competition here does not refer to the man down the street who also runs an outlet that does more or less what you intend to do. Types of competition refers to the other *kinds* of businesses that may compete with you. Thinking about them now keeps you aware of who, besides the obvious competitors, you are going to have to keep an eye on. Fast-food outlets, for example, compete with some regular restaurants and with supermarkets as well as with each other. Bookstores are not the only purveyors of books. Drug stores and supermarkets sell them as well in many areas. If you own a small soup and salad place just down the street from a Burger King, wouldn't you want to know as soon as possible that Burger King is adding a salad bar?

The issue of substitution or obsolescence asks you to consider how vulnerable your business is likely to be to technological change. When automobiles came in, the people who made buggy whips had to adapt or die. The advent of the coated paper and plastic milk containers did the same thing to milk bottle manufacturers. While this problem tends to belong mainly to manufacturers, it can also affect some kinds of retail operations and service operations. Consider the need for chimneysweeps in modern America. Or the need for people to sell ice. While there is still some need for both, there is nothing like the level of need there used to be in the "good old days."

As you consider your product/service in these lights, then, do not discard a basically sound idea. Rather, think about what you could do if your particular disaster comes to pass. Consider other potential markets for what you intend to make or sell. (Some buggy whips are still needed on racetracks. Bottles are still used for numerous products.) Consider other products or services that use similar skills. (Whip-makers would probably also do well at making belts, etc.) This is the beginning of contingency planning for your business— disaster-proofing by anticipating adverse events and preparing a course of action "just in case."

The real point is that, if you have thought about these issues in advance, and if you have some notion of where to head if disaster strikes, the disaster usually does not look quite so disasterous. With any kind of luck, it will not happen during your lifetime, but if you consider the possibilities in advance, you can make a judgment about whether the level of risk is one you are willing to accept. The risk will not go away or be reduced because you choose not to look at it.

Who Will Your Business Perform Its Function For?

At this point you have a beginning definition of what your business is going to do and some inkling about its priorities. Will the entire world beat a path to your new front door? More to the point, do you *want* the entire world to beat a path to your front door? Could you possibly handle that volume of business? Not a chance! Somehow, then, you have to narrow your sights.

In considering who you will do business with, you want to start with a look at the total potential market for whatever it is you're selling. Then choose a discrete part of that total that you believe you can serve better than any of your competitors. (In Chapters 4 and 5, we will consider how to determine whether the subgroup you have chosen is large enough to support your business, given your market and financial situations.)

You might begin to make these choices by simply closing your eyes and visualizing your place of business in some detail. Does it have young people in jeans in it? Is there Top 40 music (loud) in the air? Are the clothes on your racks pure silk and cashmere? Are there thick carpets on the floor? In short, begin to analyze your vision. It will not be sullied by analysis. Analysis, in fact, is the only way to really begin to make it come true.

With some ideas about your customers fairly firmly in mind, you can begin to use your pictures of them to develop your image of what your business will be like. If you are manufacturing industrial goods, will your buyers respond better to a shirt-sleeved, shop-floor type salesperson or to a suited-and-tied type? If you are running an accounting service, what will make your particular clientele feel most comfortable with your service? What do your buyers read, listen to, look at when they make decisions related to whatever you will be selling? Do these differ from what the rest of the total potential market looks at?

Many of these issues will be explored in greater depth in later chapters. For now it is sufficient to note that if you can identify specifically who you want to buy whatever you sell, you can begin to develop your business to appeal to those particular customers. We hope that you will do it better than your competitors—unless you manage to find a niche in the market in which you will have no competitors. Your goal—and you have accepted the assignment by the very fact of opening your doors—must be to make your entire operation consistent with the needs and views of your particular purchasers.

One of the best early ways to consider your customers (as opposed to the customers of other people in your field) is to use your powers of empathy and imagination to climb inside their heads and be them. In the role of one of your customers, consider the product/service you outlined in your basic business

FEATURE 3.1
Defining Products for Customers

A recent study examined why products fail in the United States. A principal author of that study, Modesto Maidique of Stanford University, claims that in the 224 electronics products studied, "the key was that the product added value to the customer. It's not the technology that matters, but how you shape it for the customer. The key is to find something that will make a difference in your customer's business.

"The person that establishes the value of what you do is not you internally; it's not some panel of blue-ribbon scientific advisers or scientific judges; it's the customer. And if that's the person that's setting the value of your activities, you just have to be very close to him as a philosophy and as an intricate part of the way you manage your business. I think that cuts across all segments of American business.

"And small companies tend to be very close to the customer because the marketing guy, the guy who visits customers, the guy who does the design, the guy who makes the decision is often the same person. But in a large bureaucracy, you're likely to have the decisions made by someone who hasn't seen a customer in years.

"Remember that marketing has to encompass the definition of what a product is. Marketing is not just promotion, sales and advertising; marketing also includes product planning. You can't go in saying, 'Well, we've got a super-fast technology here, and obviously speed is going to do a lot for this guy . . . ' You've got to go in and say, 'What's your business all about? What do you need? What is it in the market that you'd like to see that isn't there?' "

definition. Picture yourself as this customer walking into your place of business. See the place you envision through his or her eyes. See your goods or personnel through the person on the other side of the counter/desk/table.

When you climb back into your own persona, you will have a whole new view of your prospective business. Think particularly about what looked

Figure 3.2   Developing a basic business definition

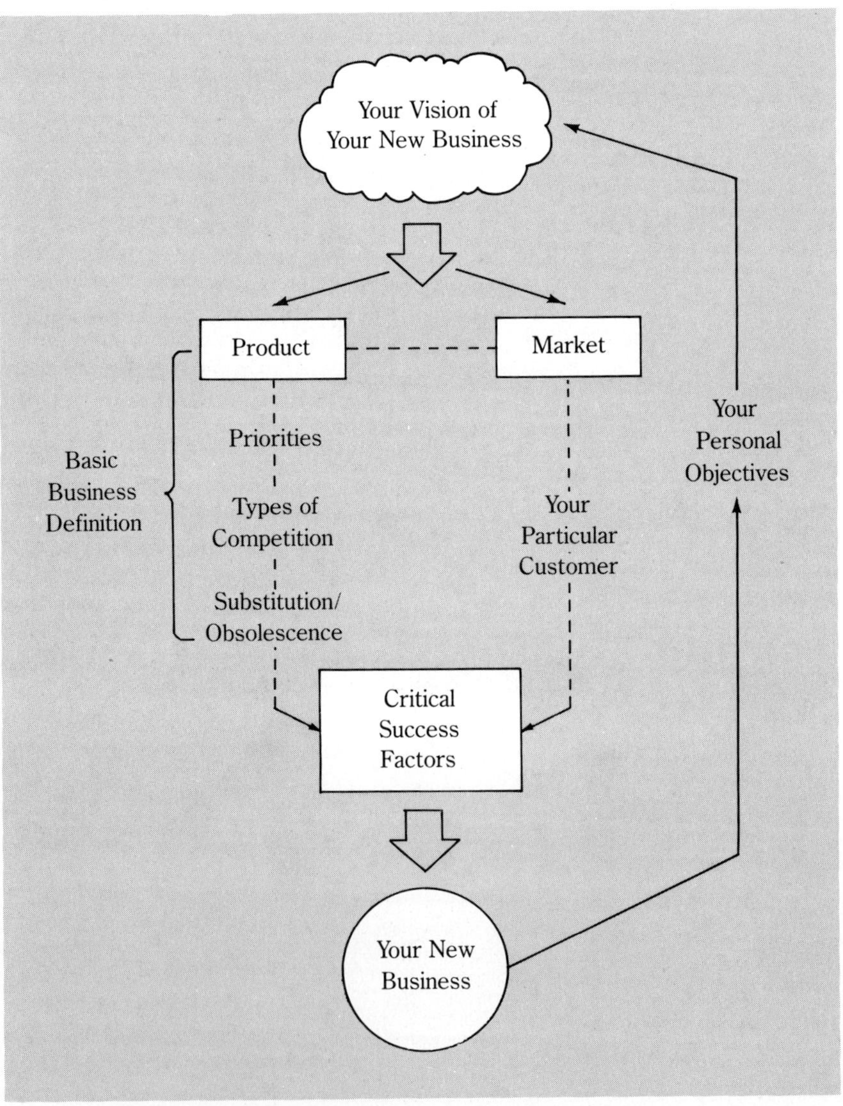

different to you in your two roles. Consider what you (customer) particularly liked or disliked about the experience of walking through your (owner's) place. Then fix whatever needs fixing. Your goal, remember, is to make life easy and nice for your intended customer. Those people will make your dream live or die.

CRITICAL SUCCESS FACTORS

When you "became" your customer, what things struck you as very important about the place of business you were touring? Did you find the place easy or hard to get to? Did it matter to you? Why or why not? All the things that struck you as important as a customer and all the things that strike you as important as the owner are worth considering as items in your list of critical success factors.

Critical success factors are those areas of your business in which you expect your decisions to be crucial to your success or failure in this particular business. In addition to your role-playing analysis, a preliminary analysis of some of your competitors will help here. The underlying question to which you are seeking answers is: "Why does one business in this field succeed while another fails or is marginal?"

Obviously, all of your decisions will contribute to making or breaking your new venture. The ones that you believe are really critical, however, should get priorities in your time, your effort, and your money. They are the ones that really have to be right.

The list of critical success factors for any business will vary, depending on the basic business definition—what the business will sell and to whom it will sell it—and the owner's vision of what she wants to do with the business. But every business/market segment combination has them. Early consideration of what should really be paramount in your planning and development will permit you to focus your energies and attention where they will do the most good.

Since it would be next to impossible to list critical success factors for enough businesses to make it worthwhile, a pair of examples might serve to show how the basic business definition influences what is critical. Let's look, then, at two health spas:

1. The Hilltop Health Spa, which you have defined as "a club that will provide an elegant and social environment for upper and upper-middle income men and women who are more interested in health and fitness than in losing weight."
2. The Valley Spa, which you have defined as "a useful place at which middle and lower-middle income women will be able to lose weight and shape up in safety and with proper nutritional assistance."

Obviously, in either case, the real trick is getting enough members to support your establishment and yourself. The question we are really getting at when we address critical success factors is one level beneath the concern for adequate membership in our health clubs. What will be critical in getting enough of our target market to sign up?

Let's look at Hilltop first. Within limits, your target market here is not likely to be very concerned about the price. It is a group that likes to see and be seen among members of its own kind of people. What this group is most likely to buy in a health club is:

- Facilities (top-of-the-line equipment, pool, Jacuzzi, saunas, etc.)
- Atmosphere (They will probably want to be as comfortable as possible while doing something as inherently uncomfortable as exercising. And they will probably want a juice bar or lounge in which to talk with their friends.)
- Service (Will you offer a masseuse? Valet parking?)

Furthermore, these clients will probably be unwilling to wait for any of these things while you phase in operations. For this group, you'll probably have to be close to perfect the day you open.

Valley, on the other hand, seeks a very different crowd. They will be at your spa for a very specific purpose—to lose weight. They are unlikely to care, within limits, whether they know anyone else there (except, perhaps, for one friend or so who is there for the same purpose and to provide moral support). They are quite likely to be seriously concerned about your price and your payment terms. In a health spa, they will probably buy:

- Classes (Will times be convenient? Is instruction provided? Are they tied to specific class schedules? How large are classes?)
- Availability of aid/information about diet and diets (Are programs individually tailored, and are they monitored?)

These two health spas will have very different critical success factors. And one in common. The owner of each has to make a critical decision about where to locate the club. (For most consumer-oriented businesses, location is a critical success factor. It is discussed in depth in Chapter 5). As the owner of Hilltop, you would need to find a large, landscapable area in or near an enclave of the people who will make up your market. It must have adequate parking facilities. If it is to be in a city, you would try for a downtown location, preferably on the top of a tall building. It would need to be convenient to financial district-type offices and some serious shopping boutiques as well, if possible.

Locating Valley would probably be somewhat easier, though no less critical. Your site would not need to be able to support a pool, but would require water lines for shower facilities. You would want a middle-income area, preferably with some parking and probably, if it makes sense in your area, served by public transportation. A primary concern if you are locating in a city would be the safety of the area. You would want to be near the normal shopping places of the people you hope to attract.

Beyond location, the critical factors for each spa will differ. For Hilltop you will need to have the ability to raise very large amounts of capital. You are projecting an expensive image and you will have to go "top drawer" on everything. You will be laying out massive amounts of money before you will even be able to ask for memberships. This will go largely for physical improvements and also for a classy advertising campaign and for the training of staff members—not only in the specific tasks that they will be doing, but also in the attitudes and manners that they will have to display to make your spa a success. A large amount of your concentration and effort, then, should be directed toward arranging for the funding of the business.

While Valley will also require an outlay of capital before you can ask for memberships, the sums will not be so staggering. You really need only minimal facilities to start and you can grow in the directions that seem most appropriate given the people who actually sign up. While it is theoretically possible for an entrepreneur to finance Valley himself, unless he is extremely wealthy, he will need help (investors, bankers, probably both) to get Hilltop off the ground.

Staffing decisions will probably be more critical for Hilltop than for Valley. At Hilltop you will need not only lots of staff, but also the right kinds of people on staff. They will have to be flexible, able to work with groups and on a one-to-one basis. They will undoubtedly need whatever credentials are appropriate in the field. They must know—or be trained—in when and when not to notice problems and intervene with help. They must be extremely attentive and available, but relatively unobtrusive. By contrast, Valley's staff needn't be as flexible or as deferential.

Advertising decisions, as they are commonly understood, will probably be more critical to Valley than to Hilltop. Advertising will probably be the major way of letting Valley's target market know that you are there and what you can do for them. To sell Hilltop, on the other hand, it would help a great deal if you were a member of the group you were trying to attract. Failing that, it would help to know some of the members. You will be trying to promote word-of-mouth publicity. Your advertising will probably be more like promotion—gilt-edged invitations to an opening cocktail party, rather than a full-page ad in your local paper. For Valley, then, the critical advertising decisions will center on choices of media, messages, and size, while for Hilltop the critical promotional gambit might be breaking into the right social set.

Results will also be critical to Valley in a way that would not be relevant to Hilltop. Valley's clientele is seeking something specific—weight loss. It will be important that Valley be able to produce those results—in at least a few cases—and to publicize them to its market. Hilltop's crowd, on the other hand, is looking for undefined things. A specific kind of result probably would not move them very much unless, of course, you have discovered the cure for aging (in which case you should not waste your time on a health spa).

Please note that in both cases the critical success factors grow out of the variables contained in your basic business definition: your product or service and your definition of your particular customer group. All businesses have those factors which, if not handled well, will kill the business. Identifying those factors in advance and planning to give extra time, thought, and attention to decisions affecting those factors can go a long way toward minimizing your risk at your grand opening.

PRELIMINARY BUSINESS OBJECTIVES

Now that you have some notion of what your business is going to do, for whom it is going to do it, and what is likely to be critical to it in the process, you can begin to consider what its objectives could rationally be. As noted in Chapter 2, these objectives should fit with your personal objectives for going into a venture of your own. Beyond this kind of issue, it is very much your ball game.

At this stage in your business planning, you should view the objectives for your business as extremely preliminary. You have not yet collected any hard data nor as yet done any serious feasibility work. In general terms, however, you should sit down with your basic business definition and your list of critical success factors and consider where you want this business to go. Do you want it to be the biggest seller of "x" in a five-county radius? Do you, on the other hand, want it to be the top-of-the-line, recognized taste leader in the "x" field?

Each different broad general objective for your business carries a different set of implications for what you will stress and how you will do business. A market-share-based objective (to be the largest purveyor of "x") is likely to require a low-price high-volume strategy—a McDonald's approach to the market you have chosen. The drive to build a quality image (the "class" in your field) might result in a high-price, special services approach to your market. This kind of approach was used quite effectively by Hewlett-Packard in the calculator field, for example.

While at this point in your development process you do not really want to choose your objective definitively, you certainly want to begin thinking about your options, given the product/service and the target market you have identified as your own. You also want to begin to consider what potential objectives may be mutually exclusive in your particular field. Most of all, at this point you want to look again at your choice of business in terms of whether any of the potential objectives for the business are likely to move you closer to your personal objectives. If the answer is "not likely," you might want to alter your business plans. On the other hand, if it is your personal objective that appears to be unrealistic in light of further consideration—for example, "I want to be a millionaire before I'm 23," you might want to reconsider that side of this equation. It's your life, your goals, and your business to arrange as you wish—subject, of course, to the constraints of reality.

SUMMARY

A basic business definition is a statement of what (specifically) you are going to sell to what specific groups of people. It is intended to serve two major purposes. First, it is intended to serve as a touchstone to help to keep you on track as you plan for your business startup. At very least, it should be specific enough to send you loud signals when you are about to make major changes in your original business concept. Such changes can, of course, be made, if you still desire them after thinking them through in terms of your original vision. Second, your basic business definition can help you clarify your vision of your business for those others with whom you might want or need to discuss your business plans—your bankers and your employees, for example.

In accord with your basic business definition, you want to consider two other issues that relate to the level of competition and risk in your intended area of business. You want to consider other types of businesses that compete with yours or with parts of your business. Second, you want to consider the risks that your business will probably face from technological change. In both cases, you want to begin considering what steps you might take to protect your business (from these competitors) or to permit your business to reposition itself (in a new technological world) by identifying alternative uses for your products or of your skills. (This kind of thinking can also be very useful when you consider expansion or diversification later on—even if disaster does not strike.)

Finally, as part of providing a framework for decision making for your business, you need to consider its critical success factors, those factors that can really make or break your business. These factors derive from your basic business definition in that they vary with your product/market choices. Defining these factors in advance permits you to allocate your planning time and effort to critical areas in accord with their importance to your new venture.

FOR YOU TO CONSIDER

1. Discuss the advantages and disadvantages of keeping at least part of your life separate from the life of your business.

2. Describe what a basic business definition is and why it is helpful to a new entrepreneur to develop one for his or her venture.
3. List types of competitors for the following and consider why they are competitors.
   a. Florist
   b. Building contractor
   c. Soft drink manufacturer
4. Discuss two potential responses to a technological change that permits or encourages your customers to substitute some other product for yours.
5. Define "critical success factors."
6. What factors will be critical to the success of each of the restaurants located as shown below?
   a. In a retirement community
   b. In a suburban shopping mall
   c. At street level in a skyscraper in the financial district
   d. In a neighborhood shopping center
7. Why begin to define critical success factors so early in your business planning?
8. Discuss the need for "fit" between your personal objectives and your objectives for your business. Why might you want to consider preliminary objectives for your business before you do all the basic research?

4. There's No Sale Unless Somebody Buys

Research is to see what everybody else has seen,
and to think what nobody else has thought.

Albert Szent-Gyergyi

You have by now developed an initial definition of what *you* want to sell and to whom *you* want to sell it. You have also considered the major factors that will be critical to your business success. Essentially, you have considered what you want to do, how you want to do it, and what you believe is vital. This is where too many would-be entrepreneurs stop.

While defining your end of the transaction is extremely important in the early stages of new venture development, it does not formally recognize that there are at least two parties to any business transaction. You cannot be a seller unless someone out there is willing to buy. You will not be a seller for long unless there are enough buyers out there to support your operations and yourself.

The question this chapter deals with is how you determine whether there are potential buyers out there for your business. Specifically, this chapter will help you to address such issues as:

1. How to define what information you need in your initial market research,
2. Where and how to get that information,
3. What to do with it once you get it.

HOW DO YOU START: DEFINING YOUR MARKET

You have already given the topic of your market some thought if you have created the basic business definition and developed the critical success factors for your business (Chapter 3). In very broad outline, you already know:

"

1. What you are going to sell,
2. To whom you are going to sell it,
3. What you need to take special care about in the process.

The beginning of your initial market study is already here. Your job will be to refine these definitions further and to begin to quantify answers to the questions you identify in the process of determining what your basic business definition really means in marketing terms.

Businesses stand or fall, often entirely on the basis of the quality of their underlying market research. One young man in a small midwestern town, for example, decided to open a car wash. The nearest competitor was miles away in the nearest medium-sized town. His car wash was going to use the best in new methods, efficient service, and wax jobs. He just knew he'd do well. After all, his would be the only car wash in town.

In less than a year, he was bankrupt. Unable to understand why this had happened, he took his problem to an instructor of small business management at the local college. Together they worked through the basic market research that should have been done prior to opening. They found that:

1. Most people in town drove to the medium-sized town at least once a week to shop or to do other business.
2. During the spring, summer, and autumn, numerous charity car wash days were held by local schools, churches, and youth groups. Many of these had become community events.
3. The young man would have had to wash every vehicle in town once a week to pay for his equipment and expenses.

By contrast, consider the restaurant business developed by Marketing Corporation of America (MCA). They began by looking for business fields in which they would not be competing with their marketing consulting clients. The restaurant business was one such field, and a potentially good one, since MCA had found that more Americans are eating more meals away from home. Use of moderate-priced restaurants was rising. Rather than stopping there, however, and determining that they had enough to start their restaurants, MCA spent two more years researching their consumers' preferences in food and decor.

Admittedly, for a small new venture this would be overkill—Who has two or three years to spend on research?—but the results are impressive. In a field which has one of the highest small business mortality rates, MCA's Baker's Garden and Tanglewood chains of restaurants claim sales per square foot that are double the industry average.[1] Essentially, MCA decided what it was going to sell (food/meals) and to whom they were going to sell it (average women). They then considered what they had to take special care about—in this case, prices, type of food, location, and decor.

While the MCA route is a bit extreme for the average entrepreneur, the underlying idea clearly works. More important, the average entrepreneur can go a long way toward quantifying her own market data without spending years and bundles of money in the process. Balance is the critical factor. What you are seeking is the happy medium between the young man of car wash fame (bankruptcy) and the MCA approach—"We try to reduce everything to a number" (and are willing to spend 15 percent of our annual budget to do it).

Segmenting Your Market

Beginning with your starting point, your basic business definition, you need to define more closely your particular market segment—those people who are to buy whatever it is you're selling. As you have already undoubtedly noticed, your specific product (or range of products) must match your specific market segment—the subset of all potential users of products like yours who could use your specific product(s). If, for example, you plan to open a shoe store, it should be immediately obvious that you cannot possibly sell all styles and sizes of all manufacturers to all people who might wear shoes. Aside from the cost of holding the inventory, you would need a massive emporium just to display your wares. So you choose. And you make your choices along certain parameters that divide the main market, shoe-wearers, into manageable segments. We have shown some possible segmentations for this market in Table 4.1.

Table 4.1 Market segmentation—retail shoes

Potential Wearers	*Types of Product*	*Price Range*
Toddlers	Sport	Low
Children—male	Casual	Moderate
female	Dress	High
Young adults—male	Specialty	
female	Work	
Adults—male		
female		

Within the parameters for your industry, you can segment the market in any way you choose. This may well be determined by how much stock you can carry in a retail or manufacturing business or your range and expertise in a service business. You may, as a shoe-seller, choose to sell only children's shoes (Stride Rite) or shoes from a narrow range of manufacturers (Florsheim/Thayer McNeil) or a full range of shoes in a given price range (Fayva). As part of your marketing strategy, you may decide to specialize by function, as some running/athletic shoe-sellers have done (Athlete's Foot).

Once you choose your basic product or product line, you can select any number of parameters from each column—keeping in mind the cost implications of your choices and the inherent market limitations (Will a top-of-the-line buyer shop in a store that carries low-priced lines?) Such a list of market segments can simply help to ensure that you have looked at all your alternatives. Various market segments for a construction business and a stationery manufacturer might look like those shown in Tables 4.2 and 4.3.

Table 4.2   Market segmentation—construction business

Potential Users	*Types of Service*	*Price Range*
Architects	New construction	Low
Developers	Single-unit	Moderate
Homeowners	Multiple-unit	High
Companies	Residential	
	Commercial	
	Industrial	
	Renovations	
	Demolitions	
	Additions	
	Rehabilitations	
	(same subcategories	
	for most service types.)	

Table 4.3   Market segmentation—stationery manufacturing company

Potential Users	*Types of Product*	*Price Range*
Young people	School supplies	Low
Adults	Social stationery	Moderate
Businesses etc.	Business stationery etc.	High

You can, of course, choose to segment your market in some entirely new way. Some of the more spectacular marketing successes have come through defining new market segments and meeting their needs. Timex did it with watches. Before Timex, watches were very special things, gifts reserved for graduation, weddings, and similar occasions. Timex developed a new mechanism (pin-lever rather than jewel movements) that made watches cheaper to make and, therefore, available to almost anyone. Far from being family heirlooms as they used to be, watches have become almost disposable. What Timex did was develop a totally new market segment.

L'Eggs did it in the pantyhose business. Before L'Eggs, a woman could buy pantyhose in a department store (expensive) or in a five-and-ten (inexpensive). L'Eggs figured that there had to be a middle to that market. So they began manufacturing a distinctively packaged, medium-priced pantyhose to be sold in supermarkets and drug stores. They won their bet, as did Timex, but resegmenting an established market can be very risky and expensive.

Quite probably, for example, you have never heard of Gablinger's Beer. It did exist—once. In the 1960s, its manufacturer, Rheingold, decided that there was probably an untapped segment of the beer market in dieters who liked beer. They made Gablinger's as a premium (high) priced beer and sold it as a low-calorie drink. Gablinger's had a very short life. As it turns out, there is a sizable market for light beers—beers for beer drinkers who are somewhat concerned about their weight. (Please note how different this is from "dieters who like beer.")

In short, although there have been big winners, it is not recommended that you try a totally new segmentation of your market unless you have some new technology or you know the market very well.

Parts of the Marketing Mix

As you can see, you are beginning to focus your attention on your particular buyer and what that buyer will like and respond to in terms of product type and price range. Both product and price are parts of the notion of a "marketing mix"—those factors that will reach your particular buyer and help him to buy your product as opposed to someone else's. Other parts of this "mix" (place and promotion) are discussed in later chapters (see Chapters 5 and 11).

The key idea is the notion of "fit." Do your choices of product/service and price range "fit" your proposed market segment? Your objective is consistency. Nothing should jar your consumers and prevent them from buying whatever it is you are selling. To maintain consistency once you have determined who your customers are, it helps a great deal to know something about them: where they live, how they live, what they like and don't like, how many of them there are, what defines them and makes them different from all other segments. And this is where market research comes in.

WHAT IS MARKET RESEARCH?

Market research is, at base, simply the systematic collection and analysis of information relating to the market for your establishment, your products, or your services. It need not be frightening or elaborate. It is simply a means of getting the information necessary to make intelligent decisions about your business. But, as we saw earlier, initial market research efforts can range from none to overkill. The key lies in defining what you need to know such that, when you are finished with your research, you have a better basis for decision making and you have not collected a thousand minor variations of the same information. In short, the key is planning your questions and your research process.

Consider data collection. There is an unlimited amount of information that exists or that could be developed about the potential customers you targeted in your basic business definition and your market segmentation grid. The amount of time and money you spend chasing it could therefore also be

FEATURE 4.1
Getting to Know Your Market

Despite the current ease of accessing computerized data bases, the numbers of would-be entrepreneurs who fail to do market research remains high. "The market is so huge that you can't even define it. Everyone needs one of our units. If we only get 1% of that market, we'll be unable to fill all the orders." So the line goes. "The fact is that few entrepreneurs really do a lot of research," says the director of USC's Entrepreneur Program. "Which is why a lot of them go belly up." But it doesn't work—as Systel Computers found out the hard way. Systel conducted little market research on its Report/80 computer, "None at all, really, unless you would characterize consumer rejection as a form of market research," notes President B. J. Moore.

Only *after* they junked the Report/80 did Systel begin to do market research. Despite the cash shortage, they committed $4,200 to focus groups to find out whether and how to sell their new Systel II. They started their research before the final design state so that they could configure the machine to the tastes of their market. They not only got design help, but they also found that the security of having a toll-free number to call would be a significant selling point. They added one.

Perhaps the most difficult situation occurs when an entrepreneur is facing a market that has no parallels, nothing for comparison, nothing documentable. Experts then suggest shifting from quantitative to qualitative research, like the focus groups used by Systel. This could also include one-on-one interviews or discussions. These same experts remind us that entrepreneurs often ask questions in ways that reflect their bias in favor of their concept. They thus counsel against having venturers ask the market survey questions. Or they urge "perspective." A professional survey, however, may cost more than $10,000.

Adapted From Joanne Kelleher, "Getting to Know Your Market," *Venture* (May 1983): 70 ff.

unlimited. A single mail questionnaire survey large enough to have any promise of telling you anything useful can cost thousands of dollars. The time of a professional in this field will cost you (conservatively) $500 to $600 a day. If you do all the data collection yourself, and if you collect all information related or tangentially related to your business field, your potential market and your competitors, you will find that you have a very handy excuse for never proceeding with your plan. All your time and energy will be consumed by the process of finding and making sense of your market data.

The relevant words in the definition of market research, therefore, must be "systematic" and "analysis." In short, there must be method in this madness. To be systematic, you have to know the direction in which you want to go, have some sense of what the destination will look like, and understand what you need to get there. To be capable of useful analysis, the questions that you ask and the data that you can collect must be compatible. You must ask questions that the data can answer. And when you get the answers, you must be able to fit them into some pattern that makes sense in terms of your business.

What Do You Want to Know?

Obviously, your overriding question is: "If I open my business as described, will it succeed and prosper?" Equally obviously, since they don't give guarantees in the new venture game, you will not be able to come to a definitive "yes" or "no." The absolute best you will be able to get is a high probability—and you will undoubtedly feel more certain of the probabilities on the "no" side. This is a judgment question that cannot be answered directly by any data you might collect (short of opening shop and keeping records). However critical it is for you, then, it is not a good market research question.

What are good market research questions are those with answers that lead you to better judgments about the overriding question. Thus, while market research cannot guarantee success, it can go a long way toward preventing failure. It does this by helping you to analyze information about factors you have already identified as critical to your success or by signaling the likelihood of a lack of buyers before you sink money, time, or effort into actually launching your business.

In general, you will be looking for data about three main areas: your industry, your customer, and your competitors. Obviously, the specific items of interest will differ from business to business. Only the broader issues will be raised here.

Industry information.   What is going on in your industry? Are there any trends developing? Any potentially devastating regulations coming? What factors in the general economy affect your industry? What do economists and industry experts have to say about what is likely to happen?

A now-defunct boat manufacturer ignored industry trend data to its detriment. Despite figures showing a growing number and proportion of sales of fiberglass boats, this manufacturer chose to build only in wood. Despite actually seeing the new sleeker lines of boats built by their competitors, this company built broader, chunkier boats. They built them. They could not sell them. These former entrepreneurs either did not believe in the data they collected or they believed that, somehow, the world would be different for them.

Customer/consumer/client information.   Who buys your kind of product/service? In your target segment of the market, how many potential buyers are there? How much does each generally spend on your product/service a year? How far will they travel to get your product/service? Where do they live? Where do they go? What do they read, listen to, like to do? How much money do they make? What about your product/service matters to them?

The 1983 difficulties of the video games manufacturers stemmed from a classic misunderstanding of who was buying their video games machines. They thought that the games buyers were basically different from those who bought home computers. As multipurpose computers (those with games as well as other functions) moved into more homes and their prices dropped—some to below games-only prices—the games makers discovered that the buyers were really one and the same group. There was then a rush to add plug-in computer keyboards to games machines and to build inexpensive multipurpose home computers. Industry experts now expect that "two or three years from now video games (machines) will be considered a piece of history."[2] (And if, as you read this, you can barely remember home video games machines, they were clearly right.)

Competitor information.   Who else is out there selling to your target market segment what you plan to sell? What products/services can (do) substitute for yours for these consumers?

Part of the video games problem was the failure to believe that a computer could (would) be substituted for the games machine when the price became right. While these are different products, they clearly meet the same needs for the consumer—except that computers apparently do it better. Thus, when fierce competition in the home computer market dropped prices to under $100, the games-only manufacturers were in trouble.

In a similar vein, the fast-food industry changed the nature of competition in the food business. (Note: This is not only the restaurant business.) Not only did they compete with each other and against the lower-to-moderately priced independent restaurants, but they also were found to compete with supermarkets. In the kind of substitution mentioned in Chapter 3, a fast-food meal was seen by consumers (the only ones who really count here) as an alternative to dinner at home. ("Don't cook tonite! Call Chicken Delite!")

New sources of supply provide a kind of competitive substitution that is often easy to overlook. Under the heading of "competition," then, you need to consider *all* potential sources of supply for your product and customer—not only the similar store down the street, but also the mail order house and the factory outlet store, etc.

Defining the Questions

In retrospect, it is usually fairly easy to spot what went wrong in a company that fails. The trick is in figuring out in advance where the problems are likely to be and dealing with them early or avoiding them altogether. The key to this trick is data—the answers to your own list of industry/customer/competitor questions. Unfortunately, you cannot go to a handy little data book and flip to "Retailers: Bicycle. Fresno, California." You have to dig up the data yourself (unless you can afford to pay someone else to dig it up for you).

Data generally comes in three varieties: statistics, pictures/diagrams/descriptions, and opinions. Pictures, diagrams, and/or descriptions include anything that will tell you something about what your customers may do with or like about products similar to yours or about how your competitors approach their businesses. Sometimes, for example, "How It Works" articles (descriptions, pictures, and diagrams) have been done about products. These can be useful in refining your product itself or in defining what about your product is particularly important to users (your potential customers). Statistical and opinion information are the types you have used for years in all your school papers. We will discuss forms and sources for these types of data later in this chapter.

The real point of raising the question of data in a section on formulating questions is that you have to tailor your questions so that you can get answers in one or more of these forms. And, if your data is going to be largely statistical/demographic, as is often the case, you will have to sharpen some of your target segment definitions. If you do this, what you will be looking for will be in terms similar to the terms of the information you find.

Assume, for a moment, that you were going into the shoe retailing business. Using your market segmentation grid, you decide to sell women's high-priced dress and casual shoes. You now need to define more specifically "woman" and "high-priced" in such a way that the demographic data (the data about where such people live, who they are, and how much money they make) will be helpful to you.

Think about your store. What age range of women do you expect to be buying most of your shoes? You have already decided that your shoes will be expensive. That suggests that, in general, your clientele will probably be more middle-aged than very young. The style of your shoes will be unlikely to appeal to the very young or very old. You can say, therefore, that you tentatively expect your main age range target to be 35–55-year-old women.

This does not mean that no well-heeled 25-year-old will ever walk into your store. Nor does it mean that a spry grandmother of 70 will not like and be able to wear your shoes. It simply means that you expect *most* of your customers to be between 35 and 55 and that you will make marketing decisions on the basis of this group.

It also may turn out that the demographic data you find as you work with the sources we discuss later in this chapter does not precisely coincide with your original age range target. Suppose, for example, that the age groupings in the data you find are slightly different—25–34, 35–44, 45–54. Despite the slight difference from your original range, you probably want the last two categories, 35–54. Remember how loosely your original age range was developed before you treat it as if it were carved in stone.

The second item you need to define for your shoe store research is what it takes to be able to afford your high-priced lines. Here you would want to define a range of family income that you would expect a consumer to have if she is to be willing to spend x dollars on a pair of shoes. Since information about family incomes is available, you have defined your consumer in another way that will help you find out more about her.

No matter what your business, you will have to define your trading area or the geographic scope of your real market. While one generally thinks of a trading area as strictly a retailing concept, many kinds of wholesalers and manufacturers are subject to geographic limits. These may occur because the product is perishable or because the cost of transportation or the time it takes to transport the product is high. While one likes to think of trading areas in terms of neat circles of x miles in radius around your home, store, or town, the demographic data doesn't work that way. Designations are generally by town or county and, sometimes, by sections of a major city. You will have to be able to define by these measures in order to make optimum use of existing data.

In short, good market research questions must have three attributes.

1. They must reflect consideration of what you really need to know about the industry, the customers, and the competition.
2. They must be capable of answers in the form of statistical or demographic data, some form of pictures, or expert opinion.
3. They must be defined in terms consistent with those of the data you expect to collect.

Particularly because of the last requirement, it is wise to get to know the sources of data and the types of data available before you complete the planning stage of your market research.

FEATURE 4.2

Some Generic Market Research Questions

I. Industry
  A. What is the title generally given to the segment of the industry that interests you?
  B. How large (in dollars and units) is your industry?
  C. Is the market growing? Shrinking? Remaining about the same?
  D. What are the key products/services in your industry?
  E. What economic trends affect your industry? What are they indicating?

II. Customer
  A. How many are there in your target segment in your relevant area?
    1. Where do they live (or congregate)?
    2. (Consumers)   How old are they?
                     How much money do they make (have access to)?
                     What do they read? What do they do in their spare time?
    3. (Businesses)   How large are they? Number of employees? Sales? Are they profitable? How profitable?
  B. How much does each spend a year on your product/service?
  C. How do they spend it? All in one place? All at one time? Contract?
  D. Are they buying more or less of your product/service?
  E. Why do they buy as and from whom they now do?

III. Competitors
  A. How many of them are there that are relevant to your business?
  B. How well are they doing? And how are they doing whatever they are doing?
  C. What are their strengths in the market you want to enter? Weaknesses?

Finding Out: Data Sources

Your market research need not be as expensive or elaborate as MCA's or Procter & Gamble's to be useful to you. The trick is to think low cost and stay close to home. Basically, there are two kinds of market research: primary and secondary. Primary research is the information you collect from the horse's mouth, so to speak. If you ran a mail survey or interviewed people on the street, you would be doing primary research. You are asking potential users of your product or service what they think, feel, and know about the product or service and whether they do or would buy it and buy it from you. As you can surmise, to get reasonably valid answers requires talking or writing to a great many people. Primary research is thus expensive, as we noted earlier. MCA, for example, was spending 15 percent of its income on this kind of research alone.

Sometimes, primary research can be done with creativity rather than with money. A Small Business Administration (SBA) Management Aid, for example, told the story of a discount store owner who wanted to find out what in his store particularly attracted customers. Rather than commissioning a study, he offered all his customers free peanuts (in shells)—all they could eat. At the end of the day, he could trace the traffic patterns by the trails of peanut shells. It was cheap, easy, and effective.

In general, because of the normal cost and difficulty of primary research, secondary research is done first. We shall follow that practice here. Secondary research makes use of the primary research done by others and published or otherwise available to you. This cuts your cost and the time it will take you to collect the relevant data. The obvious drawback of using secondary sources as opposed to your own research is that the terms in which others collected data may not be precisely the terms you would like. It is generally easier and certainly less expensive to adjust your terms rather than to do your own primary research.

To do adequate secondary research, you need to have a fairly good idea of what information sources are out there and how the data they contain relate to what you need to know. Thus, the next section of this chapter includes a brief survey of some of the major potential sources of information that you may need to know in order to do your initial market research.

Secondary sources: government.   The federal government is perhaps the largest producer of useful marketing data. Your customer research, if you are a consumer-oriented firm, will be greatly aided by the *Census of Population* and related data done every 10 years (in 0-ending years) by the Department of Commerce, Census Bureau. It will be particularly useful to you if you are starting your business in a 3-ending year when most of the data is actually out and is not yet very outdated.

The Decennial Census is easily the biggest questionnaire survey in the country, covering, by sampling at least, such out-of-the-way questions as whether your house has indoor plumbing and telephones. It is usable by anyone at no cost. Your local public or university library undoubtedly has the volumes for your state at very least. If you happen to be lucky enough to live in a city with a depository library, you will have all federally published documents available to you there.

This census breaks down the data on age, sex, race, income, labor force participation, etc., by urban/rural, by state, by Standard Metropolitan Statistical Area (SMSA), and by city and town.

The Census Bureau also publishes data that will help if you are selling to other businesses and/or if you need data about competitors in your field and area. It produces censuses of Manufactures, of Wholesale and Retail Trade, of Construction, of Services. These are published for years ending in 2 and 7. While these show only aggregate data by similar areas to those used in the population census, they can be useful for figuring out averages and total numbers, as well as concentrations of industries in specific areas.

The data is organized within geographic divisions and by industry. Industry groupings are coded using the Standard Industrial Classification (SIC) Code. A two-digit code represents the broad industry category (20 is "food and kindred products," for example). The three-digit level is more specific (201 = meat and meat products). While the code goes to some seven digits, only four or five are used routinely. You will probably find an SIC Code manual wherever you found the census.

Within each SIC Code group and geographic division, the data shown generally includes some measure of sales or shipments, numbers of establishments, total payroll, production payroll, employment, and other useful data. You might use this information in any number of ways, including figuring out the size of the average competitor, approximate wage levels in your field, and determining the size of the market for your product/service in your state or area.

In addition to the various censuses, the federal government publishes other data in other forms. *County Business Patterns* is an annual item, done by the Census Bureau, showing first-quarter statistics. In *US Industrial Outlook,* another group in the Commerce Department makes projections about what the next few years are likely to bring to many industries. As a new businessperson, you should notice that all this data comes out of the Commerce Department—it is truly your government working for you.

On the whole, the federal government (and some state governments) is a veritable gold mine of useful information for entrepreneurs and for operating business owners. It also publishes a number of directories and guides to governmental data sources. The major ones are listed at the end of this chapter.

Secondary sources: trade associations.   While some industry trade associations exist only to lobby and to plan next year's convention, most provide real services to their members (and, sometimes, to potential members). Often, these services come in the form of research reports on such issues as industry standards or statistical forecasts or the meaning of annual industry statistics. These are especially helpful to their small business members who would not usually be able to spend the money to develop such reports on their own. In addition, trade associations often identify trends in their markets and actually conduct customer research—the expensive kinds of primary research that you are unlikely to be able to do.

Trade associations thus may be able to assist you in a number of phases of your business-building work. Initially, their data can help you to define the market and determine how large it is. Their data can help you with your assessments about competition as well. Many associations also collect financial information from member companies and aggregate and publish it or otherwise have it available. This material will be invaluable when you begin to consider the financial requirements of your business and the probability of reaching your sales and profit goals (see Chapters 7, 13, and 15).

Your problem is most likely to be gaining access to the data. Some industry associations publish such information in their magazines/journals. Your library may have back issues on file. Failing your library, a local association member may have a back file and may permit you to use it. (Please keep in mind that you are preparing to be her competitor.) Sometimes a letter to the association itself will bring a wealth of useful information—and it costs only 22 cents to ask.

If you don't know the relevant associations or where they are, you can start by asking local people in your line of business. If there are none available, try your library for a copy of *The Encyclopedia of Associations* or *National Trade and Professional Associations of the U.S. and Canada.* Failing both approaches, try writing to the American Society of Association Executives (1101 16th St. N.W., Washington, D.C. 20036).

Secondary sources: magazines and journals.   In addition to trade association journals, many general business magazines and newspapers carry articles or data that may be relevant to your line of business. These often also include the opinions and forecasts of industry experts in your field. The *Business Periodical Index* at your library indexes many of these publications by subject matter, title, and author. Reading such publications can give you a good sense of who the experts are and who the competition is. Often such general publication articles will give you a panoramic view of the current state of your chosen industry, noting major issues and current trends and problems all in one place.

Of particular interest is *Sales and Marketing Management.* This publication does its own research on a number of businesses across the United States. It prints such data as the Effective Buying Income (EBI) of families in a given city, county, or retail area. It often reports on how much is spent in selected types of retail establishments in a year. It makes projections of EBI and its other data. Your library probably has it. Table 4.4 presents a part of the Regional and State Summary of Retail Sales for 1983.

Other secondary sources.   One useful secondary source is probably less than 100 yards away from you as you are reading this. It is a copy of your telephone company Yellow Pages. Here the telephone company conveniently

Table 4.4 1983 Regional and state summaries of retail sales (excerpts)

	1983 Total Retail Sales ($000)	% Of U.S.	Per Household Retail Sales	Retail Sales by Store Group						Sales/Advertising Indexes		
				Food ($000)	Eating & Drinking Places ($000)	General Merchandise ($000)	Furniture/ Home Furnish./ Appliance ($000)	Automotive ($000)	Drug ($000)	Sales Activity	Buying Power	Quality
NEW ENGLAND	**74,516,465**	**6.2808**	**16,412**	**17,210,510**	**8,344,013**	**8,606,204**	**3,074,975**	**9,674,960**	**2,304,116**	**118**	**5.8219**	**110**
Connecticut	18,924,988	1.5951	16,791	4,189,893	2,070,743	2,210,881	850,435	2,497,121	568,810	120	1.5857	119
Maine	6,778,499	.5713	16,174	1,536,091	644,269	734,960	236,084	1,039,716	226,142	117	.4761	97
Massachusetts	34,652,979	2.9209	16,441	8,107,419	4,156,529	4,217,429	1,417,992	4,183,354	1,100,113	119	2.6911	110
New Hampshire	6,110,998	.5151	17,672	1,533,735	603,085	630,272	276,092	904,423	163,745	126	.4403	108
Rhode Island	4,913,000	.4141	14,017	1,119,814	550,895	564,588	171,949	603,646	161,794	102	.4068	100
Vermont	3,136,001	.2643	16,488	723,558	308,492	248,074	122,423	446,700	83,512	118	.2219	99
MIDDLE ATLANTIC	**176,386,920**	**14.8675**	**13,000**	**44,369,411**	**17,877,580**	**20,408,651**	**8,177,398**	**27,486,586**	**4,872,541**	**94**	**16.1142**	**102**
New Jersey	40,473,188	3.4114	15,170	10,333,027	3,961,042	4,239,809	1,960,347	6,617,800	876,778	107	3.5295	111
New York	81,561,943	6.8748	12,513	21,322,586	8,768,912	9,359,087	3,976,309	10,966,920	2,478,433	91	7.6953	102
Pennsylvania	54,351,789	4.5813	12,403	12,713,798	5,147,626	6,809,755	2,240,742	9,901,866	1,517,330	91	4.8894	97
EAST NORTH CENTRAL	**199,401,172**	**16.8075**	**13,161**	**45,602,005**	**20,813,685**	**26,713,833**	**8,428,230**	**32,554,361**	**7,837,971**	**95**	**17.4524**	**99**
Illinois	56,422,590	4.7558	13,346	12,349,052	6,217,395	7,267,025	2,517,204	8,766,791	2,292,633	97	5.0462	103
Indiana	26,497,281	2.2335	13,511	6,043,817	2,654,876	3,241,485	987,884	4,462,203	1,210,950	95	2.2033	94
Michigan	44,657,436	3.7641	13,825	9,781,000	4,369,551	6,635,322	1,923,787	7,927,202	1,803,544	97	3.8476	99
Ohio	50,755,270	4.2782	12,702	12,591,140	4,974,047	6,929,600	2,090,871	8,319,467	1,864,083	94	4.4198	97
Wisconsin	21,068,595	1.7759	12,133	4,836,996	2,597,816	2,640,401	908,484	3,078,698	666,761	88	1.9355	96

Source: *Sales & Marketing Management Magazine.* Copyright July 23, 1984, Survey of Buying Power. Reprinted with permission.

lists all your local competitors for you by trade category. (In some areas, businesses of interest mainly to other businesses are listed in a separate "business-to-business" Yellow Pages.) While the Yellow Pages does not offer much data, you can get a quick count of a given type of business, some sense of the location of concentrations of companies, and, sometimes—if you look at the display advertising—a sense of the type of customer the business seeks.

Another source of data for you may be local media outlets, if your business is consumer-related. Radio, television stations, and newspapers often compile certain demographic data and spending pattern information about their listeners (readers) in order to justify their advertising rates. If you have any idea about what your target customers read or listen to, call or write those media outlets for information. Since you are a potential new advertiser, you are likely to get whatever data they have. If you don't know what media serve your area, check the volumes of *Standard Rates and Data* (library) for names, addresses, circulation, and other data.

Other organizations exist essentially to help businesses succeed in their areas. Local Chambers of Commerce and mall or area merchants' associations are often helpful with information about the local business climate and about area consumers. They may be particularly helpful in defining your effective trading area. It is certainly worth a letter or a phone call to find out.

Primary market research.   The standard kinds of primary research are the expensive and complex kinds—mail, personal and telephone questionnaire surveys, focus groups, and the like. To be done properly, such surveys usually require professional assistance—in questionnaire design (to assure neutral questions) and in analysis (often requires computers). If you have done your secondary research well, however, you can probably succeed without the expensive kinds of primary research.

But you do need the hands-on experience of talking to people in and connected with your proposed kind of business. You will need to fill in the blanks left in your secondary research. These are likely to include such nitty-gritty items as the normal terms of trade in your business and such specific questions as why your potential customers now buy from one of your competitors as opposed to another. In each case, the particular blanks will be different. In all cases, creative research is limited only by your imagination. The peanut shell "study" mentioned earlier was one of the more creative efforts. A few additional ideas are noted here as triggers for your own creativity.

One issue that is often difficult to get a handle on is the real boundaries of your effective trading area. If you have a general location in mind for your business and if you are in an interstate area (for example, Pennsylvania, Ohio, and West Virginia) or in a state like Florida that identifies its cars by county of registration, a little primary research can help. Simply go to parking lots near your intended site and count cars by place of origin as shown by the license plates.

An easy way to find out who supplies whom in your local area and, sometimes, what sells well or doesn't sell at all, is also available to you. A walk

FEATURE 4.3
"How to Snoop on Your Competitors" from *Fortune* Magazine

There are many other ways you can find out what your competitors are up to that are completely legal, if sometimes ethically questionable. The legal use of intelligence-gathering has increased dramatically as more and more companies learn how cheap and effective it is.

Businessmen believe that competition has intensified. In industries where growth has slowed, executives realize that most of the increased business they need will have to come out of the hides of their competitors. Companies have realized that without taking the behavior of their competitors into account, their strategic plans don't work.

The techniques fall into four broad categories. The first covers ways of getting information from competitors' employees, past or present:

- Milking potential recruits
- Picking brains at conferences
- Conducting phony job interviews
- Hiring people away
- Interviewing competitors' consultants
- Debriefing their design consultants
- Debriefing their former employees

The second category consists of techniques to get information from people who do business with competitors:

- Encouraging key customers to talk
- Getting customers to put out phony bid requests
- Grilling suppliers
- Infiltrating business operations
- Pumping buyers

The third general category consists of ways to find out what a competitor is up to from published material and documents available from public sources:

- Help-wanted ads
- Labor contracts
- Studying aerial photographs
- Obtaining Freedom of Information Act filings

The fourth category is direct observation:

- Measuring rust on the rails
- Taking plant tours
- Doing reverse engineering
- Buying competitors' garbage

From "How to Snoop on Your Competitors," by Steven Flax, *Fortune* (May 14, 1984): 28–33. Reprinted by permission from *Fortune* magazine.

around the backs of some kinds of establishments will present you with their trash/throwaway collection area. Often the markings on cartons and boxes will tell you about the suppliers of the particular establishment and something about what is being stocked. While it is not suggested that you wade knee-deep into piles of soggy refuse, uncrushing stray papers as you go, it seems wasteful to pass up information in plain sight—yours, at no cost, for a quick walk.

If your business is a public sort of business, another way to find out about your competitors is to simply go to their establishments and see how they do business. If it is a restaurant, eat there. If it's a bakery, taste. By the time you have made the rounds, you will have some new ideas about what you want to do and a clear picture of some things you never want to do. You'll find that the same old place looks different when viewed from the perspective of a competitor.

Another approach to finding out about competitors is to talk with suppliers in your field and with real, live customers. Suppliers deal with many firms in a field and are likely to be helpful with general information. They will rarely discuss specific customers, since the disclosure of a client's business details would be a quick way to lose clients. (Would you deal with a supplier who would talk about your business that way?) Customers, on the other hand, are likely to be very specific and frank—something to remember when you are actually operating.

Just keep in mind that your potential suppliers and customers have an interest in your eventual decision. If you go ahead, your supplier has a potential new customer, and your customers, a potential new source of supply. If you succeed, everybody wins. If you fail, however, the supplier will have had one- or two-time sales and will suffer no direct loss. Customers lose nothing if you fail. Talk is cheap, but it will be your effort and money on the line. Thus, as you use information sources, particularly informal ones, you need to evaluate and be aware of inherent biases of those sources and modify your conclusions accordingly.

NOW THAT YOU'VE GOT IT, WHAT DO YOU DO WITH IT?

As was noted earlier, when you are chasing data it is often easy to forget that your original objective was getting answers to your list of questions—not the answer to the overriding will-I-succeed question. The answers to your list of market research questions were intended to help make the judgment of whether or not you are likely to succeed.

You now know how many potential customers there are in your trading area. You know who you are likely to be sharing them with and what the strengths and weaknesses of your competitors are. You know what is going on in your industry, who trades with whom, what the major trends and threats are. You are ready to begin making judgments about what is likely to happen if you do what you plan.

The judgments must happen on two levels. The first level of judgment should be fairly objective. The second level is almost purely subjective.

The first level of judgment requires that you make estimates. At this level, for example, you must estimate how much of the potential market you can shift away from your competitors and how much of any market growth you are likely to capture. This is not the place to be overly optimistic. A spot of conservatism, in fact, might be appropriate. Perhaps the best approach is to make three separate estimates—one showing your sales (buyers times average amount of expenditure for your product) if you do really well, one showing near-disaster levels of market, and one that is a mid-range, most likely estimate. This "bracketing" technique will give you a sense of the range of reasonable results so you can at least look at them.

Actually doing this, in conjunction with your market data, requires a leap of faith—and some significant reality testing. The leap of faith comes between the assessment of market and competitive data and the estimate of what your company is likely to be able to actually sell. There is no sure way to predict this amount accurately. It takes your combined understandings of your industry, your market, and your proposed business, developed through your formal and informal research, to come up with a reasonable number. But there are some fairly concrete ways to test the numbers after you have developed them. Feature 4.4 provides a list of questions you might use in considering what your sales volume might be and whether the number you estimate is reasonable in your industry and market.

I recently encountered a business proposal from what was intended to be a spinoff from a large corporation. They had done most of their homework, finding out that the total market for their one-time-only product was 3,000 units, maximum. Their business proposal called for them to sell 750 units in their first year and a thousand in their second. Even leaving aside the issue of competition, this company's "long-term" venture would run out of market within three or four years! (And it would be unreasonable to expect their competitors to stand by doing nothing to counter this frontal attack.)

This company did part of the job. And failed to make the final check of reasonableness. The waste of energy would have been preventable by the simple expedient of cross-checking their projected sales figures with total market data. As a long-term diversification, this particular project simply did not make sense.

A second set of estimates will work with the first set that you just made. In your research, particularly in the trade association material, you will have probably found a great deal of industry average (or industry segment average) financial and operating ratio data. These are the items that tell you how and how profitably your competitors' businesses (in the aggregate) function. There will be a great deal more about this in Chapters 7, 13, and 15. For the time being, you can use selected ratios for specific purposes.

You probably have found out, for example, what the average return on sales is for your industry. This is a profitability ratio, telling you how much in profit a group of companies makes as a percentage of how much it sells. (A return on sales of 10 percent, for example, tells you that, for every dollar in sales, the company made—after deductible business expenses—10 cents.) You also learned something about how your competitors' firms worked in your research. You have probably developed this understanding through many parts of your research: reading, observation, talking with people, financial and operating data. You will be combining this information with your intentions about running your own business.

The idea is to estimate the relative profitability of your business to theirs. Is part of your strategy, for example, to sell at a lower price than they do? If so, unless you have found new ways of reducing costs, your return on sales will probably be lower than theirs. Are you planning more and more expensive equipment or staff or promotion? If your costs are going to be higher than your competitors' costs, and you are going to sell at the same price as they, your return on sales will be lower. What you are after is a very rough idea of what your return on sales could be. If you then apply this percentage to your sales estimates, you will have some idea of what you might make out of this business.

From here on, the judgments are highly personal. You and you alone must look at those numbers and decide:

1. Whether that range of potential profit and the ownership compensates you for the risk you are taking and the work you will be doing,
2. Whether that range of potential profit will make you feel successful.

FEATURE 4.4
Questions for Estimating the Market for Your Products/Services

A. Market Size
   1. How large is the potential market for my product?
   2. How large is "my" target segment of this potential market?
   3. What trends have impact on this market?
      a. Are these trends increasing its size? In what segments?
      b. Are they expected to continue?

B. Expenditures

1. How much does the average customer spend in one year (or at one time) on my products/services?
2. Do they tend to spend it all with one supplier or to spread it among many suppliers?
3. What are the trends in these expenditures? Prospects?

C. Competitors

1. How many competitors will I have?
2. How is my existing target segment currently distributed among them?
3. Are we dividing a growing pie? A shrinking one? A stable one?
4. What will they do if I proceed to open my business as planned?

Example: Suppose you wanted to open a nursing home. There are 20,000 people over 70 years of age in your area. There are three other nursing homes. Your research has shown you that 5 percent of older Americans live in nursing homes. That's an estimated nursing home population of a thousand in your area. Existing facilities can provide only 750 beds. You know, also from your research, that while the average age of Americans is increasing, people are staying healthier.

You could figure that, at present, you would probably be welcomed into the market. Existing nursing homes are probably strained to the limit—750 beds for a probable thousand users. (If I were you, I would be particularly careful to find out *why* this is true, since markets generally fill their own needs unless something—regulation, perhaps—stands in the way.)

To see whether there is potential in the home, you would consider area population projections. You might have found that the total area population (now 167,000) is growing at 1 percent a year. In five years, it is expected to include 15 percent, rather than the current 12 percent, of people over 70. If you assume that better health will reduce the number of nursing home residents from 5 percent to 4 percent within your time frame, you can conclude that the total market for nursing home beds in five years will be:

```
167,000 at a compound annual growth rate
   of 1 percent                                = 175,500 people
      of which 15 percent will be over 70      = 26,325 older people
      and roughly 4 percent will live in
      nursing homes                            = 1,053 residents
```

If you have also learned that a nursing home day sells for $50 and the average return on sales in the industry in your area is 2 percent after tax, then your 200-bed home should return:

```
$50 × 200 beds × 340 days occupancy = $3,400,000
                          × .02 = $   68,000
```

Throughout this part of the work, keep in mind that you are deciding whether it is worthwhile (to you) to continue the planning process. While a "no" is permanent—you stop planning—a "yes" at this point costs you nothing more than planning time and effort.

Your market research was absolutely necessary to let you make this judgment on as sound a basis as possible. If you decide to continue planning for this venture, the research you have already done will be inordinately helpful in making decisions about location, promotion, competitive strategy, and other areas, as you will see in the next chapter.

SUMMARY

Market research is the process of systematic collection and analysis of data designed to answer a series of specific questions about the industry environment, customers, and competition of a particular business. Data can include statistical/demographic material, pictures/diagrams/descriptions, and expert or informed opinions. Questions must be developed to be capable of answers—answers in the same terms as the question.

There are two types of market research: primary and secondary. Because of the complexity and expense of collecting adequate data in primary research, small businesses are generally limited to secondary data sources supplemented by highly creative primary research. Such secondary sources include governmental statistics about population and about business and industry, trade association material, and information from general business periodicals. Primary sources can include competitors, suppliers, and customers who are in or who deal with the type of business under investigation.

The purpose of this initial market research is to permit you to estimate your potential market and potential sales and return on sales so that you can make a reasoned judgment about whether this business will provide what you need for success. Should you decide to continue planning for this particular venture, the research done will also be useful in making later decisions about various aspects of your developing operations.

FOR YOU TO CONSIDER

1. What is a target market segment?
2. Choose a type of business in retailing, one in manufacturing, and one in services and develop a market segmentation grid for each.
3. How does the concept of "fit" apply to marketing?
4. What is market research?
5. What three attributes must a good market research question have?
6. Why do you need to redefine your questions before you can collect market-related data efficiently?

7. What is the difference between primary and secondary market research?
8. List three sources of data useful for market research. For each one, list two items of data you would expect to find and how you might use each item.
9. From what sources would you be most likely to get opinions from industry experts about the future of your kind of business? Should you treat this data any differently from the way you would treat demographic data from a census? How?
10. What is "bracketing" and how does it help you to make go/no-go judgments?

NOTES

1. Donna Sammons and Bruce Smith, "To Market, to Market," *Inc.* magazine (June 1983):60.
2. "Price War Blasts Open the Home Market," *Business Week* (June 13, 1983):104.

FOR FURTHER READING

The following publications are published by and are available through the U.S. Government Printing Office, Washington, D.C.:

Small Business Administration publications:

Association Services for Small Business. SBA MA 7.002.
Basic Library Reference Sources. SBA SBB18.
Learning About Your Market. SBA MA 4.019.
Marketing Research Procedures. SBA SBB9.
Marketing for Small Business. SBA SBB89.
National Directories for Use in Marketing. SBA SBB13.
Practical Business Use of Government Statistics. SBA.

U.S. Department of Commerce publications:

Directory of Federal Statistics for Local Areas: A Guide to Sources.
Directory of Federal Statistics of States.
Directory of Non-Federal Statistics for States and Local Areas.
Measuring Markets: A Guide to the Use of Federal and State Statistical Data.

5. Helping Your Customer to Buy

Every firm competing in an industry has a
competitive strategy, whether explicit or implicit ...
[T]here are significant benefits to gain through an
explicit process of formulating strategy....

Michael Porter, *Competitive Strategy*

Once you are convinced that your potential market is large enough to satisfy your requirements, you have to devise some method for capturing your share of that market. To accomplish this, you have to ensure that your particular target market segment has some reason for considering your business as opposed to the business that has been supplying it for some time. To help you to develop those reasons—and to build an approach to your market around those reasons—is one of the major purposes of this chapter.

At the most basic level, there are only two reasons for a person to switch from one satisfier of a need to another. Either the person perceives some particular benefit from the new or different product or service, or the new product or service is infinitely more convenient (which is, in itself, a perceived benefit). Viewed from your perspective, however, making your business more convenient for your customer is an early business planning decision—you have to decide where to physically put your business. And you need to do it relatively early in your planning cycle, because so many other factors (not the least of which are financial) are contingent upon your location.

This chapter is intended to help you to do two major pieces of your business planning: begin to develop your marketing strategy, and to choose a location from which to build your business base, a base consistent with your customers' needs and priorities and that enhances the developing image of your business. Obviously, however, to have an image for your business, you must have a very clear notion of what needs you are really trying to satisfy for your target customers. That, therefore, is where this chapter begins. By putting perceived benefits and consistent location together with your defined target customers, you will be able to create a marketing strategy that is compatible with your basic business definition and with the critical success factors you defined in Chapter 3 and refined in Chapter 4.

WHAT YOU ARE REALLY SELLING: PERCEIVED BENEFITS

The late Charles Revson, founder of Revlon, is said to have observed that "In the factory, I make cosmetics. But in the department stores, I sell dreams." This is a very graphic and succinct way of stating what was discussed in the last chapter: No matter what you want to sell, it will not move unless it is what the customer wants to buy. In Revson's case, he knew that few women would buy a list of chemical elements and coloring. But he also knew that many women *would* buy a better chance to attract a man, or a more healthy look, or a more dashing (but risk-free) approach to life. So what he sold was the dream, not the chemical compound.

Once you have decided on the products or services you want to sell and to whom you want to sell them, your next job is to figure out how to do it. This involves helping your customer to buy your version of your product or service as opposed to the versions offered by your various competitors. In short, you need to separate the "cosmetics" from the "dreams."

This involves a close analysis of your product or service to find out what there is about it that is likely to attract your clientele. Why do people buy this product or service, anyway? Why should they buy your version of it when they have been buying Company X's version for the past couple of years? If you were your customer, what would your response be to your version of this product or service? Why?

One approach to doing this kind of analysis is to examine what it is your competitors are really selling and to whom they are selling it. Going back to your market segmentation grid (Chapter 4) might be of some use here in identifying market segments to which your competitors might be appealing. A look at television commercials for pantyhose, for example, will give you some indication of the potential for differentiating one product from another product that is essentially similar in function. Consider the "Gentlemen Prefer Haynes" commercials. Compare them with the "No Nonsense Pantyhose at a No Nonsense Price" ads. Think, for a moment, about the consumer toward whom each campaign is aimed. The ads are not really talking to the same people at all. Haynes is really selling sex appeal, while No Nonsense is selling economy. Both brands of pantyhose have the same actual function.

Both brands of pantyhose undoubtedly have very similar features. They are sheer, for example. And they come in a variety of shades. And so on. Each probably has some functional advantages over other similar products—one may have been tested to last twenty minutes longer than another or be some percent more sheer or have 52 more size/color combinations. But are any of these the real reason a woman buys one brand over another? Are these features and advantages what those ads are really selling? Actually, what is being sold is some *benefit* that the customer perceives in the product—looking better (Haynes) or saving money (No Nonsense).

Please note that the customer is helped to perceive this particular benefit in the product by the manner in which she is told about the product. The benefit may be real, but it does not have to be real. The only requirement is that the customer believe it exists and is a benefit. Helping your customer perceive those benefits is a large part of your job as a seller. This aspect of your job will be discussed at length in Chapter 11. Before you get to how to tell your customer about the benefits of your product or service, you must first define its features. Then you have to determine its advantages over all (most?) competing products or services. And finally, you have to look at your target customer and figure out what that person can be helped to perceive as the benefit of your product or service to him or her.

Consider what 7Up has done to the soft drink market in recent times. It has cheerfully redefined what used to be a mere feature into what is now perceived as a real benefit. Its lack of caffeine used to be simply a fact. Following a major ad campaign by 7Up, it turned into a benefit (aided by physicians' warnings about excessive caffeine intake in general) to which other soft drink manufacturers were forced to respond—either to copy or to claim that they had always been without caffeine.

Suppose, for a moment, that you have developed a new kind of instant camera. Its optical system is markedly different from all those cameras now on the market. It can take pictures, using your new film, in extremely low-light conditions and produce a finished picture for the user faster than any existing instant camera. What are you going to sell?

Obviously, you are going to sell the cameras and the film. But what are you *really* going to sell? You are extremely excited about your brilliant technological advances. But are these what will sell your camera and film to the instant camera market? They are features that might turn on three graduate engineers.

Your camera and film will have a metering system that reacts .05 seconds faster than anything on the market today and a new type of film that is more light-sensitive than anything currently available—definitely advantages. But will those facts alone sell? Probably not—except to those same engineering types who would be fascinated by the technological characteristics of your product.

You have to begin with a definition of the people who buy (or who are likely to be able to be induced to buy) the basic product you are selling—instant cameras and related film products. If you had done your market research, you would know that, generally speaking, these products are not sold to serious

Figure 5.1   Selling your product to your customer

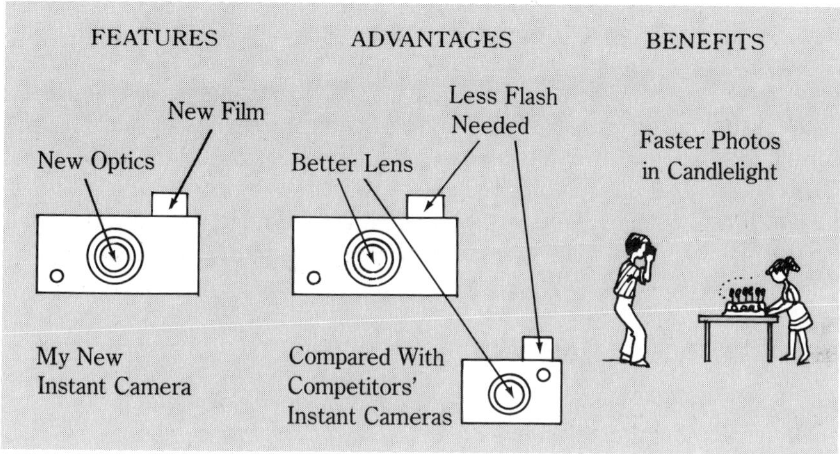

camera buffs. They are sold (as you can tell from most of the advertising for them) to just plain folks who want to take them to parties and who want the immediate feedback of the instant processing. Rather than "artsy," serious photographs, instant cameras appear to be for candid, "fun" snapshots.

So how do you pitch your new equipment to these people? You look at why they buy instant cameras and film in the first place, rather than purchasing the generally more sensitive and flexible regular cameras. First, there's the instant feedback, seeing the picture and being able to pass it around while the party is still going on or while Grandpa is still playing with the baby. Second, there's the low level of hassle and set-up generally associated with instant or snapshot cameras. There's no significant film-loading problem. Built-in flash modules take care of exposures without extra lighting gadgets. They are take-it-and-go-type cameras. (While there are undoubtedly other reasons, these two should do for our purely illustrative purposes.)

What they are clearly looking for is speed and reasonable flexibility without hassle. And your new camera and film can give them more of both because of your technological features and advantages. Think of it! The buyers of your camera and film can get to see their pictures *even faster* than they could with a standard instant. Since your flash is not needed until well after those of other available instant cameras, purchasers of your gear will have fewer poor pictures due to "flash washout" or whatever you choose to call that phenomenon. (Your term ought to be catchy because, with any kind of luck, it will become a new "buzzword" among customers—and that will sell your gear. "The Blahs" was a disease created by Alka Seltzer which, of course, its product could cure. "Halitosis," a 1950s euphemism for "bad breath," also began as a non-word, intended originally to sell a mouthwash product.) Also, *everybody* knows that naturally lighted pictures are better (right?) and your gear can give customers longer natural light time.

Out of the features and advantages of your product, then, you have developed what could be perceived by your potential market as the benefits of choosing your product over similar and competing products. You have taken a careful look at your product as your consumer would and determined what about it would fill the customer's need better. It's the benefits that you sell. Just as Revson sold the dreams, you need to determine what benefits your particular customers will buy—and help them to see those benefits.

COMPETITIVE ADVANTAGE AND DISTINCTIVE COMPETENCE

From your point of view, as business owner, the special benefits that you can sell to customers are advantages that you hold over your competition—your

FEATURE 5.1
Developing Competitive Advantage

Century Hotels is a group of five small hotels in New Orleans founded by Mark Smith. New Orleans has about 26,000 rooms. Century runs 402 of them. Despite its size, Century is maintaining its share of the market. It does so by capitalizing on the fact that its hotels are small.

"We can't get the main body of a convention to come to us," Smith says. "But we can get the top guys. We'll get the executives or the board of directors who don't want to stay at the convention hotels."

Nancy Hoose, the head of sales and marketing, relies on direct mail efforts (30,000 pieces a month) and on personal calls. She maintains good relations with travel agents, corporate travel departments, and with other hotels that can direct overflow business to Century. She stresses the value to a small hotel of repeat business.

Century essentially sells personal attention. Julio Rios, Vice President of Operations, noted that when you have a small guy competing with big ones, you have to be able to say "Tell us what you need, and we'll do it." It is probable, however, that even he had not envisioned what it took to accommodate the cast and crew of Clint Eastwood's movie, "Tightrope." Against an offer of discounted rooms from one of the big hotels, Century knocked out walls to make rooms large enough for daily screenings, set up a special dining room in which to feed the crew at night, and provided special maid service while the crew was shooting. Century got the business.

Adapted from Sanford L. Jacobs, "Hotel Chain Exploits Its Size to Compete With Big Rivals," *The Wall Street Journal* (January 9, 1984):21.

competitive edge or competitive advantage. Your instant camera, for example, offers increased low-light capability and faster picture output. A competitive advantage, more than one if possible, is nice to have because it gives you some flexibility in differentiating your product and permits you to look at a broader range of competitive marketing strategies and positions. It permits you to sell the customer something that nobody else has or can sell.

Whatever it is that you have defined as the benefits of your product or service must be perceived by the customer as real and as a special benefit in order for it to provide you with a competitive advantage. While the emphasis in Chapter 11 will be on ways of convincing your customers, it should be noted here that if your perception is not communicated to and shared by your customers, your edges—whether real or not—will not be useful to you. You will not be permitted that flexibility that comes with product or service differentiation.

A case in point concerns the relatively recent differentiation among chicken products sold in supermarkets. Years ago, chicken was chicken, and that was that. Then, along came Frank Perdue, who managed to convince consumers that his chickens were better. After all, they were yellower and fatter and didn't everyone know that yellower chickens were better? They didn't, of course, until Mr. Perdue told them. But it seemed reasonable. Pretty soon, it was true. And Perdue chickens could command a premium price.

Another company tried to cash in on the idea of essentially differentiating a product that had never before been differentiated—lobster. It didn't work, and you can figure out why it could not have worked by comparing lobster with chicken and considering how consumers deal with each. First, at the time of this great experiment, lobsters were not farmed, merely caught. Consumers basically understood that you could not really choose which lobsters crawled into your lobster pots or your nets. Chickens, on the other hand, were grown in captivity. What they were fed could be controlled. Quality could be assured.

Second, lobsters must be sold live and are rather a delicacy. When you want one, you buy it where you find it, rather than shopping around. Chicken, on the other hand, is carried by every store any time. It is already neatly in plastic wrap when you get there. A brand tag can be placed on top. You would not have to peer into murky tanks and sort out the branded creatures while they were moving around, doing battle with one another.

Finally, while chicken is made often by almost everyone, lobster is eaten most often by people who are out in a restaurant. This implies that the major purchasers of lobster are restaurateurs and that any brand marks would be gone by the time the end consumer even saw the lobster. It would be difficult to develop enough attachment in end consumers to a branded lobster to force restaurants to specify, by brand, in purchasing. Would you leave a restaurant because it did not have your brand of lobster? Would you go to a restaurant because it carried the right brand of lobster?

The point is that it was apparently more reasonable, though not necessarily more relevant, for consumers to consider branded chicken than to think about branded lobster. Perdue has his competitive advantage (now being attenuated by the addition of other brand-name chickens). He is expanding into Cornish hens and chicken franks. The lobster company is no longer in the lobster business.

In addition to being perceived as real, to be a competitive advantage, a product or service difference must be perceived as having some value to the purchaser. Consider the golf ball. One ball may be yellow while another is white. A "so what?" might be appropriate. If, however, your bright yellow ball makes it easier to find on golf courses, you may have something to sell. Instant benefit. Instant competitive advantage. Instant additional options for your market strategy.

Close kin to the notion of competitive advantage is the notion of distinctive competence. While competitive advantage is generally linked to the features and advantages of the product or service itself, however, distinctive competence generally refers to some special skill or ability in making or distributing the product or in developing or delivering the service. As in the case of a feature or an advantage being turned into a benefit for purposes of developing marketing strategy, a distinctive competence generally *creates* some advantage that can be turned into a benefit, if you choose.

You have a special skill in low-cost production of widgets, for example. This produces a situation in which your costs of production are likely to be below those of your competitors. In terms of marketing strategy, this means that you can sell your widgets at a lower price than can your competitors. If yours is a highly price-sensitive market, you can turn this into a benefit—lower cost. If your market is not particularly price-sensitive, you might simply want to increase "quality" (however that is defined in the widget business). Your benefit would then grow out of whatever "quality" features you have added. Alternatively, you might simply decide that you'd like to make more money per widget than your competitors. This would add no benefit for your customer—but would create a major one for yourself. Any of the above approaches to the widget market is feasible for you because of your distinctive competence in manufacturing cost control.

MARKET DEVELOPMENT AS A MARKETING STRATEGY

As was pointed out in Chapter 4, approaching or defining a new target market segment for your type of product or service is fairly risky. It is generally also expensive. It may be, however, a valid market strategy if the features, advantages, and benefits of your product or service really meet a newly defined need or meet a need for a newly defined group of people.

If, for example, you really believe that the features of your newly

FEATURE 5.2

Developing New Markets

Tofu (toé-foo) is not a basic American staple. But Chandri and Gary Barat of Legume, Inc. would like to make it so. Tofu is bean curd, a white, cheesy, almost tasteless ingredient. It is a dietary staple in the Orient. At present, U.S. citizens are most likely to find it in Chinese restaurants.

The Barats hope to change all that—without spending the millions of dollars in advertising generally needed to give a new product any prayer of success. "Our idea was to put it in finished products in ways that Mr. and Mrs. Average American can understand." Thus, Legume's ravioli have tofu fillings, rather than cheese fillings—reducing the calorie, fat, and cholesterol levels of the finished product. They expect such reductions to help sell their products as Americans become more concerned with health, fitness, and diet.

The four-year-old company has "borrowed from everyone to stay alive," says Gary. In 1982, a private sale of stock saved the company from bankruptcy. "[The Barats] have brought the company from nothing to where it has a certain status," says the investor who arranged the financing. "These people are totally committed to what they are doing," says a stockbroker who is also an investor in Legume, Inc.

Legume products are now in health food stores nationwide and in a few supermarket chains on each coast. Its sales were only $40,000 a month in 1983—$20,000 less than its breakeven point. While it cannot yet afford such expensive marketing techniques as taste samples, Barat believes that "we've proved we can make a product and that there is a market for it."

Adapted from Sanford L. Jacobs, "Company Finds a Niche Selling Frozen Foods Made With Tofu," *The Wall Street Journal,* (January 24, 1983):25.

developed instant camera and film will give it advantages over conventional 35mm single lens reflex cameras, you might want to ignore the fact that, heretofore, serious camera buffs did not shoot instant cameras. Going this route, however, means that you will have to help your target consumer through two issues, rather than just one. First, you will have to get him to consider a product type he has never before considered. Then, and only then, can you get him to consider your specific brand of this product type.

Your pitch to this consumer will obviously have to be very different from the one you developed for your earlier shot at the instant camera market. In fact, if you try to sell to the serious folks, you might do your strategy irreparable harm if you also try to sell the same version of the product to the party/candid instant camera user. (You might go with two versions of your camera, each pitched at a different level of the market.)

You would need to go through the same type of analysis, however. What features and advantages of your product would provide benefits to this target consumer? The answers are likely to hinge more on the quality advantages that your product can provide—for example, the deeper color provided by your new film technology, the greater sharpness of definition, etc. What might sell them are such benefits as instant feedback without loss of photograph technical quality (as opposed to speed and less flash usage).

Your price levels would have to change as well. It is unlikely that any serious camera buff would believe that a camera priced for the candid/"fun" user could possibly be really good and as inexpensive as your party version would have to be to sell in that market.

In short, developing a new market segment in which to sell your product will undoubtedly give you a competitive edge in the new segment. You would be, for a while at least, the only guy in that segment, the only real choice for customers in that particular segment. This may happen, however, only after you manage to convince members of this new target segment that your product really can meet their needs or that they have a need your product can fill. This extra step can be expensive and is not always assured of success.

GENERIC MARKETING STRATEGIES

As you can see, developing a marketing strategy, an approach to your particular target market segment, is a process of rearranging the variables in such a way that you have a benefit to offer your intended customers. The variables that lend themselves most easily to being factors in this process of market strategy development are price, promotion, and quality (however that is defined or perceived in your type of business).

Aside from developing an entirely new market for your product or service (discussed above), there are two major general directions from which to approach your market. You can offer fantastic price or marvelous quality. Either approach will clearly differentiate your product or service from those of your competitors.

Michael Porter of Harvard has found that the most profitable companies in any given field are those at the ends of the price/quality spectrum. Companies in the middle of this continuum tend to be less profitable and are often marginal in terms of industry success and company viability. According to Porter, firms that are "stuck in the middle" lack the resources to become low-cost leaders or to differentiate or focus their products well enough to capture the higher margin market segments.[1]

Your objective, therefore, will probably be to get your company as close as possible to one of the ends. The remainder of this section is devoted to an examination of the requirements and implications of being at either end of this spectrum.

Firms in three industries by position on pricing/profitability continuum

Industry	*Low Cost/* *High Volume*	*Stuck in* *the Middle*	*High Margin/* *Low Volume*
Lift Trucks	Toyota, Komatsu	Clark	Hyster
Electric Motors	GE, Emerson	Franklin	Baldor, Gould
Internat'l Autos	GM	Fiat	Mercedes

Source: Michael Porter, *Competitive Strategy: Techniques for Analyzing Industries and Competitors* (New York: Free Press, 1980). 42–43.

Low Price

Low price is generally associated with some minimal level of quality. This is what is usually referred to as "value" in advertising copy (Woolworth's "Our Tradition, Values" ad line, for example). This is not the same as being a discounter. Discount operations take regular goods and sell them at below regular market prices. Being a low-priced company in a market, on the other hand, refers to having one of the lower regular market prices for a given product or service type in the first place.

In general, the game at this end of the market is to be the low-cost producer in the market. If you manage that, then you have the greatest flexibility in pricing in the market—your distinctive competence in producing provides you with your competitive advantage. If you are a manufacturer, this probably means that you have developed a new or modified production process for your product. If you are a retailer or a service producer, you have either found a new way to cut your costs (most off-price or discount stores, for example, have few salespeople and even fewer store amenities) or you are willing to make less in profit per unit of product or service sold or both.

Figure 5.2   The profitability continuum

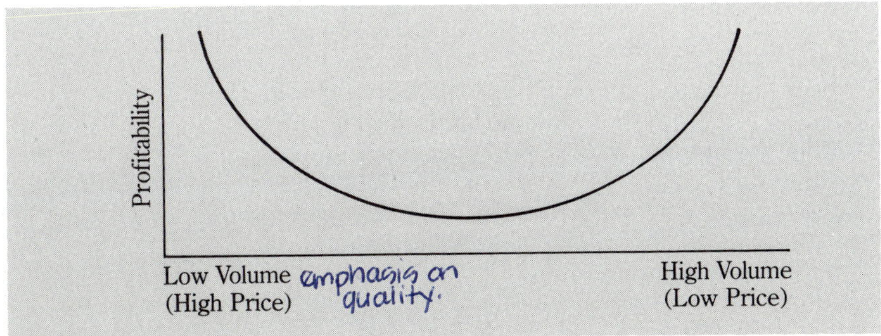

[Adapted from Michael E. Porter, *Competitive Strategy: Techniques for Analyzing Industries and Competitors* (New York: Free Press, 1980).]

If you are planning to make less in profit per unit, you clearly will have to sell a lot more units than a company in the middle of the price/quality spectrum. Low price implies low margin, which requires high volumes in order to make the whole operation worthwhile from a financial point of view.

In some few industries, generally those in which there are major economies of scale (the more units you make, the cheaper it is to produce each one), it does not make sense to bother entering unless you can be *the,* or close to the, low-cost producer. One such industry is the semiconductor industry, in which the major producers so dominate because of cost advantages that it would be virtually impossible for a newcomer to enter the market and survive with a standard product. In such industries, if you cannot differentiate your product significantly or develop some technological advance that lowers your production costs, find another industry to enter.

FEATURE 5.3

Generic Marketing Strategies: High-Volume, Low-Cost Operations

Home Depot hardware stores is now a chain of 19 stores based in Atlanta, Georgia. "Just four walls and a ceiling," says the chairman and chief executive Bernard Marcus. "When we hit a city, we lower prices overnight."

Home Depot, Inc. provides a low-budget approach to selling hardware to the do-it-yourself market. Its stores are large enough to accommodate all its stock, removing the need for costly warehouse space. Marcus notes that, if there is not enough room for an item on the shelf or on a rack, " ... it goes on the floor. We'll just stack it up, 15 feet high." Since the stores are also warehouses, forklift trucks are sometimes seen in the aisles during shopping hours.

Home Depot also cuts costs by buying directly from manufacturers—in volume. "We price at wholesale level or better," says Marcus. "As our volume goes up, our policy is to lower prices."

The one "frill" that Home Depot offers is advice. Each store has 115 to 160 salespeople trained in do-it-yourself tasks. In effect, Home Depot will help its potential customers become real customers by teaching them how to do it as well as selling them the materials with which to do it.

This strategy apparently works for Home Depot. Sales have more than doubled each year since its beginning in 1979. In 1982 its stock was one of the fastest growing nationwide in over-the-counter trading. It is a classic of the high-volume/low-cost marketing strategy.

Adapted from L. Erik Calonius, "Two Hardware Chains Try Different Ways to Attract New Do-It-Yourself Customers," *The Wall Street Journal* (December 28, 1983):sec. 2, p. 1.

High Quality

At the other end of the continuum you find the companies whose advertising stresses quality rather than price. Now "quality" is a highly elusive attribute, but if you can convince customers that your product or service has it, you are in great shape. You can command a premium price in the market. This allows you to make a greater profit per unit sold—assuming that your costs are about average for the industry—and you can therefore sell fewer units and still be profitable.

In fact, sometimes the fewer units you have available for sale, the more your market will compete to get them. After all, if the supply is limited and you can't get product *x*, it clearly must be a wonderful item. If folks are competing to buy, the price can rise and nobody will much care. This is the philosophy that encourages the notion that the diner with the most trucks at it must have the best food in town—even if you have to wait to get it.

Projecting a "quality" image usually involves some general kinds of support for the product or service, although the specifics differ from industry to industry. First, the establishment from which the product or service is sold must reflect the quality image you are selling. If you sell clothing at outrageous prices, the carpets on the floor should probably be outrageously

---

FEATURE 5.4
Generic Marketing Strategies: High-Cost, Low-Volume Operations

The most expensive perfume now on the market is for men only. It is put out by Bijan Pakzad, whose shop on Rodeo Drive in Beverly Hills admits customers one at a time by appointment only.

In a sense, the perfume is a bargain. It is one of the less expensive items one can buy of Bijan's. His suits start at $1400 (bullet-proofing extra) and he will sell you a set of crocodile luggage for $20,000. The perfume, on the other hand, will cost you a mere $250 an ounce. Unfortunately for true bargain-hunters, it comes only in a six-ounce bottle ($1,500). Pakzad claims that "If the bottle is small, it is not masculine enough. It is not bulky. It is not strong." Therefore, your $1,500 will get you not only six ounces of the perfume, but also a hand-blown, hand-cut Baccarat crystal bottle.

Despite the price, it is reported that there is no shortage of buyers. The heir to the Saudi throne, for example, is said to have bought seven bottles at the same time to give away as gifts.

The high-price/low-volume strategy has clearly been extremely successful for Bijan Pakzad.

Adapted from Christopher Bertelli, "This Perfume for Men Leaves Impression on Senses—and Wallets," *The Wall Street Journal* (September 5, 1984):sec. 2, p. 1.

thick. Second, you will have to support your product or service both before and after the sale. You can expect, for example, to have to have appropriately classy advertising in appropriately classy places. Your returns policy will have to be more liberal, for your customer will really always have to be right. You can also expect to have to provide more service and/or better warranties to your customers than will your low-price business cousins.

Market Structure

In general, this kind of market structure exists because people seem to be unable to conceive of paying relatively small amounts for high-quality goods or services. Two examples should serve to make this point. The first has to do with a small consulting company that did not charge the normally high consulting fees. Its costs were not as high as those of larger firms because of its minimal overhead. When it bid for a project, therefore, it showed up as low bidder by a very large margin. When potential clients compared the bids or proposal price estimates, they routinely chose against this company simply because, at those prices, it was thought that the company simply could not be any good. For the consulting company, the solution was simply to raise its prices to the standard levels. Thereafter, it did quite well at winning contracts.

The second example has to do with the sale price of a trade book from a prestigious university press. The publisher decided to test the sales of the book at a range of prices before it chose the final selling price. Since this book was properly academic and put out by this very serious publishing house, the book sold best at the highest price the publisher tested. Needless to say, that was the final price of the book, giving joy to both publishing house and author. (The book is not this book.)

The hand-held calculator market is almost a perfect paradigm of this differentiated price/quality structure, accepted and encouraged by both the manufacturers and the clientele. At the beginning of the calculator craze in the early 1970s, a great many companies made calculators. All of them cost a great deal (a four-function Commodore, for example, went for $140). Then, as the price of the chips which ran them came down for the major producer, Texas Instruments, TI began to take over the low end of the market. Competitors (Commodore, for example) could not match TI's price performance and they dropped like flies from the market. Pretty soon, TI very nearly owned the low-price market.

But there was also a market for the "quality" calculator. Hewlett-Packard backed its calculators with a year's full warranty and a great deal of slick advertising in all the right places. It also found ways to meet special needs for various segments of its market. H-P was the first to provide specialized functions for business applications as opposed to scientific applications, for example. H-P did not lower prices to meet the price competition that developed in the mid-1970s. In fact, virtually the only times H-P lowered prices on current models were when new, more advanced models were taking over the line. Unlike Commodore, Hewlett-Packard is still very much in the hand-held calculator market, moving toward increased capabilities, as is the entire market. It dominates the quality calculator market.

LOCATION: AN ESSENTIAL ELEMENT OF MARKETING STRATEGY

Conrad Hilton was once asked what were the three most important factors in the success of a hotel. He is supposed to have replied, "Location, location, and most important of all, location."

As you can see, how well you meet what your customer expects of you and your operation can be critical to your success or failure. If you go back to the critical success factors that you identified in Chapter 3, you will probably find that most of them are related in some way to what you believe your target market segment expects from your business. One of the earliest decisions that you will have to make (other than the purely internal decisions about your legal form and types of financing) is a decision that is greatly influenced by customer expectations and your choice of broad marketing strategy. It is the location decision—one every entrepreneur must make.

Deciding where to locate is such a complex decision that large consumer-oriented companies—for example, McDonald's, Hallmark—have staffs of specialists to handle this aspect of their operations alone. This does not mean that a reasonably careful, thoughtful, plain old person cannot make a perfectly adequate decision. It is simply noted to give you an opportunity to consider how critical the location decision is thought to be.

Consider this decision, the one regarding where you will locate your business, as a marketing decision. If you are planning a retail business or a business that will serve the public directly, a restaurant or a photocopying place, for example, the implications of your location decision are immediately clear. If your customers cannot find you easily, you're probably in big trouble. And that's even *before* you open your doors.

If your business is a manufacturing business or one that deals in industrial or business products (as opposed to consumer products), the decision about where to locate your company may be just as critical, but a good deal less obvious. Brief thought, however, should help you see how your location tends to affect most of your business operations.

Suppose, for a moment, that you are planning on opening an aluminum can crushing plant. You will make money on the difference between what you pay the people who sell you empties plus your costs and what you can get from the big aluminum smelting plant in Pittsburgh, for example. Your key marketing challenge is how to ensure that you have enough material to keep your plant busy and to get a good price and a good deal from the smelter. Your best strategy, then, is to minimize your costs to permit yourself the greatest amount of pricing flexibility in obtaining your critical material—empty cans. Where should you put your plant in relation to your buyers and sellers if you intend to use trucks to pick up and deliver your input and output?

You can assume that the equipment will probably cost you the same amount no matter where you put it. There may be some differential cost of land between a location near your town and near Pittsburgh. Assume, for the sake of example, that there is none. Clearly, then, your tradeoff will be in the cost of transporting the uncrushed cans versus the cost of transporting the crushed cans. Since your trucks can only carry a fixed volume of stuff, a long run will be less expensive on a per pound of aluminum basis if you crush the cans first. You would locate near your source of empty cans. This cost-minimizing would permit you, if necessary, to pay a premium price for the empties you purchase, if supply is a problem, thereby ensuring yourself a favorable competitive position in the empty aluminum can-buying market.

If, on the other hand, there is not enough supply of empties available from your town alone, you might edge farther from your town in the direction of Pittsburgh. You would try to locate at a point that ensures a large enough supply of empties while minimizing the distance over which you have to transport uncrushed cans. Since your profit is in the spread between income and cost, your location will be critical to how well (if not whether) you prosper.

In an even simpler example, let's say that you will manufacture motorboats for the recreational boating industry. Depending on how you look at it, your customers will be either the dealers to whom you sell your boats directly or the end users who eventually purchase your boats. In either case, the competitive situation requires that a given size of boat with specific characteristics sells only within a fairly limited price range. Also, boats are rather expensive to transport. Thus, the price expectations of your market dictate that your plant be located within a relatively short distance of your end users. Beyond this area, your transportation costs will require either that your price rise out of range, or that your margin drop out of sight. In either case, you won't profit well from your business.

If you have chosen to go with a high-price, high-quality marketing strategy, you may have some greater flexibility about where to locate your plant. You expect that your customers will pay the small premium that additional transportation costs will add to their purchase price. If, however, your marketing strategy has you pointed toward the low-priced end of the market, any additional cost could well kill you.

Deciding Where to Locate

One location consideration is common to almost all businesses: the issue of whether to buy property and build or to lease or rent your location. While this decision is clearly partly a financial tradeoff, there is also the issue of the optimum use of your probably limited funds. Even if you could purchase a building relatively inexpensively, for example, do you want to commit that large a portion of your potential startup funds to a long-term investment in property as opposed to, say, a larger investment in inventory? Probably not, particularly when you are not absolutely certain about whether or for how long this specific property will meet the needs of your business. It should be noted, too, that the Small Business Administration will not back loan requests for real property purchases for companies in startup situations. They are considering these same variables.

Partly because of the uncertainty of the long-term value of this particular site to you, you want to lease or rent, and you want the lease to be as flexible a one as you can negotiate. (One *does* negotiate a lease, not merely sign it. See your lawyer.) You would hope to be able to sublease the premises should you need to move prior to expiration. You would probably also want to have the owner do as many alterations and modifications as you can persuade him to do so that the space better accommodates your business. Failing that, you might agree to pay for alterations and improvements through increased monthly payments. Since you will have to have such changes made anyway, you would probably rather pay for them in small doses over a long term than in a lump sum before you open for business. The rationale is similar to the rationale for leasing as opposed to purchasing the site itself.

Beyond these lease/purchase issues, your major considerations differ, depending on the basic orientation of your company's business. Decisions about where to put manufacturing facilities are often less complex than those required for locating retail operations, so those will be discussed first.

For a manufacturing firm, major location issues include:

1. The transportation cost issues outlined briefly above.
2. The availability of an adequate supply of labor of the quality necessary for your business. If your business requires specialized skills, you need either people educated enough to absorb your training, or an area attractive enough that you will be able to draw the requisite labor skills to your site. Your place must be nice enough to keep them after they've seen your plant.
3. The availability at your site of adequate utilities (Do you require special electric lines for your equipment, for example?) and adequate space for efficient operating layout or process flow.
4. The availability in your space or building of the means to move products

and materials around or into and out of the place—for example, adequate freight elevators, loading docks.

5. The proximity of your site to the means of transportation you intend to use for moving your raw materials and finished goods into and out of your plant site—for instance, how far from the nearest airport? rail line? major highway interchange?

6. The availability of space into which to expand when your business outgrows its initial boundaries. You want to relocate manufacturing operations as rarely as possible because of the general hassle associated with such a move. You also usually do not want to split operations among several sites unless there are market, cost, or operations reasons for doing so. Lack of expansion space does not count as an adequate reason.

You should also be particularly aware that many states and localities are actively seeking any legal business that will bring jobs into their respective baliwicks. Many places have agencies (called "economic development agencies" or "area planning agencies," etc.) whose lives are devoted to searching for such businesses and to making their lives easier once they agree to locate in the designated area. "Making lives easier" can consist of smoothing out various zoning difficulties, assisting with transportation arrangements and hiring and training, and sometimes even offering tax incentives to the incoming business. Do not throw such agencies out of your office!

Location decisions for businesses oriented to the retail or consumer markets include a good many more variables than do those for manufacturing operations. They deal directly with their publics—and you know how strange and complex customers can be.

In addition to the lease considerations, which all businesses essentially share, retail operations must consider the fact that they usually expect their customers to come to their place of business, rather than simply shipping their product to their customers' locations. This implies that you had better be where they expect to find you. (The only real exceptions to this come when you have found such a unique product or have such a massive competitive edge that you are absolutely certain your customers would hunt you down in the Antarctic if you decided to locate there. These are extremely rare.)

Quite naturally, locations to which a broad range of retail customers normally flock tend to be relatively expensive locations. Many experts, however, actually view rent or lease costs as a tradeoff against advertising costs. They argue that if you have located in a non-standard area for your consumers in order to save money on rent, it will take you more advertising money to let your potential customers know where you are and what you can do for them. You will also have to convince them to go out of their way for your place. They also point out that this high level of advertising expense is likely to be required throughout the life of your business.

To their general observations must be added the note that it is difficult enough to start a small retail operation. You do not also need to add the uncertainty connected with having to entice your consumers into altering their normal patterns of life and shopping. What you really want to do is to put your store in their way so that they cannot possibly miss it.

To fit the notions of your customers about where your retail location should be, you need to consider what type of goods you are going to sell. In very broad terms, there are two types: shopping goods (items that people like to browse through and around for before purchasing, like mink coats or clothing or jewelry) and convenience goods (that people tend to pick up wherever they are, like a quart of milk or a dozen eggs or some rolls). Essentially, you want to locate within or near coveys of stores with a like type of goods. You would not, for example, want to locate your posh fur salon between a supermarket and a discount drug store. Nor would you want to put your discount food warehouse next to the classiest department store in the area. This all comes back to the notion of "fit" between your operation and your intended customer. If you really jar their notions of what you should be like, they will avoid you in droves.

Once you have decided to locate with or near other stores rather than off in the woods by yourself (which might not be bad for a crafts shop or an antiques place in the right kind of region), you still have a number of choices. There are at least three levels of shopping area to which you may be able to attach yourself—in addition to local business strips and downtown locations.

Neighborhood centers are generally built around a supermarket or a drug store. They serve 7,500 to 20,000 people within a 6- to 10-minute drive from the stores. The stores tend to be convenience-type stores. Such a center might be a good place for a hardware store, beauty shop, or bakery, for example.

Community centers serve a 10- to 20-minute driving radius and a population of 20,000 to 100,000. The anchor stores are usually variety or discount department stores or one of the smaller department stores. Here there is often a mix between shopping and convenience goods. A major supermarket, for example, as a one-end store and a discount department store at the other end or in the middle. In these centers, you want to locate your shop closest to the stores with similar types of merchandise.

Regional centers are the monster places that have become the rage lately in both suburbs and cities. A rural or suburban regional center will serve 100,000 to 200,000 people. In a city, such a center or mall may well serve many more and is often a tourist attraction as well. There is usually more than one major department store. These serve as anchors for an area of mainly shopping goods stores. Sometimes there is a drug store in the area—truly for convenience.

In addition to these types of shopping areas, a new variety seems to be growing. This is the **specialty center,** which dedicates its space to a specific kind of retail store. There are now "discount malls" that house a collection of manufacturers' discount outlets. There are also centers built around home remodeling and repair.

When you are looking for a place to put your retail operation, you need to be especially aware of the terms of the lease you will be asked to sign. Pay particular attention to what it is that you are actually leasing. In many planned shopping centers, you are leasing the bare space—and we do mean bare. Sometimes, an enclosed mall location includes only three walls. You get to do the storefront yourself. Leases tend to be in "legalese," so you definitely want your lawyer to look them over carefully before you sign anything.

While you are usually expected to make any alterations necessary to your space to make it accommodate your business, you can sometimes negotiate a deal in which your landlord does some alterations in return for a higher lease payment. While this is probably more costly to you in the long-run, it spreads your payments over a long period, therefore giving your outlet a better chance of having a long run.

Organized shopping centers usually also require additions to the basic lease cost of the site you are using. While total rent in a downtown location is just total rent, a shopping center may require fees based on square footage or store sales. These are simply requirements that you all contribute to the upkeep of common areas of the center and/or to common advertising programs. For these fees, you generally also get to belong to the center association. This is sometimes a very active organization that contributes significantly to the success of stores in that center. In fact, the strength and effectiveness of the center association should be a major consideration in choosing a shopping center location.

You also want to be particularly careful about who owns any improvements you may make to the space. A small business owner who merely wanted his displays to be sturdy attached them physically to the floors and walls of his leased location. A while later, when he decided to move his operation, he discovered that, under the terms of his lease, anything attached to the premises was the property of the landlord. It was an expensive way to learn to read all the print on leases.

Given the fact that you will be paying out serious money to finish your retail location so that it meets your needs, you want to ensure that you can remain in that location at least long enough to recoup your investment. You therefore want to pay attention to the duration of your lease and to options to renew and terms of renewal.

Traffic Studies as Decision Aids

Now that you have an overview of options available to you in terms of retail locations, how do you decide on one? Essentially, you go back to your market research data to remind yourself of the demographic characteristics you started out looking for in your customers. Then you either find or conduct traffic studies in the area (or exact spot, if you have one in mind) in which you plan to locate. In Chapter 4, we discussed using a variant on this form of primary research to determine the boundaries of your potential trading area. Your objective now is to find out whether enough people and/or enough of the *right* people pass your site to support your operation, assuming you can draw *x* percent of them in.

Quite often, you will find that somebody has already done most of this work for you. City offices or Chambers of Commerce do traffic studies in some places, particularly for areas in which they are trying to build (or rebuild) the business base. Area merchants' associations usually do them for the same reasons. Almost all mall merchants' associations have traffic studies for the malls themselves.

If you find you need to do one yourself—or are mistrustful enough of what people are telling you to want to supplement or check their conclusions— traffic studies can be done fairly simply. Either you or someone you hire simply stands outside the proposed location and counts. This should be done at various times of the day and/or evening and on various days of the week. If you are selling convenience goods, your concern is the volume of traffic passing the location. If you are selling shopping goods, the quality of the traffic is of greater concern. To estimate "quality" of passers-by you will have to determine what clues your counters should look for. Clearly, a quality count will be less accurate than a straight head count.

One thing that you need to consider in making such a count is the probable purpose of the potential customer's trip. In the most obvious example, if you are planning to be on a major artery between the suburbs and downtown, the inbound side of the road will be jammed during morning drive time. People are unlikely to stop for a quart of milk, however. The outbound side will be jammed during afternoon drive time when harried people are quite likely to stop for that quart of milk. Where do you want to put your convenience store?

As a new, untried small business, at least one option is probably closed to you. You are unlikely to be able to get into the major regional shopping malls. In these places, investment by the developers is so large that they are unwilling to take chances on anything. You represent a risk to them. After all, how does it look for a mall store to go out of business? They generally tend to stay with known names (which, themselves, act as a draw to the mall) or at very least with franchisees with known names.

SUMMARY

Both your marketing strategy and your location must be consistent with your basic business definition, particularly with the notions of your target market. To ensure this consistency, you must analyze the features and advantages of your product or service to determine what differentiates you from your competitors and to identify what will turn on your intended customers. In short, you need to identify the benefits of your proposed product or service in such a way that your customer will understand them immediately. The basic marketing strategy of your business must be built around these benefits.

In terms of marketing strategies, companies in a given field generally fall along a continuum. At one end are those that compete on price, offering some minimal level of quality. At the other end are those that offer quality and service and for which price is not the overriding consideration.

The location decision is an early business decision that can contribute to the overall consistency of the business with its market. By locating your business to maximize some competitive advantage or to be convenient to your particular customers, you can go a long way toward ensuring the success of your business.

FOR YOU TO CONSIDER

1. Describe the differences between features, advantages, and benefits, and explain why you should sell only benefits.
2. What is a "competitive advantage" and why is it really nice to have?
3. Define "distinctive competence." Does it relate to competitive advantage?
4. What are the difficulties in developing a market as a market strategy?
5. Describe each end of the price/quality continuum of market strategies.
6. Why are location decisions discussed in the same chapter as defining market strategy?
7. Why is leasing a site usually preferable to owning for a new small business?
8. List the major location considerations for a manufacturing company.
9. For a retail operation, why is the type of good or service important in your location decision?
10. Describe the major levels and kinds of shopping centers. What does each offer?
11. List the key things to consider in leasing a location.
12. Why do you want a traffic study of your potential retail area? Who usually does them? If you have to do one yourself, what are critical things to remember?

NOTES

1. Michael E. Porter, *Competitive Strategy: Techniques for Analyzing Industries and Competitors* (New York: Free Press, 1980):34–44.

FOR FURTHER READING

Abell, Derek. *Defining the Business: The Starting Point of Strategic Planning.* Englewood Cliffs, N.J.: Prentice-Hall, 1980.

Kotler, Philip. *Marketing Management: Analysis, Planning, and Control.* 5th ed. Englewood Cliffs, N.J.: Prentice-Hall, 1984.

Levitt, Theodore. "Marketing Myopia." *Harvard Business Review,* September–October, 1975.

Porter, Michael E. *Competitive Strategy: Techniques for Analyzing Industries and Competitors.* New York: Free Press, 1980.

Small Business Administration publications:

Factors in Considering a Shopping Center Location. SBA MA 2.017.
Learning About Your Market. SBA MA 4.019.
Locating or Relocating Your Business. SBA MA 2.002.
Marketing Strategy. SBA 1009. (book)
Store Location: Little Things Mean a Lot. SBA MA 2.024.
Using a Traffic Study to Select a Retail Site. SBA MA 2.021.

CASES FOR PART 2

SALLY JONES AND "NEIGHBORS"

The more Sally Jones thought about her restaurant, the more she liked the idea. She had taken courses in business in college, though, and she knew that she would have to go beyond the mere notion before she could even begin the serious work. She decided to start by listing what specifics she could about her as-yet nonexistent restaurant.

This was really "making it up as you went along," she chuckled. But it was O.K. What she was trying to do was to translate her images into words so she could create a reality. The beginning of her list looked like this:

Specific items re restaurant

1. Light: Either a storefront or some other structure with giant windows.
2. Smell: Like baking bread, homey.
3. Real art work on the walls, not standard "store prints."

At about this point, Sally really looked at the list. It immediately occurred to her that it was missing most of the *big* issues. She began a second list, then, essentially documenting that she recognized the importance of the issue, but that she had no really clear perception of how the reality should look.

Specifics	*Need to get specific (fast)*
1. Menu: limited, but mainly different each day. Soups, breads, desserts are major items.	1. Size. (She alternately saw a large, spacious place, and small, close-but-not-cramped one.)
2. Sell wine and beer, not hard stuff. (She knew how hard it was to get a liquor license in her area.)	2. Atmosphere. (Options: intimate—but then the windows would have to go. Homey. Elegant.)

She knew that these lists were far from complete. In fact, she expected them to keep growing and changing as her ideas developed. But they were a start.

She also knew that the clientele she would be seeking would differ, depending on her choices in the specific areas. It was also vital to begin to focus on those items that were key to her success in the restaurant business. These, too, she believed, would vary according to her choices.

1. Develop two different basic business definitions for Sally's restaurant. Make them as different as you can while remaining within Sally's frame of reference as shown above.
2. What are the critical success factors associated with each of your pro-

posed basic business definitions? Be able to discuss why they differ in the ways that they do (if they do).
3. Which approach do you recommend for Sally Jones? Why?

•   •   •

Sally could almost see her restaurant in her mind's eye. It became clearer the more she thought about it and visualized it. It would be decorated simply—wooden butcher block tables, Breuer chairs, lots of plants, lots of light (natural at lunchtime and indirect after dark). The table linen would be brown and the tableware would be cream and brown ironstone. It looked beautiful. She felt good knowing that her name would be on such a peaceful, successful place. The food at Sally's would, of course, be marvelous.

Having been to marketing classes, however, Sally knew that she would have to do some market definition and some market research if she really intended to make her new restaurant work. She already knew some things about who she wanted as customers—people pretty much like herself. Her lunch crowd would be largely young to middle-aged housewives, and at dinner she wanted to attract their whole families.

Table 1   *Population and housing units by town, 1970 and 1980*

	Population		Housing Units	
Town	**1980**	**1970**	**1980**	**1970**
Bethel Park	34,755	34,758	11,994	9,507
Mount Lebanon	34,414	39,157	13,356	13,152
Scott Township	20,413	21,856	7,832	6,477
Upper St. Clair	19,023	15,471	5,879	4,305
Total	108,605	111,242	39,061	33,441

Source: U.S. Department of Commerce, Census Bureau, Census for 1970 and 1980 (Washington, D.C.: U.S. Government Printing Office).

Her choice of market was dictated largely by two factors unrelated to market size or condition. First, Sally wanted her place of business to be near her home so that she could get back and forth quickly. Second, she knew that her target group liked her kind of cooking. All her friends had told her so often enough. Her suburban Pittsburgh area made attracting large numbers of business people or workers extremely unlikely.

Hence, she decided to consider her primary market as "her kind of people" from the four communities surrounding her home. They were all middle to upper-middle-class family areas. She believed, however, that if Sally's became as good as she expected, her real drawing area would be a great deal larger. In Pittsburgh, a good restaurant could draw people from all over the area. And the word got around pretty fast. Many times, she and

Don and their friends had traveled way out to the northern suburbs—through or around the city—just to try out a new place that someone had heard was good. Sometimes, it had even been worth the trip.

Sally also knew that she would have to determine how she would develop her restaurant to appeal to her chosen target group. This would involve a sharp focus on the advantages of her restaurant over others in the area and an acute sense of how to sell these factors to that market. At present, she saw her main advantages as her food and the sense of peace and well-being that she could create through controlling the atmosphere (or, to use the current phrase for that notion, "ambiance"). She knew she would have to fit these into an overall approach to marketing her place.

Table 2   Effective buying income—selected data, 1980 and 1982

1980:	EBI		Households with EBI of (000)		
	Total	**Median Hous.**	**$10 to 14.999**	**$15 to 24.999**	**$25 +**
U.S.	$1,814,166,815	$19,146	13.2%	28.2%	32.5%
Pennsylvania	93,369,946	19,488	13.1	31.6	32.6
Pittsburgh M.A.	18,444,923	19,805	12.1	32.8	33.0
Allegheny Co.	12,519,816	20,172	11.8	31.2	35.0
1982:			**$10 to 19.999**	**$20 to 34.999**	**$35 +**
Pittsburgh M.A.	21,875,467	23,706	22.7	32.8	25.7
Allegheny Co.	15,000,200	$24,493	21.9	32.0	28.0

Source: *Sales & Marketing Management* (July 27, 1981 and July 25, 1983).

Her efforts in market research produced the data in the accompanying tables for her to consider. It consisted of two kinds of data: population-based data and data on spending in eating and drinking places. She also counted about 800 restaurants in the Pittsburgh Yellow Pages—excluding McDonald's and the like with whom she was not competing. Only about 45 restaurants of all non-fast-food types were operating in her four-town primary market area. Most, she had never heard of. Of those she knew, only five were decent, producing food that was at least edible in a reasonably clean, nice atmosphere.

Based on this data, she concluded that a restaurant like Sally's could work in her chosen area.

1. How and why might Sally Jones have reached this conclusion?
2. Do you agree with her conclusion? Why or why not?

Table 3 Retail sales—selected data, 1980 and 1982

1980:	Total (000)	Per Household	Eating and Drinking PI (000)	% of Total
U.S.	$965,745,665	$11,792	$87,309,502	9.0%
Pennsylvania	46,622,536	10,932	3,993,498	8.6
Pittsburgh Metro.	9,307,129	11,157	835,387	9.0
Allegheny Co.	6,280,810	11,571	614,806	9.8
1982:				
Pittsburgh Metro.	10,211,133	12,350	964,371	9.4
Allegheny Co.	6,948,475	12,757	718,229	10.3

Source: *Sales & Marketing Management* (July 27, 1981 and July 25, 1983).

Table 4 Projections compared with 1980 and 1982 estimated data

	Pittsburgh Metro Area			Allegheny County		
	1980 est.	1982 est.	1987 proj.	1980 est.	1982 est.	1987 proj.
Households (000)	834.2	826.8	823.9	542.8	544.7	542.0
Av. house. EBI	$22,111	$23,706	$43,886	$23,065	$24,493	$46,886
Retail sls. (000000)	9,307	10,211	16,307	6,281	6,948	11,325
Ret. sls./household	11,157	12,350	19,793	11,571	12,757	20,895

Source: *Sales & Marketing Management* (July 27, 1981 and July 25, 1983).

3. What other information, if any, should she have gathered? Where should she have looked for it? What should she have done with it had she gotten it?
4. Based on your understanding of her objectives and her target market, what location specifications would you recommend to Sally Jones?
5. How would you expect her to define her competitive edge? How would you define her competitive edge?
6. How should she position her restaurant in terms of broad marketing strategy?

ROB KING AND "KING FINANCIAL"

For what may have been the first time in his career with Consolidated National, Rob King began to enjoy going to work. He looked upon the days as an opportunity to study and learn. He began to really watch the bank customers he knew were owners of small businesses. Unfortunately, since these people looked and acted pretty much the way everybody else did, observation was not particularly fruitful. It seemed to Rob that they may have been slightly more assertive and confident than the average bank customer, but he honestly couldn't be sure that this observation didn't come more from his own perceptions of how things should be than from reality.

Rob also had to figure out a way to get to the actual small business loan paperwork. Like most larger banks, Consolidated National had a separate small business lending group. This had its good and bad points, from Rob's perspective. On the negative side, it created difficulties in his information collection process. But on the positive side, once he left the bank, he would be insulated somewhat from any difficulties that Helm could create. He was certain that Helm disliked him personally and would go out of his way to sabotage Rob's clients and, therefore, his new career—if he could. The departmental separation might cushion that to some extent.

Table 1   *Sole proprietorships, partnerships, corporations—1974, 1978, and 1981 (000)*

	Proprietorships	**Partnerships**	**Corporations**
1974	10,874	1,062	1,966
1978	12,018	1,234	2,377
1981	13,000	1,461	2,813
Annual % increase	2.8%	5.4%	6.2%

Source: Internal Revenue Service in *The State of Small Business: A Report of the President.* (Washington, D.C.: U.S. Government Printing Office, 1982): 70.

To solve the problem of access to specific small business lending data, Rob began to strengthen his ties to a few people he knew in the small business lending group. It helped that their offices had been near Rob's all these years. He also decided that he needed to do some more formal work on small business formation and financing if King Financial was really going to succeed.

Rob's first shock upon beginning his lunch-hour/after-hours research program on small business was the discovery of exactly how little was known about small business. This amazed him, since he also found out that virtually all enterprises were "small businesses"—depending, of course, on what definition of "small business" you liked.

Rob decided, almost immediately, that he would avoid the conflicting definition problem altogether by choosing as his field the very small, very new, or just-beginning business. This market segment had two additional advantages to Rob. He wouldn't have to hire lots of high-powered (expensive) staff people at the beginning of his career. He could also avoid head-to-head competition with the larger, established consulting and accounting firms in the area. There was also the hope that, if Rob did his new job well, the companies would grow—and King Financial would grow with them.

Table 2 New business incorporations—1973, 1978, and 1983 (estimated)

	Number	**Percent Change**
1973	329,358	
1978	487,019	47.9%
1983 (est.)	596,178	22.4%

Source: Dun & Bradstreet. Various issues of *The Wall Street Journal.*

Rob's formal research also turned up a number of relevant facts for King Financial. He found that about 80 percent of all small businesses relied on bank financing for their startups and operations. Acquiring such financing was consistently cited as a major problem by owners of smaller companies. Rob found this information heartening. He would be offering service where it was needed most.

He also found that, among the many problems cited as reasons for small business failure, those relating to capitalization and funding appeared frequently. Small businesses had generally higher debt levels and shorter-term debt than larger companies. This made good financial planning a survival issue. But small businesses were also generally cited as being painfully short in the planning area. Rob saw the business mission of King Financial expanding to provide this vital financial planning and control service to his intended market as well.

Table 3 Data by census region: Pacific vs. U.S.

	Pacific	**U.S.**
Incorporations % change 1–6/82 to 1–6/83	+2%	+2%
Bankruptcies % change 1–6/82 to 1–6/83	+14%	+7%
Share of employment growth (firms <100 employees)	18.6%	100.0%
Share of employment (firms <100 employees) 1982	15.7%	100.0%
New business incorporations (1983, first half)	37,074	300,045
Business bankruptcies (1983, first half)	8,269	32,951
Business failures (1983, first half)	2,959	13,134

Source: *The State of Small Business: A Report of the President.* (Washington, D.C.: U.S. Government Printing Office, 1984): passim.

Table 4   Data for California vs. U.S.

	California	U.S.
Business incorporations (1983, first half)	26,772	300,045
Business incorporations (1982, first half)	26,680	281,494
Proprietorship income (1982, last half) ($mil)	$24,631	$219,326
Proprietorship income (1983, first half) ($mil)	$27,974	$249,334
Total business receipts (1980) (proprietorships)	$62,261	$505,885

Source: *The State of Small Business: A Report of the President.* (Washington, D.C.: U.S. Government Printing Office, 1984): 79.

Table 5   Enterprises by size class and industry division—1976, 8, 1980, 2

	Total	1–19 Employees	20–99 Employees
U.S. TOTAL			
1976	3,338,453	2,972,629	298,088
1978	3,736,594	3,320,471	343,143
1980	3,971,068	3,523,907	366,968
1982	4,369,726	3,903,412	382,146
MANUFACTURING			
1976	316,935	231,418	65,247
1978	335,501	246,091	68,886
1980	351,999	257,513	72,289
1982	377,145	280,832	73,960
WHOLESALE TRADE			
1976	342,764	306,445	32,571
1978	374,892	333,935	36,457
1980	400,217	355,682	39,468
1982	435,885	391,897	39,255
RETAIL TRADE			
1976	1,150,692	1,063,898	78,957
1978	1,162,922	1,066,918	87,367
1980	1,197,429	1,095,175	92,195
1982	1,266,821	1,163,250	93,070
SERVICES			
1976	638,211	563,154	55,170
1978	804,746	713,457	67,993
1980	881,518	780,189	75,298
1982	1,022,869	905,463	87,162

Source: Small Business Administration in *The State of Small Business: A Report of the President.* (Washington, D.C.: U.S. Government Printing Office, 1984): 65–66.

Despite diligent searching, Rob turned up very little information on the potential local market for his services. What data there was tended to be national and, occasionally, state-level. The data that Rob considered most useful is shown in the tables.

When his formal research was in its final stages, Rob set up a lunch with a friend in Consolidated's small business lending group. In casual conversation, Rob learned about some of the special issues in small business lending, particularly about Consolidated's leverage ratio limits, security requirements, and personal guarantee policies. He also learned about businesses that the bank preferred not to lend to because of their inherent risk levels. He already knew that the specifics of these policies varied from bank to bank and, sometimes, even from loan officer to loan officer. He resolved to strengthen his ties to small business lenders at the two other big banks in the area. "A *very* useful lunch," smiled Rob, as he cheerfully paid the bill.

Rob felt that he was ready to get serious about King Financial. Bubbling with confidence and enthusiasm, he decided to tell Ginny about his new career over the weekend.

1. Should Rob King be ready to go ahead with his plan for King Financial? Why or why not? If you said that he should not be ready, what more does he need to find out or to do before he is ready? How should he find out or do it?
2. Is Rob King looking at the right numbers, given his initial notion of what he wants King Financial to do? If not, what should he be looking at? Where and how should he find it?
3. What is Ginny's response likely to be? Why? How should Rob deal with it?

• • •

As Rob King considered the market for consulting services, he found that practitioners seemed to come in a number of varieties. There was the large consulting firm. Some of these were attached to accounting practices, while others were freestanding. Particularly the freestanding ones tended to work with large corporate clients. Most of the attached consulting practices had small business or "private company" consulting groups. While each of the large houses was known for a specific specialty, or series of specialties, most of them would handle a broad range of consulting projects. These firms were generally expensive to hire and use.

The medium-sized consulting companies were generally freestanding and, quite often, limited themselves to one or two specialty fields. One, for example, operated only in the field of employee benefits—pensions, health care benefits, and the like. Another only developed bank accounting systems. This was, obviously, a broad category, and fees ranged from ones as large as the big houses to somewhat lower fee structures.

The very small firms and independent practices also covered a broad range of project work and fee structures. While some independent consultants held themselves out as able to do anything for anyone, these people tended not to last in the business, because, obviously, they really couldn't be that wonderful and that versatile. They stumbled fairly quickly—and word generally got around to potential clients rapidly and effectively.

The best strategy, then, for an independent consultant appeared to be to specialize by skill and/or by industry. Most often, such specialists also had a network of other independent or small consultants to whom to refer business that was outside their own fields. It was generally understood that such referrals worked on a two-way basis.

Rob also found that, for reasons unknown, clients seemed to equate quality with price in the consulting business. Except when bidding some kinds of government contracts, the low bidder—particularly the *very* low bidder—was rarely chosen for a consulting assignment. This appeared to have little to do with the expertise of the consultant or the quality of the proposal.

Given all this, Rob King knew that he had two major tasks to perform before he even got to develop the structure and operations of his business. He had to define his field or fields and get a rough notion of where his fee structure would stand relative to those of other independent and group consultants. He also had to begin to develop that network of other consultants whose work and judgment he trusted—after all, he would be the source of their referral to *his* clients.

1. Develop a basic business definition and critical success factors for King Financial using what you know about Rob King and about the market he found in his market research efforts (see tables above).
2. Develop a basic marketing strategy for King Financial.
3. What, if any, competitive advantage does King Financial have? How should Rob use this (these) advantage(s) to create "benefits" for his potential clients? If you cannot find a competitive advantage, how should Rob proceed?
4. How should Rob go about building his network?

DANIELLE MACKIE AND "DANIELLE DESIGNS IN CERAMICS"

For the first time in a long time, Danielle Mackie took out all the pieces of her work that she had had shipped to her new place. Some of her work was, of course, at home with her parents. Other pieces had been given to various friends and relations over the years. She still had a good bit of the stuff around. This evening, she pulled it all out and arranged it in her living room. She wanted to look at all of it in what would be, for her, an entirely new way.

Once she had her pieces massed in the room, she began to examine the array. She tried to divorce herself from the process of creating the pieces and look at the mass of her work as if she were a buyer trying to find the perfect item. She then began to examine each piece closely in turn. She tried for the same level of detachment.

She then backed up and tried it again, trying to replicate her own attitude on recent trips with friends to galleries in Boston and New York in which various pottery and ceramics objects were being displayed and sold. On the whole, her work did not look bad to her in comparison. It was, however—even she saw it—of variable quality. While one piece might be startlingly clean in design and clear in conception and workmanship, another was less well articulated. She might even call one or two pieces "muddy."

Such variability, she knew, would never do. If nothing else, pieces by Mackie would have to be consistent. She knew this from her long discussions with the gallery owners she had met on that last and many earlier trips. Consistency was a critical quality to such sellers. Consistency would, therefore, be critical for her own success.

As she looked at her pieces, she tried to envision the person who might like one of them enough to buy it. It finally occurred to her that the buyer would depend largely on where and for how much she would offer to sell a piece. This realization forced her next decision. Despite the fact that she had been making items of clays for years, she had no idea what her talent might be worth "on the street," so to speak. She decided that there was only one way to find out—and that was to take some pieces out for a test.

She did not want to go to any of the galleries she knew without a fairly clear notion of what her prices should look like. There weren't enough outlets as it was and she didn't want to show any of them that she was a rank amateur. This left only one real approach for her testing—one of the numerous art shows/crafts fairs that ran in New England during the spring and summer. Since it was now early winter, the delay would give her time to make some pieces especially for sale.

She began on one or two fairly elaborate pieces and, for the first time, she kept track of how long it took her to complete a piece—conception to finished product. She was appalled at how long it took. She'd apparently never noticed because working with her materials and her tools had always been a complete escape for her. Her objective had always been precisely to lose track of time. This new information gave her pause. It implied that the prices she charged would have to be astronomical if she intended to make a living from her work. "Mother was right again," she sighed, considering giving up her dreams of Danielle Mackie, successful artist and craftsperson.

But the dream had tight hold on her now. She could no longer just put it aside. Her life at the museum was peaceful, but boring. It simply couldn't compare with the freedom she found when she was at work in her "studio." She began to get her brain into high gear. There had to be a way to work this out. She could see, for example, a young housewife buying one of her pieces for $50. She could not see a society matron paying $1,000 for one of them. She *could* see a no-longer-very-young woman buying one of her more creative pieces for up to $500 or $600. Danni, of course, preferred the creativity involved in what she thought of as her "better" work, the $600 variety.

Slowly, a plan began to evolve. "Why not develop two markets for my work," she thought. "If I can make enough items in the $50 category to sell in relative bulk, then I get the rest of the time to do the work I really want to do—the more unique, distinctively 'Mackie' pieces. And no more 'Please catalogue these slides, Miss Mackie.' This is beginning to sound better and better!"

1. Comment on Mackie's "two market" approach to building her ceramics business. Do you see any special problems inherent in this approach? If yes, what are they and how might she deal with them? Explain why you believe as you do.
2. Develop a basic business definition for each of her proposed markets. What critical success factors will be of prime concern for each market?
3. How well does each of these markets meet what you believe to be Danielle Mackie's needs and objectives?
4. How might Danielle Mackie go about doing market research for her prospective ceramics business? What should her key research questions be?
5. Do you believe that her intention to show her wares first at an art show or craft fair is a wise decision for her? Why or why not?
6. Develop an initial marketing approach for each of Mackie's two market segments. Explain why you have made the choices you made.

ED JAMES AND "OAK TREE BOOKS"

Ed James was considering the potential market for his bookstore in the Washington, D.C. area. He had tentatively decided that a place in the Wheaton (Maryland) mall would be a good spot for it.

There was one other bookstore in the mall area. It was an outlet of a chain of booksellers. It handled the standard run of paperbacks and popular hardcovers. It was not actually in the mall area, but, then, the mall itself was not all of a piece. It was actually a pair of outside operations, one strip including a supermarket, liquor store, bank, and Phone Center store, and then a square, including a major department store and other shop-type retail establishments. The bookstore was in the strip part.

There were also other stores in the area, including a second bookstore. These, however, were separated from the twin mall areas by the mall parking lot and a major road. The bookstore in this group was part of a discount chain operation, a subsidiary of a major drug store chain. It handled mainly paperbacks and manufacturers' closeouts.

Ed was rather confused about exactly what kind of a bookstore he wanted to own and operate. When he pictured the ideal bookstore, he saw a large, comfortable place with chairs for people to sit down in while they looked over his books. The place was done in dark wood, just like a library. He had to remind himself continually that the objective was to sell books, not to serve as a resting place with reading material for weary shoppers. He had no vision to replace this dream bookstore.

He knew that the Department of Commerce expected the book publishing industry to grow in sales by more than 10 percent a year, and that 80 percent of this increase would be from inflation. They expected 2 to 3 percent growth per year in the number of volumes printed. (*U.S. Industrial Outlook,* 1980).

Table 1   Survey of book purchasers, 1975 (bought a book in last six months)

What they bought:	Hardcover	19%
	Paperback	81
Where they bought:	Full service bookstore	45%
	Paperback store	84
	Department store	20
	Newsstand, supermarket, stationery	24
Income:	$20,000 or more	32%
	$15,000–19,999	21
	$10,000–14,999	12
	$ 7,500– 9,999	12
Education:	College graduate	46%
	Some college	20
	High school graduate	23
	Some high school or less	11
Age:	under 18	8%
	18–25	29
	26–34	23
	35–54	29
	55 or older	10

Source: B.M. Compaine, *Book Industry in Transition* (White Plains, New York: Knowledge Industry Publications, 1978).
Note: 46% of books bought by top 10% of purchasers.

He also knew that the American Booksellers Association expected it to become progressively more difficult to make a profit selling books because of the squeeze between costs and the willingness of people to pay higher prices for books. There was also a growing number of discount booksellers operating in larger cities. As yet, none was operating in the specific area he targeted.

In terms of product, he did not think that he wanted to run just another paperback place. While he knew that his dream "library" was out, he did want his place to have a certain amount of class. Some trends in the book business seemed to favor his desires. Adult hardcover books were selling again, largely because of the outrageous price of paperbacks. Children's hardcovers were not moving very well, however.

Ed had begun to collect data about the people in the Washington area in the hope that it would help him to decide what to sell, to whom to sell it, and where to locate his prospective bookstore. The data he had collected to date are shown in the accompanying tables.

Table 2   Income and poverty status in 1979: 1980

	Wash. D.C. SMSA	MD.	VA.	D.C.	U.S.
FAMILIES: NUMBER	757,450	1,094,875	1,391,076	134,504	58,975,810
Less than $5,000	36,039	63,355	92,686	16,805	4,297,235
$5,000–7,499	25,120	48,702	74,607	9,735	3,652,477
$7,500–9,999	28,593	58,865	89,889	9,148	4,112,637
$10,000–14,999	74,012	133,870	213,083	19,311	8,651,778
$15,000–19,999	81,780	150,059	206,729	15,953	8,930,918
$20,000–24,999	88,400	152,168	198,879	13,761	8,413,980
$25,000–34,999	160,270	239,006	264,329	19,691	11,325,422
$35,000–49,999	155,384	161,415	159,084	16,457	6,260,836
$50,000 or more	107,852	87,850	91,793	13,643	3,330,526
MEDIAN	$27,515	$22,850	$20,423	$18,893	$19,908
MEAN	31,757	26,177	24,071	25,730	23,177
PER CAPITA	10,276	8,255	7,704	9,123	7,371

Source: U.S. Department of Commerce, Census Bureau, Census for 1980 (Washington, D.C.: U.S. Government Printing Office, 1980).

1. How can Ed best use the data he has collected?
2. Is the data he has collected adequate to help him in his decisions about who to sell what to? If yes, what do you recommend he do? If no, what data (specifically) does he need in addition to what he has? Why does he need each piece of data you recommend? Where do you suggest he get it?

Table 3   Data for Montgomery County—*Sales & Marketing Management* estimates

Population	599,500	Total retail sales	$4,424,712,000
Median age	33.1	General merchandise	709,782,000
% of population:		Drug stores	160,245,000
18–24	10.5	Total Effective Buy. Inc.	9,438,485,000
25–34	18.3	Median household	39,441
35–49	21.9	% of households by EBI group:	
50 and over	24.6	10,000–19,999	12.0
Number households	220,100	20,000–34,999	24.5
		35,000 or more	57.3

Source: *Sales & Marketing Management* (July 25, 1983).

Table 4   Language and educational status: 1980

	Wash. D. C. SMSA	MD.	VA.	D.C.	U.S.
PERSONS 5–17 WHO SPEAK:					
Only English	575,345	853,645	1,089,552	101,862	42,922,138
Spanish	17,915	14,054	12,005	2,750	2,947,051
Other lang.	33,583	29,780	32,333	3,855	1,582,047
18 AND OLDER WHO SPEAK:					
Only English	2,002,444	2,845,919	3,675,989	452,111	144,309,205
Spanish	68,577	42,266	46,699	16,857	8,170,555
Other lang.	170,190	158,971	129,769	26,139	10,273,757
EDUCATION—25 AND OLDER					
Elemen. school	170,921	434,123	673,795	63,244	24,370,124
High school					
1–3 years	198,058	397,533	500,497	64,367	20,320,142
4 years	538,605	805,471	897,778	102,828	45,691,481
College					
1–3 years	332,162	366,722	459,146	56,073	20,800,462
4 or more	595,994	493,974	599,922	111,800	21,593,443
% of H.S. grads.	79.9%	66.7%	62.5%	68.0%	66.3%

Source: U.S. Department of Commerce, Census Bureau, Census for 1980 (Washington, D.C.: U.S. Government Printing Office, 1980).

Table 5   Median age and average persons in households

	Wash. D.C. SMSA	MD.	VA.	D.C.	U.S.
MEDIAN AGE:					
All	30.1	30.3	29.8	31.2	30.0
Females	30.8	31.3	30.9	32.3	31.3
PERSONS PER:					
Household	2.68	2.81	2.78	2.39	2.75
Family	3.28	3.29	3.27	3.30	3.27

Source: U.S. Department of Commerce, Census Bureau, Census for 1980 (Washington, D.C.: U.S. Government Printing Office, 1980).

• • •

Ed James had decided that he would continue his work in developing his bookstore. He believed that there was enough market for another bookstore in the general area he had chosen, but he needed to consider two additional issues before he went ahead with his plans. He wanted to do a bit more research on the particular retail area he had selected as his location, and he wanted to give some consideration to what, if any, specialties his bookstore would target.

In support of his efforts in this stage of his planning, Ed collected information about the local retail areas in the general vicinity of Wheaton, and on Wheaton itself. The information he collected is shown below in Tables 6 and 7. (Wheaton Plaza is in Major Retail Center [MRC] 18.) He also began to collect articles about up-and-coming specialties in the bookstore specialty business. He knew that specialty and non-book lines could make or break a bookstore, and he wanted to stay as close to the books themselves as he possibly could. After all, he thought, I want this business because I love the things.

Table 6   Kinds of retail businesses by Major Retail Center (MRC) And Central Business Districts (CBD)—Washington D.C. area, 1977

	Washington	Major Retail Centers				
	CBD	**1**	**2**	**14**	**17**	**18**
Retail stores	896	130	64	257	238	201
Sales (000,000)	476.4	206.2	41.7	152.6	221.4	209.8
Convenience goods stores	368	32	19	74	60	53
Sales (000,000)	140.9	28.3	21.3	36.1	47.3	31.0
Shopping goods stores	388	77	26	93	116	94
Sales (000,000)	286.1	116.9	14.2	—	51.9	122.4
Department stores	3	4	1	0	1	3
Variety stores	4	0	0	1	3	1
Grocery stores	23	4	2	6	11	10
Eating and drinking places	304	19	11	59	39	30
Apparel and accessory stores	182	22	8	23	32	34
Misc. shopping goods stores	143	28	12	32	37	25

Source: U.S. Department of Commerce, Census Bureau, U.S. Census of Retail Trade, 1977 (Washington, D.C.: U.S. Government Printing Office).

Through these articles, he found that there was a growing interest in old and rare books. There was even an Antiquarian Booksellers' Association of America that held shows and assisted dealers and collectors. While this field was certainly attractive to Ed, he figured that it would probably not produce a steady stream of money—unless he devoted a great deal of money and time to searching for and selling specific items to a specialized, difficult-to-build client list.

A more interesting specialty appeared to be a kids-only bookstore. This would fit right in with Ed's intention to provide community service as a

Table 7   Statistics by MRC and kind of business, 1977

DEPARTMENT STORES	MRC 1	MRC 14	MRC 18
Establishments	4	–	3
Sales (000)	67,804	–	*
Pd. employees wk including March 12	1,106	–	*
VARIETY STORES			
Establishments	–	1	1
Sales (000)	–	*	*
Pd. employees wk including March 12	–	*	*
APPAREL AND ACCESSORY STORES			
Establishments	22	23	34
Sales (000)	18,244	9,184	16,673
Pd. employees wk including March 12	314	219	470
EATING AND DRINKING PLACES			
Establishments	19	59	30
Sales (000)	*	24,995	*
Pd. employees wk including March 12	*	1,296	*
GROCERY STORES			
Establishments	4	6	10
Sales (000)	*	*	13,554
Pd. employees wk including March 12	*	*	127
MISC. SHOPPING GOODS STORES			
Establishments	28	32	25
Sales (000)	11,796	*	8,281
Pd. employees wk including March 12	217	*	251

Source: U.S. Department of Commerce, Census Bureau, Census of Retail Trade, 1977 (Washington, D.C.: U.S. Government Printing Office).

*Number not provided because would permit determining item for single unit.

marketing edge over the chains and discounters. He knew that books for children and young adults represented about 10 percent of sales in chain stores, but that the depth of children's books and the knowledge about them was lacking in most of such establishments. He was pretty sure that he didn't want only children's books, but he became convinced that a separate room or part of his shop for children and young adults would help him to make it as a bookseller.

1. Prepare a market segmentation grid for Ed James' business. Recommend the segments he should choose to serve and explain the reasons for your choices.
2. Comment on James' choice of location for his prospective bookstore. If you do not approve of his choice, explain why and set out more appropriate (yet realistic) location criteria for him.

PART 3
FOUNDATIONS OF YOUR BUSINESS

CHAPTER 6
Choosing Your Legal Structure

CHAPTER 7
Getting Money to Start

CHAPTER 8
Insuring Your Assets

6. Choosing Your Legal Structure

John D. Rockefeller had a problem. He wanted to control a large number of companies and, essentially, to control the competitive situation in oil in the late 1800s. The Sherman Antitrust Act stopped him from doing it on his first try.

The State of New Jersey made his second try a breeze by being the first state to permit a corporation to hold the shares of other corporations without special legislative permission. Rockefeller set up the first "holding company" there. New Jersey's law even permitted him to sell shares to the public in his holding company. Thus, he could use other people's funds to broaden his empire and his control.

Other people followed Rockefeller's lead, and it was soon discovered that building holding companies—some of which actually "held" very little—was the best get-rich-quick scheme that had ever been legal in the United States.

And you thought that the legal form a company could take didn't matter! Not only did it matter to John D. Rockefeller, but it matters today, to you. For while you may not be intending to build an empire based on odd accounting and watered stock, what you can and cannot do in your company is often determined by the legal form you have chosen for it.

In this chapter we will consider the legal forms available to you for your new venture. You will also be introduced to your key advisers in the process of beginning and running a business—your lawyer and your accountant. A caveat: these chapters are by no means intended as a substitute for said advisers. The intention is to make you aware of the broader tradeoffs in determining your legal structure and initial financing in the hope that you will be a better and more knowledgeable client. You will also have some background to use in considering who are to be your advisers. *Do not read this chapter and assume you can go it alone.* Whatever you spend now on a good lawyer and a good accountant is likely to save you more in money and general hassle in the long run.

CHOOSING YOUR ADVISERS

Because the issues involved in structuring a new business are so complex, and because your choices about who is to advise you at this critical juncture are so important to the future health of your business (and of yourself and your family), it is wise to take some time in your very early planning stage to find good advisers. Now this sounds as if it should be simple. Your local phone book undoubtedly has pages of listings for lawyers and accountants. But you don't want just anyone who is certified. You need specialists. Similarly, while a friend of Uncle Harry's may turn out to be the lawyer you want, the fact that she is Uncle Harry's friend should not be the deciding factor.

You are looking for:

1. Advisers who know, understand, and have worked extensively with small businesses—preferably ones in your field,
2. Advisers with whom you feel comfortable and with whom you can really talk.

These people will be key to the successful building of your dream. You must be able to tell them about that dream, and they must have the capacity to help you get there—or, at very least, direct you around some of the chasms that cross your path. If your business is inherently complex or closely regulated, you must perhaps stress experience with your specific kind of small business. Examples of businesses of this sort would be health service operations, real estate development companies, or various types of music production businesses.

The fastest way to find candidates for your advisory positions is to talk with other owners of small businesses in your field. If you don't know any, you can start with lists from your local professional associations (County Bar Association, local chapter of the American Institute of Certified Public Accountants), which will probably be listed in your Yellow Pages under "Associations, Professional." A banker, if you already know one, may also be extremely helpful in suggesting advisers. After all, the bankers probably see many lawyers and accountants in their lending work.

Once you have developed your initial list, begin a sort of interviewing process. Talk to these professionals individually until you find those who seem "simpatico" and who also seem to know their (and your) business. Do not be afraid to talk about money and how fees are structured. While this should not be the deciding factor, it is perfectly reasonable for you to want to know how you will be charged for services. Though you should not expect to get a fixed quote—no one knows specifically what you will require by way of service—be a bit wary of a professional who will not even give you a per-hour figure. Not knowing what the tab is likely to be creates stress and prohibits planning—two things you really don't need just now.

Unless there is a specific reason why you expect to need professional "clout," a professional from the largest firm in town is unlikely to be the best person for your purposes. Many large firms have cutoff sizes below which

FEATURE 6.1
The Importance of Good Advisers

"I think the most important thing any entrepreneur can do is go to the right people for the right advice," says Hinda Schreiber, who, with her partner, began a successful sports equipment manufacturing company. They used the services available to them through the Small Business Administration.

Other women—even those with business backgrounds—find that they need more specialized advice or a different type of assistance. Ruth Lambert, partner in a $2 million real-estate forms business, for example, claims that, while men have no difficulties with calling in a consultant, women feel the need to do it all themselves. "Men have no personal script against getting help. But women do; they get into 'I made the apple pie all by myself.' "

Women like Ms. Lambert are developing their own solutions to the problem in mutual aid. She and her partner, Dianna Minnick, joined a group of 10 women business owners. The group meets monthly. Its purpose is to provide members with advice and assistance. "The forthrightness is priceless," says one member. "You get suggestions that are real and actionable," adds another.

This group is sponsored by American Woman's Economic Development Corp. (AWED) out of New York, but similar groups exist or can be started. Members learn from each others' experiences. "The women act like a board of directors," says Paula Sprague, an AWED adviser who guides the roundtable discussions. "There is no better forum for business owners than to have eight or nine people sharpshooting at them."

Adapted from "Job Strategies: How I Made Big Bucks," *Glamour* (September 1984):216; and Sanford L. Jacobs, "Women Chief Executives Help Each Other With Frank Advice," *The Wall Street Journal* (July 2, 1984):21.

they know it will be unprofitable for them to provide service. Even if the firm doesn't have such a lower limit, you are unlikely (for a couple of years, at least) to be able to demand the levels of attention and commitment you require from a firm driven by large fees and prestige.

As usual, there is an exception to this general rule. Some major professional firms have special small business groups, developed on the assumption that small businesses eventually become large clients. These groups may be an option for you. Their definition of "small," however, may be giant in relation to your business plans. You may have no desire to become significantly larger. If you opt for this kind of professional advice, find out in advance how the firm staffs such units. You want a particular person to handle your business, not a revolving group of people. When and if you outgrow their small business unit, you want to retain your relationship with *your* accountant or lawyer. You don't want to have to train a new person every two years or so.

A final note: Once you choose a lawyer and an accountant to be your advisers, two things seem to occur with amazing frequency. First, there is a tendency to view these professionals as permanent in your business life. Second, there is a tendency to view their advice as if it were orders. Avoid both of these tendencies. If one of your advisers is not working out, he or she is replaceable. And, in the final analysis, the risks and rewards of running your business are yours. Your advisers are there to advise. Their willingness to accept risk may be quite different from yours. Ask questions. Have them develop alternatives. Listen with care and respect to their advice—after all, that's what you're paying them for—but consider it as advice. Think about what they have recommended and then make your own decisions. Win or lose, in the final analysis it's your business.

WHY THE LEGAL STRUCTURE OF YOUR BUSINESS IS IMPORTANT

While the decision about what the legal structure of your firm will be probably did not make your list of critical success factors, it is extremely important to you personally. While it does not relate to your product or your market, it nevertheless will have a major influence on how well your business contributes to your personal objectives.

To some extent, the form of your business will dictate how you may and may not raise money. It will determine how and on what you pay taxes. It will determine many of the legal hoops you will have to jump through to actually get your business off the ground. It will determine, to some extent, your legal liability in business matters. In short, the form you choose for your business will have far-reaching effects in your day-to-day business dealings—and certainly in your tax affairs.

There used to be rules of thumb about the "right" legal form for businesses. In the early days of this century, corporations were viewed as "not quite nice" as forms under which to do business. It was felt that a proper gentleman should not have to hide behind the creation of a legal "person" if he was doing business honestly. More recently, new entrants to the business arena were advised by books and articles to incorporate immediately. They would, it was widely asserted, reap tax benefits as well as the benefits of reduced liability.

In real life, of course, it is not nearly so simple. There is no single best way to organize your firm legally. This is why the decision about legal structure is the first in which you should call upon your advisers to guide you. Your eventual choice will be based on what you expect the business to do, what you expect it to make in profit, what you personally own outside the business, what your financial needs are, and a host of other legal and financial issues.

The remainder of this chapter will outline your three main choices with respect to the legal structure of your new venture. Again, it is not intended that this discussion be the sole basis on which you make the decision. It is intended, rather, as a guide to your initial consideration of the issues involved and as a basis to assist you in asking the right questions of your advisers and of the circumstances surrounding your business startup.

You have three basic options for your legal structure: sole proprietorship, partnership, and corporation. Each is discussed in a separate section below. You can move your business up in complexity, from proprietorship to partnership to corporation, with relative ease. It is somewhat more difficult to reverse the process, however.

Sole Proprietorships

A sole proprietorship is just what it sounds like—a one-owner company. You and you alone may invest in it. You and you alone are responsible, in legal terms, for its profits or losses—not to mention its contracts and obligations.

This form is extremely easy to set up. If you are planning to use your own name under which to do business, all you have to do is to acquire the appropriate licenses and permits for your type of business. These licensing and permit requirements vary by state and city or county. Your lawyer will know or know where to find out. Alternatively, check the *Directory of Professional and Occupational Licensing in the United States* at your library for state licensing requirements. Call your state and county and city and ask about other license and permit requirements. If you have any doubt about whether you will need a certain kind of permit, check. Failing to get a needed permit is serious. Permit and licensing requirements are independent of your choice of legal structure. They are related to your choice of business.

The various tax numbers you will need to do business legally and properly are also independent of your business form. For most businesses, these will include sales tax and employer I.D. numbers. Since these requirements also vary across states and areas, check. Other businesses in your field, if you happen to know their owners, can be helpful here. You might also check with your local Chamber of Commerce. If they don't have the data you need, they will surely know where to call to find out.

If you are planning to use some name for your business other than your own—for example, The Happy Hour or Copies Supreme—you will have to file a DBA certificate (for "Doing Business As"). This is usually done at your county clerk's office or city hall. Call and ask. Generally it is an inexpensive, one-time process. The only possible hitch is if someone else in your area is using the same name. They will let you know if you have to choose a new name.

This ease of formation is a major attraction of the sole proprietorship as a business structure. Additional advantages to this form, particularly for highly independent types, is that you don't have to share anything with anybody—except, of course, for Uncle Sam and his state and local tax cousins. Your decisions are solely your own. In the purest sense, you succeed or fail on your own. The drawback to this method of operation is that you also have nobody to talk to who is as involved in the business as you are. Some people find this very lonely.

The ease of operating a sole proprietorship extends to what has to be filed by way of tax forms and other data. Essentially, it, as a business, doesn't file any extra forms. You, as the proprietor, file Schedule C (Profit or Loss From Business or Profession) and Schedule SE for self-employed individuals, along with your normal Federal 1040 tax form. The same approach is followed by states and localities that tax separately.

The federal government views a business loss as an offset to any other income you may have. Many states and localities seem to view business losses as a form of "funny money." They view a business loss as a zero rather than a negative offset to other income. This seems a bit unfair, since businesses often show losses in their early days and since the same governmental entities are rather quick to claim a piece of the profits that eventually result. In any case, if this factor will make a difference to you, find out what is done with losses in the governmental units that can tax your sole proprietorship—that is, *you.*

What governmental units tax is the entire net profit of your business for the year in question. It does not matter whether you put it back into the business or not. Furthermore, you cannot pay yourself a salary for your efforts in the business. You may take an owner's draw against profits, but this is *not* deductible as an expense of the business. (In real life, this should not matter to either you or the tax people since you would be taxed on it as either wages or profits at the same rate, your own individual tax rate.) Please note, however, when you make your business projections for your sole proprietorship, that just because you cannot deduct the cost of supporting yourself, the expense does not disappear. This simply means that the bottom line of the business will need to be large enough to cover your personal expenses. Eating is a fairly necessary pastime—even for an entrepreneur.

As the tax structure indicates, the law does not make any distinction between you and your sole proprietorship. And therein lies one of the major disadvantages of structuring as a sole proprietorship. Since you and the business are legally indistinguishable, you bear unlimited liability for anything that the business does, does not do, owes, contracts for. What this means in real life is that, if your proprietorship fails to pay a supplier, for example, that supplier can recover what is owed not only from your business, but also from your personal assets if the business is unable to cover the full amount. Similarly, if the business is sued, your personal assets—everything you own personally—are also at risk. Thus, if the business you plan to enter is at risk for numerous lawsuits—for example, a ski school or an exercise clinic—a sole proprietorship may not be the form of choice for you.

Another disadvantage also follows from the notion that you and your sole proprietorship are essentially the same. When you die, so does it. Obviously the assets do not collapse on the spot, but the business as it was no longer exists. Any assets will, of course, be part of your estate, but if you don't want the business to be broken up, you will need to make provisions for that in your will.

Finally, the sole proprietorship form of organization reduces by two the number of ways you can acquire financing. First, unlike corporations, you will not be able to issue bonds. (This is a matter of merely passing interest since, even if you were to incorporate, it is extremely unlikely that you would be able to issue bonds in the near future.) Second, you cannot offer to sell shares in your business to anyone else. This can be a serious drawback if you require more money to start your business than you have or can raise by yourself. You can still borrow money, of course—if you can find a lender. This is sometimes more difficult for a sole proprietor because there are the assets of only one person to serve as collateral for a loan—and that one person has probably already sunken everything salable into the business.

Choosing a sole proprietorship, then, is essentially a tradeoff of increased risk and fewer financial options against ease of startup and operation and total independence. As you will see in the next sections, the other forms structure the tradeoffs differently.

Partnerships

In a partnership, two or more people share ownership of the business. Partnerships range in size and complexity from a two-person, 50/50 arrangement to the 1000-person giant accounting/consulting partnerships. A partnership, particularly a small partnership, is still relatively easy to set up and is still relatively free of additional paperwork requirements. In fact, a partnership operates very much like a multi-person sole proprietorship.

Partnerships come in two major varieties. A general partnership is the standard, "vanilla" form of partnership. If it uses the names of the partners—like Dewey, Cheatam, and Howe—no registration is required. If the partnership will run under some other name, like The Legal Beagles, a DBA certificate must be acquired just as it is for a sole proprietorship. The general notion is that the tax people should be able to relate the business with the people who are to be taxed on the profits from the business.

The partnership as a business is not taxed. It must file an informational return with the Internal Revenue Service, Form 1065. This form shows the total profit or loss from the partnership and the distributive share of that profit or loss assigned to each partner. As in sole proprietorships, the share of the total profit or loss belonging to each partner is taxed—regardless of what is actually done with the money. Each partner is taxed at his or her own individual tax rate. The partner attaches Schedule E to Form 1040 and is also responsible for paying social security taxes on the earnings (Schedule SE).

Please note that the business can accumulate capital (as can a proprietorship). This money, however, will already have been taxed to the proprietor or to the partners. The profit generated from the accumulated capital is taxed as the business generates it.

Although it is not absolutely required, every partnership should write and sign a partnership agreement. This agreement should be approved by—if not actually written by—your lawyer. It is also wise for each partner to have a separate lawyer to protect the interests of that specific partner. While it may sound as if I am attempting to create business for the legal community of the entire world, you will begin to understand why you might want this level of legal involvement as we discuss further the joys of partnership.

The partnership agreement should be very specific about a number of items. It should, at minimum, contain:

1. The name and address of the partnership.
2. The names and addresses of the partners.
3. The initial contributions of each partner and the form(s) that each contribution will take (money, labor, ideas, etc.).
4. How responsibility for future contributions will be divided.
5. How long the partnership is to last.
6. How work is to be divided among the partners.
7. How profit is to be divided among the partners. (In the absence of an agreement, the Fed assumes that it is split equally among the partners—not by percentage contributed.)
8. How much each partner will be permitted to take out of the partnership each year (in draws against profits).

9. How decisions will be made and what is to be done if agreement cannot be reached (arbitration, coin flips, etc.).
10. What is to be done if one partner wants to get out or becomes incapacitated or dies. (Will the partnership carry key man insurance? Are there buyout arrangements?)
11. What procedure is to be followed in adding partners.
12. How the partnership can get rid of clearly undesirable partners, for example, the one who forges checks or buys politicians (and gets caught).

There seems to be a widespread reluctance to take proper legal precautions when dealing with family members, particularly parents or spouses. "They'll think I don't trust them," or "We don't have to think about troubles now," or "They'll get angry and back out of the deal."

Please consider what you are really saying about the potential for success of this kind of partnership for you and your family. If you can't discuss how to handle uncomfortable situations in a time of high enthusiasm, how likely is it that you will be able to cope when actually facing difficulties? A good agreement protects everyone from the really sticky conflicts by letting you all decide in advance. Will Uncle Jack's son get a job at the firm even if he cannot tie his shoes? What will be done if Aunt Eliza, a partner, fails to perform her proper duties to which she agreed in the partnership agreement? Will all the cousins become partners when they get older, or will they be added in the same way as another outsider? Dealing with all the forseeable potential problems in advance and in writing is not a lack of faith. It merely assumes that, once you are operating, you will have enough to do without arguing over the things that could have been handled in advance.

The reason for this inordinate stress on making it all legal and putting it all in writing lies in the way partnerships generally operate. Decisions must often be made while one partner is on vacation, out of town on business, at home with the phone system out of order. *Any one general partner can commit the entire partnership to some contract.* Thus, if your partner is suddenly overtaken by a mad urge to purchase the Brooklyn Bridge or 600 tons of pork bellies, the partnership is stuck—assuming that the contract is essentially valid in and of itself. A good agreement will give you some hope of recovering something from your crazed partner if the decision was not his to make in the first place. Assuming, of course, that he has anything upon which to recover.

Which brings us to another difficulty with partnerships. Like sole proprietorships, general partners in a partnership bear unlimited liability for debts, etc., of the partnership. This does not mean that a 20 percent partner is liable for 20 percent of the debt. Each partner is liable to the full extent of her personal assets. A creditor can collect from any partner at the creditor's option. Now, if you have very little money and precious few assets, this probably shouldn't bother you much. You have little to lose and would also be

PROFILE
Newbury Comics—A Partnership

Begun in 1978, in 1984 Newbury Comics grossed $1.5 million and is a great deal more than just a store selling old comic books. The partners, Mike Dreese, 28, and John Brusger, 27, now make independent records, run a rock music magazine, and sell punk and New Wave paraphernalia. More growth is expected.

The two partners appear to be a perfect match. A friendship that began when they were freshman roommates at the Massachusetts Institute of Technology has matured into a good working relationship. The shared value system that originally brought them together still remains. In most other respects, however, the partners seem startlingly different from one another.

Brusger is the operations partner. He handles the numbers and the orders. It is his inventory system that maintains adequate records for the business. Dreese, on the other hand, is the dreamer. To the extent that there are long-range plans, they are Dreese's. By his own admission, he tends not to finish what he starts. The two, together, check and balance each other. Says Dreese, "If I were by myself, there would be no one to say, 'You are screwing up.' "

Not surprisingly, their private lives are very separate and different from one another. Brusger is married, lives in a suburb, and is able to forget the business when he is not working at it. Dreese is single, lives in the city a few blocks from one of the stores, and worries about the business most of the time. Despite—or, perhaps, because of—these differences, Newbury Comics is working.

Adapted from Neil Miller, "Double Takes," *Boston Phoenix* (July 24, 1984):19.

an unlikely target for the creditors. If, on the other hand, you have something worth protecting—like the family jewels, or hereditary shares in the family oil company—this may be a serious consideration for you.

As you can see, then, you want to be extremely careful about who your partners are. From a financial viewpoint, they become your alter egos. Their decisions put you at risk. You therefore need people who not only know their business, but who also have good judgment and can be counted upon to do the "right" thing in any of the tight places you are likely to get into in your business career. Needless to say, people like this are few and hard to come by. Your best friend from high school may be a great person with whom you get along famously—and a great carpenter, besides—but before you take her on as your partner, reconsider her as someone who will have full access to your pocketbook and checkbook as well.

Partnerships are like proprietorships in terms of their lifespans as well. The partnership dies when a partner dies—unless, of course, it ends by agreement prior to any such unhappy event. If proper arrangements for continuing beyond the death of a partner have been made in the partnership agreement, a somewhat reorganized, and essentially different partnership can continue.

But consider what happens if proper provisions have not been made in the partnership agreement. The share of the partnership assets of the deceased partner become part of her estate. She has willed her assets to be divided equally among her three children. You now either have three new potential partners—who you may or may not like—or you face a situation in which the partnership share must be sold off to meet the requirements of the estate.

Or consider further your potential exposure in divorces, particularly in community property states. You and your partner are each happily married when you begin operations. Your partner divorces, and the bulk of what is divided in his half of the property settlement is the assets of the partnership. These must be sold off to satisfy the requirements of the settlement. Many, many partnerships have closed down because of such forced dismantling.

While a good partnership agreement can help to protect you from some of these hazards, it will probably not be totally effective. Even your lawyer is not omniscient. You have to contribute to the general level of safety by choosing your partner(s) with extreme care.

There may, however, be good reasons for considering a partnership structure. Aside from the ease of getting in and of continuing operations, it is generally easier for a partnership to borrow money than it is for a proprietorship. First, since more than one person is contributing to the original stake, it is likely that less money will have to be borrowed. Furthermore, a lender can look to the assets of more than one person to collateralize a loan, making loan approval more likely.

Another advantage of a partnership form is that it permits a better mix of skills in the ownership group than there can possibly be in a sole proprietorship. In deciding to start a business, you will consider your areas of strength and weakness. One way to supplement your skills is to find a complementary partner. Of course, this complementary character gets a piece of your company in return for those skills. Your tradeoff, however, may be adding an additional source of skill for equity in your business or not having a business.

Finally, there is a highly intangible advantage in having someone to talk to who is as concerned with the success of the business and the business problems as you are. Entrepreneurs often feel that they are talking to themselves and that nobody really understands what they are going through. They are largely right. And partnership is one solution.

For those of you who are particularly concerned with the liability issues in partnerships (since you have some wealth) and who don't have the urge to manage the company, there is an alternative form of partnership that might be worth considering. Alternatively, if you are an entrepreneur who doesn't mind sharing the profits, who doesn't have much money for startup, but who *must* have full control of the operation, this alternative might suit you as well.

It is a limited partnership. In this form, the limited partner is essentially making a straight investment in the company and waiting to see what happens. While there must be at least one general partner in a limited partnership (the person the creditors can chase), the liability of the limited partner(s) is restricted to only the amount invested originally or agreed to be invested in the future.

The limited partner may not take an active part in the management of the company. Should the limited partner participate in management, he is deemed to have become a general partner, losing this limitation on his liability. Since limited partners often are the people with the money, it is usually to the advantage of creditors to acquire access to the assets of limited partners as if they were general partners. Creditors are not shy about challenging the reality of designated "limited" partners. Thus, it is probably unwise to try to pass off your independently wealthy spouse or parent as a limited partner. It would be difficult to convince a judge that they really never discussed the management of the business with you.

FEATURE 6.2
Dangers in Limited Partnerships

Limited partners have always been considered relatively powerless in the management and running of a partnership. They used to accept this role. But as larger numbers of limited partnership investments go bad, limited partners are coming to life as a significant force. Investment in this form is slowing. Limited partners are taking the general partners to court. Some are complaining to regulators and letting them take the general partners to court. In short, limited partners are beginning to exercise some strength.

The main issue appears to be the competence of the general partners and what, if anything, limited partners can do about it if the general partners are not performing their jobs properly or well. The answers are coming in through judicial decisions and through changes in the law. By 1984, 21 states had adopted a uniform limited partnership act giving limited partners the right to vote on certain issues—including the removal of the general partner(s). The act was pending in two additional states.

Adapted from John D. Williams, "Limited Partners Grow Aggressive in Relations With General Partners," *The Wall Street Journal* (August 2, 1984):27.

For the entrepreneur who really only needs or wants the money (and no hassles about the management), finding a true limited partner can be sheer heaven. They are a rare commodity, however, in a startup situation, because few reasonably wealthy people are willing to invest sizable sums with no control over how the company is being run. That's probably how they got to be wealthy in the first place.

Under any kind of name, *all* limited partnerships must file certificates describing the partnership and its arrangements. These must be sworn by each partner, whether limited or general. Again, your lawyer will have all the specifics for your state and will know where to find the requirements of other states, if that is relevant.

Corporations

A corporation is a "legal person," separate from you as the founder and owner. From this simple fact stem most of its advantages and disadvantages as a legal form of organization for your new venture.

First, it is by far the most complicated legal structure to set up. This is because you are creating a wholly new legal entity—almost like bringing an immigrant or a child into the United States. You have to let all the relevant authorities know that it is there. In fact, you have to get the permission of the relevant authorities for it to exist legally. For corporations, the relevant authorities are state governments. While each state has slightly different fee structures and rules, and may call things by slightly different names, the general process for incorporating can be described.

Setting up your corporation.   You apply to the state for a certificate of incorporation, which may also be called a charter or articles of incorporation, depending on your state. You tell the Secretary of State who the incorporators are (not necessarily future shareholders), where the business will be located, and who the initial directors are (who will serve until the first stockholders' meeting). Some states require that there be more than one incorporator. It is quite possible, however, that there will be only one owner—you. Therefore, please note that your corporation will not necessarily be larger than it would be had you organized as a proprietorship. It may well be smaller than a partnership.

You must also state a business purpose. You want this to be broad enough to permit you some flexibility in the future, yet narrow enough so that people have some idea what your company does. You will also have to state the numbers, types, and par values (or no-par) of the shares of stock you want authorization to issue. Par value is the minimum amount for which you can sell a share of your stock. Generally, par is set low. You can, of course, sell a share for more than its par value.

In choosing the number of shares to issue, you want authority broader than your immediate requirements. You don't want to go through additional difficulties when you need or wish to sell additional stock. You may be authorized for more shares than you plan to sell initially.

Some sidelights are necessary about authorizations for shares of stock and about actually selling shares. First, in some states, your zeal for a large number of authorized shares may be somewhat dampened by the fact that the state fee for incorporation may be based at least in part upon the number and/or the value of the shares you are authorized. Strike a balance between present cost and future need.

Second, you want to be extremely careful about regulations of the U.S. Securities and Exchange Commission (SEC) and various laws in your own state relating to the sale of stock. Believe it or not, the SEC is not trying to make your life difficult, but rather to protect potential stockholders from abuse and fraud.

They are really not interested in your stock issue if:

- Your issue is small.
- It is not available to the general public.
- The buyers are people who mean to invest in the company rather than speculate in your stock.

Their rules, for you then, would generally be mere formalities—filing proper forms and the like. Failing to take care of such formalities, however, can become far more troublesome than the filings. Your lawyer undoubtedly knows what to file with whom. Just make sure it gets done. It's your neck on the block. We will touch on these issues again in the next chapter.

In addition to charging you fees for registering this emerging legal "person," the state has something to say about its name. There may not be two corporations with the same name in the same state (for instance, Standard Oil of California, Standard Oil of Ohio, etc.). Also, your name may not be misleading. This has led to some fairly odd behavior on the parts of various state regulators. In Massachusetts, bank examiners closed down a middle-school classroom project designed to teach about banking because the youngsters used the term "bank" in their name and they were not properly chartered. (A charter would have cost hundreds of dollars.) While this is obviously extreme, the general idea is reasonable and commendable.

Developing your corporation.   If everything is in order, the state will permit you to incorporate. Then the fun really begins. You must hold your first formal shareholders' meeting. This should probably be run by your lawyer, and it may be one of the odder experiences of your life if you or you and a friend or relative are the only shareholders. You must formally adopt the by-laws of the corporation, which have to do with how often, where, and with what notice the board of directors shall meet, how many directors there will be, issuance of stock, and similar formal items. At this meeting, the first real board of directors is voted into office by the stockholders, and corporate officers are formally chosen. There's nothing like voting with only two potential voters.

A word about boards of directors is in order here. It is not mandatory that members of your board be major shareholders—or shareholders at all. Since the board of a corporation technically runs the company (can fire its president, make distributions to shareholders, and other such significant acts), it behooves you to find the best people you can for these spots. These people are elected by the shareholders to serve until the next election. If you choose them properly—and convince them to work with you—you could have a source of real talent at your fingertips.

Providing advice is, in fact, a proper role of the board, as described in all the textbooks. Along with being legally responsible for the assets of the corporation, board members are supposed to serve as advisers to the corporation. Finding appropriate board members can, thus, be a major factor in the success of your company. But you need not only to find them, but also to convince them to become involved in the affairs of the company. For this reason, most new companies begin with shareholders as board members. To entice potentially useful skills and knowledge onto your board, then, you may wish to offer a small amount of equity participation in the company. You could also offer to pay board members a small amount plus any expenses incurred by attending board meetings. In a very real sense, you can approach the problem of assembling your first board of directors as a test of your powers of persuasion.

In addition to electing your first board, two special elections might be considered. The first, done prior to issuing stock, is to elect to issue said stock under section 1244 of the *Internal Revenue Code*. If your company plan for issuing stock and the amounts of stock qualify, your common stock may be issued with highly beneficial treatment of losses for shareholders. Under section 1244, any losses suffered by the shareholder can be treated as ordinary losses for tax purposes, rather than as capital losses—when the shareholder sells or when the company folds up. For investors with other income, this treatment permits them to reduce their overall federal tax payment by potentially significant amounts. While this may not be a particularly pleasant thought for you at your very first stockholders' meeting, keep in mind that this kind of tax benefit is much-beloved by those with enough money to worry about how to offset their ordinary income. These are generally also the people with money to invest.

The second election you might consider is the election of Subchapter S status for your corporation. This might make deep-pockets investors even happier. It rates discussion in a separate section and some detail below.

You have now created a separate, new legal creature. It can sue and be sued. It can make contracts. It is a separate being from you for tax purposes. It will continue to exist even if you die or decide to leave the business. Its shares of stock provide an easy way of transferring ownership. While a new group of shareholders might use existing mechanisms to markedly change the company, the corporation itself would require no alteration.

Unlike the other forms we discussed, getting money out of your corporation is not a simple matter of making withdrawals from what are essentially your own funds. This creature you have created owns its own money. Its profits, on which it is taxed at corporate rates, can be reinvested or paid out to shareholders in dividends. The board decides. Should they decide to declare a dividend, each share of the same class of stock gets the same amount of money, say, $.02 per share. When you as shareholder receive this money, it is taxed as dividend income to you. The same money is, in effect, taxed twice— a serious drawback to the corporate form. (You would also be taxed on your salary from the corporation as your regular income. It is a tax-deductible business expense for the corporation.)

On the positive side, the corporate form may provide some legal protection for your personal assets. Although corporations theoretically offer limited liability (limited to your investment in the company), in real life this generally doesn't work out for small businesses. First, almost no banker will lend to a small business, particularly a new small business, without requiring that the owner(s) guarantee the loan with personal assets. Bankers report that 95–97 percent of their small business loans carry such guarantees. The bank thus has full access to your assets.

Second, the "corporate veil" can be "pierced," if it can be shown that the corporation was set up not for good business reasons, but to avoid liability. Under these circumstances, your corporation will be ignored and creditors will be able to treat your assets and those of your "partners" as if you had structured your company as a proprietorship or a partnership. Unlimited liability would be the result. Such practices as mixing corporate and personal financial transactions are often critical here. While the corporate form might make some people feel better, then, we recommend good liability coverage (see Chapter 8) and less emphasis on the liability protection of corporations.

Subchapter S corporations.   As you can see, most rules regarding corporations were set up to deal with the large corporations—General Motors, IBM, and their ilk. Profits were taxed because of the nature of corporations as legal persons. Dividends were taxed because the people who got them were usually not parts of the corporation and viewed their shares as merely sources of income. Clearly, a small corporation does not operate this way. The owners generally work there. Essentially, small business corporations operate like partnerships—with slightly greater liability protection.

FEATURE 6.3
Characteristics of Different Legal Structures

Note: Items noted below are generalizations. What is best for your company will depend on your personal financial situation and on the type of business you are beginning. Please see the text for details and consult your lawyer and your accountant before making a final decision regarding your legal structure.

Issue	Proprietorship	Partnership	Corporation
Size of ownership group	One person.	Two people or more.	One person or more.
Income taxes	Business not taxed. Entire net income of business taxed as personal income.	Business files informational return. Entire net income of business taxed as personal income of the partners.	Business is taxed. When dividends are declared, dividend income is taxed as income to shareholders.
Establishment	Easy to start.	Easy to start.	Requires filings with, approval of state. Costs money.
Life	Dies when you do.	Dies when a partner dies or earlier, by agreement.	Independent of your lifespan and those of shareholders and managers.
Liability	Unlimited liability.	Unlimited liability for all general partners.	Liability limited to investment in company in many cases.
Taking money out	At will, assuming availability of profit.	By agreement, assuming availability of profit.	By vote of the board of directors, assuming availability of profit.
Getting loans	May be difficult. Equity and assets of only one person.	Possibly easier. Equity, assets of more than one person.	Depends on size and ownership of company.

It seemed incongruous to everyone that small corporations should pay such a heavy price for that level of protection. So the Subchapter S Corporation was developed. This is a corporate form that is taxed as if it were a partnership. The total profit for the year is divided among the shareholders according to their proportions of stock. Each shareholder is taxed on the full amount at her own individual rate—whether or not the board actually distributes the profits as dividends. The personal assets of the shareholders are as protected as they can reasonably be.

The federal government created this form specifically for small, closely held corporations. Thus, a corporation electing Subchapter S status must meet certain requirements. At present, there may be no more than 35 shareholders, none of whom may be non-resident aliens. They must all be people, as opposed to corporations, although some types of trusts may hold shares. All shareholders must agree to the election of Subchapter S status. The corporation may have only one class of stock (which is why you want to look at this election before you vote to have more than one class of stock). At present there is no size limit in either sales or assets for a Subchapter S corporation. These rules have changed often in the recent past. If this sounds like a good deal for you, check current rules.

Subchapter S is a federal designation. Many states do not recognize it as other than a regular corporation. They tax as if you were General Motors. If the tax treatment of a Subchapter S is the crucial feature for you—and it certainly should be one of the more important items—check the treatment by your state of Subchapter S corporations.

SUMMARY

This chapter outlines the major features of the three basic legal structures for your company: sole proprietorship, partnership, and corporation. It also considers two variant forms, the limited partnership and the Subchapter S corporation. *This chapter is not intended to substitute for a thorough consideration of the entire matter by your major advisers: your lawyer and your accountant.*

Proprietorships and partnerships are essentially magnified people. They are taxed as if their income was your income—whether or not you actually withdraw the money from the business. Through them, creditors and litigants have full, unlimited access to your personal assets. They die when you or your partner does. But they are rather easy to set up and not particularly demanding in terms of extra paperwork and regulatory hassles.

Corporations are legally separate entities from the people who own and run them. They exist independently of you and can continue after you're long gone. They are taxed separately and, when their profits are distributed to you as a shareholder, you are taxed on the dividends (double taxation). While this feature may be limited for small businesses, corporations provide some relief from the unlimited liability feature of proprietorships and partnerships.

Limited partnerships and Subchapter S corporations are mixed forms. The limited partnership provides *to the limited partner(s) only* the limitation of liability to the extent of the investment. The other side of the deal is that the limited partner may not participate in management of the company. The Subchapter S corporate form permits the corporation to be taxed as a partnership, if it meets all the requirements.

As you can see, the tradeoffs are numerous. They include the level of risk you are willing to accept, corporate versus individual tax rates (which involve your personal income level and what you expect the business to produce in profit), and the cost and relative hassle of beginning and maintaining your legal structure. As noted at the outset, this decision is critical to several of your later decisions, notably how much tax you will pay and how you may raise money. This decision should not be neglected. It may well be difficult or impossible to correct later.

FOR YOU TO CONSIDER

1. Who are the primary members of your advisory team? Why do you need each?
2. What is a "good" lawyer or accountant? Where and how do you find them?
3. Why does the legal form you choose matter to you? Can't you just change it later?
4. Discuss the advantages and disadvantages of the sole proprietorship.
5. Discuss the differences between the general partnership and the limited partnership. Discuss the advantages and disadvantages of each.
6. Do the same for regular and Subchapter S corporations.
7. What is "double taxation"? Why do you care (if you do)?
8. Discuss "limited liability" in the context of small businesses.

FOR FURTHER READING

Adams, Paul. *The Complete Legal Guide for Your Small Business.* New York: Wiley, 1982.

Corley, Robert N., O. Lee Reed, and Robert L. Black. *The Legal Environment of Business.* 6th ed. New York: McGraw-Hill, 1984.

Hamilton, Harper. *How to Prepare Your Own Partnership Agreement.* Boulder, Colorado: Hamilton Press, 1978.

Shilling, Dana. *Be Your Own Boss.* New York: Morrow, 1983.

Small Business Administration publications:

Incorporating Small Business. MA 6.003.
Selecting a Legal Structure for Your Business. MA 6.004.

7. Getting Money to Start

"The first important lesson operators of a new business usually learn is that success depends on more than a good idea. All too often it's a lack of adequate financing that blights a budding enterprise.

"The two partners ... purchased and rebuilt 10 cars ... By the end of the test, Automotive Import Recycling had sold all 10 cars and taken orders for 8 more.

"[I]t needs to move to a larger space to build volume to a profitable level, and it needs a lot of money to do it. ...

"Because of a lack of capital, the company works only on a cash basis. ... [It] can afford only a limited inventory of parts. This prevents it from buying at bulk ... which means paying 30% to 50% more for parts and material. ...

Wall Street Journal

No matter how expensive or inexpensive you expect it to be to start a business, it will inevitably cost more than you think it will. This is partly due to an almost universal optimism among new venturers and partly due to the fact that nobody can predict the costly problems that almost inevitably arise in the early operational stages of any small business. The only way to approach planning for the startup cost of your business, then, is to plan to raise enough initial funding to cover several "unexpected" emergencies. Please note: This does not mean that you should overestimate costs of operation and startup, but rather that you should plan a contingency amount over and above your expected costs.

As stated in the *Journal* piece quoted above and as noted in Chapter 2, a major cause of difficulties, including bankruptcy, in small businesses is the lack of adequate startup and operating capital. This chapter is intended to help you to make a broad estimate of your initial needs and to consider the various potential types and sources of funding to meet these needs. We will be discussing how to make precise estimates of your requirements in Chapter 14. It is assumed throughout that you are unlikely to be able to fund your own startup alone. It may also be that, even if you happen to be one of those rare people who can put up all the initial funding, you may not choose to do so.

You will see, as the chapter progresses, why this information follows the chapter on the options open to you in structuring your company. Essentially, your choice of legal form may define some funding sources out for you. You need, therefore, to have some notion of how much money you will have to be able to acquire beyond your own funds as you consider your legal structure.

"BALLPARKING" YOUR INITIAL REQUIREMENTS

To make a rough estimate of the kind of money you are talking about needing to start your business, you will use information you gathered for your assessment of your market (see Chapter 4). Of prime value to you here will be the financial ratio information that you probably collected from your industry associations and/or your industry journals. If you happen to have friends who run businesses similar to the one you are planning, you might want to talk with them about their costs. (Don't be surprised, however, if they turn you down—particularly if you intend to operate in or near their market areas. You stop being a close friend fairly rapidly when you become a competitive threat.)

As you recall, you used the return on sales industry average ratio (net profit divided by net sales) to determine whether your potential customer base was likely to produce a return that would satisfy you as an owner. We will start with the same figure here. You can work this same figure in reverse.

First, you need to decide what you want to get out of the business in profit for the first year. (Remember that most industry average data is from corporations. Under that form, owners' salaries are part of expenses and do not have to come out of net profits. If you are a sole proprietor or a partner, you will have to adjust your figures by taking what you expect in salary-type compensation *out of* your desired net profit figure. Desired net profit, then, is intended here to represent the money you earn for taking a risk, rather than money you earn by working for the company.) Your initial year is not the best time to be greedy. You will be in good shape if you survive the first year with any profit. But that will become obvious to you as you work out the amount of initial funding you will require to meet your more grandiose profit targets.

Suppose that the average return on sales in your field is 5 percent. We can assume that this is after-tax money, since all we are doing here is trying to get

PROFILE
Laura Chenel: On Raising Not Enough Money

When Laura Chenel moved to a farm in northern California, she bought a goat as a pet to keep her company. She liked the animal so much that she got another goat, and another, until, almost accidentally, she had acquired a herd of them. She then discovered two problems. First, she would have to go to work just to keep the goats in food. Second, she had to figure out something to do with the milk they gave. She solved both problems at once by making and selling goat cheese for a living. Her sales now exceed $250,000 a year.

When she first got serious about making cheese, she sold her house and some of her goats and went in search of a plant. When she found the right spot, it turned out that the owner wanted to sell, not rent. "Suddenly I had to come up with $10,000." Some friends lent it to her, with only her word as collateral. Chenel had no business training or knowledge. She had no idea what the business was worth, nor any understanding that it was under-capitalized. She found out the hard way.

"I would have saved a lot if I had had more money to begin with. For instance, I wish I had bought a pasteurizer at the start; I've thrown a lot of money away waiting this long." To get her milk pasteurized, she had been taking it by truck to a dairy 45 minutes away. At most, her truck could carry 12 cans of milk at once. In summer, this translated into four trips a day. "I've been spending $1,000 a month and a lot of labor; if I'd had the money in the beginning, the pasteurizer would have long since paid for itself." Chenel recently took out her first loan for $50,000—to buy the pasteurizer.

Adapted from Ruth Reichl, "The Making of an Entrepreneur," *Working Woman* (August 1984):99.

a rough idea of how much you'll need. If your industry average data specifies pre-tax return, work on that basis. If you will accept about the same salary-type compensation as other owner/managers in your field, then the amount of net sales you need in the first year is 20 times the amount of net profit you want.

EXAMPLE: Industry average return on sales = 5 percent
Your desired return for risk = $10,000

$$\frac{\$10,000}{.05} = \$200,000 \text{ in net sales Year 1}$$

Once you know about how much you will need in sales to meet your profit target, the rest is usually fairly simple—for "ballpark" calculations. Somewhere in your industry average data there is likely to be information on average inventory turnover and average sales-per-square-foot of selling space (for retail businesses, obviously). Again, working these numbers in reverse, you can come to the approximate amount of inventory that will be needed on average and the amount of space required to meet your profit goal. (Most people believe it wise to overstock 10–15 percent at the outset to cover what one hopes will be an opening week surge of business.) You also should have rough estimates of the cost of the necessary type of space in your area. Or, again, industry average data might suffice at this point.

We can try out this approach on Jan's Junque Shoppe. Suppose that Jan found that the average inventory turnover in this business was three times. That means that sales for an average year is three times the average inventory. Since she already knows that, to make the profit she wants, she needs $200,000 in net sales, figuring her inventory cost is easy:

$$(\text{Sales} / 3) \times \text{inventory cost as a percentage of sale price}$$

Now, from other industry average data that Jan had collected, she knew that the average cost-of-goods-sold for the industry was 60 percent of total sales. Since her total cost-of-goods-sold is inventory cost (She is not a manufacturer, merely a retailer), her average inventory cost would be:

$$(\$200,000 / 3) \times .60 = \$40,000$$

Since she wants some extra inventory available for opening, however, her initial inventory cost would be:

$$\$40,000 \times 1.15 = \$46,000$$

If she continues to use industry average data for her ballparking, she might find the following:

Item	Average % of Sales	For Jan's Junque
Equipment costs	30%	$60,000
Space	12%	2 mos. deposit = $4,000
Legal and accounting	5%	$10,000

If this is the full list for Jan's Junque, then the amount that Jan has to come up with to start is:

$$
\begin{array}{r}
\$\ 46,000 \\
60,000 \\
4,000 \\
\underline{10,000} \\
\$120,000
\end{array}
$$

Some industry associations provide data on such startup costs, as do such groups as the SBA and the Bank of America's *Small Business Reporter.* Since some of these costs also vary with your state and area, take care to adjust as required.

The SBA also recommends, as do all the experts, that you add to your startup requirements at least three months' worth of operating expenses to see the business through until it begins to bring in money. To this provision we would add enough to ensure that you can eat, feed your family, and keep a roof over your head during this time period.

Assume, then, that industry average operating expenses are 35 percent of sales (Sales − 60 percent of sales − 5 percent net profit = 35 percent). If Jan's operation is going to be about average, her operating expenses will be $70,000, or almost $6,000 per month. Her "extra" business funds should be about $18,000.

She also needs to live during the period prior to the time at which the business is bringing in an income. She needs at least $2,000 a month to pay her mortgage, the car payments, food, and similar items. She wants to have at least six months' worth of living expenses on hand as she starts her business—$12,000.

Thus, in total, Jan needs $120,000 + $18,000 + $12,000, or $150,000, to start her business.

The difference between what you need and what you have available in your various bank accounts (and are willing to kick in to the business startup) is the amount of money you will have to raise from somewhere. Quite probably you are shocked and somewhat depressed at the notion of having to find this huge amount of money. Do not quit yet! The next sections of this chapter examine your options for raising any amount of money within reason.

TYPES OF MONEY YOU CAN RAISE

Aside from your own money, there are two basic types of funds that you may be able to raise: equity and debt. They cost you in different ways, and they provide different benefits. But first consider two major overriding (and possibly contradictory) notions.

1. You may not want to consider your only funds to be the loose cash you have in bank savings accounts.
2. You may want to think bigger than you have been thinking in terms of the amounts of money you may be able to raise.

Against all the advice of "experts," a good many entrepreneurs have financed their startups on the proverbial shoestrings. Mary Flatt, founder of Eastern Onion (the belly-gram and singing telegram people), started with $700 from selling her car and a loan from an old friend for $500.[1] Gary Dahl, creator of the Pet Rock, began production out of order deposits.

While this is clearly a tenuous and scary way to start, it can be done. Therefore, before you go to others for funds, consider your own asset base. Do you really need two cars? Can you safely borrow against the equity in your house? If the answers to these questions indicate that there may be more personal funds available, then ask yourself whether you are prepared to commit these funds to your startup.

On the other hand, a common entrepreneurial error is seeking less money than is really needed for startup. Numerous entrepreneurs claim that if your idea is sound and your plan is likely to succeed, finding money is not really a problem. They point to the gigantic amounts of money looking for profitable investment homes. We will discuss the size and requirements of this pool of investment funds later under "Venture Capital." Suffice it to say that if your business is the right kind of business, these entrepreneurs may well be correct.

Equity Funds

Equity is one of the two types of funding available for business startups. Equity is the kind of funding that represents ownership in the business. If you were to clean out your bank accounts and sell off your car, putting all the money into your business, that money would be your equity. If others put equity money into your business, they will own part of it. In sole proprietorships and partnerships, equity is the owners' proportions of the total owners' equity or net worth of the company. In corporations, ownership interest is represented by shares of stock. (See also Chapter 13.)

Essentially, equity is risk capital—money put into your business with the hope of gain (dividends, capital gains), but with no guarantee of even keeping the original amount of the investment. If your firm goes under, you and other equity investors have last claim on any money that might be realized from the sale of the assets of the business. In bankruptcies, the amount that remains after the creditors are paid off is often nothing.

You can sell equity in your business to anyone you can find to buy it and at any price you can convince a purchaser to pay. If you want to be a sole proprietor, however, you will be the only person who may hold equity (ownership interest) in your company. If you are a corporation, your number of shares will be limited by your corporate charter. Increases in this number must be legally approved by your board of directors and by your state government.

It should be noted here that selling shares of your corporation to your Aunt Tillie does not constitute "going public." "Going public" means that you are offering shares of your stock to the general public, usually through an underwriter. You expect that your shares will thereafter be traded in the public financial markets.

Such an offering is subject to scrutiny by and registration with the Securities and Exchange Commission (SEC). The SEC will be interested in the sale of your equity only if you are a corporation, are selling shares out of your company's home state, are selling shares to more than 35 reasonably sophisticated purchasers, or are selling more than $100,000 worth of stock to more than 100 people, aided by advertisement and/or commissioned sales types. If your issue falls within these limits, you may have to file certain forms to that effect. Your lawyer should know. It is unlikely that you will need to worry about going public in the initial phase of your new venture.

Despite the fact that you will probably not have to meet SEC disclosure requirements, most investors (except possibly Aunt Tillie and other close relatives) will want to see some basis for believing that they will get an adequate return on their investments in your company. In addition to dazzling them with the sheer beauty of your concept, you will need to provide them with projected financial statements (which are discussed at greater length in Chapter 15). These will show what you expect the business to be like over the next three to five years. While these will be projections, they must not be fairy tales. First, your potential investor may know something about the type of business you've chosen. In that case, he'll spot your puffery immediately. Second, you want to maintain a decent long-term relationship with your shareholders or partners. Telling tall tales early in the relationship is unlikely to provide a good working base. Finally, fraud is not only bad business, but it is also punishable by law.

For an entrepreneur, equity financing has certain advantages. Chief among these is the fact that you are not legally obligated to pay the money back. In real life, however, unless your investors are really philanthropists, they will want some return on their investment. Since they are placing their money at significant risk, they will probably want a greater return than they could get by putting their money in a safe savings account or Treasury note.

In small companies, this return is generally limited to some distribution of the earnings of the company. The notion of capital gain—the idea that an investor can reap the benefit of the growth in value of the company itself—is there as well, but in small companies there is often no way for an investor to realize such gains. This is because the equity interests are not traded as are those of public corporations. In small, closely held companies, such capital gains are usually realized when a company is sold or is valued for estate purposes—or when the company actually does go public.

The main drawback to financing your business with equity, of course, is that equity represents ownership interest. And with ownership goes a certain measure of control. An owner with 51 percent of the equity of a company can control the company, simply by outvoting all others. An investor with 49 percent or less of the company may exert effective control, if there are a number of other owners and those others fail to agree on a course of action. If they do agree, the fact that you started the company is not relevant. You lose. (Note: It is not legal to run your corporation for your own benefit at the expense of minority shareholders.) Clearly, giving up ownership is a major tradeoff in financing decisions for a new venturer.

Other factors that reduce the obvious attraction of equity financing are largely financial. First, you have to share the profits of your venture. (You also get to share the losses, if any.) Second, the amounts taken out of the company by owners as dividends (in corporations) or as draws (in partnerships and proprietorships) are not tax-deductible to the company.

Selling Equity in Your Company

Equity in your company is generally traded for either money or skills required by the company. A classic error of new entrepreneurs is to view shares of the company only in terms of money invested. In fact, unless all equity participants (partners or shareholders) bore equal responsibility for the development of the concept and the business and will bear roughly equal operating responsibility, money invested should not be the critical factor in determining shares of your business. You are contributing the concept and the labor and are often taking other risks as well—for example, being out of the labor market. This "sweat" is what gives your investor (partner) a chance of making money on his investment. This "sweat equity" ought to be considered as a major factor in determining the voting and profit shares of your business.

One alternative approach to determining shares in your company is a return on investment approach. Your non-managing investor or partner is investing a sum of money on which a return is required/expected/hoped for. That level of return in relation to your earnings projection provides a means of dividing company equity. If your investor needs to make a return of 20 percent per year for five years on an investment of $90,000, and your projected earnings over five years will total $400,000, a 22.5 percent share of the company would be indicated for this investor—even if you did not add any monetary contribution at all. (This assumes that the original investment remains in the company and that some agreement is made about distributing the income if the company is a corporation.)

As you can see, the process of determining who should get what for her investment is not a mechanical, divide-A-by-B issue. It is a negotiated settlement in which items other than dollars can become part of the deal. Such issues as board seats or payout (how much of corporate profits or partnership net income will be taken out of the company) can also become factors in the negotiation. The real question for you is: How much of your company are you willing to give up to get what you need? Be reasonable, but don't give away the store. Remember, this business started life as your company.

Debt Financing

Debt for a company is very much like debt for an individual. You have to pay the money back. The lender will charge you interest for the use of the money. You have to pay on a specific schedule. Failure to meet the agreed-upon schedule (default) can result in serious consequences, including later difficulty in obtaining loans, loss of the business, and/or loss of other assets.

Any interest you pay on your business debt, however, is tax-deductible to the business. It is considered a normal business expense. Thus, if the business shows profits, the federal government will cover part of the cost of carrying your business debt through reductions in your taxes.

Debt does not result in the division of ownership in your business. This does not mean that the people or institutions that lend you money can exert no effective control over your business. Control is simply exerted contractually rather than through ownership. Generally, if you are borrowing for anything other than a short term (a year or less), the loan contract will contain certain covenants regarding what you may or may not do and/or what you must do financially in your business. Such covenants may include not taking on any additional debt without specific lender approval and/or maintaining or exceeding certain financial ratios. These covenants are designed to protect the lender by strengthening or maintaining your ability to repay the loan. Thus, indirectly, they are aimed at keeping your business financially strong.

Failure to comply with the agreed-upon covenants results in technical default on the loan. If your business should fail—despite these precautions

---

FEATURE 7.1
Particularly Risky Firms

If your banker isn't leaping over the desk to lend you money to open a restaurant and cocktail lounge, here's why. Loans to eating and drinking places caused the biggest number of losses last year for small banks (assets below $500 million), according to a survey by Robert Morris Associates, the bank lending officers trade group.

Loans to oil and natural gas drillers caused the most write-offs at bigger banks. However, loans to real estate agents and managers led the sour-loan list of banks in the San Francisco Federal Reserve district. Asked to predict high-loss industries for the current year, the bankers put eating and drinking establishments first, general contractors in residential construction second, and subdividers and real estate developers third.

and the best efforts of you and your lenders—debt holders get their money before equity owners get anything.

Working with bankers.   Because of the difficulty of getting a loan for a new venture and because of all the requirements associated with major borrowings, entrepreneurs often view lenders (usually banks) as a necessary evil— necessary because they have the money, and evil because they create the requirements that, in turn, require paperwork and inconvenience. Many entrepreneurs view this process with distaste, if not outright alarm. Some eventually conclude that a banker's sole aim in life is to harass new small businesses.

In fact, the only way banks make money is by making loans that pay interest. These interest payments cover their costs and provide them with their profit. Like you, they are not in business to give their product or service away. What most of the annoyance is really about is to assure the banker that she is likely to get the bank's money back as you claim she will. If your loan is large enough, your performance may mean her job.

Each requirement is designed with that assurance in view. As mentioned earlier, covenants are designed to help assure that your business remains strong enough to repay. Equity requirements—the requirement that there be a specific amount of ownership money in the business for every dollar of bank money—assume that if you have enough of your money in the business, your personal financial interest will make you take care of the bank's interest as well.

Banks will also want to see something besides your projections backing their loans. Pledges of collateral, co-maker/guarantor requirements, and personal guarantees are the usual methods for putting something tangible behind your fledgling company besides your good looks and honest face. They permit the bank to recover its money from someone or something even if your business fails. Putting up some property as collateral involves pledging to turn that property over to the lender should you default on the loan. Often the lender physically holds the item of value, say your stock certificates, the deed to the family farm, etc. Co-makers and guarantors are other people, presumably with some assets of their own, who essentially pledge to cover your loan should you not prove able to do so. In a co-maker arrangement, the other person is equally responsible with you for the payments. If the person is a guarantor, the lender can only chase him after you fail to pay up.

Do not be insulted or surprised when your banker asks you to guarantee the loan with your personal assets, if any. This is standard operating procedure for small business loans, particularly for those in which there is really, as yet, no business. It not only covers the bank, but it is also a measure of your confidence in your own business plan.

FEATURE 7.2
Interest Rates for Smaller Companies

Despite the relative difficulty of carrying the costs of loans, smaller companies pay higher interest rates for them than do large companies. Banks usually cite one or both of two reasons for this interest rate gap.

1. Market factors, and
2. Additional expense required to monitor smaller companies.

In addition, as smaller companies have recently suffered high failure rates, many banks are also adding a risk premium to their interest rate calculations.

Market Factors

Deregulation of the banking industry has spurred competition—as it was intended to do. However, the competition is for the business of larger corporations. Such companies are often offered rates below prime, discounted, to get new business on the bank's books. The bank's other business, loans to smaller companies, for example, has to make up the difference between what the bank must pay for funds and what it lends those funds out for.

Part of this market dynamic has to do with options. While large companies can sell commercial paper if bank credit gets too expensive, small companies have no other real options. Furthermore, many small company owners do not shop around for the best financing terms.

Expense

While small business lending is riskier for a bank than lending to large companies, at least one recent university study concluded that, rather than being more expensive, lending to small businesses may well be more profitable to a bank. This Southern Methodist University study found that small companies leave larger balances in their non-interest-bearing accounts than do large companies. The bank makes money by lending this "free money." Profitability was, thus, 2.7 points higher for small business loans.

Despite all this emphasis on property valuable enough to cover their potential losses, banks generally do not like to take property. They do so only as a last resort. Trading in property is not their business, and they usually do not make money at it. They would rather help you succeed so that you can repay in money as originally agreed.

Since the bank's basic interest lies in the success of your business, you should use, rather than fear, your banker or potential banker. He makes loans to small, new businesses in the hope that they will eventually become large, profitable clients for the bank. Particularly if your bank has a separate small business lending group, it is likely that your banker will know at least as much about your kind of business—and more about the general climate for small businesses in general—as you do. He has valuable information—if you decide to use it. Under the best circumstances, your banker can become an additional member of your expert advisory team.

You can and should begin to learn from bankers even before you sign your first loan agreement. You will be presenting your business plan and supporting documents to a number of bankers. A number of them will say "no." The policies of banks differ and their perceptions of risk differ. When you hear a "no," find out why. There may be some reparable flaw in your plan. Or the banker may know something about your business or location that you don't yet know—maybe a new traffic pattern is about to reroute traffic from in front of your proposed door to a street half a mile away. If it is something in your plan itself, and if a number of bankers say "no" for essentially the same reason that you can see no easy way around, you might want to reconsider your entire plan carefully. You might, in this final analysis, consider whether their reasons make enough sense to you to rethink the notion of laying your money down.

Negotiating a loan.   In a process somewhat akin to the negotiations surrounding a private equity sale, you will be negotiating with bankers. You are looking not only for somebody (anybody!) to say "yes," but you are also looking for reasonable terms for the loan and a banker with whom you feel reasonably comfortable. The bankers are looking for the same things. They assess you, personally, as well as your business plan and figures. In fact, for an as yet nonexistent business, their assessment of you is likely to be more important than their thoughts about the proposed business. Each of you is looking at the beginning of a long, potentially rewarding relationship. Your personal interaction is an important part of this relationship.

Loans, particularly the terms and conditions under which a loan is granted, are negotiable. You do not have to accept a loan simply because you applied and it is offered. A banker you like may be worth paying an extra quarter-point in interest rate to you. It is probably not worth an extra two percent. If you have found a banker you like, and if you have other options, try negotiating.

If you do negotiate, it is helpful to be aware that certain things are probably non-negotiable. Also, consider what your choice of terms to renegotiate is telling the banker. To focus on equity requirements, collateral requirements, and personal guarantees immediately tells your banker that you lack confidence in your plan and are nervous about backing it. The banker also generally has superiors to answer to. Those people, not knowing what a good soul you are, will demand to know how the bank's exposure is being covered. Your banker is probably unable to deal on these issues and you may frighten her about the safety of the loan by trying to back off yourself. You do not want to increase her perception of the riskiness of your venture.

In fact, the more confidence you can give your banker about the potential future of your business, the better. Perhaps the most comforting thing you can do for your banker is to provide clear evidence of proper planning for your venture. Your business plan should demonstrate (not "state," "demonstrate") that there is a market for your product or service and that your pricing, volume, and cost estimates will produce a viable, profitable business. Your banker will be particularly interested in knowing (and in seeing whether you know) exactly how much money you will need and for how long you will need it. Saying, "Oh, I guess about $40–50,000 ought to do it," will simply not be acceptable. Your banker will also want to know when you will need the money, what you intend to use it for, and how and when you will pay it back.

Your written financial statements (Chapter 15) will make this clear, but you want to use your meetings to increase your banker's confidence in you and in your ability. You should therefore be prepared to discuss your plan and statements, showing that you are in full command of the facts and implications. You will inspire little confidence if you turn to your accountant at the merest mention of a number. Save him for really technical questions, if any. And make very sure you are fully coached before the meeting.

Confidence is really the name of the game. Your business has, as yet, no track record. But you do. Lenders are big believers in track records. Even with a proper business plan and a good presentation, be prepared to discuss your experience in the kind of business you propose and your personal credit history. Many lenders prefer to put their faith (and their money) behind a good, credit-worthy person with a good idea than to back a disorganized person with a potentially great idea.

Interest-free loans.   A favorite financing trick of a new, particularly a new, young entrepreneur, is the "interest-free family loan" or the loan that will be paid back "whenever the business can afford it." This is a particularly dangerous approach for the lender (with whom you presumably have a positive relationship). The major dangers here lie in sole proprietorships and partnerships. If your business runs into difficulties, it is likely that your creditors would dearly love to gain access to some additional assets. By taking a highly unstructured "loan," you have exposed your lender to the threat of being declared to be truly a partner. Voila! His or her assets become accessible through the implied "partnership."

To guard your relatives and friends as lenders, a structured, *written* loan agreement is an absolute necessity. It can be as simple as a handwritten, signed paper stating the amount of the loan, the interest rate, and the dates on which payments will be due—the first of the month, the 15th of the month. Even such a simple document also affords protection should either party die before the loan is paid off. The loan would be a claim on your estate or an asset to your lender's heirs. Make sure that your lawyer approves (if not writes) the agreement.

Free Money

About now, you are probably wishing that someone would come along and give you money that will cost you neither control nor interest. Well, if you are considering the right kind of company in the right field at the right time, it is theoretically possible to get something akin to that kind of deal.

The "right fields" in this case are those that are more or less related to the social services—for instance, running day-care centers, providing employment to people who the powers that be are interested in seeing employed or other services of similar social interest. If this sounds like your business, you might consider setting up as a non-profit corporation. You will have to qualify under Section 501 of the *Internal Revenue Code*. Talk with both your lawyer and your accountant.

Please note that "non-profit" does not mean that you must starve or live on a pittance. It merely means that the earnings of the company cannot be used for the benefit of the people running the business. It does not mean that you cannot take a decent salary.

Being a non-profit corporation may make you eligible for various types of government grants and/or grants from various private, non-profit charities or foundations. While this is not quite free money, in that you have to come up with fundable proposals and you generally have to account for the money carefully, you do not have to sell equity or go into debt—or not, at least, to the extent that you might have had to as a profit-making firm.

The non-profit area is extremely complex and usually not of very broad interest to entrepreneurial types. It is mentioned here as one option for those interested in the right fields. If you think you might fit the description here, consult your lawyer.

Other Sources of Startup Money

We have looked at the most common sources of funds for businesses—banks and every friend and relation you may have. But there are at least two other sources of funds with which you should be familiar. Both venture capital and funding through the Small Business Administration (SBA) are often talked about by new venturers, but are generally little understood. Clarification is needed before you can determine whether these avenues really are options for you.

Venture capital, though a highly diverse field, is generally an equity-based funding approach. There are wealthy people and companies out there who are seeking high-risk, high-return businesses in which to invest. Unlike Aunt Tillie, who is prepared for a long-term investment with modest return, venture capitalists usually invest for a maximum of seven years, after which they hope to get up to 500 percent on their money. This can usually be accomplished only by going public with a high-technology or research-based product. To provide further assurance of returns, venture capitalists generally prefer to invest after the startup phase.

While venture capitalists are generally not interested in the day-to-day operations of your firm, they will often seek seats on your board of directors

FEATURE 7.3
Developments in Venture Capital

The amount of venture capital money available for investment in smaller companies has grown rapidly in recent years. This explosion of available money has created a number of changes in the venture capital markets and processes. It is still true, however, that the firms most likely to be able to find and use venture capital funds are those that can grow rapidly in earnings and can be taken public in a relatively short period of time.

1. Venture capitalists are investing earlier. As more venture capital dollars chase the companies that already have prototypes or products in the later stages of development, competition in that segment of the field is becoming extremely intense. As a result, more venture capitalists are willing to invest in startups, providing seed money to not-yet-companies in which they see "potential." In the 1970s, only about 10 percent of all venture capital financings went to these kinds of companies. In recent years, as much as 45 percent of venture capital financings are going to early-stage companies.

2. Venture capital fairs and conferences have been growing as vehicles through which companies can make structured presentations to numbers of venture capitalists at once. Subsequent meetings with individual venture capitalists often result in deals for financings. Estimates indicate that 60–70 percent of conference participants find the money they are seeking through these conferences. (Note: There is generally a screening process for companies seeking participation in such conferences.)

3. As more money is chasing appropriate firms, the firms are becoming more sophisticated in considering terms offered by the venture capitalists. An increasing number of companies are saying no to any involvement with venture capitalists, preferring to rely on less demanding forms of financings.

so that they can assure their eventual return. As with any other equity deal, your arrangement with a venture capitalist is a negotiated arrangement. But keep in mind their time frames and their need of eventual public offerings. If your business is unlikely to be able to produce 500 percent within five to seven years, and/or if you want to remain a private company, put visions of well-heeled venture capitalists out of your head as a source of funds. They will not be interested in you.

There is, of course, an exception to this general rule. The SBA funds some venture-capital-type companies designed specifically for small businesses. These Small Business Investment Companies (SBICs) may be somewhat less stringent in their requirements than commercial or private venture capital firms.

Despite these SBICs, the SBA deals mainly in debt financing. Among potential new venturers, there is a fairly general misconception about how they do it, however. It is widely thought that the SBA is a major funding source, a lender of last resort—and at below-market interest rates, besides. Actually, there are relatively small direct lending programs at SBA. The maximum loan is $150,000—if there is any money available.

The majority of the SBA's financial assistance to small business involves loan guarantees. If you, as a small business owner or prospective owner, are unable to obtain financing for your business on reasonable terms (given the current market) on your own, you may take your bank rejections and your plan to the SBA and ask for help. The SBA may then guarantee your loan from the bank for up to 90 percent or $350,000, whichever is less. This significantly reduces the risk to the bank, since a federal agency will cover most of the bank's loss should you fail to pay up. The bank is not required to make the loan. At best, you owe money to the bank at roughly average interest rates.

Since the founding of the SBA in 1953, it has assisted in the financing of more than 461,000 businesses—or about 15,400 a year. (There are an estimated 13 million small businesses in the United States today.) The agency claims to have created 33.4 million hours of work and added $468 billion of additional gross national product.[2]

Not all businesses are eligible for SBA aid, although most are. According to 1983 issues of *Inc.* magazine, the SBA process is often lengthy and is sometimes ill-equipped to evaluate high-technology companies. If you want to check eligibility requirements or availability of loan funds, call your regional SBA office.

SUMMARY

There are two major forms of financing for a new venture, equity and debt. Most businesses are financed initially with a mixture of debt and equity. While it is possible to finance entirely with equity, unless you are planning a low-startup-cost business, such a program will leave you with little flexibility—unless, of course, you and/or your investors have a lot of money. Building a business on your money alone may result in an undercapitalized business, forced to cut corners and unable to weather the kinds of financial crises to which most new small businesses are subject. It is virtually impossible to finance your new business with debt alone because no institutional lender would touch such a deal.

Potential equity sources are yourself, partners, and anyone else you can convince to purchase a share of the company. The corporate form makes selling equity simpler because there is an easy vehicle—shares of stock—for selling ownership interests. In general, equity investors are interested in a reasonable return on the money they invest in your company. Venture capital, a specialized type of equity arrangement, is not an option for all entrepreneurs because of the required return on venture capital investments.

Potential lenders to new businesses are generally banks and assorted friends and relations of the entrepreneurs. Lenders other than close relatives are seeking safety in their business lending. They are interested in covering their potential losses and in being repaid—eminently reasonable considerations given the fact that banks are businesses, too.

To an entrepreneur, each financing method offers advantages and drawbacks. Equity does not need to be repaid, but it divides ownership, control, and profit. Debt is expensive in dollars, but it is partly underwritten by the government through the tax structure. It does not divide ownership, nor does it threaten your control (unless you default), but it is more structured than equity in terms of how it is obtained and how it is repaid.

The choice, of course, is yours. It will be based on your personal preferences, your tax situation, and your abilities. In the end, after all, it is your company.

FOR YOU TO CONSIDER

1. How can you get a rough handle on the amount of money you will require to start your business?
2. Describe the two main types of financing available for business startups. From the point of view of an entrepreneur, what are the advantages and disadvantages of each?
3. How do you go about selling equity in your company? Can you do this if you are a sole proprietor?
4. Describe two ways of dividing the ownership in your company. Which method do you prefer? Why?
5. What is the Securities and Exchange Commission and why might you care?
6. Why is venture capital not an option for most new small businesses?

7. What is a banker looking for when you come in to talk about a loan for your business startup?
8. What are loan covenants? Co-makers? Guarantors?
9. Why is it not a good idea to try to negotiate your way out of a personal guarantee for your loan?
10. What special considerations should you have about personal loans to be used in the business or loans to the business from family and friends (particularly if you have chosen not to be a corporation)?
11. In terms of financing, what is the main thing that the Small Business Administration can do for you?

NOTES

1. Robert Shook, *Why Didn't I Think of That!* (New York: New American Library, 1982): 10, 89.
2. "Small Business." *Wall Street Journal* (July 25, 1983): 13.

FOR FURTHER READING

Hayes, Rick Stephen, and John Cotton Howell. *How to Finance Your Small Business with Government Money: SBA Loans.* New York: Wiley, 1983.
Silver, A. David. *Up Front Financing.* New York: Wiley, 1982.
Bank of America. "Financing a Small Business." *Small Business Reporter,* 1980.

Small Business Association publications:

The ABC's of Borrowing. MA 1.001.
Handbook of Small Business Finance. 045-000-00208-0.
A Venture Capital Primer for Small Business. MA 1.009.

8. Insuring Your Assets

"Finally, in case all else fails, you can get insurance
on your insurance from Professional Indemnity
Agency of Pleasantville, N.Y. The policy, also
backed by Lloyd's of London, pays your legal
expenses when you sue your insurance company
over a claim that has been denied."

Inc. magazine

Once you have actually begun a real company and you are considering
acquiring some assets or a partner, you have to begin to think about protecting yourself and your fledgling company from all the hazards that the world can
inflict on it—and on you. As was noted earlier, a good insurance program may
well be more valuable protection to you than the incorporation of a small
company. In fact, the reason that this chapter on insurance follows so closely
on the heels of chapters on legal organization and initial financing is that
insurance protection should be mandatory at the time of your first acquisition
of any property. Unfortunately, it is not mandatory, if you acquire assets with
your own funds. (No bank will permit you to purchase any assets with its
money and not insure them.)

While insurance agents often score almost as badly as used car salesmen
on trustworthiness scales, they are, in fact, extremely helpful to small
business owners—if you find the right ones. They can help you in many
positive ways. More important, perhaps, they can keep you from some of the
more serious consequences of the rigors of the world at large. Yours need not
be one of those uninsured new businesses that never opens its doors at all
because of the unreimbursed loss of its assets through theft or fire or other
type of loss.

In this chapter you will find out about the real nature and purposes of
insurance. You will find out what kinds of insurance you *must* purchase, what
kinds you probably *should* purchase, and how to decide about the optional
types. We will discuss what you can insure and will consider some of the terms
that insurers and their agents use in the business. You will learn, in fact, more

than you ever thought you wanted to know about insurance and how to purchase it.

Our assumption is that, even though you are prepared to take the risk of going into business, you are not into risk for its own sake. You do not feel the mad urge to expose yourself to greater risk than necessary. In short, given the opportunity and the right terms, you would prefer letting some other outfit take some of the risk for you. And that's what insurance is really all about.

WHAT IS INSURANCE?

Insurance is the kind of bet you make when you really want Team A to win, but you think that Team B might well beat them. If you bet on Team B, you will win either way. Either you will have your winnings (Team B wins), or the team you really wanted to win (Team A) will have won.

When you purchase insurance, you are essentially betting that some specific disaster will happen to you or to your assets. The insurance company is betting that it won't occur. If that specific disaster occurs, the insurer will have lost. But you will have won in the sense that you will be restored to the condition you were in before the disaster. If the specific disaster does not occur, you win because you do not have to go through the problems of insurance claims, the distraction from the basics of your new business, or the need to reassemble the basic tools of your trade.

While betting against your own luck seems a rather strange way of approaching a venture so inherently hopeful as starting a new business, it makes sense if you think of it as a tradeoff—which is another part of the definition of insurance. Essentially, you will have reviewed your capability to survive a disaster—or merely a string of annoyances, such as a series of thefts—and found that, if it all hit at once, you probably could not make it. You choose to pay a budgetable small amount (premium) every month (or quarter, or year), rather than risk an unpredictable major loss coming at some time when you may be financially unprepared to deal with it.

And why, you may wonder, should any company want to make such a deal with me? Not to mention making a business out of taking on this kind of risk? Well, needless to say, it is not really as crazy as it sounds. An insurance company has an edge that you don't have. It collects large numbers of the same kind of risks into one program. You have only your one building or two motor vehicles. This collecting of large numbers of similar risks into one program permits the insurer to predict, quite accurately, the incidence of the peril against which it is insuring. It permits the insurer, in short, to play the probabilities.

To understand how this works, you need to understand a bit about probability. Let's say that in the streets of a specific city of half a million people, there were 50,000 muggings last year. The year before, there were 49,000 and the year before that there were 51,000. You could observe that, if you walk the streets of that city, the chances of being mugged are, on average, 1 in 10 in a year. If an insurer were to write an anti-mugging policy in that city, and could cover all the people in town, it could count on losses stemming from 1 policy in 10.

You don't particularly care, however, about the average. You care about *your* chances on the days you happen to be in town. For you, as an individual, the chance of being mugged is, essentially, random. It could happen any time on any day. It would be 1 in 10 if you were in town today. It will be 1 in 10 if you go to town next week. If you were mugged today in this town, there is no guarantee that it would not happen again to you on next week's trip. (Of course, you could take various steps—known in the insurance business as "loss prevention"—to minimize your own risk. You could travel with three large bodyguards, for example.)

The point here is that, as an individual, you cannot predict a specific event by looking at the average for all events of its kind. An insurance company collects enough risks of a similar kind so that it *can* use the averages to predict its numbers of losses. This ability to predict its losses permits it to set premiums to cover all the losses and to cover its administrative costs and make a profit.

Essentially, then, insurance is a mechanism for moving money around among people or companies that are exposed to similar perils. You pay your premium (as do the others). If you are the "muggee" this day, the insurer takes your money and the money of some other covered individuals or businesses and covers your losses. If someone else is mugged, the company uses his premium payments and, perhaps, some of yours to cover his loss. Since you cannot predict when or whether the specific peril is going to strike you, or the extent to which you will lose, this kind of arrangement may not be a bad deal for you.

KEY INSURANCE NOTIONS:
RISK, INTEREST, AND INDEMNITY

If you assume that the people who run insurance companies are not irrational, much in the insurance business that seems odd and esoteric will begin to make a good deal of sense. We can start with the notion of what can be insured.

An insurance person looks at the world and sees two very different kinds of risk. First, there is the risk of loss about which the loser can do very little and in situations in which the loser cannot win. Despite the fact that you locked it and parked it under the lights, your car is stolen, for example. There is no way you can gain. Locking and lighting your car are merely efforts to maintain what you already have. This situation is defined as "pure risk" and it is what insurance is designed to deal with.

The second kind of risk is called "speculative risk." It includes situations in which the loser had a chance of winning and to which said loser specifically exposed himself. If you play the ponies, for example, one must assume that you do so in the hope of winning lots of money—although you might (probably will) lose money. Speculative risk is not insurable.

From the point of view of an insurer, the difference between pure risk and speculative risk makes sense. Pure risk operates on probabilities, regardless of what the insured may do. (Of course, it is assumed, and generally written into policies, that the insured will take all possible, reasonable precautions to avoid the occurrence of losses.) Speculative risk, on the other hand, depends on some actions of the insured—she bets on a horse race, for example, or invests in the stock market. Please note that speculative risk gives the individual risk of loss, but also the possibility of gain. This possibility of gain is another feature of speculative risk.

An insurer is in the business of playing the odds. No insurer in his right mind, however, would bet on the actions or choices of anything so illogical or unpredictable as a single human being. If the insurer were to guarantee your winnings at the track, for example, he would essentially be betting that you were a good handicapper and that you were operating rationally to choose the horse you expected to win, rather than, say, going for an outside long-shot just for the odds. For similar reasons, an insurer will not guarantee that some speculative endeavor will be financially successful. The success or failure of your business, for example, will depend on, among other things, your skill and judgment. These are things on which insurers will not place their bets.

Thus, while you can insure almost any pure risk (if you are willing to pay the premium), you cannot insure away the risk of any of your speculative endeavors—your basic business risk, for example. The cost to you of covering your insurable risks will vary with the type of risk and the predictability and frequency of the occurrence of loss. For example, it was said that the legs of a famous dancer were insured for a million dollars by Lloyd's of London. The premium was undoubtedly astronomical since leg injuries are fairly frequent and since there were probably relatively few pairs of legs being insured—few situations over which to spread a fairly high level of risk. Fire insurance, on the other hand, is likely to be relatively inexpensive (compared with the potential loss) because there are many insured objects and the risk is fairly predictable and not outrageously high in most places.

Insurable Interest

Another notion, which makes sense when insurers are viewed as basically of sound mind, is the notion of "insurable interest." It goes hand-in-hand with the idea that insurance is designed to compensate you for financial losses from covered perils, should they occur. The issue in the concept of insurable interest is whether you stand to suffer a financial loss.

Let's say that there is an old, ramshackle building just down the street from you. You know that it is only a matter of time before the place goes up in smoke—either by accident or by design. Unless you owned it, you would not be permitted to purchase insurance on it because you would stand to lose nothing if it did burn down. You have no insurable interest in it.

Furthermore, you have to maintain your insurable interest in order to collect on any policy except a life insurance policy. Had you owned that firetrap when you wanted to insure it, you could have purchased insurance for it (assuming it met codes and requirements). If you sold it before it burned down, however, you would not be able to collect on your policy even had you continued paying the premiums. Once you sold the building, you would no longer stand to suffer a financial loss if there was a fire. You would, therefore, not have had an insurable interest at the time of the loss.

The one exception to this rule is for life insurance policies. For these, too, you have to have some insurable interest when you purchase the insurance. You may not insure, for example, a gangster on whom you know there's a contract (unless, of course, you are related in some way or his imminent demise will in some demonstrable way injure you financially). Once a life insurance policy is in force, however, all you need to do is to continue to pay the premiums in order to collect in the event of the death of the insured.

Indemnity

Property and casualty insurance (the kind that you will use predominantly in your business) is generally "indemnity" insurance. Its purpose is to restore your loss, to "make you whole again," in the financial sense, in case of covered perils. It is specifically written to not permit you to profit from the occurrence of a covered peril. Essentially, your insurance policy attempts to prevent you from collecting more than your financial losses from a given incident.

This notion of indemnity, that the insurer will indemnify, but not exceed the covered loss, spawns three related insurance notions: pro-rata liability, coinsurance, and subrogation. Considered in terms of the intent and limitations of insurance, they do make some sense.

Pro-rata liability is what prevents you from taking out three identical $50,000 policies on the same piece of $50,000 property—and collecting on all three. If you actually did this, each insurer would pay only one-third of the loss up to the policy maximum. You would have been paying those two extra premiums for, essentially, no financial gain. That is the idea.

Coinsurance in anything but health insurance means the part of the coverage that you choose to be responsible for yourself. Property policies, such as your fire insurance policy, generally include a clause stating that you must insure "to x percent of value"—usually 80–90 percent. This means that the policy premiums are set as if the value of the property is covered to that extent. This will be considered "full" coverage under the policy. If you choose to insure to some lower proportion, it is understood that you are taking on a portion of the risk of loss yourself.

Assume, for example, that the policy on your $100,000 building requires that you insure to 90 percent of value, or $90,000. Assume further that, being strapped for cash, you decide to insure only $50,000. If your building is destroyed completely, your insurance policy will pay only 5/9 of your loss. You are on the hook for the rest.

Please note that this proportion will hold for any loss claimed against the policy. A more modest claim will result in the same 5/9 payment, maximum, from your insurer. You have chosen to bear the rest of the risk by choosing not to insure to the value stated in the policy. As you can see, for a small business, this is probably not a wise move.

Subrogation is another way in which insurers prevent you from collecting twice for a specific loss—activity which would violate the indemnity principle. Essentially, this provision in all policies states that, when your insurer pays you for a claim, you also grant your insurer the right to recover its loss from any third party who might have been the cause of the loss in the first place. If there are losses to you beyond the amount paid you by your insurer, you retain the right to take the third party to court for the remainder of your loss (and anything else you want to try).

Suppose, for example, a truck crashes through your storefront in the middle of the night. You make a claim against the relevant insurance policy. Your insurer pays off and you can repair the damage. Your insurer sues the driver and, presumably, his company to recover the amount they paid you. You are technically not concerned with the outcome of their suit—except that your policy will undoubtedly require that you assist the insurer in such suits in any way possible.

In short, as you can see, insurers are not in the business of being philanthropic or of offering you the opportunity to profit from a covered peril.

WHO SELLS INSURANCE?

The actual insurers are the companies whose names you know so well from television ads and ads in magazines and newspapers. While there are variants in specialties and lines of business, there are two basic types of insurance companies with which you might do business: stock companies and mutual companies. They differ in ownership and, usually, in some operational aspects.

Insurance companies in general are regulated by the states in which they do business. This makes them somewhat variable from state to state. The discussion of them here is thus necessarily general in nature. Its generality should not bother you, however, since this section is merely intended to show you the broad range of options and the really major differences.

Stock companies are those owned by the shareholders as is any regular corporation. Aetna, for example, is a stock company. They sell you insurance policies under which the corporation assumes responsibility for your potential losses. Your only rights are to continue to pay premiums and to collect if there is a loss covered under the terms of your policy.

Mutual companies, like Mutual of Omaha or John Hancock, on the other hand, are technically owned by the policyholders. As a policyholder, you get some say—albeit miniscule—in the operation of the company. Technically, mutual companies are not run for the profit of the people running the company. Surplus funds are supposed to be plowed back into the general pool to reduce the future premiums of the owners/policyholders.

While this sounds as if it should offer you a much better deal, it doesn't seem to offer reduced premiums in the real world. And it does provide the possibility of one additional pitfall. As an owner, you may be partially responsible if the mutual company misestimates its potential losses and, in fact, runs out of money before it runs out of losses that it has contracted to insure. This unknown level of risk, and its unplanned-for appearance is precisely what you were buying insurance to avoid in the first place.

The chance that you will be held financially responsible, or assessable, for such misestimates is avoidable in most cases, by the simple expedient of reading the policy to find out whether you would be assessable under its terms. If so, you should probably skip that particular policy, since you would be simply substituting a new risk for the ones you are trying to avoid. If you are not assessable for excess losses, the policy will insure you as well as any other policy with the same terms and limits. As with a stock company, excess losses will probably come out of the reserves of the company. The misestimate would be corrected for in the following year's premium rate.

The person from whom you actually buy insurance can be either an agent or a broker. Used properly, a good insurance person can be a significant addition to your advisory group. This person can help assure that you are adequately covered for those risks for which you need coverage. He can help ensure that you have such coverage without duplication at the lowest reasonable cost to you.

A good insurance person should be willing to do these things for the same reason that a banker is prepared to spend time on small loans to new businesses. Small businesses tend to grow into larger clients who may well be profitable clients in the future. And small business owners rarely forget those who helped them in the beginning.

As you can tell from television ads, the differences between agents and brokers are blurring—assuming that they were ever clear except on the law books. An agent is technically in the employ of an insurer (or she may be agent for a number of insurers without competing lines of business). Depending on the company, the agent may be able to commit the company to underwriting certain kinds and levels of insurance policies. This ability may get you your insurance policy slightly faster. A broker, technically, is an independent business person, licensed by the state and able to purchase insurance from any source. This person technically works for you and would theoretically not be able to commit companies to insurance policies.

In real life, it doesn't make much difference, these days, which way you go. What you want is a person who knows insurance and who is willing to assist you over the long term with your business insurance. The same rules should apply to your search for an insurance person that applied to your search for your other advisers. In general, however, you are likely to see your insurance adviser less frequently than any of the other people on the team.

AVOIDING INSURANCE ALTOGETHER

People tend to be superstitious about insurance. Odd though you may think it, some people do not buy life insurance because they feel that the terms of the bet will somehow bring on their demise. Lest you be one of these people who feels that the act of purchasing insurance somehow calls forth the covered disaster, a brief piece about the alternatives to purchasing insurance is in order. There are essentially three such potential alternatives. A short discussion of each should convince you that you really have no alternatives.

First, you can simply assume the risk yourself. As already noted, this approach exposes you to the probabilities with absolutely no way to spread the risk among numerous similar items. If you opt for this approach, non-insurance, it is hoped that you have done a good job of "loss prevention" (doing everything possible to see to it that disaster does not occur) and that you have the ear of Providence and do a lot of talking in that general direction.

A second option is to self-insure. Under this approach, you would put away a given amount of money every period against the day when disaster does strike. Your downside risk here is that something happens before you have stashed enough cash to deal with the problem. Given your probable size at your opening, and the fact that you are unlikely to have large amounts of excess cash, loss prevention and prayer would again be recommended.

This second option has an additional drawback. While you are putting money away to deal with potential losses, the Internal Revenue Service will insist on seeing this as part of your profit. Unlike the premiums you would pay to an insurer, you would retain access to your reserve funds. In general, the IRS sees money over which you retain control as money that is not deductible as a business expense.

The third and final option may have some merit on a limited scale for a new small business. It is to avoid buying insurance by transferring the risk directly to another party. The most common approach to this is the leasing arrangement. Motor vehicle leases may be written so that the owner, rather than the lessee, is responsible for insuring the vehicles. You may be able to work an arrangement like this on leased premises. Here, too, however, it will be expected that you take all possible care of the property so that the insured-against situations do not come to pass. Some thought on your part will undoubtedly produce other potential transfers relevant to your business.

As you can see, while the major alternatives to buying insurance may be reasonable for large companies with sizable risk pools of their own, they make little sense for new small businesses. The only real alternative you have is to hope that nothing happens that can put you permanently out of business. Given the odds on making a go of a small new company at any time, it would be beyond comprehension for you to decide to increase the odds against you for little reason. Your real question should not be whether to buy insurance, but rather how much and what kinds.

DETERMINING WHAT INSURANCE YOU NEED

The government of your state makes some of your insurance decisions for you. For example, it generally mandates that your employees be covered by workers' compensation insurance, that your vehicles be covered in specific ways, and that your business contribute to the state's unemployment insurance funds. These types of coverages, therefore, are not part of your decision-making process.

Deciding on the kinds of coverages to purchase should never be solely a question of how much money you expect to have lying around loose. (We already know the answer to that question will always be "none.") Obviously, however, the amount of money that you can spring loose is a factor in limiting the kinds of coverages you will be able to buy. The focus of the decision should be the requirements of the business itself and your ability to maintain it in the face of various insurable risks.

There are essentially three issues to consider in determining whether or not to buy insurance:

- The probability of loss,
- The magnitude of loss, and
- The magnitude of the premium.

Each notion is discussed briefly below. The brevity is a reflection of the fact that nobody can make these decisions for you. The best anyone—including your insurance agent—can do is to advise you about the things that you should consider in reaching your conclusions.

Probability of Loss

While it is theoretically possible that Denver will be flooded in the spring melt-off this year, it is highly unlikely—and, if it happens, it is to be hoped that folks in Omaha and elsewhere have something akin to very large arks. Flood insurance, therefore, should probably not be very high on the list of coverages needed by a Denver small business owner. On the other hand, because the Mississippi floods with amazing regularity, flood insurance in the lower Mississippi valley should be a serious consideration. (It is generally available through the federal government, rather than being underwritten by regular insurance companies.)

The point here is that a prime consideration in your insurance decisions is how probable it is that some specific peril will strike your business. It is fairly likely, for example, that you will be exposed to theft, burglary, robbery, fire, and various other common perils. It is less likely that your business will be destroyed by tornado, earthquake, or flood—except in certain parts of the country. These area-specific issues should be the main concentration for your analysis of probability of loss.

Magnitude of Loss

Your second major question has to do with how much it matters whether a specific peril occurs to your business. Will the sheer size or magnitude of a loss in a given area impair your ability to operate in some significant way?

Mark R. Greene, in his Small Business Administration booklet, *Insurance and Risk Management for Small Business,* tells the story of a company that found it was insuring an old building that was slated for demolition in the near future. Had it burned, it would have actually saved the company some cost. (They cancelled the insurance.)

While you are unlikely to have such a clean situation, similar considerations should apply. If you own three old pickups, for example, and are really only using two, you might consider whether carrying collision for them makes sense. If they are really old and if one is damaged, you might simply want to retire it in favor of the third one you have in a sort of reserve.

Obviously, "magnitude" is a relative term, depending on your business and your resources. You basically need to set a figure on the amount of financial loss that your business is likely to be able to absorb and then insure potential losses (with high probabilities) above that figure. This analysis clearly rests on the resources of your business and on your ability and willingness to cover losses to the business with your own resources. Assuming there are more potentially serious losses than you have the money to insure against, you should rank order perils by impact on the business and by probability and then work your way down the list until you run out of possible insurance money.

It is here that **magnitude of premium**—how much it will cost you to insure a given situation—becomes a consideration. How much will you gain,

FEATURE 8.1
Insurance Against Computer Fraud

Not surprisingly, as the computer takes over more and more businesses, computer crime has become a key issue. Insurance companies are struggling with issues of how to create adequate coverage without going broke. Thus, there are numerous forms of coverage now, most covering the really large companies that rely on their data bases or data transmission capabilities.

But the problems with which the industry is wrestling in the field of computer fraud are, essentially, the same three issues facing the average insurance user:

1. **What is the probability of loss?** While everyone will agree that computer crime is growing, many companies do not report incidents for fear of encouraging more attempts and for fear of alarming their clients. It is thus difficult to determine the average incidence of computer fraud.

2. **What is the magnitude of loss?** There are two issues here. Because companies often do not report, it is as difficult to estimate losses as it is to develop averages. Moreover, there is an issue about the nature of a loss. What is it that an insurer should insure? The cost of reproducing lost data? The actual amount of financial loss? The confidentiality of data or the confidence of clients? Depending on what is insured, the magnitude of loss will be easier or more difficult to determine.

3. **What should be the magnitude of the premium?** Right now, premiums vary a great deal throughout the industry—as could be expected, given varying definitions of probability and magnitude. Neither insurers nor insureds can yet measure or quantify potential losses or probabilities.

In a real sense, in computer-fraud insurance, we can watch insurance in development.

financially, by paying the required premium for a given insurance? (The issue of how high a deductible you should choose is also a part of this analysis.) If one of those three old trucks, for example, is worth $400, does it make any sense to pay $150 to insure it against collision for a year? Particularly if there is a $100 deductible on the policy? In agreeing to a deal like this, you would essentially be paying $150 a year for a maximum potential return—if the truck is totalled—of $300.

SOME STANDARD KINDS OF COVERAGE

If your business is like most, you will want to purchase such coverages as fire insurance, crime insurance, and liability insurance. These are such common types of coverage that they are often sold in groups, as umbrella-type policies or multi-peril programs. These multi-peril policies differ from one another in their specifics by company and, often, by location. Your best approach is to actually *read* the policy (before you buy), find an agent you trust, and ask a lot of questions. (Note: In some areas, fire and crime policies are difficult to come by because the probability of occurrence is too high to make the policies profitable for insurers at anything like a reasonable premium. For such circumstances, the federal government, recognizing the necessity of such insurance, set up pooling programs, known as FAIR plans, and a federal crime insurance program. If you are in such an area, check the requirements and provisions of these programs. Your agent can help.)

Property Insurance

Insuring your physical property has one additional pitfall. It lies in the way insurers generally interpret "value" for such policies as fire policies. In general, "value" is not considered as the cost to you of replacing the asset. It is seen as the cost to you of replacing the asset *given its age and prior use*. Thus, if you have a building that is supposed to last for 40 years and it burns to the ground after 10 years, your insurer will view its "value" as three-fourths of the replacement cost. Assuming that the replacement cost of the building is $100,000, and the building burns to the ground, the most you could get from a standard policy—assuming you have carried enough insurance to avoid becoming a coinsurer—would be $75,000.

The inability to actually rebuild or replace your assets with the insurance money can be avoided through the purchase of replacement cost insurance. To ensure that you are not a coinsurer under the new circumstances, you will have to carry "x percent to value" of the maximum you would now be able to collect—the full $100,000. This discussion should also make clear the need for frequent and careful appraisal of insured assets.

Liability Insurance

A good liability policy is invaluable to a small business. (Vehicle liability and workers' compensation, as noted earlier, are requirements, not options. They are discussed separately.) People, these days, are seriously into suing others, and any protection beats total exposure. Consider the following scenarios—which actually happened to small companies.

- A diner in a restaurant bit into a hamburger, hitting a small, imbedded stone and breaking a tooth. The diner sued. The issue became how the stone got there and whether the stone could possibly have gotten through the restaurant's grinder. The restaurant sued the supplier and everything got rather messy. The restaurant was initially responsible for getting its patron's tooth fixed.

FEATURE 8.2

Hazards on Your Business Premises

It is well known that you are required to keep your business premises in reasonably safe condition. You are also required to inspect your premises and equipment periodically to ensure that they are still reasonably safe for those using your premises. These terms are, as you can see, rather vague, and recently courts and juries are interpreting them very loosely. That is, if a case can be made for owner neglect or negligence, an award is generally made.

"The duty to inspect played a part in a recent Washington, D.C., case in which a 51-year-old woman fell through the seat of a wrought iron chair in a department store restaurant. The fall worsened her degenerative disc disease. ... During the trial, her lawyer established that the chair had never been inspected in 20 years of use. The jury returned a verdict for $175,000."

Your responsibility extends beyond those who are actually doing business on your premises. You may even be held responsible for accidents and hazards to trespassers—if you can be assumed to have known that trespassing was going on. Children, particularly, are protected in this way. The courts are removing distinctions, as well, in this area. "A man's life or limb," said the California Supreme Court, "does not become less worthy of protection by the law ... because he has come upon the land of another without permission or with permission but without a business purpose."

Insurance is a necessity for protection in this growing field of litigation. Policies of $1,000,000 on premises liability can be purchased for as little as $500 a year. But care and inspection are absolutely critical.

Adapted from Fred S. Steingold, "Do Your Business Premises Present a Public Hazard?," *Inc.* magazine (November 1983):189–90.

- A hardware store was washing its floors. To alert its patrons to the potentially slippery floor, it placed a large floor sign in the doorway. A patron slipped and broke his leg. Despite the sign, the store was held responsible for the injury.

And these are just normal, everyday, low-risk businesses. Consider the potential exposure of a ski school or ski lodge, a health spa, or any other business dealing with exercise/fitness/use of the body.

Clearly, a liability policy is a wise move. Obviously, the cost of such a policy will depend upon the type of business you are running and its general likelihood of attracting suits. Do look at them, but remember, the higher the premium, the more the odds say you are likely to need the coverage.

Other Kinds of Insurance

As noted earlier, you can insure just about any pure risk—even the payoff from your insurer. A list of some types, with notes if appropriate, follows. Its purpose is to give you clues as to the types of things you might want to consider for your specific type of business before you sit down with your insurance agent.

- Product liability insurance.
- Bonds:
    Fidelity Bonds—against thefts by employees.
    Surety Bonds—guarantee that certain pieces of work will be done.
- Business interruption insurance—covers certain costs while you are rebuilding after a loss; can also cover shutdowns at key suppliers' or customers' operations that will effectively shut down your operation.
- Key person insurance—to cover certain expenses while you are finding and training a replacement.

You can now also purchase such coverages as pollution insurance, glass insurance, insurance against lawsuits alleging sexual harassment, and practically anything else. Consider what makes sense for you and your business by assessing each in terms of the three measures discussed earlier: probability of loss, magnitude of loss, and magnitude of premium.

Required Coverages

These are straightforward. You simply comply with the law in your state. A few notes, however, might save you from inadvertent non-compliance (which is no defense if you are caught), inadvertent gaps in optional coverages, and/ or excess cost in compliance with the laws.

The requirement to insure your vehicles has been discussed, as has the notion of transferring certain insurable risks by leasing said vehicles. It needs to be pointed out, however, that your business may be liable, even if it owns no vehicles, for actions of your employees while driving rental or leased cars or trucks. You may also be liable for acts of your employees when they drive their own cars on company business. These are risks you may want to insure that do not come under the required vehicle insurance provisions, even though they sound as if they should.

Workers' compensation is required of employers of more than a given number of employees. This minimum number varies from state to state. Most systems work on a job category risk system. Under these programs, a butcher will cost more to insure for on-the-job injury than, say, a check-out clerk or a secretary. This is for the obvious reason that the job is more dangerous and more prone to injury. When you purchase your workers' comp plan, then, take care that your positions are properly categorized and

FEATURE 8.3
Business-Disruption Coverage

Business interruption insurance is trickier than most to understand and, therefore, to buy. While you can buy such insurance to cover your own business or damage to your own business through perils which occur to your major supplier or major customer, the terms are often not what they seem. In this area, in particular, you will need to read and understand your policy.

Business interruption insurance usually covers your fixed expenses *until the damage is repaired.* But it may take you longer than this to get back in the market and resume normal operations.

Another issue that often arises is how deductibles are stated and paid. "An oil refiner thought the five-day deductible in its business interruption policy meant that it absorbed the loss in business for the first five days. When fire wiped out 20 percent of its production, the company filed a claim after the fifth day.

"The refiner's daily gross income was $200,000; it was losing $40,000 a day due to the damage. However, it learned that the five-day deductible meant five days' gross—in its case, a $1 million deductible. That was far more than the company ever expected to absorb itself."

The key here, as in insurance dealings in general, is to understand what your coverage really is. Ask questions before you sign. And it helps a great deal to know what you need to ask questions about.

Adapted from Sanford L. Jacobs, "Business-Disruption Coverage is Inadequate at Many Firms," *The Wall Street Journal* (October 3, 1983):33.

counted. In this way, you will not be paying high rates for essentially low-risk jobs. You should also evaluate the categories and the positions within them periodically to ensure that they have not changed in level or nature of the risk since your last analysis.

Your contributions to unemployment funds also begin with a minimum number of employees. The number differs among states. The cost is generally based on payroll dollars and, sometimes, partly on performance in employee retention.

One potential way around both of these coverages is a risk-transfer approach. Rather than actually hiring employees, you subcontract work, or particularly risky parts of the work, to other companies or to outside, independent parties. If you choose this route, however, you should be aware that governments frown on the use of this ploy solely as a means of avoiding your responsibilities as an employer. If your "subcontractors" really work for you for 40 hours a week, 52 weeks a year, have work space in your office, and meet other tests, they may well be considered employees no matter what you call them.

If they really are subcontractors, and if you pay any of them more than a specified amount (check current federal regulations), you must report their earnings to each relevant individual and to the federal government. This is done on one of the numerous variants of the 1099 form.

OTHER USES OF INSURANCE

Until this point, we have been discussing only one use of insurance—its value in providing protection for you and/or your business against specific perils in the world outside your business. But there are at least two other ways in which insurance can be used in your business to enhance its safety and viability as a business. The first has to do with ensuring the continuation of a specific ownership group. The second involves the attraction and maintenance of an adequate employee group.

Ownership

As you recall, when we discussed possible legal structures for small businesses, a major problem was continuity. It was pointed out that a major factor in favor of forming a corporation is the ease of transferability inherent in a structure based on shares of stock. A major drawback of a partnership form was the potential for difficulty following the demise of a partner and the distribution or passing of her interests through the estate.

The scenario is clear, common, and frightening for any owner of a two- or three-person company. Old Jack, a prince among men, dies and leaves his share of the partnership or his 33.3 percent of the shares of the company to his no-good son, Ebenezer. You are suddenly in business with a man neither of the other participants can stomach. But since neither of the remaining participants has a great deal of excess money (and, besides, Ebenezer is likely to want a price that is outrageously high), you can't get rid of him. After he wreaks havoc for a while among you and alienates all your customers and suppliers, the business folds—all because good old Jack had a terrible son.

The above scenario works for any small company. But as we noted in Chapter 6, there is an additional danger in a partnership. If old Jack was inconsiderate enough to have a number of heirs and not enough assets to go round, the partnership itself might have to be sold off to satisfy the requirements of his estate.

Not surprisingly in a chapter on insurance, there is a way around all this that rests on simple insurance mechanisms and a little foresight on your part as well as on old Jack's. You essentially insure each others' lives for enough to purchase the deceased partner's equity in the business. This obviously requires not only the insurance policies and some method for ensuring that the premiums be paid properly, but it also requires that there be some agreed-upon method for valuing the business—and, hence, old Jack's share thereof—for purposes of such a sale. All of this should be handled by lawyers and agreed to in writing by all parties to the agreement. You don't want any trouble with Ebenezer for any reason.

Employment

As you have no doubt figured out by now, unless you have enough family members to staff your business, it will probably be difficult to attract and retain the employees you need to run the place. As a small business, you are inherently less attractive to most people because you lack prestige, because you lack the funds to pay large salaries, and because the opportunities for advancement are likely to be very limited for at least a few years. (We discuss this issue in greater depth in Chapter 10.)

One way in which you can sweeten the pot a little for your prospective employees is through the benefit package you offer. Large firms in a number of industries, notably the high-tech industries, often compete for employees on this basis. For a company that is unlikely to be paying top dollar, the benefit package is even more important. Many employee benefits are insurance-based.

Depending on normal practice in your industry, you might consider providing group health insurance benefits, group disability, and group life insurance policies for your employees. In general, these programs are volume-based. Thus, once again, you get the short end in terms of higher premium costs simply because you are small.

It is not always necessary to pay 100 percent of the cost of these benfits, however. Many employers, for example, pay only a proportion, or sometimes a dollar amount, toward a given health benefit policy. It generally pays to compare rates, but be very clear on the actual coverages being gained for the premiums being paid.

Finally, there may be a way around high premium rates for such employee benefit-type coverages. Many associations of small business and Chambers of Commerce offer their combined bargaining power and large numbers to their members through joint contracts. While it will cost you the amount of the dues over and above any insurance costs, the tradeoff in rates might be well worth the expense. In addition, membership in such organizations is often good for business, whether or not you use their insurance buying power. Such memberships are generally tax-deductible. Check your local Yellow Pages and/or ask your banker about such groups in your area.

SUMMARY

The rules regarding insurance generally make sense, when viewed in the context of what insurance is intended to accomplish. It is not intended to insure against risks you choose to take on and in which you have a hope of gain. It deals only in "pure" risk. It is not intended to permit you to profit from your disaster, but rather to make you as you were, insofar as a financial mechanism can do so. In other words, it indemnifies you. It is also not intended to allow you to bet on events that have no financial effect on you or your business—hence the concept of "insurable interest."

From these very basic notions stem many of the limitations and prohibitions in insurance policies. Considered from the perspective of a serious purchaser, they make sense, since the basis of the insurance mechanism is to move money around from those who have not suffered a loss to those who have. The game-players simply raise the cost to everyone in the system. The insurers take their cut in all cases.

Despite stories you may have heard about those who have never bought insurance and who have never had a loss, insurance should be considered a necessity for a new small business. If you are purchasing assets with borrowed funds, insurance on them is undoubtedly a requirement of your financing. Should you take less care of assets purchased with your own funds?

In the plethora of possible kinds of insurance to buy, your state will dictate the terms of at least three required coverages. Assuming you own vehicles, you will have to insure them. If you have more than a minimum number of employees, you will have to carry workers' compensation and unemployment insurance costs.

Beyond these required coverages, you should probably carry, at minimum, fire and crime insurance and an appropriate level of liability insurance. Factors to consider when making choices about what coverages to purchase and how much of each to buy should include: the probability of the risk you are considering insuring against, the importance of the loss to the business if you do not buy the insurance and the relevant disaster occurs, and the cost of the insurance relative to the size of the potential collection on a claim.

FOR YOU TO CONSIDER

1. What is insurance?
2. What is the difference between pure risk and speculative risk? Why does it matter to insurers?
3. Why can insurers take on these risks while you cannot?
4. What is "insurable interest" and why is it important to the discussion of insurance?

5. What does "indemnity" mean?
6. Describe three "alternatives" to buying insurance. For your small business, is any of these really an alternative?
7. What are the three main factors to consider when approaching a decision to purchase a specific insurance?
8. What coverage will you be required to purchase? Is there any way to avoid buying such coverage?
9. Describe two uses of insurance that do not specifically involve the restoration of a loss due to an outside peril. Given your proposed business, does either of these make sense for you to consider further?

FOR FURTHER READING

Bank of America, "Crime Prevention for Small Business." *Small Business Reporter,* 1982.

Small Business Administration publications:

Insurance Checklist for Small Business. SBA MA 2.018.
Insurance and Risk Management for Small Business. SBA 045-000-00209-8.
Preventing Burglary and Robbery Losses. SBA MA 3.007.
Preventing Retail Theft. SBA MA 3.004.
Risk Management and Insurance. SBA 045-000-00184-9.

CASES FOR PART 3

SALLY JONES AND "NEIGHBORS"

In her initial research, Sally Jones had come across the news that starting even a small restaurant could cost between $100,000 and $250,000. This scared her to death. Their *house* had only cost $70,000 in 1977! And, of course, they still had a sizable mortgage on it. The very notion of asking Don or her father or her uncle for that kind of money was crazy. She knew that any, or all, of them would roar with laughter—and properly so. But she had fallen in love with the idea of her restaurant. There *had* to be a way to get it done. After all, if 800 other people in the area had managed, she certainly could.

The more she considered the matter, the less reasonable it seemed to try to build Sally's alone. She simply would not be able to raise enough money. She began thinking about partners. There was, of course, the family, but she had already concluded that there was not enough money there to do the whole job. She next began to consider her close friends. Two of the three hated to cook—which was probably a lucky break for their families, since they were not very good at it anyway. That left Janice Barker, probably her closest friend.

Sally and Janice had been friends for five years. Although proximity had originally brought them together (the Barkers lived just down the street), a real compatibility between the two had developed over the years. And Janice Barker was in much the same position as Sally. Each had two young children, now in school. Each was married to a corporate mover who expended great deals of energy and time at his respective office. Their children played together much of the time. Sally's husband, Don, and Janice's husband, Jim, had also become friends, golfing or playing tennis together when their schedules worked out. The two families often socialized as two couples or en masse.

Best of all, Janice could cook. Her specialty was baking. She could do more for a cake or pie than even Sally's mother could. This skill could complement Sally's magic with main dishes and soups. Sally just knew she could work with Janice over the long term.

As she reached for the telephone, however, she paused, considering that with a partner, her name alone could not be over the door. The pause was brief. She didn't seem to have much choice, and she was committed enough now to the concept to be prepared to make some sacrifices to get the thing going. She called Janice.

"Hi, Janice. I've got a really great idea and I think you'd be the perfect person to do it with me!"

"Oh, hi, Sal. That's quite an opener. Why do I have the feeling that you are about to totally disrupt my life?"

"Because I am. But you'll love it. Guaranteed. D'you know how for the last few months we've both been complaining that we have nothing useful to do now that the kids are in school? Well, I've come up with our answer. We're going to start our own restaurant—give your peach cobbler to the world, not just our kids. What d'you say? Is it worth talking about some more?"

Clearly, Janice was prepared to talk about it some more. In fact, the two friends spent most of the next afternoon in discussions. They eventually renamed the place "Neighbors" and agreed that their respective skills just about perfectly complemented each other.

They also decided that their next big move would have to be to convince their husbands that they were not completely crazy. Knowing Don and Jim, they were sure the real issue would be money. They therefore decided to use the number $150,000 for opening costs. While they knew this was not really even a ballpark figure, it wouldn't be worth their energy to develop a better one unless they could convince the men not to oppose their plan. They would develop a better ballpark number and a real estimate later in their planning process.

Sally also knew that banks generally shied away from financing large proportions of new restaurant operations. This was because of the high failure rate and because there were few hard assets from which to get their money back should failure occur. She figured that they would have to come up with a way to raise at least half of their startup funds themselves before a bank would even listen to them.

They decided to get Don and Jim together over dinner at Sally's on Saturday. They planned a phenomenal dinner, figuring that their ability with food was, after all, what they were selling. Janice, of course, would bring dessert.

Dinner was marvelous, as usual, and over coffee and cake, when the kids had disappeared, the four neighbors got down to business. Sally and Janice outlined the concept and the reasons behind "Neighbors." Don and Jim were, at first, totally disbelieving. As they listened, however, it began to dawn on them that their wives really thought they wanted to open a restaurant!

"You are telling us that you want to raise about $75,000 within our families so that you can borrow *another* $75,000 from a bank to open a restaurant on the basis of these estimates and the fact that you're great cooks?!" Don was astounded.

"Of course not," said Sally. "We know that we've still got a lot of work to do. But we're talking orders of magnitude here. Is this possible? Then we'll see if it's really feasible within our financing limitations. We want to know that you two will be with us in this—or, at least, behind us. We promise we won't ask you to do any of the work."

"And think of the longer-term gains," added Janice. "We can build a real nest egg for the kids' college, maybe even have those vacations we always talk about—and rarely get to go on. The fact that 'Neighbors' will be a partnership will give each of us lots of flexibility."

"But isn't a partnership risky?" asked Jim. "Couldn't we lose the house and everything if you two go bust? And, if you take money from other relatives as well, won't they stand to lose everything, too? On the other hand, if you *borrow* money from us and from other relatives, won't the bank think of that as debt so that you still won't be able to get a bank loan?"

After a great deal more skepticism, Sally and Janice finally got agreement to the notion that they should continue to work on the idea. Don and Jim agreed to listen to them further when they had somewhat better opening cost data and when they had figured out how to solve the liability problems.

1. Discuss the tradeoffs inherent in Sally's choice of a partner. How would her venture be different had she chosen a family member or a non-cooking friend? Which approach do you recommend for her?
2. Are there any alternatives to the partnership structure that Sally and Janice have chosen? What are they? How would each solve the problems raised by Jim at dinner? Which legal structure do you recommend for "Neighbors" and why?

•   •   •

Sally and Janice knew that their next task had to be to get a better handle on what it would cost them to open "Neighbors." That, they figured, would go a long way toward convincing Don and Jim that they were serious about this. They were not yet ready to try for a final estimate, of course, but they wanted to develop a reasonable ballpark figure that came from something other than what someone else said it might cost to open a restaurant.

They also wanted to do some heavy thinking about the alternative ways of reducing their own required investment in the business. It was clear to

Table 1   Figuring your restaurant startup costs

Rule of thumb:	Budget cost of land and building (with equipment, etc., ready to open) at no more than $4,500/seat **or** combined cost of facilities should not exceed a conservative estimate of one year's sales. (Note: This involves *building* the building.)

Budgeting for the interior—1980 costs: (160-seat restaurant)

Kitchen equipment (new)	$80,000
Tables and chairs	50 per seat
Silverware, napkins, dishes, menus, etc.	6,000–10,000
Preopening promotion	19,000

About 20 square feet per seat is normal, exclusive of kitchen space.

Source: Dewey A. Dyer, *So You Want to Start a Restaurant* (Boston: CBI, 1981).

them that the sheer size of the numbers had made their husbands nervous. But, first, of course, they had to come up with a believable number in a reasonable way.

They set to work and found the information in Tables 1, 2, and 3.

1. Using the information in the tables, develop a ballpark opening cost figure for "Neighbors" as a 100-seat restaurant.
2. At what points and by what means might Sally and Janice be able to reduce their up-front outlays to start "Neighbors"—without doing violence to their concept or quality level? Do you recommend any of these approaches to them? Which ones? Why? For those you did not recommend, why do you think they are bad ideas for "Neighbors"?

Table 2   Initial investment requirements restaurant—1981

Specifications:	Annual gross sales	$300,000–$500,000
	Floor space	3,000 square feet
	Seats	100 (table service)

OPENING COSTS:	**Range**
Leasehold improvements	$135,000–$225,000
Fixtures and equipment	
Dining area	9,700– 21,700
Kitchen (500 sq. ft.)	40,000– 70,000
Lease deposit (first and last months)	2,000– 4,200
First two weeks' food inventory	2,000– 5,000
Subtotal	$188,700–$325,900

OPERATING COSTS (first three months):	
Owner's salary	$ 3,000–$4,500
Payroll (6–8 employees, 35 hours @)	7,800– 10,400
Food supplies	12,000– 30,000
Insurance, taxes, licenses (excluding liquor)	650– 850
Professional services	250– 700
Rent (two months not in opening cost)	2,000– 4,200
Cash reserve	2,000– 4,000
Subtotal	$ 27,700– $54,650
TOTAL	$216,400–$380,550

Source: Bank of America, "Restaurants," *Small Business Reporter* (1981): 11.

Table 3   Selected ratios in the restaurant industry

From Dun & Bradstreet (1983–84) for 1983:

Sales to inventory (times)	61.2×
Assets to sales (%)	32.4%
Gross profit or gross margin	46.5%
Inventory as % of total assets	7.5%
Profit after taxes	4.4%

From Dun & Bradstreet *Key Business Ratios,* 1980:

	< $50,000	$50,000–$2,000,000
Eating places with assets of:		
Sales to inventory (times)	32.9×	26.3×
Profit on sales	.9%	1.5%

From Robert Morris Associates *Annual Statement Studies* (1983) for 1982:

Retailers/restaurants < $1 million assets

Cost of sales (CGS)/inventory	27.0
Gross margin (%)	55.6
Inventory/total assets (%)	7.3
Sales/total assets	3.4
Lease % rental expenses/sales	5.0
Officer's compensation/sales	5.4
Profit before taxes (%)	2.6

Source: Dun & Bradstreet, *Key Business Ratios,* Business Economics Division (New York: 1983–84); and Robert Morris Associates, *Annual Statement Studies* (Philadelphia: 1983).

• • •

Sally and Janice also knew that they would have to provide insurance for their investment—and that insurance could be one of the potential ways of reducing their own liability in case of trouble. They knew that they would have to cover their employees for workers' compensation. Even if the state did not require it, they knew that their lessor and/or their banker would require them to carry good property loss coverage. This would include insurance against fire, smoke, water, vandalism, and similar perils. They were pretty sure that they should add burglary and theft insurance to this package, but were uncertain about what other coverages to price and consider seriously.

They knew they were not yet ready to consider the employee benefits insurances.

1. Consider and make a recommendation to Sally and Janice about carrying liability insurance. Explain the reasons behind your recommendation.
2. Consider and make a recommendation to them about business interruption insurance. Support your recommendation.

3. Given their (probably very) limited initial budgets, would you recommend any other kinds of insurance to the two friends? Which and why?

ROB KING AND "KING FINANCIAL"

Rob King intended to structure King Financial for minimum cost to start. Thus, he determined that his first "office" would be his converted study at the house. He knew this might appear unprofessional, but he frankly doubted that he would be entertaining clients in his office very often, particularly in the beginning. General practice was for the consultant to go to the client or to meet the client outside both offices for lunch or cocktails or such. Thus, particularly since his address was not particularly bucolic-sounding, Rob figured he could at least begin operating from his home.

As long as he took this and any other cost-cutting methods, he figured that he could finance his startup out of the family savings. The kids would not be headed for college in the near future. By the time they were, Rob hoped that King Financial would be thriving and he would not have to worry too much about the magnitude of college bills. He knew that Ginny felt somewhat differently about borrowing from the kids' future.

He also had a decision to make about the legal form he wanted for his company. People often told him that the corporation was the only way to go. This route, however, would increase his startup costs—and, to some extent, his operating costs. Some people even said, though he'd never seen it, that banks preferred dealing with a corporate entity. Rob could not really see why it would make a difference to a bank. Particularly since he did not expect to make massive amounts of money in his first years of operation, he was unsure about what he might gain from structuring King Financial as a corporation. A partnership was out of the question. King Financial would be his and his alone.

1. Comment on Rob King's location plans.
2. Do you see any alternatives to "borrowing from the kids' future"? What are they and which, if any, would you recommend to Rob? Why?
3. What legal structure should Rob King adopt for King Financial? Why did you recommend that legal structure?

DANIELLE MACKIE AND "DANIELLE DESIGNS IN CERAMICS"

Danielle Mackie was really getting caught up in the potential of her fledgling ceramics business. Her trip to the New England trade fair she had chosen was a rousing success. Buyers wanted to place orders for multiple copies of three of the pieces she had developed for "bulk" sale. Happily, she had chosen an early show and the buyers wanted her goods for Christmas sale. That gave her some time to get her operation together and to do the actual production work.

Even more important to Danni was the fact that a number of her "creative" pieces had sold to precisely the people she had hoped would be interested—middle-aged, wealthier women who sought a touch of distinction, something unique to set their homes (and their taste) apart from others otherwise just like them. In this process, Danni's personality and genuine love of talking about her work and her materials appeared to be as much of a selling point as the piece itself. It had not hurt, she congratulated herself, that she had thought to create a brief note about each piece (signed by Mackie, of course) as part of the "package" for each of her better pieces.

Another useful return from her trip was a series of invitations to talk further with owners of small galleries in the New England/New York area. She knew that this represented not only respect for her work, but also a recognition that it would probably sell. She would have to prepare carefully for these meetings.

Suddenly, she was running out of time. She had worked herself into a position in which she had two choices. Either she could commit to the ceramics business or she could give it all up and go back to cataloguing slides at the museum as her full-time, sole profession. Not surprisingly, she was not enamored of the idea of giving up the heady feelings of success and satisfaction she had experienced at the show. This meant, in effect, that she had a matter of months to structure a business that would keep her fed and clothed and that would work for her over time. During the same period, she would have to develop new pieces, a portfolio, and the production approach for her "bulk" pieces. She would also have to have her talks with gallery owners so that their businesses might serve as her outlets for the tourist and Christmas seasons. The total job seemed quite overwhelming. This was definitely not, she thought, the nice, peaceful pace of museum life! Amazingly, her education would be quite a help in this process. At least she started out knowing what had to be done.

And the first thing on her list was to consider the legal requirements for her company. She asked her father for the name of a local lawyer. When Danni called to discuss the business, however, Ms. Kiner pointed out that her group specialized in criminal law. This was definitely not what Danni needed. Kiner then described the kind of lawyer needed and provided a referral to a specialist in small businesses. This Mr. Harald had done work with a number of crafts cooperatives and independent craftspeople and would know and understand the special problems facing artists and craftspeople as they developed businesses around their skills and talents. Kiner believed that Harald would be helpful to Danni well beyond the simple mechanics of setting up a business and getting the proper licenses and permits.

Danielle Mackie was immediately struck by the notion of a cooperative, but believed that she had too little time just then to look into it. She expected, however, to maintain a relationship with Harald. Thus, when she was ready to consider the matter, she would have access to information. Her immediate priority was to get her show on the road. Harald seemed to be just the lawyer to help her through the legal hoops.

Her next most immediate problem was money. While her kiln and her tools were more than adequate for the hobby level of work she had been turning out over the years, she knew that the capacity, particularly of her kiln, would not meet her current or her expected needs. Kilns were extremely expensive, with second-hand ones selling for more than $1,000. She would need financing, and she was not ready to talk with her ever-practical parents about either a gift or a loan. She did, however, have the orders from the buyers she had spoken with at the show. "That should help at the bank," she thought.

1. What possible problems do you see on the horizon for Danielle Mackie at this stage of her planning? What do you believe she should do to minimize their effects or avoid them entirely?
2. What advice do you expect Harald to give her regarding the legal structure she should adopt for her business? Why? What kinds of permits should she probably consider investigating? What steps might she have to take to prepare her business to comply with the various tax authorities?
3. Assuming that Mackie's only assets are her car (a 1980 Volvo), her old kiln, and a small interest in a family farm in Connecticut, what would you need as a banker to finance her operation? Would you do it under any circumstances? Explain your answer.
4. Inherent in the nature of Danielle Mackie's operation are certain processes that might be dangerous to health and property (the kiln, the chemicals in glazes, etc.). What implications does this fact have for her business planning? How should she handle the issue(s)?

ED JAMES AND "OAK TREE BOOKS"

The more Ed James considered his bookstore, the more he realized he was looking at a major undertaking. He was also beginning to see its inherent risks. While the risks didn't bother him particularly, prudence required that he begin to consider ways to reduce the risk—personal as well as financial.

He knew he wanted to operate the bookstore by himself as much as possible. He would want some additional funds available in case the store required more than he expected. You don't become rich teaching English—particularly in private schools. Even if you add coaching the debate team after classes. He expected that his requirements would be fairly short-term, however, since his Aunt Hattie had told him he would inherit everything she had one day.

While he loved his Aunt Hattie deeply, he recognized her demise as inevitable. He had not examined her income tax returns, or anything equally tacky, but she appeared to live well, in a large house in suburban Silver Spring, with clothes bought from the better stores in the area. In the years when she was feeling spry, she traveled extensively. Her more recent trips had included tours of Egypt and the Middle East and of China and the Far East.

Ed James also counted among his friends a number of parents of former students who, he hoped, would assist him in his new career. Some of his earlier students had, themselves, gained some wealth and status by now. There was some value to being well-liked by one's students, he grinned to himself.

He knew that before he really got his plan rolling he would have to decide on a legal structure for his business. He had discussed some options with a lawyer friend. He was leaning toward sole proprietorship, but he didn't like the sense of exposure inherent in that form. He figured he would have little trouble finding a partner who would not hassle him about the operations of the business. But he feared the consequences of an incorrect choice.

He also knew he might need additional financial backing in the future— for the short term. On his own, he was not a particularly credible candidate for a bank loan. He hoped, however, that he could sell a banker on his special suitability to run a bookstore. But a wealthy backer certainly would not hurt. He did not want to ask Aunt Hattie because he knew how negatively she felt about the notion of his departure from the Academy.

1. What dangers do you see in Ed's approach to his bookstore that Ed himself does not seem to see?
2. What options does Ed have regarding his legal structure? What are the advantages and disadvantages of each structure for him?
3. What legal structure do you recommend that Ed adopt? Why do you believe that this form meets his needs better than the others?

· · ·

As Ed James began to think more and more about money—how much he'd need and where he could get it—he began to get more and more worried about whether his savings would be even in the ballpark. On a whim, he had asked a contractor about the cost of panelling and shelving an average-sized store with dark wood. His shock at the answer (well into the five-digit range) was so great that he knew he should not have even asked. To calm himself down (and to cheer himself up a bit, he hoped), he decided to take a serious first cut at what a more reasonable bookselling establishment was likely to cost to open.

He recognized that this first cut would provide him with only an order-of-magnitude estimate for the "average" bookstore. And he knew that his bookstore couldn't be just "average." He wanted to try to adjust his very rough cut cost estimates by some factors designed to correct for those "gimmicks" he had considered as potential competitive edges:

- Children's Corner
- Reference/quotation services
- Book review/homework help hotline
- Community resource for phone numbers, data
- Those others that he had talked about before

He hoped that these numbers would look more reasonable, if not make him wildly happy. (He expected Aunt Hattie to dance at his Grand Opening.)

According to the *American Booksellers Association Financial Profile* (1981), the average bookstore was about 2,400 square feet in size, with annual sales of about $260,000. Average rent costs were about $5 per square foot—but he knew that rents in the Washington area were high compared with those in most other parts of the country. Rent, for the ABA average store, was about 5 percent of total sales. Rent expense was larger, as a percent of sales, in stores doing a smaller gross sales amount.

The same source told him that the cost-of-goods-sold (essentially his inventory costs) averaged about 65 percent of total sales for almost all size categories of bookstores. Inventory turnover averaged 2.9 times for the ABA sample. An earlier study showed inventory turnover at 4 times. Still another source told him that a really gross estimate for one-time opening expenses for the average bookstore, fixtures, cash register and the like, would run about $70,000.

Perhaps the most shocking thing to Ed was the data he found on the profitability of the average bookstore. Clearly, he was not going to winter in Acapulco on his profits. Before tax, the ABA sample averaged 4.9 percent in net income. Including their estimate of 4 percent for owners' wages, the average bookstore made a net profit before tax of only 0.9 percent. The one cheerful note in all this was that the median unadjusted pretax profit was 2.3 percent of sales. This indicated to Ed that there was a wide disparity among bookstores in profitability. (He also noted that the average owner's wages totalled about $6,850. This figure made even the Academy look good by comparison.)

He had been saving part of his military pension for the last five years so that his savings now totalled $40,000. He would, of course, continue to receive his military pension, regardless of what he did by way of work. It ran about $15,000 per year. What he really wanted the bookstore to do was to replace his earnings from the Academy—$12,000 per year before taxes. He owned nothing of any value except his old Chevy, which hardly counted. Aunt Hattie was doing just fine in the health department.

1. Estimate about how much Ed James needs to open and operate his bookstore. How much will he need to raise from outside sources?
2. What expenses will be affected by each of the "gimmicks" he envisions as providing his competitive edges? Will these effects be large or small? Will they continue over the life of the business, or will they be one time costs (or both)?

3. What are his options for getting the money he needs (short of knocking off Aunt Hattie)? How do you recommend that he proceed to finance his bookstore?
4. Given your financing recommendation(s), what, if anything, does Ed need to prepare or develop? What should his next steps be?

PART 4

STRUCTURING OPERATIONS

CHAPTER 9
Operations: Getting Your Show on the
Road

CHAPTER 10
Personnel Requirements: Who's Minding
the Store?

9. Operations: Getting Your Show on the Road

Skimping on space planning and interior design is
a bit like hiring a chauffeur and equipping him
with a bicycle.

Marita Thomas, "Facilities Planning," *Inc.*

Now that you have considered what your business will be, the legal form it will take, how you intend to finance it, and what protection you intend to provide for it through insurance, it seems reasonable to begin to put the actual operation together. Structuring the operations of a business is really a two-part discussion, done here in this chapter and in the one that follows. The first critical factor is the physical assets and resources you need to make, or sell, or perform whatever it is you said you were going to. The second factor, discussed in the next chapter, is the human resources you will require to make your business work the way you intend it to work.

These two factors, the physical and the human factors, operate very differently, depending on the business you have chosen and the way you intend for your business to operate. In some kinds of businesses, it is the hardware that is important—the cable television distribution business, for example. For others, notably consulting companies and other types of service sellers, it is the caliber of the people that is the critical factor. In some fields, which factor is of prime concern depends on your vision of your business. A restaurant, for example, can rely on equipment, à la McDonald's, with the people being largely interchangeable. Alternatively, your restaurant can rely on the skills of its chef and service personnel.

While the relative importance of these two factors is infinitely variable, both must be included in your pre-opening considerations. Now you need to determine what your optimum mix of the two will be.

We have chosen to start with the hardware/space considerations for two reasons. First, almost all businesses require some space, a physical factor,

190

out of which to operate (even if that space will initially be your spare room or a corner of your garage). This is a logical place to begin to consider what a business requires. Second, it is frankly easier to consider physical needs than to define the qualities required of personnel. Structuring the physical aspects of the business first, then, will give you more time and ammunition with which to develop definitions of the human requirements of your business. Also, in a purely practical vein, you will need a place to put your people once you have hired them.

The physical requirements of your business include your space, the equipment you need, and the material you will use to make or sell whatever it is that you are making or selling. In Chapter 5 we began to talk about the location of your place of business. And, in one sense, location is a marketing decision. What we will look at here are the physical characteristics of your space—the location itself—which is definitely a set of operating considerations. The aspects that will be discussed briefly include size, layout, structure, utilities, and renovations. For your own business, other factors may be relevant, but this section should start you thinking in the right directions.

FEATURE 9.1
Avoiding Space and Equipment Costs as a Path to Profit

Colby Computer

Early on, Colby had decided to have high-quality casings for his computers, some of which are intended for heavy-duty industrial and military use. [It] arranged for the frames to be produced by Western Diecasting, Inc., a well-regarded local company, which agreed to accept stock in partial payment. As a result, Colby was able to reduce his start-up costs.

Xicor Inc.

Xicor started with little more than an idea about a new kind of chip. "We didn't have the money for a technology trip," Klein [president and chairman] recalls ... "Not having the money made us do everything right the first time."

[Klein] eschewed fancy offices, working initially at the home of one of his engineers, and he arranged to have Xicor's original manufacturing work done overseas, in Switzerland. "We wanted a product, not a fancy building," he says.

From Joel Kotkin, "Why Smart Companies are Saying *No* to Venture Capital," Reprinted with permission, *Inc.* magazine, August, 1984. Copyright © 1984 *Inc.* Publishing Company, 38 Commercial Wharf, Boston, MA 02110.

The segment of this chapter addressing equipment needs will focus on various options for obtaining the equipment needed to begin your operation. Finally, we will look at ways of finding and dealing with potential suppliers and at ways of estimating how much material you will require for efficient operation.

SPACE: HOW MUCH IS ENOUGH?

Clearly, your place needs to be large enough, but not too large. The trick lies in figuring out what meets this definition for your company. In some businesses, there are general guidelines in those industry averages that you should still be keeping handy. Most retail operations, for example, have data about average sales per square foot. The average successful bookstore, for example, has sales of $75 per square foot—$93 if you count only selling and display space. Based on your knowledge of average profitability (and your expected relationship with that average), you can approximate the amount of space you will want.

In certain businesses, notably restaurants and bars or lounges, the local authorities have limits on the minimum space you must have to serve a given number of people. In some ways, this makes your job somewhat easier. Do not, however, choose and sign for your space before you check out what these limits are in your area. It could wreck all your projections to discover—after you have a long lease or you actually own the place—that you can have only three quarters of the tables you banked on.

Size limits potential profit. This critical item was over-looked by a former small business owner who rented a very small shop because it was inexpensive and because he wanted to "test" his concept and his comfort with being an entrepreneur. He planned to sell crafts patterns, yarn, and all the related paraphernalia. When we finally got a look at the operation, we found that the size of the place limited the selection the owner could provide, thereby cutting out most potential customers. More to the point, we found that, even had he sold out the place each month, he would not have been able to make a decent living—and there is no way that a store of this type could have an inventory turnover rate of 12 times a year.

Another interesting item that is often forgotten in the initial size calculation is the fact that you have to keep your excess stock somewhere. Many prospective entrepreneurs seem to expect the imminent introduction of the sky hook. (Forecasters say that this invention may take a few more years.) In the absence of this technological advance, storage space is necessary for almost all businesses.

Where that space is may be important to the success of the company. In a restaurant or bar, excess inventory really needs to be not only on the premises, but also physically accessible by staff. In businesses in which stock moves more slowly—a paint store, for example—you may be able to get away with stashing some of the excess in your garage or basement if the conditions in those places will not damage your goods and if they are well secured. (Remember to check your insurance coverage if you intend to maintain some inventory off-premises.)

A final option may be possible, depending on the type of business you have chosen, the reliability of suppliers, and the normal terms of delivery to your customers. You may be able to let a warehouse-based distributor keep the inventory for you, drop-shipping small lots as required. This option will generally involve a cost tradeoff of leasing/buying additional space versus the increased costs of supplying your needs in this fashion.

Some industry data sets include information about the average proportion of selling space to total space. If your assembled data does not do this, do not fail to make provision for storage space yourself. Later in the chapter, we will discuss how to determine how much inventory you should keep handy.

Room to Grow

As was noted earlier, you want your initial space to meet your size requirements for a number of years. Moving a business of any type is invariably a major annoyance, even if it is a people-based business that requires only that new stationery be printed and new phone numbers be learned. It dislocates your staff and your customers or clients.

This aspect of your space planning, then, depends entirely on your plans for the growth of your business. If, for example, you wish to remain small and exclusive, you need give little attention to this factor in assessing an initial space for your business. If you plan to expand your business by opening additional units, rather than by increasing the volume of your first unit, the same conclusion follows. If, however, you intend to become the largest company of your kind in the northwest in the next five years, for example, and if the economics of your business dictate that this means single-plant operations, then growing room is a major consideration for you.

How much growing room you will require depends upon the speed with which you plan to grow. Coupling your peak expected volume by, say, year five of operations, with your expected sales output per square foot figures should give you the basis for a reasonable estimate. Do not make the mistake of acquiring space too far ahead of yourself, however. Space is generally one of the major expenses of an operation, and more space means more expense. You do not want to overburden the present with your plans for the future. As an alternative, try to negotiate a shorter lease and resign yourself to moving in five years.

Suppose, for a moment, that you expect your business to do a sales volume of $300,000 the first year. You want it to double by the fifth year. You can get space for $15 per square foot. Average sales per square foot in your industry are $200. Your calculations would look as follows:

Expected first year sales	$300,000
Square feet required @ $200 per	1,500
Cost @ $15 per square foot	$ 22,500 (7.5 percent of sales)
Intended fifth year sales	$600,000
Square feet required	3,000
Cost @ $15 per square foot	$ 45,000 (15 percent of first-year sales.)

Your question is whether you want to overburden your new store with a single cost item that you don't yet absolutely need that will eat up 15 percent of your first year's sales. You should also consider how your place will look at a $600,000 size, but with $300,000-level inventory in it.

A final consideration is the cost of moving as a tradeoff with the extra rent cost. If you estimate that the cost of moving—including extra advertising costs to let your customers know where you are—would be $70,000, for example, you might simply resign yourself to a move. You would have paid more than $100,000 over five years to save $70,000 if you chose to take the larger space initially.

The Shape of the Space

Another important factor in helping your business succeed or fail may well be the shape of the space you choose. While this sounds a bit overstated, consider trying to control shoplifting (without major investments in security) in an L-shaped shop set up as shown here.

Figure 9.1 The shape of your space is an important factor.

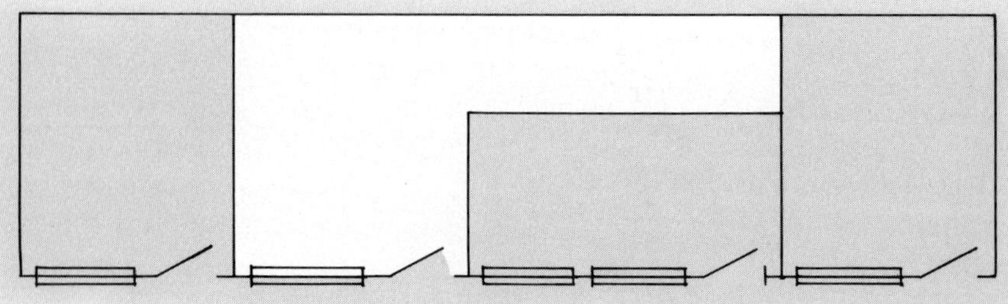

Physical layout may be even more important for a manufacturing operation. In many instances, the flow of an assembly process is critical to the profitability of that operation. A shoe manufacturer, for example, had space on a number of floors in an old building. His staff spent time and energy moving goods from one floor to another. This was particularly difficult on those days (which were numerous) when the elevators in the old building were not working. A new, one-floor manufacturing space, though more expensive in and of itself, increased the productivity of his workers more than enough to offset the extra expense and increase the profits he took in on every unit shipped.

The moral of this story is to consider carefully how you will set up your operation in the space you are considering *before* you actually sign on the dotted line. If the layout of the space will make your operation harder to control or more expensive to operate, you probably do not need the extra headaches—even at a very good price. In fact, the excellent price you are getting may be because of some operational cost tradeoff that you would have to make to use that space. Consider carefully what that cost might be. If your particular business will not incur that cost (for example, you are selling antique brass cannons and do not really have to worry about anyone slipping one into his pocket) you might really be getting a great deal on the space.

The Condition of the Space

In this section, the "shape" we are discussing is the structural condition of the property you are considering for your operation. For most businesses, the normal building code approval will be adequate. If, however, you intend to use a great deal of heavy equipment, you must be sure that the floors and the rest of the structure will be able to handle the load. You certainly do not want the place coming down around your ears. A similar rule applies if your equipment will generate a high level of vibration or a series of sharp shocks to specific areas.

While this kind of analysis normally applies to manufacturing businesses, consider your business carefully before deciding that this does not apply to you. If you are going to run a bowling alley, for example, or a health spa, people will be using heavy items which, while they *should* not be dropped or thrown on the floors, often are. A little care in advance beats possible difficulties later.

Do not attempt to decide on your own if your current favorite site is structurally capable of handling the stresses you intend to put on it. If there is even enough question for you to pause to consider the matter, call a professional engineer to have a look.

Utilities, Amenities, and Renovations

If a space you are considering does not have all the attributes you want for your business (and few ever do, somehow) you will want to consider the cost of renovating, remodeling, or adding to the space. Find out in advance how costly this will be to do and whether or not what you want is possible given the particular space.

While rugs and plants and panelling and such are important parts of the cost picture here, they are not the key considerations. You are likely to have to do those things in any site you choose. In terms of your choice of physical space, however, your questions should run more to whether the place you are considering has the capability to bring in the type and amount of electric service you will need, for example. One manufacturer being moved in an urban renewal program found that the cost of replicating the electric service he had at his current site would be the major cost of his proposed move.

Redoing plumbing is another, often-costly consideration. If you will need significantly more water or water in different places than the site you are considering now offers, check the cost of the additions or changes before you jump in. Make sure it can be done. And find out who is going to pay for it. As we noted earlier, the cost of some renovations and changes may be undertaken by the lessor in return for increased monthly payments. This may be a good deal for a cash-poor new company. Whatever arrangement you come to, make sure it is spelled out in writing in the lease document.

Costs

Obviously, the cost of your space will vary with the desirability of your location and the amount of available space of the type you seek in the area you want. Clearly, you wouldn't put a warehouse on the best block in town. The price would be prohibitive given the return on warehousing operations. In this phase of your planning, then, your industry average space cost as a percentage of sales is likely to be of little help unless your area is very close to the national average in most respects.

Given this, you will have to figure your space costs based on your local reality. In general, they will be comprised as follows:

(selling space + inventory space + growing room) × (cost per square foot)

While space costs are generally quoted in annual dollars per square foot, you will actually make payments on a monthly basis—either to the lessor or to the bank (unless you have financed a purchase yourself). Usually, if you will be operating on a rental or a lease, a deposit of at least one month's rent will be due at the beginning in addition to your current payment. Plan for it.

To this amount, your space costs of operation, you will have to add the cost of any renovations that you have not been able to convince the lessor to do for you and include in the lease cost. This, like your first month or two of rent, will be incurred before you can open the doors of your establishment. Do not make the fairly standard error of planning your funds as if you could sign a lease today and open shop tomorrow.

Space costs are generally considered to be "fixed costs"; that is, you have signed a contract stating that you will pay the agreed-upon amount each month for the entire agreed-upon period whether or not you have any customers. Although, as you will see in Chapter 13, this does not really mean that they are unalterable forever, contracts for such costs should not be taken lightly.

FEATURE 9.2

Productivity Difficulties for Smaller Companies

When he was at the Harvard Business School, nobody told Mr. Sontag it would be like this. "But I found out quick that knowing about quality circles and robots won't help when you're out of time and money and you've got to get stuff out the back door."

His problem? An old, largely unautomated plant that makes electric motors in competition with some of the giants like G.E. Even on the new production line, all but 2 of the 30 steps required to assemble the motors are done by hand. It takes four hours to make a motor. The company must cut that to one hour to make a profit on the product.

With a large capital expenditure budget, that would be easier. "When you only have $400,000 to spend, you can't just order up a batch of $100,000 robots ... The very last thing I need is some Harvard M.B.A. to come in here and tell me to get a new computer system."

Given this paucity of capital budget, and the custom orders in some lines, Sontag has shifted to encouraging employee productivity rather than machine productivity. Lawrence Fulco, a Bureau of Labor Statistics economist, however, notes that "People get the idea that if you get all the workers in the U.S. into a room and give them a pep talk, productivity would go up. But there are other factors, like how materials are ordered, moved and stored."

In addition to working on these aspects of the business, Sontag stresses employee morale. He has instituted merit raises and profit-sharing. He formed an employee social organization and has an annual company picnic. Meanwhile, he seeks a "manufacturing wizard" who doesn't mind getting his hands dirty.

EQUIPMENT: OPTIONS AND TRADEOFFS

While most people believe that only manufacturers need be seriously concerned with equipment issues, in fact some kind of equipment is needed by any business. Even an independent consultant requires some mechanical or electronic support for operations (such as the computer/word processor on which I am typing this or the calculator I carry around to my clients' offices). A simple retail operation needs, at very least, some kind of cash register and/or safe, racks or shelves to use for merchandise display, and some kind of theft-control gear. In these days of choice, even a telephone system raises the kinds of issues discussed in this section.

Thus, even if your business is not based on its equipment, as a manufacturing company might be, do not disregard the major issues raised here. Draw up an equipment list as described below. Only then should you determine the level of effort you want to expend to acquire what you need. Make this determination with the understanding that equipment exists to save you time and effort (computers, for example), and it is up to you to make the relevant tradeoffs between time and/or effort and cost.

Particularly if your company is equipment-based, part of your space consideration had to be the size and amount of equipment that your business will require. This segment of the chapter looks at the three main options you have for acquiring the equipment you need and discusses some of the tradeoffs inherent in choosing each approach. Equipment costs also fall into the category of fixed costs. Once you have made a series of choices, it is not generally easy to go back and start over. Once again, careful consideration is needed to minimize your risks of choosing incorrectly for your business.

In this area, as in determining the amount of space you need, you are really on your own—but with guidance from industry sources and from this book. Many industry associations offer help in defining your basic equipment list, either through direct help or through articles and/or advertisements in their journals. Check through their materials carefully, and before you start acquiring, make a list of what you need, about how much it will cost, and about how long you expect each piece to last. This list is intended as your own personal guideline—and as a guard against over-eager salespeople.

Over-eager salespeople are relatively rare, however. In fact, most equipment salespeople can be of great assistance to you in developing your equipment list. In general, they want a good, longer-term customer in you—and that will not come to pass if you initially acquire too much equipment (or the wrong equipment) and it puts you under. Talk with them. Listen to what they have to say, keeping in mind that their business is handling equipment for businesses like yours. But reserve judgment.

Your list will also help you to see which items of equipment are critical to your decision-making process. For example, a fairly expensive piece may be important, but if you expect to replace it in three years, then your choice is less critical here than on an item that you expect to be using ten or fifteen years from now. The list will help you to concentrate your research and your effort on the items that will really count for you in the longer run.

Research is a key notion in equipment acquisitions. You need to find out a great deal about the state and trend of technology in equipment for your industry. You need to be acutely aware of the market for new and used equipment in your industry. Most important of all, you need to have a good idea of the capabilities and capacities of the various types of equipment that you could use in your business and how these features fit with how you intend to use the equipment. While you can get help in considering these issues, ultimately the choices must be made on the basis of your concept of your business—a concept that only you, at present, know intimately.

New or Used?

In most industries, there is a market of some kind in used equipment. The strength and size of this market is one of the key factors in making a decision about whether you look at used equipment or consider only new equipment. The size and strength of the market for used equipment are generally determined by two major factors: The speed with which technology is affecting the equipment itself, and the turnover rate of businesses in your industry.

Technology affects equipment markets in two ways: size and price. If there have been few technological advances in equipment for your industry, there will be a stable market in used equipment. Prices will be fairly high as a proportion of the price of new equipment—after all, it lasts for a long time and, generally, there will be very little difference between the productive capacity of an old machine versus a newer one. Much of the leather shoe manufacturing business is a good example of this kind of business. A profitable manufacturer in this business was (as of 1979) actually still operating a machine made in 1901. It was built of wood.

On the other hand, an industry in which technology is making rapid changes in the equipment used—telecommunications, for example—is likely to have a large market in used equipment that is no longer state-of-the-art. Because the equipment is technologically "old," prices are likely to be lower and more volatile since changes are still occurring. You will not know how far behind the industry leaders you will be until after the wave of change has passed.

The turnover rate of businesses in your field obviously affects the supply of used equipment. If businesses come and go with amazing speed, chances are (unless it is a very high-tech industry) that there is a massive market in used equipment. The best example of this kind of industry is the restaurant business.

As a beginning entrepreneur, it is likely that your first impulse is to acquire everything spanking new. The impulse is understandable, if expensive. Definitely check your entire equipment list for the difference between new and used equipment prices. It is very likely to change your mind.

Aside from price, the questions that you should be asking yourself about your new/used alternatives are:

- Is there a technological difference between new equipment and what is now available in the used equipment markets? Does this difference make any real difference in my particular business?
- Are there problems in compatibility of old and new equipment? (Can I get some of what is needed new and some old?)
- Is the used equipment market large enough in my industry and area to permit me to get what I need fairly easily, or is the search itself likely to be costly?

The issue of how much difference a technological advance makes to your particular business is often difficult to pin down. Obviously, if an advanced machine were less efficient or had less capacity than all existing machines, it would not sell very well for its manufacturer. However, whether *you* need those extras and whether they are worth the extra cost to you are different issues. If a machine, for example, has massive capacity that you are unlikely to use for a number of years, do you really want to acquire that capacity now, paying for it until you need it? Or would it make more sense to trade it for a larger capacity machine later?

Obviously, the answers to such questions go back to the factors that affect the total market for used equipment in your industry. If there is likely to be a major technological advance between now and when you will finally make full use of the machine, you certainly do not want to lock yourself in to an outmoded item. As you can see, the issues are complex and involve your predictions about what will be happening in your field. Again, research helps a great deal.

One word of caution if you decide to go with used equipment. A piece of new equipment generally comes with a warranty/guarantee from the manufacturer, and it is sometimes available with instruction (if necessary) and service contracts. Some or all of these items may not be available with used items. Be sure to consider the costs of the missing items, if you need them, as part of the costs of the used equipment.

And to minimize potential service problems of used equipment acquisitions, be sure that someone who knows what she is looking at checks over any used equipment that you may be considering acquiring. This is less necessary if you are buying an item from a respected dealer who will provide some warranties and some service than if you are buying, say, restaurant equipment at auction or in the sale of a business. Do not forget the cost of such consultant services as part of the tradeoff cost of acquiring used equipment.

Lease or Buy?

Once you have decided what to acquire, you need to decide the basis upon which you want to acquire it. Your two options are to purchase the equipment or to lease it. This is largely a financial decision, although in some instances, there is a technological component as well.

As was true when we discussed buying versus renting a site for your business, your major concern must be with the scarcity of cash in your fledgling company. Since leasing equipment generally requires significantly less up-front cash outlay than the down-payment required to purchase, the bias is toward leasing. Additional advantages of leasing include the possibility of reducing your required lease payments through leaving the tax benefits with the lessor. At the beginning, your company is not likely to be able to use such benefits to their greatest extent anyway. Finally, you will not have to go to the bank for as much financing. This conserves the borrowing power of your company—however miniscule that may now be—against possible severe need in the future.

Leasing may be a wiser option for you if your equipment is subject to high technological risk. Any computer-based business or many businesses in the medical field are in such a position. At the end of a lease, you may simply return the equipment to the lessor and be done with it. You can then simply lease new, state-of-the-art items. Had you bought the now-technologically obsolete equipment, disposal would be your problem. The risk would be yours. Please note, however, that this risk transfer service does not come free. In an industry in which technology is making equipment obsolete at a rapid pace, a lower resale value will be folded into your lease cost.

In fact, the kind of lease you write makes a significant difference in your ability to trade equipment in this fashion. Most equipment leases are "financing leases"—that is, they are long-term and non-cancellable, and they are intended to cover the full costs of the piece of equipment (plus financing costs plus the leasing company's profit) over the course of your lease. (Your site lease does not meet this test. It is an "operating lease.") Of the two main variants on the financing lease, only one, the conventional true lease, really allows you to return the equipment to the lessor. Under the alternative, the conditional sales agreement, your only real option is to buy the equipment at a predetermined nominal price.

As usual, however, there are tradeoffs. Under the conventional true lease form of a financing lease, the lessor gets all the tax benefits. Under the conditional sales agreement form, you would be considered the owner, for tax purposes, from the beginning of the lease. As noted earlier, however, in your early years, you may not be able to reap full tax benefits from leasing anyway.

There are, of course, also disadvantages to leasing equipment. First and foremost, you do not own the equipment—and never will unless and until you opt to purchase it from the lessor at the end of the lease period. While you are responsible for service, it is not at your option. It must be by the book and for the inspection of the lessor (which is not a bad idea, in any case).

In addition, a lease is no easier to get out of than a debt. In fact, closing out a loan is a good deal easier. Suppose you borrowed to purchase a piece of equipment that you no longer wanted. You could simply sell off the equipment (assuming your bank approved) and prepay the debt. Or, if you were doing really well, you could simply prepay the debt, paying whatever penalty you agreed to. You are usually into a lease, however, for the full term at the full price.

Finally, there may be additional costs to leasing as opposed to buying. First, a lease is complicated and will require the services of your lawyer and your accountant to evaluate properly. In addition, if you will not be in a position to use the tax benefits, such as the Investment Tax Credit (the credit that the federal government gives to businesses that purchase capital equipment), the lease may be more costly to you than the purchase. You can use such benefits only if your company is profitable enough to be required to pay taxes in excess of the credit. If you are a corporation, you can carry some of the benefits forward.

What it all basically comes down to is the tradeoff between cash out now or cash out over the longer term. Since a dollar today is more valuable than a dollar is likely to be in a year or two, a present value calculation can let you compare the cost of a lease versus the cost of a loan in current dollar terms. You will find the major differences to be in the timing of the payment amounts and in the ways the tax benefits are handled. Initially, however, your choice here is likely to depend more on your amount of available cash and borrowing power than upon the results of a discounted cash flow analysis described here in Feature 9.3.

One of the nicer things about leases is that they are negotiated agreements. Unlike loans, which are usually payable in monthly installments, leases can be written so that payments coincide with the times when your business is likely to have money. Note: This does not mean "anytime your business happens to have money," but rather at specified times when you expect there to be funds in the company. This, in itself, may be a major argument for a lease in your particular business.

As we noted when discussing locations and bank loans and equity deals, remember that you are negotiating a deal, not simply accepting a final offer. There are many potential lessors in most industries, and they are competing for your business. (You might be big someday.) At least take a shot at a good lease arrangement, remembering that the leasing company has to make a nickel or so on this deal, too. Don't be greedy or unreasonable. A few quotes will give you a reasonable range and terms. But don't just sign the first agreement that comes past, either.

FEATURE 9.3
Discounted Cash Flow Analysis of Lease vs. Purchase

The purpose of discounted cash flow analysis is to recognize that today's dollar is likely to be worth more than tomorrow's dollar. The analysis discounts future dollars as they come in, by the year they come in, and provides answers in terms of today's dollars. The discount rate is thus critical. It is, in effect, an inflation estimate. We have used 7 percent here.

Equipment cost: $50,000
Bank loan: $40,000 (20 percent down payment)
   3 years, 15 percent
   $1,387 per month
   $49,900 total loan payments

Economic useful life: 5 years
Lease: (conventional true lease)
   4 years, 14 percent
   $1,366 per month
   $65,600 total lease payments

Year	*0*	*1*	*2*	*3*	*4*	*Total*
LOAN:						
Downpayment	$10,000					$10,000
Loan payment:		$17,519	$17,519	$17,519		
Interest expense		6,000	4,272	2,285		
Depreciation		5,000	10,000	10,000		
Payment net of tax benefits (Tax @ 50 percent)		$12,019				$11,233
			$10,383			$ 9,069
				$11,377		$ 9,287
Investment Tax Credit		$(5,000)				$(4,673)
Total after tax present value cost						$35,016
LEASE:						
Annual payment		$16,392	$16,392	$16,392	$16,392	
Tax @ 50 percent		8,196	8,196	8,196	8,196	
Payments net of tax benefit		$ 8,196				$ 7,660
			$8,196			$ 7,159
				$ 8,196		$ 6,690
					$ 8,196	$ 6,253
Total after tax present value cost						$27,762

As you can see, the lease option is less expensive for this particular company in this specific situation. A large part of the differential in expense is the loan requirement for a 20 percent downpayment.

It should not be assumed that this is always true. If you have the funds or the borrowing power to have a real choice between a lease and a loan, each with specific terms, you must do your own analysis each time.

Certain things have not been costed in this kind of analysis. At the end of the loan, you would own the equipment outright—and still have two years of tax value through depreciation. At the end of the lease option, you would have (probably) the right to purchase the equipment for a small sum. If you returned it, however, you would get to start all over with nothing. How much weight these factors should carry depends entirely upon your intended use and period of use of the piece of equipment.

Another Possible Approach to Financing

If you happen to be in the right kind of business, there may be an even easier way of financing your equipment than with a loan or a lease. In some businesses, the people who manufacture the equipment you need have a selfish interest in helping you get into and succeed in the business you have chosen. It is not at all uncommon in such industries for the manufacturer to offer very good terms on its own financing of your equipment.

In general, businesses in which this practice would be found are those in which the idea is continuing public recognition for the manufacturer and for the sport or business. Bowling alleys, for example, display the names of their equipment manufacturers prominently. The manufacturers have a significant interest in advancing bowling as a public sport. They help alley owners to start and grow leagues. They sponsor tournaments. And they help finance the equipment. In general, equipment manufacturers in such fields will be of significant help to you in all aspects of getting your business off the ground and in keeping it flying. Use them well.

THE WHO, HOW, AND WHEN OF SUPPLY

As Napoleon once pointed out, an army travels on its stomach. His point was well-taken. An army can neither march nor fight without provisions, supplies. Supply lines, therefore, were, and still are, critical pieces of military strategy and tactics. Supply is an equally critical aspect of your business planning—unless your only real product is an idea or something equally intangible. If you do not ensure adequate, low-cost, timely supplies of whatever it is you will need, you can kiss your new company goodbye.

Fortunately, supply is not a particularly difficult aspect of your business to do adequately. To do it well requires some care and consideration, but will result in a probable advantage over most other businesses in your field. Help is available, often from suppliers themselves. Listen to anything that might be useful—the price is right—then make your own judgments.

Start your supply operations in the same manner as you began your equipment search. Make lists. The one thing that you cannot afford to do is forget to order something small, easily overlooked, but critical to your success—salt for your restaurant, for example. Make a gross estimate of about how much of each item you expect to use over a given time period. As you begin, this volume estimate may be as rough as "lots" versus "not much." What you are seeking here is some yardstick by which to set priorities for your attention.

Make note of the unit of purchase and begin to estimate a range for the unit cost of each item on your list. (You will no longer be buying shirts, for example, in units of one. You will be purchasing for resale in lots of a dozen.)

With your list in hand, begin to talk with suppliers in your field. You have already talked to some of them while in the process of your initial market research. Go back to your notes from those talks before you initiate new ones. You are interested in price, minimum order quantities, and delivery lead times, among other things.

You should be particularly interested in the supplier's relations with other smaller companies. And you want to know whether you can talk with some of those other smaller accounts. The worry is that, as a lone small account, you will get last choice (if there is any supply left) and delivery whenever it is convenient for the supplier. To some extent, you cannot avoid this until you have grown a great deal. But if you are one of a number of small business accounts, and if the existing accounts are reasonably satisfied, you have better odds of getting what you need when you need it.

Be prepared for one major change in what you were told in your earlier talks with suppliers. When you asked about normal terms of trade before, you were asking about the general case. You are not yet the general case. Expect, therefore, to be asked for cash on delivery for your first few shipments of whatever. This is not personal. Your supplier is in business just as you are. Ask yourself what you would do if a person you had never dealt with before came into your place with no track record and no credit history and wanted to walk out with a sizable amount of whatever you were selling. Cash on delivery, right?

Sometimes, suppliers will go in the other direction, extending your initial payment terms because they know you are new and probably strapped for cash. You might try to negotiate an arrangement like this, but do not be disappointed if the attempt fails. Plan to pay up front.

Your basic interest is in a group of suppliers who are stable (that is, likely to be in business for the long haul) and who will be able to assist you in other ways than selling you goods or materials. A number of additional services often provided by suppliers are discussed in Chapter 11 on advertising and marketing. While one of your major concerns is price, be sure to consider these additional services when deciding which suppliers are really offering low price.

Another issue to bear in mind is the notion of backup. To run your company, you will really need what your suppliers are selling you. If one or two items are particularly critical to your operation, you might try to ensure that at least two of your suppliers handle those items. If anything goes wrong with one supply line, you may still be able to operate normally. Obviously, this approach will become a lot easier to implement as you grow larger, or at least better established, yourself.

While you are establishing relations with potential suppliers, you must also begin to refine your estimates of how much of each item you will need over a given time period. (You can't order "some" of something.) If you will be dealing almost exclusively with one distributor, in setting up a bookstore, for example, you can expect assistance in this area from your representative. Keep in mind, however, that he works for the distributor and, as such, his first goal is to make profitable sales for them.

If, as is the more standard case, you will need to figure out what you need more or less on your own, you still have some guidelines. In the industry average information you collected earlier, there should be statistics that relate to inventory requirements and inventory turnover rates, for example. An initial inventory calculation was shown in Chapter 7 (p. 144).

Alternatively, if you are manufacturing something, you can work out the inventory requirements for yourself by using your estimates of unit sales to figure out how much material you will need. You know, for example, how much wire goes into one of your toy robots. You also know how many toy robots you intend to produce in your first month. The amount per unit times the number of units is the base amount you need. (You also probably want some extra, or "buffer stock," so that you do not run out at a critical time and are not entirely dependent on your supplier's schedules.)

While your first cut at the amount you need of a given item should be a well-considered one, do not expect to nail it dead-on the first time. Your estimates will get consistently better as your business develops a history and you have a better basis for your estimates. Keep in mind that a slight overestimate generally beats an underestimate—unless you know that you can get virtually instantaneous delivery of the item whenever you need it. An underestimate means a halt in production or a lost sale. Usually, an overestimate simply carries a small cost. (This does not hold true for massive overestimates, which can seriously erode your profits.)

Assuming that you can estimate your needs reasonably accurately, you can use a formula to figure out your least expensive and most efficient ordering pattern. This is referred to as the Economic Order Quantity (EOQ). While it will probably not be immediately useful to you because you do not yet know some of the numbers (total amount used per year, cost of placing an order), keep it in mind for later.

The EOQ is unique for each inventory item you use. It is therefore most useful for those items that you use and purchase in sizable quantities. It would probably not make sense, for example, to bother with EOQ for an item you use 10 of a year. The EOQ might well be a 10-year supply for you.

$$\text{Order quantity} = \sqrt{\frac{2 \times \text{total amount used per year} \times \text{cost of ordering}}{\text{cost of carrying inventory} \times \text{cost per unit}}}$$

The EOQ approach has a number of significant drawbacks, particularly for a new small company. It assumes that you will be financially able to purchase and store goods in the most efficient quantities. While the storage costs go into the "cost of carrying inventory" term in the formula, there is no way to account for whatever cash limitations you might have. In fact, it assumes that there is no real space limitation, either. It costs the space rather than permitting you to place an absolute limit on it. The formula also assumes that you will purchase and use the particular item you are investigating at an even pace throughout the year. If any of these conditions—cash availability, space availability, or level inventory utilization—is not the case for your company, EOQ will be of limited value to you.

SUMMARY

To begin actual operations of your business, you will need at least some space, some hardware, and some goods and/or materials to either sell or make into whatever you are planning to sell. Getting these items in line—and on time—will require some planning on your part.

In addition to the marketing considerations already discussed with regard to your location, planning for adequate space in which to operate involves determining how much space you need for sales, storage, and growth. It includes consideration of such factors as the physical shape and condition of the space given the use(s) you intend to make of it. It also includes estimating the cost of that space, given what you will need to do to it to make it usable for your business purposes.

Obtaining the equipment you need for the business is also a vital operational consideration. Equipment, here, includes not only heavy machinery, but also any other hard items you need to get into and stay in business—including such items as cash registers, safes, electronic devices, or shelving.

(You have a number of options for acquiring the equipment once you have determined exactly what you will require. In most industries, you have a choice between new and used equipment. You will usually have the choice between purchasing with a bank loan or leasing from a leasing company. In some industries, you may also have the option of financing an equipment purchase through the equipment manufacturer.)

Finally, you have to stock the place with whatever you will be selling or with the wherewithal to make whatever you will be selling. Here, too, the keys are complete lists of the items you will need, and good estimates of the amounts and costs of the items. As in equipment acquisitions, your interests are in price, delivery times, and payment terms. Keep in mind, however, that unless you are leasing equipment, (you will undoubtedly have longer term, more frequent contact with your suppliers than with any other outside group with which you will interact—except, it is hoped, your customers.)

FOR YOU TO CONSIDER

1. What three size issues do you need to consider when you determine how much space you will need to begin operations?
2. Assume that you are starting a small retail candy shop. Why might you be offered space at a phenomenally good price per square foot? What should you consider before you sign on the dotted line?
3. Address the same questions as if you were planning to open a health, fitness, racquetball, and swimming facility.
4. Why should your initial equipment list include the length of time you expect each piece of equipment to last?
5. How does the speed of technological change affect the markets for equipment in a given industry? How does it affect your choices about how you will acquire your equipment?
6. Why might you want to acquire used equipment versus new equipment?
7. What are the advantages of leasing over buying equipment? Vice versa?
8. Why might you care about the other accounts serviced by a given supplier?
9. Discuss three key issues in making decisions about who you should choose as your suppliers.
10. Discuss two approaches to determining how much of a given item you should stock, and discuss how the EOQ approach will work once you actually get into operation.

FOR FURTHER READING

Bank of America. "Equipment Leasing." *Small Business Reporter,* 1982.
Chase, Richard B., and Nicholas J. Aquilano. *Production and Operations Management: A Life Cycle Approach.* 4th ed. Homewood, Ill.: Richard D. Irwin, Inc., 1985.

Small Business Administration publications:

Can You Lease or Buy Equipment? SBA MA 2.014.
Capital Planning. SBA 045-000-00193-8.
Computers for Small Business—Service Bureau or Time Sharing. SBA MA 2.019.
Purchasing for Manufacturing Firms. SBA 045-000-00181-4.
Purchasing Management and Inventory Control for Small Business. SBA 045-000-00167-9.
Retail Buying Function. SBA 045-000-00177-6.
The Equipment Replacement Decision. SBA MA 2.005.

10. Personnel Requirements: Who's Minding the Store?

"I still have to remind myself not to get involved in the day-to-day details."

"There's no way the company can grow if you're doing it all yourself."

"You have to select people with demonstrated capabilities, tell them what results you expect and largely leave them to decide the means by which they will be obtained." The good boss then monitors the results.

Sanford Jacobs, *Wall Street Journal*

In the last chapter, we talked about the physical resources that you would need to put into your new company. We deferred the discussion of the human resources required because it is inherently more difficult to define personnel needs than it is to describe a machine or some raw materials. By now, however, you have been working out the functioning of your operation in fine enough detail so that you should already have a fairly strong image of the human resources you need. This chapter is intended to help you to focus on the "people" aspects of your company—an easy task, if you're the lone operator of a sole proprietorship. For most entrepreneurs, however, this is one of the more difficult tasks, simply because it is not concrete.

Earlier in your planning, you almost assuredly mentioned your employees as one of your critical success factors. Our examples in Chapter 3 had to do with the differences between the types of employees needed by two different kinds of health spa. You probably discussed the atmosphere in your place as "family-like" or "friendly" and your prospective employees as "high-caliber"

210

or "superior" or, at least, "better than average." That's all very nice. But these statements hardly classify as operational considerations. It will be your job, in this section of your work, to give these vague notions some concrete reality.

To do this, you will have to take a hard look at the skills and qualities you need/want in your personnel. This is the relatively easy part. You will then have to figure out how you are going to get such people, train them, build them into a team, and keep them—all as a new company with very little money and few other attractions (unless you count your sterling personality, which does not pay the bills).

In addition to finding the people, you will have to organize them and determine who has how much authority and responsibility—and who supervises whom. You will also have to structure performance reviews, salary systems, and career paths for your employees. Building an employee-based business is very much like developing an instant family—with you as its sole head and truly responsible party. It is exciting and scary. But most of all, it is hard work.

The remainder of this chapter is intended to raise most of the questions you will need to address in your personnel activities. It is impossible for any such chapter to be exhaustive, because people—being people—are always coming up with new considerations. But it will help you through the basics and help you to avoid some of the more common mistakes. Moreover, it will help you to begin to think about people issues in concrete terms.

DEFINING YOUR OWN RESPONSIBILITIES

But first, a word about your job. New entrepreneurs generally go to one of two extremes with respect to their own functions within their fledgling operations. Either they expect to be able to do the entire job virtually single-handedly, or they believe that they are going to sit at a big mahogany desk with their feet up and play "boss." Either of these notions is likely to do your business in.

If you attempt to do everything, two things are likely to occur. First, things will start to slip through the cracks. Nobody is capable of keeping track of everything over long periods. Second, you are likely to be so anxious over handling all the details of everything that the big picture goes. You will be unable to develop an overall sense of where the business is, where it should be, where it is going. All long-range considerations can be consumed in the day-to-day operational details. Neither outcome is particularly desirable from the perspective of the business as a growing entity.

If, on the other hand, you want to play "boss," find yourself a large corporation and rise to the point at which you really do not have to do any more work. Then you will have minions to do your bidding, within a framework structured by others—and a president or other superior officer on whom to dump much of the responsibility. Do *not* start your own company.

If you do start your own company, you will be the one who is responsible for all serious decisions—including such major items as solving disputes among employees, dealing with the distributor who never puts enough cans of Coke in the machine in the employees' rest area, etc. If you believe that you are "too good" for such minor work, stay corporate. These things, believe it or not, can sink a small new company. They will, therefore, be of major concern to you as the owner/operator of one.

Your job within your company needs to be a well-thought-out mix of big issues and critical details. It should not just happen to you, however. Your job, like the jobs of your prospective employees, should result from thought about what needs to be done and analysis about how best to get it done. Just because, for example, you have heard that entrepreneurs should keep in close touch with the financial results of their businesses, do not decide to do the books yourself. You may be neither interested in playing with the numbers nor the best qualified person to do the job. (This does not mean that you should not know how books should be done or that you should not understand fully the meaning of what the numbers tell you as a manager, but only that doing the actual bookkeeping may not be the best use of your time and money.) In short, your job description should flow naturally from your analysis and from the lists of what functions need to be performed to get your product or service to your customer.

WHAT HAS TO BE DONE?

Once you have outlined your main scope of work, the next step in your personnel planning is to determine exactly what it is that will have to be done in your company. The level of detail here is critical. It is very easy to visualize the "front" of the operation and to overlook the "behind-the-scenes" work. For example, who, in your restaurant, is going to haul away the dirty dishes? Load the dishwasher? In your health club, who will pick up the used towels that your members insist on strewing all over the place? You are responsible for deciding whose jobs these items are parts of—and, therefore, whether they get done in the right way or at all.

One of the easier ways to begin your personnel planning, then, is to develop a list of the tasks that will have to be done—all of them—in the business as you envision it. Think about all the steps that have to be done to get your product or service to your client or customer. For a very simple retail operation, the list might look like this:

1. Purchase (and pay for) appropriate goods.

2. Accept delivery of goods. Check invoices against purchase orders. Log in goods.
3. Place goods in their appropriate places on the shelves.
4. Check once a day (twice? more often?) to ensure that all goods are where they belong. Replace items that have been moved. Ensure that shelves and goods on shelves are neat and orderly.
5. Assist customers in finding the goods to whatever extent is appropriate in the business.
6. Ring up and log sales.
7. Maintain inventory records.
8. Tally cash, checks, charge slips, with logged amounts.
9. Take cash, etc. to bank (with required paperwork).

Now, obviously, these tasks do not all have to be performed by the same person. In fact, it is unlikely that you will want the person who stocks the shelves to also be responsible for bank deposits. This list also focuses on the customer, omitting such behind-the-scenes operations as purchasing and bookkeeping. But even given this brief list, you can see that you need a mixture of skill and experience levels to get the whole thing running smoothly. Your next step is to allocate the tasks on your list to the jobs you intend to fill.

Using your own list, start with the tasks that you believe are critical enough to the business that you want to do them yourself (assuming, of course, that you are capable of performing those tasks efficiently and well). In the list above, those tasks might be 1, 2, 7, 8, and 9. If you are planning a simple, effective inventory control system, you might be able to give up task 7 to a senior-level employee (if you're planning to hire one or train one). You might also consider giving up task 2 to such an employee, if your business does not require that experienced judgment of quality be brought to the acceptance of incoming merchandise.

Note that, by giving up a task, you really give up only the first-level responsibility for it. If the shop merchandise is a mess at noon, and an employee was supposed to straighten it up at 11:30, you are not compelled to ignore the mess because it is not your job. The issue is whether you are supposed to do the straightening in the first instance, rather than seeing to it that somebody else does it. Ultimately, of course, you are responsible for the whole show. After all, it's your show.

Building Job Descriptions

Once you have decided what you are going to do on your lists, you can begin to group the other tasks into beginning job descriptions. Your first consideration should be the skills required to perform each task. Your second series of thoughts should include whether the people you want for one task will be willing to perform other tasks that you believe they might do. For example, if you need suave, experienced waiters, will they also clear tables—even though it is obvious that they are perfectly *able* to do so?

The point here is that defining jobs is only partly an exercise in pure logic. Jobs have this funny habit of involving people. And it is best to learn now that people often have strange notions of what they should and should not be required to do. If people don't like a job description—no matter how rational it seems to you—you will have trouble filling the job. You do not need to begin with built-in difficulties. It is wise, therefore, to consider generally accepted job descriptions as you develop your own.

Skills groupings or basic skills are the underlying requirements of the jobs you will be offering to potential employees. Do you need people with manual dexterity? With the ability to deal with numbers? With good communications skills? Work backwards from your lists to develop basic skills lists for each of the task groupings you have developed. Suppose, for example, that you are beginning a local package delivery service. Part of your task/skills table might look like the one shown in Table 10.1.

Table 10.1 Sample task/skills table

Task Group	*Job Title*	*Basic Skill Requirements*
Pickup		Driving (appropriate license)
Delivery	Driver	Bondable
Collection		"Personable"
Scheduling		Good with maps
Route design	Dispatcher	Good on phone and radio
Dispatching		
Cash concentration		Good with numbers
Petty cash	Bookkeeper	Familiar with bank requirements
Bank deposits		
Bank reconciliations		

When you start looking for people to fill these jobs, the items on the right are those that you put in the newspaper ad or that you tell people who might be in contact with the people you are looking for. You also outline any specific qualifications you want—like the license type for the driver, or a college degree, or a specific level of experience. Such specific requirements are supposed to guarantee that the qualities you seek will be present in your candidate. As we read more about functionally illiterate high school graduates, please consider this assumption very carefully before you base your hiring decision on paper qualifications.

Training

When you have reached the point of making a task/skills table, you also have a series of choices. The main one is whether you want to or can afford to buy employees with experience. Your alternative is finding people with the basic skills or basic characteristics and training them for your jobs. This, of course, presumes that you know enough to train them. While experience is often expensive, do not assume that by training people you will buy their undying loyalty. It is unlikely that you will.

In a classic example of the hazards for the trainers of training people, there is a small city with a two-tier economy. In the second tier, there are a number of small machine shops. The city is dominated by a single large employer that also hires machinists, but at wages well above those the small companies can afford. These small companies are essentially the training ground for the dominant employer. When the dominant employer is in a slump, all the small firms have ample, well-trained labor. Their productivity rises. When the giant is expanding, it is difficult for the small firms to even find anyone to train. Loyalty does not buy food or clothing.

The moral of this story is that, even if you are prepared to train your new employees, do not expect to get away with paying below the market rate for experienced personnel for very long. Remember that you are creating experienced personnel. They can and will sell that experience to a competitor when it becomes reasonable for them to do so. That's why they took your job at such low rates in the first place.

In yet another way, paying lower wages and training personnel may be more costly in the long run than buying experience initially. Training takes time and effort on the parts of both you and the employee. Until your employees know what they are doing, they are unlikely to be as efficient as they theoretically could be. This lack of efficiency could cost you in lost production and/or in disgruntled customers. Furthermore, if your plan calls for constant training and low wages, you have to be prepared for this cycle of inefficiency to continue indefinitely as employee turnover continues.

If your particular business can stand the turnover and the inefficiency, then, by all means, try training inexperienced help. But do set up a formal, structured training program with clear goals for each employee. Review your trainees regularly and formally. And give them clear signals about their longer term prospects with the company. (But be aware that even the fast-food restaurants, long a training ground for the totally inexperienced, are now moving toward programs of raises and awards designed to cut employee turnover rates of as high as five times a year. Even they cannot handle it.) A good compromise might be to train your first crew, or part of your first crew, and plan to move them fairly rapidly to a going market rate for more skilled practitioners of whatever it is they are doing.

For some businesses, training is not a particularly difficult activity. If you have some experienced people, it may simply be a matter of careful on-the-job training—assigning an experienced person to watch over and direct the activities of a trainee. You may have to be that experienced person, however. Keep in mind that even the most efficient dynamo can only be in so many places at once. There is, therefore, a limit to the number of people that you can train in this way.

In some kinds of businesses, the manufacturer of your equipment may provide some training on their equipment. While that can be of great help, you will still have to fit those new skills into the patterns of operation of your new business. Therefore, you do not get off the hook entirely.

In short, training an entire staff will probably overburden your new operation, which is penny-wise and pound-foolish. Molding a team is difficult enough without also building the players. Obviously, if your operation has no real parallels, you have no choice but to train, but try at least to buy some basic skills in the marketplace. Even beyond the training issues, you really want to have at least a few people around that you can trust professionally— just in case you catch the flu or have to go out of town.

How Many in Each Job Category?

Having just determined what skills you need, you next need to decide how much of each skill you will need to do the volume of business you expect in the first few months. Do not assume peak efficiency for your first few months, even if you plan to hire fully trained, experienced people. Your business represents a new team. It takes time for a team to learn to work most efficiently together. Keep in mind all the missed cues and broken plays in such all-star games as the Pro Bowl or a North-South game. All the players are good—the best, in fact—but the teamwork is lacking.

In some businesses, there are some guidelines on how many employees you should expect to have given the level of business you intend to do. In retail operations, you can usually get to an average number for sales per employee. This number may already be in your industry average data. It may also be in the notes you've taken from earlier discussions with industry people and suppliers.

Failing these simple sources, the federal government can provide some assistance at a very aggregate level. The Department of Labor's Bureau of Labor Statistics (BLS) collects data on wages and hours by industry (SIC) in many areas. Although their data-gathering has been sharply curtailed in recent years due to budget cuts, they may have the data you need to estimate an output per employee number in your industry. The Census of Business for your industry grouping will also give you assistance along these lines. Essentially, in both cases, you will be dividing some output measure by the number of employees in a given category.

BLS data, if it exists for your field/area, has two advantages over census data. First, because BLS data is used for labor-related policymaking, it tends to be more up-to-date than census data. Second, since the BLS focuses on labor, the breakdown of labor categories tends to be better. Using Census of Manufactures data, for example, you can get only "production workers" and "value added" as your number of employees and your output measures, respectively. You would divide value added by number of production workers to get an average amount of value added for each production worker.

Using this kind of data in conjunction with your own beliefs about how and how fast things should get done around your shop, you can come to an

FEATURE 10.1
Leasing Your Employees

It sounds like an odd thing to do—leasing your workers rather than hiring them and handling their payroll yourself. It is, however, one of the most recent ways developed for giving everyone a better deal. Here's the way it works.

You simply transfer your employees to the books of the leasing company. (In some cases, you have to fire them so that the leasing company can hire them immediately.) You have just lost a great deal of paper work—payroll, benefits data, tax calculations, and the like. Your employees get a much better deal. They get the same salary, but they have access to a much wider range of benefits because the leasing company can make volume deals with insurers while you cannot. Moreover (and not necessarily to your advantage), an employee does not have to quit to change jobs. He or she can simply transfer to another leasing company client.

You still retain the power to hire, fire, and give raises and promotions to those who work for you. Nothing is changed in the working relationship. All that changes are the costs. The leasing company is paid a percentage of payroll—often around 30 percent. This figure includes employer taxes and workers' compensation. This, plus the reduced costs of providing employee benefits, plus the savings from reduced paperwork, may make the ultimate figure a saving for the small business owner.

By some estimates, there are more than 24 employee-leasing companies, handling 20,000 workers. The numbers are growing rapidly.

Adapted from "Boom in Worker Leasing," *Newsweek* (May 14, 1984); "Employees: To Hire or Contract," *Venture* (August 1984):33; and "Company Leases Instead of Hiring Workers," *Patriot Ledger* (Quincy, Mass., July 13, 1984):12.

estimate of how many people you need to hire for each job category. Suppose, for example, you are planning a bookstore. Your industry data tells you that the average bookstore has 5.3 employees (including the owner) and that each does an average of $57,414 per year in business. In the bookstores in which the employees are most productive, each employee produces $62,712 per year in sales.

You are aiming for peak sales productivity (and you are developing incentives to help you reach that goal—more on that later in this chapter). You know, however, that peak is unlikely in the first months of your operation. You figure that $60,000 per employee per year is a fine goal. Your sales budget (See Chapter 15) indicates that in the first six months you will sell $100,000 worth of merchandise. You therefore should have 3.4 people ($100,000 / 60,000 × 2). If you intend to work as a full-time sales person in your bookstore, you would subtract 1 from this number. If you were planning to work half-time in sales (and the rest in administration, etc.) you would subtract half an employee. (Note: In most businesses, you can hire part-time people. In some cases, two half-time people have been shown to be more productive than one full-timer. There's less time for boredom to set in....)

A final note is necessary on the numbers of people you really need to run your business. Two impulses tend to war within entrepreneurs at this point. There is a feeling of importance that comes with having large numbers of employees. This encourages a tendency to over-hire. The conflicting impulse is to cut costs by under-hiring. The above method should temper both impulses, but it helps to be aware that they exist.

If you are likely to err in one direction or another (you do not believe that your estimates are really very sound, for example), consider erring on the side of under-hiring. If business booms, or if your initial estimates were low, it is relatively easy to add a person. Firing someone, however, is likely to be one of the more difficult things you will get to do as an owner (or a manager, for that matter).

BUYING LABOR IN THE MARKET

As noted earlier, acquiring your personnel is costly in both time and money. In many kinds of businesses, the cost of labor is the main continuing cost of doing business. You have already figured out what kinds of people you need and how many of each kind you need to make your business work in its first six months. In this section, we will discuss how to define them, find them, hook them, and bring them on board—no mean feat for a small company with no track record and (probably) very little money.

The key notion in all of this is the market for labor in your area. If, for

example, your supermarket is in an area where there are numerous unem-
ployed meat-cutters (say a large supermarket chain has recently closed), then
you will have an easier time finding and hiring good meat-cutters. You will
probably also have to pay them less than you would if you were in a market in
which there was great demand for meat-cutters. You would probably also have
a more difficult time hiring quality in a tighter market. After all, you'd be the
new kid in town.

The market for labor in your area obviously depends on what you are
looking for. If you consider the three basic skill levels at which you might
hire—specialized/skilled, semi-skilled and unskilled—you will see that it is
quite likely that there will be three different labor markets with which you
might be concerned. And the three markets are not necessarily even similar.
There may, for example, be numerous students available to provide the
unskilled services you need. Assuming that you don't particularly care about
turnover in these positions, you should have little trouble hiring for your
"gofer-type" jobs at about minimum wage.

If you choose this route, please be aware that your low-level jobs are
unlikely to feed into the remainder of your jobs. A stockboy is unlikely to
mature into a meat or produce man. He is more likely to go away to college or
get a "real job." Both you and he will think of the job in short-term terms. He
will want to leave it behind. You will not invest in training for the future, since
there normally would be no future associated with the job.

If, on the other hand, you view your lower-level jobs as training grounds for
your mid- or upper-level jobs, you have really changed labor markets. You will
be competing in the lower ranges of the higher category. You will be looking
for a "produce department trainee" (or some such title), rather than for a
"stockboy" for your supermarket. It will cost you more on the front end in
dollars and benefits. And you have also committed to train the employee and
move him up—if everything works out well for both of you.

How to Find the People You Need

Depending on your choices about the people you are looking for, finding
people to talk to is relatively simple. Actually, the trick is trying to target the
people you want in advance, to whittle down the number of people you have to
see to those most likely to fulfill your requirements.

There are a number of ways to do this. If you are looking for either
unskilled people or highly skilled people, one way to find them is to tell all your
friends that you are looking. Then you will be seeing people who are known to
somebody you know—a definite advantage in terms of general trustworthiness. If you try this with mid-level, fairly undefined jobs, however, you
are likely to see (and have to turn down) your Aunt Harriet's cousin's best
friend. Use this method with care.

Local schools and colleges can be good sources of at least semi-screened candidates for your jobs. The people in schools who handle jobs are concerned about their reputations within the local business community. They are therefore likely to be reasonably careful about who they send you.

An ad in the local paper is a tried and true method. If, however, you are in an area with more people than jobs (most of them, today), be prepared for a deluge of people you definitely do not want to talk to. A way around having to actually see these people is to use a box number at the paper. This is relatively inexpensive and can save you a lot of time on the phone or in person. Do, however, make a point of at least answering any applicant. I suspect we have all been in the position of writing to some company only to hear absolutely nothing. If I know the company, I never do business with them again.

If you do not mind paying for the service, you can actually use an employment agency to do your screening for you. The cost, these days, is usually borne by you, although you may find a deal in which the applicant pays the agency fee. Fees vary, but can run up to a third of the annual salary of the person you hire through the agency. You make the final decisions. The agency simply does a thorough screening for you, including reference checks.

Depending on your jobs, reference checks can be a very serious issue. According to numerous current reports, more and more people are giving false credentials to potential employers. Remember the Pulitzer prize winner whose paper withdrew her prize because she was not who she said she was nor did the story happen quite as she told it. NBC News reported, on February 25, 1984, about a man who was selling fake medical credentials. Hospitals are beginning to find these fake physicians practicing in their operating rooms. If experience or past history really may matter in your jobs, definitely check references. You might just want to know whether a candidate tells the truth.

Before you sit down to talk to a job candidate, review your lists and fix in your head where the job fits into your developing organization. Consider those qualities and skills you listed as vital to the position and those you are willing to teach. It is entirely fair for you to count whether you personally like a candidate or not. You are not starting a General Motors-sized operation and you will be working closely with all your employees. You have the right to at least like them. Just be careful not to let the fact that you like someone blind you to a total lack of the skills you considered vital before you met this person.

What Do You Have to Offer?

Once you find a person that you want to have on your team, you get to try to convince that person to join up. It is assumed that, while you made your job sound attractive during the interview, you did not lie about the nasty details. Every job has them. Any serious applicant expects them. Hiding them simply means that if you win (acquire the candidate) you lose. The candidate, now your employee, feels cheated, is angry, and may leave—as much because you didn't tell the straight story as for any other reason. Who wants to work for someone who opens with a lie or a very partial truth?

So we can assume that your prospect knows what the job is really like. We can also assume that she found you a basically agreeable person. (If you liked her, chances are she also liked you reasonably well.) Now, you two get down to brass tacks. Besides the above, what do you and your job have to offer to the candidate?

As a small, new business, you really have limited offerings. Someone who takes a job with you does not get the instant respect—or even recognition—that her friends get when they say they work for General Electric or IBM or any other "name" company. She will be forever explaining what she does and for whom. Also, you probably cannot come up with the salary dollars that such a large company could offer to a really hot prospect.

But don't quit now. This is simply another area of competition. People do go to work for small companies. Consider, in fact, some of the reasons you are not going to be in a large corporation. Think about what you can offer to potential employees along these lines first. And think about the risks of joining you from their points of view. (Clearly, if you are filling "gofer" jobs, you can compete with everyone else almost directly. These are minimum-wage, no-experience, no-real-future types of jobs. This section relates to your mid- and upper-level positions.)

Your hot prospect may well be working for someone else. He is thinking about whether you will still be around in a year. He does not want to leave a job that offers some security for one that offers little or none. You can sell him on your basic concept, but people are generally very conservative. You may not be able to address this concern directly, but you need to be aware that it will (should) be there in your negotiations.

And hiring is often a negotiation. If you deal with it as such, you will have developed a list (not necessarily on paper) of what your bargaining chips look like. Entirely apart from any goodies that your specific business may allow you to offer (discounts on much-wanted products, contacts with the high and mighty, etc.), you may have a number of significant advantages over a large firm in hiring. Some of these are noted in Feature 10.2.

Please note that just because you have these items in your arsenal does not mean that you have to throw them into the pot. Use what you think it will take to add this wonderful candidate to your staff. You can always add others later in your discussions or as the person works out well in your organization, if you want or have to. And always keep asking yourself whether this particular person is really worth to you what you are offering to get her. Do not get so caught up in the negotiation and in the prospect of "winning" that you forget what you started out to do—hire someone to fill a specific position.

FEATURE 10.2

Advantages of Working for a Smaller Company

1. Your size permits you to offer:
   a. The potential for learning and understanding an entire operation, rather than just a department or a unit of a company.
   b. More responsibility and authority than is likely in a large company given the same age, experience, etc.
   c. A closeness among all levels and people in the workplace.
   d. More flexibility in hours, times, job specifics, etc.
2. Your growth potential permits you to offer:
   a. A *real* shot at bigger and better things (advancement). Fast.
   b. Real participation in *building* a business.
3. Your ownership permits you to offer:
   a. Equity participation (very carefully, in small doses, to very special employees when there's no other way to get them and you really need them).
   b. Profit-sharing programs.

Wages and fringes (or salary and benefits). When you consider personnel issues, it is easy to forget that, in addition to the actual amount you will be sending home with the employee every week (month), you will have other costs as well. There are certain state and federal payroll taxes, for example. And there are the costs of whatever fringe benefits you want to or have to offer to compete in your labor market.

The basic wage package is the fairly easy part. To determine what the going wage for a job is, you can go back to your statistics (BLS and census). These will give you very rough averages. Then, check your local paper for the offering prices of various jobs in your area and industry. (Yes, read the want ads. You need to know who your competition is and what they are offering.)

When you have decided on what you are prepared to pay your new hire(s), add 6.3 percent of that to the tab to cover the employer's contribution to Social Security. You will also need to add whatever is required in your state for your contribution to unemployment funds. This differs from state to state, as do the requirements that you pay. Payment is generally based on whether your work force exceeds a generally small number of employees. The rate at which you must pay is often determined by your track record in employee turnover (which you don't have yet). Check with your state division of employment.

A major issue is fringe benefits. These are expensive and, once they have been instituted, are very difficult to take back. To be competitive in many job categories, you may well have to provide some kind of health insurance plan (see Chapter 8). If you are considering this, talk with some of your local business or trade associations. Because this insurance is particularly expensive for smaller companies, many associations have developed group plans through which the employees of their members may be insured. Even given the membership dues, this kind of arrangement usually proves to be a good deal.

Employee taxes and benefits are often quoted as a percentage of gross salaries. These figures, naturally, differ across industries and by region. Let's assume that a person's gross salary is $10,400, taxes of various types on employers on this amount are $936, and your contribution to the employee's health benefit plan is $1,200. Your total compensation cost for this employee would be $12,536. If you add another 10 days of pay for sick time and holidays ($410), your total cost for this employee would be about $13,000. Her fringe benefit package is worth about 30 percent of salary.

Along with wages and fringes go terms of employment. Taken strictly, this includes such items as the understanding that working conditions will be reasonable, buildings reasonably warm, all possible safety precautions taken, etc. Used more loosely, terms include such items as salary and performance reviews, raises, and promotions—the expectations based on which the person agreed to come to work for you. Never give an employee reason to believe that the deal on reviews and raises is different from what it actually is. Disappointment is a key cause of turnover. And when the disappointment stems from misinformation that you give or imply, you deserve the problems that come with the turnover.

Initial formal reviews for employees are generally performed within the first three to six months of employment. This does not mean that you only discuss an employee's performance at review time. Particularly given the size of your new organization, it is more likely that you and your employees will be discussing how it is all going almost constantly. (Listen to what they are saying. They may see a vital thing that you don't.) It does mean that reviews and raises should be formal procedures. Their times should be planned for by each employee and by you.

Insofar as possible, given the status of your very new company, the criteria by which you intend to judge the performance of a specific employee should be clear to that employee at all times. This not only helps the employee to perform well, but it also makes it easier for you to plan and to evaluate performance. If necessary, write down the requirements, measures, and criteria. If it is feasible, enlist the employee in defining his own goals, measures, and criteria.

The only other major requirement of your performance review system is that your employees perceive it as a fair system. If Charlie Fahrquardt, who everyone knows does as little as is humanly possible while still remaining ambulatory, consistently gets the same raise as Jon Straight, you are going to be in trouble very shortly. Under those circumstances, why should anybody do any work?

And a note of caution about fairness and employee perceptions of fairness. It seems to be virtually impossible to keep salary data confidential. Even in cases in which flat prohibitions against discussing salaries exist, employees tend to know pretty well what everyone is making. Therefore, in your hiring and promoting, you need to remain aware of where each employee ranks with

FEATURE 10.3
On the Value of Written Personnel Policies

In 1982 there were 10,000 employment-related civil rights cases filed with the U.S. District Courts. At the state level, California alone hears more than 8,000 such cases. It is becoming clearer that courts are perfectly willing to overturn management judgments if they can be convinced that a person has been treated unfairly. Such legal judgments, or out-of-court settlements, can be costly in money and time, particularly to small companies that have very little of either commodity. The key to not letting this happen to you lies in clear, well-documented, uniformly applied personnel policies.

We suspect that you are now saying what these small business owners said:

"This is somewhat of a social place, where people know each other very well." "You can't show me an entrepreneur who has built a fast-growth business who is concerned with formal policies. He wants to sell product." "If we didn't have to bother with writing all these documents, we could be doing what we're supposed to do—growing our business." All these companies have been sued on employment-related grounds. The dominant response has been, "How can this be? It's as though a member of my family wants to sue me." And then they start reviewing and rewriting their personnel policies.

At very least, lawyers say, you should put anti-discrimination guidelines and a grievance procedure in place. There should also be a performance evaluation system with progressive discipline measures to support promotion or termination decisions. The cost of an evaluation, say the lawyers, would be about $500. The cost of a suit, on the other hand, can be more than $85,000.

"Having policies in place creates the perception—and the reality—that you've made an attempt at fair play. It protects you from frivolous charges."

Adapted from Sid Kane, "Your Right to Fire," *Venture* (October 1983):36; and Ellen Kolton, "An Ounce of Prevention," *Inc.* magazine (October 1984):153.

respect to others in the company. If two people with essentially the same job are earning two very different amounts, there is likely to be a problem. Ensure from the outset that this does not occur. If you have paid dearly for a specific person who will bring something special to your company, make certain that it is clear that this person is making more because of extra or different work or because of special job-related abilities.

A word about unions.   Most new companies will not have to deal with unions immediately. If your company is in the minority that is likely to be unionized from the outset, many of the issues discussed above will be essentially irrelevant to you. The union will have developed the job categories and the wage scales and the fringe benefit package. All you really have to do is to say how many bodies you need and to pay up regularly. You will, of course, have to address these issues with respect to your non-union staff. (If it is your fondest desire to remain non-union in an essentially unionized industry, this is not the book for you. Call your lawyer for referral to a management-oriented labor lawyer. And be prepared to pay a lot.)

WHO'S MINDING THE STORE?

A story told by Stanley Marcus, of Nieman-Marcus fame, raises the final set of issues relating to hiring and shaping the staff of your operation.[1] It has to do with an old merchant, literally on his deathbed. His children had all gathered at his bedside to be with him. He supposedly opened his eyes, looked around, and said "I appreciate your interest in the state of my health, but who's minding the store?" While this story may be apocryphal, the issue is very real for all entrepreneurs. If you can't or don't want to be there, who will mind the store?

This goes directly to the issue of how you structure your team. You should, despite your initial size, be building a hierarchy. It should really be a three-team team. Team One is the top management team. You are there, of course, but so are other key staff members. Who is in this group will depend in part on your own skills and abilities. If you are marvelous at marketing and not so hot at numbers, you should already have hired a numbers person. She should be part of Team One. In short, this is the prime group of decision makers—and those to whom other employees can bring relevant problems.

Team Two is really an advisory team. This group would include your lawyer, accountant, and banker. It will also include any members of your board of directors who have any special knowledge to contribute to your operation. In fact, you should choose board members with just such expertise in mind. These are the people to whom *you* can bring *your* problems.

Finally, there is everybody else—Team Three. This group will benefit most from some standard hierarchical structure. It is comforting to most people to know where to go with difficulties and who to see for directions. Your structure does not need to be rigid as it would be in a giant outfit, but it needs to be there. Everyone needs to know who is in charge when you are not there. Everyone needs to know who to bring problems to first (unless you really want to handle *all* the details).

Developing a layered set of responsibilities does two major positive things. First, it allows you to delegate some of the work to someone you have hired or trained for that purpose. Second, it creates someplace for your employees to go within the company. A waiter, for example, could aspire to be a headwaiter, in either your current restaurant or in an expansion restaurant. He would not have to leave you to gain advancement. And you would not have to train a new person in your ways of doing things.

FEATURE 10.4
Getting Employees Involved in Your (Their) Company

Suggestion System

EFCO Corp, a Missouri maker of aluminum windows offers cash for employee suggestions that work to save the company time or money. Checks have ranged from $50 to $500. The program costs the company $2,000 a year, which it claims to recoup many times over.

President Terry Fuldner cites one recent case in which a foreman came up with a slight change in window design. He got $500. The company is saving $8,000 a year.

Adapted from John F. Persinos, "Ideas You Can Use," *Inc.* magazine (August 1984):103.

Gain-Sharing

Employees of Pontiac Foundry in Indiana are tied directly to how productive they are in manufacturing the company's products. They share in the gains that their work produces. This is not the same as profit-sharing, which is based on the company's bottom line. It is calculated, rather on the sales value added by the labor. If labor costs are below a certain percentage (the average over the past five years) the saving is distributed to the hourly employees. Office workers also get checks in proportion (20%) to their representation in the company.

The program appears to be working. Employees are taking home more. Pontiac's labor costs have stabilized. There is 30% less scrap in the operation. Management pays for significantly less overtime. Pontiac claims that there is a new spirit of teamwork and concern across the company.

Adapted from Ellen Wojahn, "'Gainfully' Employed," *Inc.* magazine (December 1983):150.

Obviously, it is best from your perspective if your second-in-command is a relative or a close friend. This practice, however, sends signals to your employees of which you should be aware. They know that they will never get to be president—unless you have elderly or sickly children. Unless you grow very rapidly, creating lots of expansion slots, this may turn off some potential talent. There is also always the fear—and often the reality—that Cousin Jack, who is a real idiot, will be taken into the business and some employee will become responsible for his inabilities (which are probably considerable).

This is not added to dissuade you from setting up a real business organization—one that will work even without you for a time. It is, rather, to alert you to what your employees will think, depending on who you slot into the truly responsible positions in your company. A good rule of thumb is to try to see what your employees will be seeing whenever you make a major personnel-related decision. It will give you a chance to pull back or at least to take reasonable preventive measures before you act. Your employees, remember, are people pretty much like you. Only they don't own the place.

SUMMARY

Personnel decisions are among the most difficult you will have to make throughout your career as an entrepreneur (or a manager, for that matter). If you do it right the first time, you will minimize your difficulties over the longer term. Your first job is to determine what skills and abilities and special knowledge you will need to run your operation. You will probably find that there are three levels at which you need help: Low (essentially without special skills), medium (with some skills, but with skills that are relatively easy to train for), and high (with very clear, relevant skills, abilities, and experience).

You may decide that you are the only high-level person you need just now. But be sure that your job has a job description and some limits that are thought out before you start. If you just let your job evolve, it is entirely likely that you may not like the result—or you may find yourself with an impossible job.

Once you have determined what you need, you have to determine how much of each type of skill you need. Using industry data, observation, and some imagination can help you to work backwards from the amount of business you intend to do to reach a number of employees needed in each category. Erring on the side of hiring too few people will minimize your hassle and allow for relatively easy corrections later on.

Having determined the numbers, you have to go out and find them and convince them to work for you. While you are unlikely to be able to offer huge pots of money to attract top staff, you do have the advantages of a smaller company with lots of potential for growth. If necessary, you can offer increased responsibility and authority, profit-sharing, and even equity participation to selected employees. By definition, you can offer a greater scope in your operation and a greater closeness and unity of purpose.

But people generally work at least partly for money. You must also structure a salary scheme that keeps you in the ball park in the competition for the labor you need. You must have a structured, clear approach to performance evaluation and salary increases. You will also have to pay various payroll-related taxes, and you may have to offer such fringe benefits as health insurance. Your system, whatever it is, must be perceived as fair by your employees.

FOR YOU TO CONSIDER

1. Once you have decided what you want your operation to "feel" like, how do you begin to turn that into concrete hiring decisions?
2. Besides what you want to be a part of a job you are defining, what else should you consider? Why?
3. What two tendencies appear as new entrepreneurs think about their own jobs in their organizations? Why should each be avoided?
4. What can a task/skills table do for you in your personnel planning?
5. Discuss the advantages and disadvantages of training your personnel from scratch. Choose one kind of business in which training might be the best way. Describe another in which training would not be a feasible approach to staffing the business.
6. How should you determine how many employees you need?
7. List three ways of finding potential job candidates. What are the advantages and disadvantages of each approach?
8. How should you determine what to offer a potential employee by way of wages, fringe benefits, and other inducements? Discuss your advantages and disadvantages as a small company in this hiring process.
9. Why should you structure a hierarchy in your company—despite the fact that this form of organization is one of the things you dislike about large companies?
10. What are the critical factors of your performance evaluation and salary review systems if you want them to work well for your company?

NOTES

1. Stanley Marcus, *Minding the Store* (New York: Signet, 1974):103.

FOR FURTHER READING

Bank of America. "Personnel Guidelines," *Small Business Reporter,* 1981.

Small Business Administration publications:

Checklist for Developing a Training Program. SBA MA 5.001.
Delegating Work and Responsibility. SBA MA 3.001.
Employee Relations and Personnel Policies. SBA 045-00000196-2.
Managing Employee Benefits. SBA MA 5.008.
Recruiting and Selecting Employees. SBA 045-000-00186-5.
Setting Up a Pay System. SBA MA 5.006.
Training and Developing Employees. SBA 045-000-00191-1.

CASES FOR PART 4

SALLY JONES AND "NEIGHBORS"

For Sally and Janice it was time to get down to the serious business of figuring out how "Neighbors" would actually work and what it would actually need. They had already decided that they wanted a 60-seat restaurant. They hoped to keep it fairly small and family-feeling. If the numbers could work out at that level, it would also minimize the help and the space they would need to open and run the place. Thus, costs would be low.

They began this phase of their work by determining their own respective roles in the venture. They figured that if they got this out of the way, each of the two could work independently on the operations requirements for her areas. This would minimize work—and probably produce better quality work since each would be operating from strength (or what it was hoped would soon become strength).

	Sally	**Janice**
Cooking	Soups, main dishes	Breads, desserts
Purchasing	Related foods	Related foods, staples, standard items
Administration	Bookkeeping, accounting	Personnel
Marketing	Advertising, promotion	Menu and logo design, art work

They already knew, using the average space requirement, how much space they would need: 60×20 for seating (1,200 square feet) plus about 500 square feet for the kitchen and other non-seating space. They could also use some additional storage area for non-spoiling inventory—canned items, paper goods, and the like. They found that most storefronts in their area would accommodate them nicely. This space would also be square (rectangular, actually) and therefore easy to work with. They might have their large, light windows after all.

Purchasing was a function they had split, but since Janice had personnel, Sally decided to handle purchasing. She began by considering the major categories of items they would need. She then sat down with the local Yellow Pages to find out which restaurant suppliers handled what. She requested price lists for relevant categories of items. She also asked them about their terms for new restaurants. Unfortunately, but predictably, she found only one or two distributors who would extend credit to them during their opening phase. She decided to concentrate on these suppliers, but not to rule out the others as yet.

Janice was having a bit more trouble. She started out by thinking about what jobs needed to be done in a restaurant. She came up with: cook or chef, waiter or server, bus person, reception/cashier. Then she thought about their intention to serve beer and wine. This would require still another person to be an almost-but-not-really bartender. The numbers of people/jobs really worried her.

She had seen numbers earlier that showed a 100-seat place using six to eight employees plus the owner. Scaled down, that meant four or five employees at "Neighbors" if only one owner worked at a time. Assuming five plus one, given the jobs required, there would be only two servers and one bus person for all 60 seats. And that included nobody to see to getting the dishes and pots washed, the garbage taken out, and other such tasks. Her staffing seemed a bit thin even to her untrained eye. Also, she noted that if only one of the women was going to work at a time, they would either have to hire a cook or trust some employee with the money. She didn't like either choice.

1. Comment on the division of labor that Sally and Janice have structured for themselves.
2. Has Sally approached the job of finding suppliers as you would have thought best? If not, explain how she should have done it and why your approach is better than hers.
3. Consider possible solutions to Janice's problems in determining personnel requirements for "Neighbors." Which solution(s) would you recommend to her? What might the consequences of your solution(s) be for "Neighbors"? Why do you believe that your solution(s) are the best way to go?

• • •

Together, Sally and Janice began to consider their equipment needs. Even using their rough data, they knew that there would be a lot of it and that it would be expensive. Their main issue, at this point in their planning, was not which specific items they needed—they expected to call in a consultant/specialist to help them there. Their concern lay, rather, in the most efficient approach to acquiring whatever specifics they needed. They knew that their choice here could be critical to the success of "Neighbors." In fact, they figured that most of the spread between high and low equipment prices on the *Small Business Reporter* list was due to the difference between new and used equipment.

Obviously, they decided, the best deal would be for them to find a site that had been a restaurant and would have some or all of the equipment still available for them to acquire and use. Failing that, they were leaning heavily toward buying used equipment. Janice talked about leasing some of the larger items, but Sally didn't think that, given the turnover in the restaurant business, there would be manufacturers or leasing companies that would lease restaurant equipment. Moreover, if they owned no major equipment, a bank would have absolutely nothing upon which to secure the loan that they hoped to get.

1. Comment on the assumption that the best deal for "Neighbors" would be to find a site with some or all equipment already in place.
2. Consider the tradeoffs between new and used equipment for "Neighbors." Which way would you recommend that they go and why?

3. Comment on each side of the leasing issue. Toward which set of arguments are you leaning? Why? Have you anything to add to either side of the discussion?

ROB KING AND "KING FINANCIAL"

Since Rob King's plans were for remaking his study into an office, he began to rearrange the room and his papers and books. He also began to consider the requirements of his prospective business. He knew, for example, that he would have to acquire a computer. A fairly sophisticated one would let him develop proposals, contracts, and reports with minimal secretarial help. It would also be essential for developing client financial statements and analyses efficiently.

Including the significantly expanded storage capacity he believed he would need, the entire system (hardware and software and peripherals) would cost him in the neighborhood of $9,000 or $10,000. He had looked into borrowing 80 percent of this amount and found that he could probably get a loan at 16 percent for three years. Alternatively, he could lease the system through a local leasing company at 14.5 percent for four years—if he was prepared to give up the tax benefits of ownership.

If he acquired the computer, he would not have to have a typewriter or a large-scale calculator. His current calculator would do just fine for his client visits. It was a quite respectable brand and vintage. He would, however, need an additional telephone line, since he could not see competing for telephone time with his wife and his kids as they moved into their teen years.

It was Rob's intention not to hire any staff on a full-time basis or even on a regular part-time basis for at least a year or two. This meant, in practice, that he would have to develop a group of freelancers that he could trust for jobs that would require extra manpower or special skills or knowledge. He should also have access to an occasional secretary (with her own typewriter) for times of overload. He had not yet decided what to do about keeping the books. He had already arranged with an accountant friend to check the books on a quarterly basis.

1. Should Rob buy or lease his computer system? Why do you recommend this approach?
2. Has Rob forgotten anything that he is likely to need to purchase or contract for his new business? What? Is this (are these) large expenses? How do you suggest he acquire what he needs?
3. Why do you think Rob has reached his primary conclusion about the personnel for King Financial? Do you believe he has chosen an appropriate approach to running his company? Why or why not?

DANIELLE MACKIE AND "DANIELLE DESIGNS IN CERAMICS"

At the same time as Danielle Mackie was beginning to get the formal part of her business in order, she also had to get into production and consider the structure of her business operations. She started by taking a good long look at her garage/studio/hideaway. In its present state, she knew it would never do as the studio/workroom of a professional. It had a number of major problems.

First, it was not wired adequately to handle a serious electric kiln. Second, there was no running hot water. While using the garden hose and carrying hot water from indoors was all right for the hobbyist, her permanent workplace would not operate smoothly with such a jury-rigged system. It would take too much time and would create unnecessary interruptions and delays. Finally, the place was too small. The difficulty was actually less the work space than it was lack of space to store raw materials and finished items prior to shipping. There was certainly no place to store packing materials, nor was there any space in which to do the actual packing.

This situation left Danielle with three main options. Unfortunately, none of them was The Perfect Solution. Moreover, each of them carried implications about the way she was going to do business. She decided that her best approach to making a decision would be to treat her current problem as a school "case." She would write down all the factors she could think of, and her best estimate of the costs associated with each option, and then she would reach a rational conclusion. Notebook in hand, Danielle Mackie began the process by stating each major option as follows:

1. Make the required alterations to her present work space.
2. Lease a separate workshop somewhere else in the area.
3. Lease or rent another living/working space that would meet her new requirements.

Two things occurred to her immediately, as she looked at her notes. First, she had blithely assumed that her landlady (not to mention the zoning board) would permit the level of activity she contemplated and the types of renovation she would need. She also had some question about whether it would make sense for her to have the work done, assuming she could get the required approvals. She was what they call a "tenant at will" in her present place. That meant, essentially, that either she or the landowner could terminate their rental agreement on a month's notice. She was extremely wary about spending money and setting up her business in a place in which she had such shaky tenure.

Second, and perhaps more important, she had really no idea of how much space she would need to operate the business she envisioned. She thought that the best approach to figuring it out might be to consider the dimensions of her major equipment. She knew she would need a wheel, a large work table, a kiln, some kind of glaze-spraying booth, and ventilation ducts to get rid of the chemicals released in the firing process and the glazing process. She might also want some of the heavier equipment used to mix clays and/or extrude them. She would also need storage space for her hand tools, for materials, for work in process, and for finished goods.

It also occurred to her that the total job, as she envisioned it, might be too large for her to handle entirely on her own. Particularly when making her production items, she thought that she might ask another potter or a student to help out. (She grinned as she saw how she was avoiding the notion of saying she might have to hire an assistant.) As her business grew, as she hoped it would, she knew that additional hands would be needed. She decided it would be wise to provide the space for at least some additional workers at the outset. Unless she was prepared to rebuild the garage, then, her current arrangement would not do at all. She crossed it out with a sigh.

Removing the stay-where-you-are option from consideration was a real blow to Danni. She really liked three things about her current arrangement—four, if you counted the low rental cost. First, she had to resign herself to the upset of a move—even if she only moved her ceramics activity. Second, she really liked her current ability to work whenever she felt either creative or energetic or both. Often, this mood struck her late at night or very early in the morning. She was afraid that the hassle of traveling to a workshop would actually reduce her desire to do the work. Finally, she saw herself as eventually showing people her work and her workshop in a reasonably rural, "craftsy" setting. Her current place fit that bill perfectly. She doubted that she could find another that would fit it as neatly.

As she analyzed her vision further, she recognized that she really saw herself as selling her work as she was working—no middlemen, no critics, no business hassle. She would get the same kinds of ego boosts periodically (often) that she had gotten at the show. Having recognized this, she tried to integrate her insight into her planning process. She started a new section, which she labeled:

Options for doing business

1. Sell goods to retailers (bulk items) and to galleries ("creative" pieces). If I do this, the only reason that it might matter where I work is my personal preference for easy access. The place doesn't need to be pretty or inviting. It can be just, well, commercial. Oh, and it needs to be easy for others to get to just in case I need help with the work.
2. Sell some goods (all goods?) out of the studio/shop. That way, I can still show off my things and work at the same time. It would still have to be convenient for workers, but it would also have to be pretty and inviting for customers or lookers. I'm sure that this kind of place will cost me a lot, but I might also be able to combine some kind of living arrangement with

this approach. I could not really do that with straight commercial space, and I have no desire to live in a warehouse. ...

She also realized that her choice between these options would have significant implications for how much space she needed. They might also have cost implications based on the existence or lack of the specific facilities she needed—the hot water, the venting, and the electrical service, to name just three.

She figured that if she ran a straight workshop—no frills, no living space—she would need about 1,500 square feet of space. If she added display space, and tried to make the workshop itself seem inviting, she would need about 2,500 square feet. Bringing in the electrical service she needed would cost only about $700—if the proper service was already available in the building she chose. It would cost about $1,500 if service had to be brought in from outside. Obviously, it would create no additional cost if the space she leased already had adequate service.

If there was water service, she might have to add a boiler and additional plumbing to meet her needs. She estimated that the cost would be close to $2,000 to have the work done properly by licensed contractors. She expected to have to add venting to almost any place she was likely to find.

Her current rent was $500 a month, for which she got 1,000 square feet of living space, plus the one-car garage that was now serving as her studio. On her wanderings to look at potential places to locate, she had found three that looked interesting. She could lease any of them for five years at the stated rates or amounts.

1. A vacant storehouse/warehouse in the downtown area. It was wired properly, probably because of the heavy equipment that had once moved whatever they used to store in it. The plumbing work would have to be done, however, along with the venting. The total space available was 1,500 square feet at $5 a square foot per year. The walls were bare and grimy.
2. An old carriage house in a suburban/rural area. It offered easy access to a state highway that ran north–south (mainly). The place had its own driveway and entrance. It had clearly been used as a garage and storage space, since it was plain, bare space. The carriage house was set in the trees. It was five miles from where she now lived. The owner offered to lease it to her for $350 a month. He also agreed to the use she planned for the carriage house, and to the renovations she would need to have made. The place would need upgraded electrical service, new piping to bring in hot water, and the ever-present venting system. It had about 2,000 square feet of usable space.
3. A rambling farmhouse with an almost-separate 2,000-foot ell off the kitchen. The ell had its own entrance. This was in definitely rural territory. The only thing that kept you from feeling as if you were in the middle of the fields and woods was the county road that ran in front of the place. It was, however, not far from a town that had a reasonable tourist popula-

tion in the summer and fall. It was also not far from a college that had an arts program. The place would require the electrical upgrade, the venting systems, and, Danni figured, some $1,000 worth of work in the ell to get it ready for use as a studio/shop. The owner would lease it to her for $900 a month.

1. Why might Mackie be avoiding the idea of hiring help in her new business? Which, if any, of these reasons are valid from a business viewpoint? Why? How do you recommend she handle the issue?
2. Develop an optimum approach to doing business for Danielle Mackie, given the needs she has outlined to this point. State the priorities you used in making the choices that you made for her. Why did you choose those priorities?
3. Given Danielle Mackie as you know her, and given the approach you just developed for her business, which of the three location options is best for her? If you don't like any of the three, describe the kind of place or places she needs and the price or prices she should be willing to pay. An unrealistic description (based on the information given in the text) is useless to her.
4. What more, if anything, does Mackie need to do before she makes a final decision about a place? If you listed some tasks, how do you recommend she go about accomplishing them? How should she use the results in making operating decisions for her business?

ED JAMES AND "OAK TREE BOOKS"

As Ed James began to get more fully involved with his bookstore plans, he began to consider the amounts and kinds of spaces he would need to accommodate his various proposed lines of business. He had decided, tentatively, to go with a basic bookstore, carrying popular hard-cover and paperback books, a semi-separate children's and young adults space, and a homework-help service line.

According to the American Booksellers' Association figures, the average square footage of selling space for a single-store bookseller selling $50,000 to $100,000 annually was 980 square feet. In the $100,000 to $150,000 range, selling space averaged 1,389. In the $150,000 to $300,000 range, selling space averaged 1,965 square feet. Total square footages were, respectively, 1,259, 1,682, and 2,355. Average sales in each of the three groupings were: $74,662, $121,970, and $202,365. Gross margins in the bookstore business ranged from 39 percent for the most profitable stores to 33 percent for the least profitable. According to the ABA data, the ability to reduce non-selling space as a percentage of total space was strongly related to the overall profitability of the bookstore.

Ed figured that he would need slightly more space than would otherwise be the case. He would first need sitting space for children and their parents in a section of the store that could be divided, visually, at least, from the main store. He would also need some space for a couple of telephones and some extra shelving on which to store the textbooks in use at the local schools for the help service. It would be particularly nice if he could figure out some way to shield these telephones from excess noise—without impairing the ability of the person on the phone to see what was going on in the store.

Unfortunately, space in his chosen area was rather expensive. Since he would be counting on foot traffic (at least in the beginning), however, good space was really a necessity. He expected to pay about $10 per square foot per year for minimally adequate space for his store. That would not put him directly in the square mall area. A space in the mall area itself would cost about $15 per square foot.

Given his intention to be more than your average, run-of-the-mill bookstore, he knew that he would have personnel requirements different, to some extent, from the average bookstore. He would also have to pay more to get the characteristics he really needed. Since he was setting himself out as a place specializing in children's books and in homework assistance, he would probably need people who parents would trust in helping to make decisions regarding their children's reading material. He, himself, was a teacher—"former teacher," he corrected himself with a grin. At least one other salesperson should probably be a former teacher. He hoped to find a retired elementary school teacher, someone who could complement his high school-level experience.

He also thought it would be a nice touch to have a teenager as an after-school member of the staff. This person would have to be a reader (which, Ed thought, might be no mean trick these days) who could recommend books to the young adult crowd.

Ed James had discovered two things about personnel in bookstores. First, he found that the average number of employees across all bookstores for the entire year was 5.27, including a working owner. The number was broken down into 1.77 full-time employees, 2.41 part-time employees, and 1.09 working owners, to be precise. He recognized that this average included the larger bookstores as well as those smaller than the one he contemplated.

The same ABA Profile told him that mid-range results for sales per employee ranged from $27,500 to $66,500. Interestingly enough, the highest sales-per-employee figure had been produced by the group that was in the middle range of profitability. Thus, profitability did not necessarily correlate with high per-employee sales. In his intended sales range, the figures looked as follows:

	Average	Mid-Range
$ 50,000–$100,000	$39,544	$28,965–52,906
$100,000–$150,000	49,537	38,877–62,261
$150,000–$300,000	62,377	43,177–64,333

He also knew that his bookstore would not have sales (or need help) precisely evenly throughout the year. The ABA Profile showed, for example, that, though the average bookstore used 5.27 employees based on the full year, the number of employees figured on a quarterly basis ranged from a high of 5.56 during the fourth (Christmas) quarter to a low of 5.13 in the second quarter.

Ed James now felt ready to begin planning his operation in some detail. He decided to develop an initial plan based on what he really wanted his bookstore to be like—except, of course, for the dark-panelled walls and comfortable chairs that he had already given up. Using this as an ideal, he could then determine where and how to cut back so as to do the least damage to his basic concepts. He knew, in his heart, that cutbacks would be necessary, so he also decided to develop priority items for cuts—a Priority One cut would be the least important item to him and, therefore, the first to go.

1. Determine how large a bookstore Ed James should be seeking. Draw (to the best of your ability) a layout that will provide the types(s) of spaces and environments that he needs. Be prepared to explain why you chose the amount of space and the layout you did. Make sure to consider the costs to Ed James of what you are recommending. (Keep in mind that he needs space in which to keep his inventory and his supplies—non-selling space.)
2. Develop an equipment list for the bookstore you have designed.
3. Comment on Ed James' staffing plans. If you believe that some other approach to staffing would be better or more cost-effective, describe your approach. For whichever approach you recommend, estimate what staffing Ed will require, how much it is likely to cost him, and how he should organize his sales staff (work hours, overlapping shifts, peak times, seasonal staffing, etc.).
4. Given what you know about Ed James, specify the items that should head his list of items to reduce or to cut. Explain clearly why you made the choices you did.

PART 5

GETTING INTO THE MARKET— AND STAYING IN

11. Getting the Word Out: Promotion

"George Washington Hill, the fabled tobacco tycoon, once remarked that half the money he spent on advertising was an utter waste. The only problem, he added, was he never knew which half."

New York Times Book Review

You would now, theoretically, be ready to open the doors of whatever operation you have been planning. You have your physical resources poised and ready. Your staff is hired and trained. You're all set. Except for one small detail. Nobody knows that you are about to do what you are about to do. To paraphrase an old line, "Suppose you throw a grand opening and nobody comes?" This chapter is designed to discuss ways of making as sure as possible that people show up—not only at your opening, but on a continuing basis.

Once you are clear about the operational aspects of your business, you can turn back to some of the issues we touched on earlier, in Chapters 4 and 5. Before you went ahead with your decision to work further on your business idea, you determined that there was enough market potential to satisfy your requirements. You also did enough competitive analysis to convince yourself that you had enough, or important enough, benefits to offer to your target market. You know that they're out there (but not necessarily just waiting impatiently for you to appear).

Your job in this chapter is to devise some method for capturing your share of your market—and of keeping it once you get the people through your door or on your customer lists. To accomplish this, you have to let your relevant people know that you are there, and you have to let them know how you can help them or how you can satisfy some need of theirs. At its most basic level, there are only two ways to do this: tell them about your product/service, or

240

put your product or service in their way so that they cannot possibly miss noticing it. (Location, the most basic form of "putting it in their way," has been discussed at length in Chapter 5.) Beyond these basics, there is infinite variety.

This chapter is intended to help you sort through some of this variety by discussing some of the major approaches to "telling them" and by discussing how one might put your particular product or service in the way of its intended customers. By putting these pieces together with your defined target customers and your basic marketing strategy, you will be able to create a

FEATURE 11.1
Creating Awareness

Does your product really need to be seen for people to turn on to it? Does it help if people can see it in action, doing whatever it is that it does for customers? Do you sell it to consumers?

If your answers to any of these questions is "yes," there may be some new and different places in which to show people your product. Airports have begun to provide display space to companies (for a fee, of course) who want to show their products to people who frequent airports. IBM shows off its personal computers with displays that actually permit passersby to play with them. (The assumption that the computers will stand up to this kind of abuse is also a major selling point.) Day-Timers also uses such displays, as does Classic Motor Carriages (showing real classic cars in air terminals), makers of leather luggage, tool makers, and other companies. Each display space also includes a handy dispenser for brochures (a "take one" box) so that potential customers can remember the display and get in touch with the company for information, full catalogues, and/or orders.

If the demographics of airports are not right for your product, consider shopping malls. Many of them rent space on a daily basis to sellers who need to demonstrate their products to generate consumer interest. If you sell to consumers, there is probably a nearby mall with the right demographics for your product. Many mall associations track the demographics of their customers and might be prepared to talk with you about them. Some malls do periodic promotions of various types of products, often art or craft products, to which "outsiders" are invited to exhibit and sell. Be aware, however, that mall managements are unlikely to welcome for demonstration and sale products that will compete with regular mall merchants.

For the policies of your local installations and for further information, contact the managers of your local airports or malls.

marketing program that is consistent with your product/service and with the developing image of your company.

In earlier chapters, the need for a consistent approach to your market and for "fit" between everything you do and your intended customers was noted. Nowhere is this more important than in the area of telling and showing people about your product or service and your company. Consistency and fit are critical to establishing and maintaining the image of your company. The advertising and promotion you do should not be permitted to mar that image in any way. In fact, your advertising and promotion should contribute significantly to building and maintaining that "right" image.

The image you are building should complement what you are really selling—the benefit(s) to be derived by the user from your product or service. As noted earlier, the "benefit" may derive from a feature of your product or from an advantage it has over its competitors. The benefit, however, is what will induce a potential customer to actually buy. Therefore, the benefit is what you sell. This chapter focuses on how to sell the benefit(s) to your target customers.

THE ADVERTISING AND PROMOTIONAL PROCESS

Particularly as the new kid on the block, you have to let everyone know you're around. In marketing terms, this is known as "creating awareness." Like that new kid, you can do this in any number of ways. You can be the loudest kid on the block. This might be the best approach if you are discounting and you are really taking on every other store in town directly. If you choose this approach, your opening sale had better be a blockbuster.

At the far other end of the spectrum, you can make your opening announcement in genteel fashion—an announcement, rather than a challenge. This would be a better approach for, say, an upscale clothing store, an accounting practice, or a Mercedes-Benz dealership. Obviously, there is a lot of territory between these two extremes. The point is that the tone and approach you use to let people know you are there must fit the nature and objectives of your business.

You can also use advertising and promotion to create and/or maintain awareness of specific products as shown in almost any television or radio hour. Here, too, the concept of "fit" applies, as it does to a business as a whole.

How you create and maintain awareness may well be crucial to your longer-term business health. People remember. If a customer is lured to your shop by your opening advertising blitz, he had better find what you have led him to believe will be there. If the reality is different from what he expects given your statements and implications, he may well leave in disgust—and never show

Figure 11.1   *Two examples of advertising that fits the image of the business.*

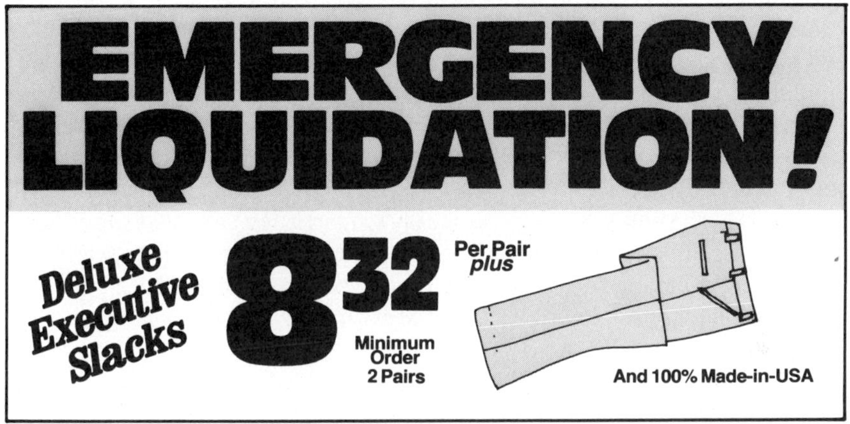

up at your door again. As they say about people in interviews, you never get a second chance to make a first impression.

Assuming your awareness-creating is going along as you planned, your next objective is to "induce trial"—get your target customer to try whatever it is you are selling (or where you're selling it). Advertising is obviously important here. In addition, promotions may be useful, depending once again on the fit with your product, service, or business image. Promotions generally include giveaways, contests, samples, and/or cents-off coupons (and any other approach you can dream up).

The underlying assumption in inducing trial is that your product or service or shop is so clearly superior to its competitors that the target will continue to repurchase or to come in again. This is the ultimate goal—a continuing customer for your business. In real life, however, they often need advertising reminders and the periodic inducement of "sales" and promotions.

Thus, as you can see, advertising and promotion are likely to be with you throughout your business life. The issues raised in this chapter include some approaches to planning your advertising and publicity, your choices about media for your campaign(s), and some approaches to determining costs and developing budgets. The basic model is a consumer product or a store, but there will also be notes relating specifically to marketing professional services and industrial products. As you will see, while these latter items appear to be quite different, the underlying principles are the same. You still sell benefits. And you still maintain consistency and fit with your intended customers.

FEATURE 11.2
Inducing Trial

For many kinds of products and services, prospective purchasers defer trial because the price is high and the results uncertain. "Will what I buy be worth the money to me?" If your product or service falls into this category, consider some form of guarantee (also, if necessary and/or possible, some way of insuring your downside risk on the guarantee).

Consider the problem for Toro Co., a maker of snow throwers, among other things. Nobody wants to buy a snow thrower if there isn't going to be enough snow to justify the expense. So Toro began a program that would refund the cost to a purchaser who bought prior to a certain date if the snow levels for the year did not exceed certain percentages of "average." If snowfall was less than 20 percent of the average, for example, the buyer would get his snow thrower free. While this program added thousands of sales according to the company, the risk was not very high according to meteorologists. They note that snowfall in Minneapolis has never been less than 20 percent of average and has been 50 percent of average (Toro's cutoff point) only four times in the last 40 years.

Services may also be enhanced in the eyes of a purchaser through guarantees. Many training/retraining programs now include the option for the participant to get a full refund if not satisfied that the course or program was worth the price to them. Some consultants also offer a limited form of such a guarantee. Behavioral Science Research, a market research firm, took this approach to clients and increased its sales significantly.

Particularly in service companies, where "results" are more subjective than, say, the amount of snow in a year, guarantees should probably be limited and conditions carefully defined. Both company and customer should be required to perform in accord with whatever sales contract you develop. In all cases, your lawyer should play a major part in developing a guarantee program.

CHOOSING MEDIA

If you begin from your analysis of your target customer, you are unlikely to go wrong in choosing media and developing advertising and promotional campaigns. Your choices about how to reach them, however, are very broad. If you are in specialty areas or industrial products, your choices are more limited. You will be looking at trade shows, personal selling, and industry magazines, journals, and trade newspapers as the only reliable means of reaching your customers. For consumer-related businesses, the choices are almost endless.

Print Media

Print media range from your basic handwritten leaflet to full-page spreads in the slickest magazines you know. The costs, of course, follow an equally broad pattern.

Leaflets are inexpensive and highly flexible. If you have access to low-cost labor to do your distribution and if you target your market by geographic area, leaflets may be a reasonable way for you to go. Please be aware, however, that it is illegal for you to use mailboxes for your leaflets. The U.S. Post Office gets rather upset. You are, after all, avoiding paying them. (That is why many supermarket "shoppers" and other such items are bagged in plastic bags that slip over your front door knob.) Keep in mind the fit with your customers, though. This is *not* the way to sell fine furs or expensive jewelry.

Direct mail is sometimes a good approach. Keep asking yourself whether your particular customer would purchase your product or service because of a mail solicitation. Your mailing piece must be very good and reasonably professional to have any chance of succeeding.

Mailing lists can be purchased to cover very specific market segments from any number of sources. Many will be listed in your Yellow Pages under "Mailing Lists." They are not extremely expensive. They are also not necessarily very good. Many may include duplicates, for example. I once used a list that listed IBM as a small business (under 100 employees) in Pittsburgh. I specified "small business." They clearly were defining that as "small business office." The list was of marginal use to me. If possible, talk to others who have used lists from the same source. Be very clear about what you want and what you will be getting.

Direct mail is also notorious for its generally low return rate. Many experts believe that a 4 percent return on a direct mail solicitation is a gigantic success. Plan your scope and costs accordingly.

Finally, check with the Post Office about bulk mail rates and requirements. For the cost of a permit ($25), you can cut your unit mailing costs by almost one third. You also have to sort by ZIP code before delivery to the post office. If you are using a list, this may be fairly simple, since many lists are already

Figure 11.2   Mailing lists can help you reach specific market segments.

MAILING LIST OF C.E.O.'s OF NEW ENGLAND'S TOP 500

NEW ENGLAND BUSINESS has tabulated New England's 250 largest industrial firms and 250 largest service firms and has made available a list of the Chief Executive Officers of those firms, along with addresses and telephone numbers. The cost of the list is $75 (15¢ per name), listed by zip code and up to date, with the rank of the companies next to the names and whether they are Industrial or Service.

Also available...a list of the C.E.O.'s of 151 of New England's top privately held companies, also listed by zip code and including addresses, telephone numbers and rank. Cost is $50, or $115 for both lists.

Write: Lesley Lloyd
NEW ENGLAND BUSINESS
31 Milk Street
Boston, MA 02109
(617) 482-8200

arranged in that order. You may also want to check into the costs of postal return privileges as opposed to stamps for return envelopes or cards. The larger your mailing, the more sense the return privilege option will make. If you are mailing outside the United States, you cannot send U.S. postage or standard postal returns. See your local post office for how to deal with this situation.

Basic costs for a mailing include: the design and reproduction of your mailing piece, the cost and cost of printing of two sets of envelopes (or one set of envelopes and one preprinted card), your list of names, outbound postage, and inbound postage. There may also be costs associated with opening and sorting the responses, if your mailing and return are large enough.

Various kinds of promotions can also be handled by mail. Sampling programs often send actual product samples through the mail. Coupons can also be handled in this way. Some companies now exist solely to collect coupon offers from area merchants so that they can send (by mail) packages of coupons and offers to area residents. This approach may also fit your needs and your customers. It is likely to be less expensive than doing your own mailing. It is also less likely to provide the individual focus you want.

Newspapers are the medium of choice for most small businesses. This is because they target specific geographic areas and because they are easy to time precisely. If your target is geographically defined, this may be for you. If, on the other hand, your target is a small area within a city or metro area, you may not want to pay for space in the metropolitan newspaper.

In most cities, you have the option of neighborhood or area newspapers. These will target your customer better and will also be less expensive. Some major papers also have sections targeted for specific subareas of their circulation ranges. The Sunday *New York Times,* for example, has a Connecticut section that is delivered only to drop points in Connecticut. It also has a

New Jersey section and a Long Island section. Advertising in such a section might be feasible for you. The *Wall Street Journal* also has regional editions.

Newspaper advertising is purchased by line, by column-inch, or by part of a page—half page, quarter page, etc. The rate depends on the circulation of the paper and on the number of times you want to run an ad or the amount of space you contract for over a period of time. Sometimes you can specify placement of your ad. If you can, you want it opposite or on the same page as something your target is likely to read and toward the top of the page. Your great sale on footballs, for example, would be nice in the sports section.

Magazines sell space by the partial page. They are generally more expensive to advertise in than are newspapers and generally reach a larger audience. Since there are so many different magazines, each targeting a specific customer, they may help you reach your specific customer more economically than other methods.

Most magazines (and some newspapers) keep track of the demographic characteristics of their readership especially for potential advertisers. They make the bulk of their revenue from advertising. What they are selling, then, is access to this set of demographics. They will be happy to tell you about them. If you cannot decide about potential placement of your ads, go back to *Standard Rates and Data* for a quick set of options and comparisons.

Many of the larger, national circulation general magazines offer deals that are very like the newspaper subarea issues mentioned above. *Newsweek,* for example, claims to be able to sell you a geographic target as small as a block. Such magazines can certainly offer coverage of areas below the national or large regional level. If such a publication will reach your targets, ask about small area editions.

Other print media include billboards, bus and/or subway cards, and some kinds of in-store posters and displays. It should be noted that in an increasing number of areas, billboard advertising is severely restricted. In using these types of advertising, pay particular attention to whether your potential customers are likely to see them and respond to them positively.

Electronic Media

Television and radio are prime places for advertising. Television comes in two main varieties—network and local. Buying time on network television is extremely expensive. It varies with the time of day and the network. Time on special events is also available—if you can afford it. A minute of advertising time on the 1985 Superbowl show, for example, is said to have cost more than a million dollars. (Of course, you purchased access to every football fan, nationwide. An estimated half of the national population watched the game. If you sold shaving cream, this may have been a good deal. For a pantyhose company, it probably would not have been worth it.)

Figure 11.3　You can target your market by area.

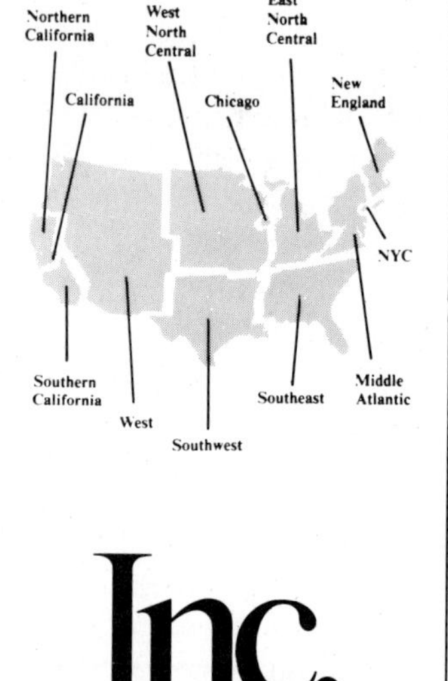

Reprinted with permission, *Inc.* magazine, 1984. Copyright © 1984 by *Inc.* Publishing Company, 38 Commercial Wharf, Boston, MA 02110.

Local television is a growing medium. It consists of the over-the-air stations that are not affiliated with one of the major networks and local cable stations. Because they can be highly targeted methods of reaching your specific consumer, they may well be good potential places for your advertising. Most stations keep the same kinds of demographics as do the print media—only they usually subdivide by time of day because that is how viewers and listeners tend to divide themselves.

According to the *Wall Street Journal*, late night television advertising is the latest rage.[1] The paper reported that some 25 million television sets are still on at midnight. At bottom, 5:30 A.M., there are still 3.6 million households viewing. Late night (early morning?) time, they report, can be one-fifteenth as expensive as a prime-time spot, allowing advertisers to reach viewers at about one sixth the cost per viewer of reaching the prime time audience. Not a bad deal!

Radio is a lot cheaper than television as an advertising medium. It is the second choice, in general, of small business because it segments its listening audience so clearly for you. There is always a rock station, a Top 40 station, a country and western station, an "easy listening" station. Some markets also offer all-news and classical formats. Radio also comes in two varieties, AM and FM. They vary in their range and thus in their prices. FM tends to be more targeted and smaller, hence less expensive and, quite possibly, more effective for you—if the demographics are right. In short, there's something for everyone. And, as an advertiser, you can choose the audience you want to reach fairly precisely.

Networks and independents, both radio and television, base their rates on their circulation, just as do newspapers and magazines. This is why there is so much good television during the periods when viewers are counted ("sweeps"). The ratings of shows and stations determine the amount that a station can charge for commercial air time. You purchase time in increments: a minute, 30 seconds, 10 seconds. (A very new notion, 90-second television commercials, is just now being tested. By the time you read this book, you will know whether they work by whether they are still around.) The aggregate amount of time you purchase will affect the overall price.

PRODUCING YOUR ADVERTISING

Actually producing the advertising you will use in the medium or media you choose consists of two main considerations: content and form. What follows is a brief outline of prime considerations for you as an advertiser as you develop your actual advertising copy.

Content

The first rule of writing advertising copy is to keep it simple. You want what you are saying to be absolutely clear to just about anybody who can read—and to some who cannot, if possible. Clarity can be enhanced by using very simple and very few words, a simple layout, and large, short headlines. If at all possible, the physical look of your ads should be similar all the time so that readers or viewers can recognize you almost from the ad alone, before they even read it. This will also cut down on your production costs, since the format part can be used over and over again.

Be very direct about what it is you are trying to say. While a good, humorous ad can be truly great, there is some question as to whether the target remembers the product (which is why you are spending all this money in the first place). Some old Alka Seltzer ads have become classics of humorous advertising, but research showed that they did not increase product sales nor did most consumers (at the time) remember the name of the product. Humor is also very difficult to do well. You run the risk of offending some people when you meant nothing of the sort.

Use each ad to make only one or a very few points about a specific product or sale item. This will reduce the clutter and leave your message clear.

And make very sure that your advertising tells potential customers where you are and how to reach you. This is particularly critical if you are somewhat out of the way or in an area unknown to some of your target people.

Form

The form in which you have to deliver your advertising to the medium you chose depends on the requirements of the particular outlet. In general, however, magazines and newspapers require camera-ready copy. This means that they want from you something that they can simply put into their production stream. If you cannot do this, you can hire professionals who will help you or do it for you. Some outlets will make up your ads for you for additional fees. Sometimes, a print outlet will help you do your ads as a service to their advertisers. Ask.

Television advertising generally has to be delivered on video tape. As you can imagine, this can become an expensive process. It does not have to be, however. If you do not need an ad to compete with the Pepsi commercials, a tape made with rented equipment and rented technical talent, with yourself or your friends and relations as the on-camera talent may work for you. This will reduce the production cost considerably. Just make sure that you won't be embarrassed by the finished product when it airs. And that your target market is likely to respond to it positively. That's the purpose, after all.

From a production perspective, radio may be the least expensive option. You can often simply write copy for the announcer to read at the appropriate time. Alternatively, you can supply audio tape for playback.

Whatever approach you use, be sure to preview your material to check for content and appearance. It is also good practice to check to ensure that what was supposed to run or air at a specific time or in a specific place does, in fact, do so.

NON-MEDIA BASED APPROACHES

Sometimes, and for some kinds of businesses, the best advertising is not advertising. In fact, some kinds of businesses are not permitted to advertise. Accountants in some states may not advertise. Physician advertising is frowned upon, although not quite prohibited. Basically, professional services are probably not best sold through standard advertising practices, anyway. Once again, consider the fit with your intended customer. Will that person choose the professional who advertises? Or is she more likely to find the service seller in some other way?

This definitely does not mean that professional service sellers should not do marketing. A common misconception of those who intend to go into consulting-type business is that the business will just happen. It doesn't. You have to go out and get it. You just do it differently from the way you sell a widget. (But you can often sell widgets in the ways you sell professional services.) You do it basically through contacts and publicity—approaches that should be utilized by all business owners to whatever extent possible.

Publicity

Publicity does not necessarily involve the kind of media hype that gives public relations a bad name among quiet types. It is simply another, very effective way of getting out the word about you and your company.

You start by considering what might be of general interest or news about your new company or your new service. Then, either by press release or by telephone or in person, you let all the media people who might be interested in on the angle you have developed for them. Quite often, they will be happy about acquiring some feature-type pieces for their local news shows or columns. This is a particularly good route if your business involves something offbeat. You are an artist who turns junk cars into sculptures of breathtaking beauty, for example. Or you began to design clothing because your mother was a model and she dragged you through every showroom in the United States before you were 10. You are looking for the stuff of a good story.

The advantage of publicity over advertising (aside from the fact that it costs you nothing) is that the word on you and/or your company appears as news, rather than as advertising from you. It is instantly more interesting and more believable. It also allows you to be less modest in discussing your awards, talents, etc. It is a route well worth some thought and effort on your part.

If you don't have any publicity-worthy items in your back pocket, you might consider ways to generate some. You might stage a fashion show for the benefit of your local favorite charity. I stress "local" because what you really want is major local interest in your new business. You might give a talk on how to invest your money safely. Obviously, what you do depends on your business, your target market, and your expertise. You can fly this kind of notion as far as your ingenuity can take it. Do not forget, however, to let the media people know what you are going to be doing so that they can provide proper coverage.

For many sellers of professional services, what sells is recognized expertise. The question for you is, assuming you have the expertise, how do you get it recognized? How better than to be immortalized in print? Many newspapers and magazines and business and trade journals are always looking for relevant material to print. Consider writing articles. Start with local papers and small journals and advance to the more important ones using your experience and prior credits. Aside from the fact that it feels good to see your name in lights, so to speak, you become a recognized expert. Selling your services becomes much easier. (This is also a good technique for sellers of industrial products and services.).

Find out about potential places to publish through such publications as *Standard Rates and Data* or, for more commercially oriented periodicals, try the *Writer's Handbook* and the *Writer's Market.* Your concern is not places that pay, but rather the places that are read by members of your target market. Your objective is not to make money from the sale of articles—though you might actually do some of that. It is to become known and to have your words in print—clear proof that you are an expert.

Personal Selling

A second non-media approach to marketing your products or services is personal selling. This set of techniques can also obviously be coupled with advertising and/or with publicity, depending on your business and your needs. Personal selling should be self-explanatory, but it is really not. There are, in fact, really two kinds of personal selling. First, there is the kind that takes place in a shop or any other establishment to which a potential customer comes to (perhaps) purchase something. In such cases, it is the job of the sales person to present appropriate merchandise to the customer so that it meets the customer's stated (and unstated) needs. Often, a good personal seller can create additional sales through making add-ons attractive and/or helping the customer trade up from the item originally sought.

The trickier kind of personal selling is done by "outside sales people." It is trickier because you not only have to do the selling, but you also have to figure out who the customer might be and what she might want. In in-house selling, remember, the potential customer has to come to you. The outside selling process, however, does not consist of simply showing up on somebody's doorstep or calling on the phone and making a pitch. To do it right requires planning along lines similar to those of all marketing programs.

The problem with unplanned sales calling is its expense. In 1984, the approximate cost of an industrial sales call was $200. How many of these can you waste before you're out of business? The trick is to make each one count. And the way you do that is exactly the same, at base, as the way you make your advertising do its job. You target your energies at those most likely to buy or be sold on whatever it is you are selling. In personal selling, this is known as "qualifying" the prospects. And you are still selling benefits, only now you might call them "solutions to problems," since you are probing for customer needs/problems and offering something to meet/solve them when you find them. Same notion repackaged slightly differently.

SETTING YOUR BUDGET

While most business owners think of marketing costs as just another expense of doing business, it will help to think of them more as a continuing investment in building a clientele or a customer base. Thinking about it in this way helps you to see your advertising and promotional outflows in longer range terms. More important, perhaps, thinking in investment terms will help you to look at your marketing costs as money that should be producing results.

The general objective of advertising, and of marketing in general, is to produce customers who will generate revenues and profits for the company. Thus, your marketing programs should be tied in some way to sales generated or desired. The questions that you will have to address include how much to spend on your entire program and how to allocate this amount among various media, programs, and time periods. A final issue, which will be discussed later in this chapter, is how to monitor and evaluate results.

All of these issues are tied to your forecast of sales or your target for sales for the upcoming year or period. There are three general approaches to setting a promotional budget. At the outset, you are probably limited to the least attractive of these, simply because of your inexperience in your own business. All three are described briefly, however, because you will want to "trade up" as soon as your accumulated information permits you to do so. (At very least, you will want to fine-tune and track media effectiveness.)

The Percentage of Sales Approach

This is by far the simplest method to use. It assumes that x dollars spent in advertising generate y dollars in sales. While you know that this is not true—some items clearly need no advertising help, and no amount of advertising will help some others—it is an easy way to calculate what your first-year advertising expense should be. You can even get some help from your now-dog-eared set of industry average statistics. Doubtless there is a ratio for advertising and/or marketing expense as a percentage of sales. Use this figure as a working base for your own calculations.

Keep in mind that your industry average data is for an operating business. You will therefore have to add an amount to cover your special grand opening advertising and promotions, if any. Many sources suggest that your opening blitz should create an addition of as much as 20 percent of your estimated normal-year expenditures for advertising. Your specific situation may call for more or less.

Consider how hard you expect it to be to launch your operation relative to other similar businesses. Are you located off the beaten track? Count on a greater cost to create awareness. Will your operation require a higher opening week campaign because of the nature or target of the business? (Remember, for example, Hilltop Health Spa from Chapter 3. A posh party was planned for their opening gun.) In short, start with industry data, but don't be misled by

FEATURE 11.3
Ad Budget Formulae

Spinnaker Software's Jay Mixter says his bosses are willing to "bet the company" when spending money on advertising. They did it to the tune of 44% of sales in 1982. "I'm not one of those people who plays with formulas and ratios. They simply don't always work. My biggest concern is finding out what it requires to compete in the industry, what the competitors are spending. And then I ask how that tracks with sales."

Stephen Hassenfeld, CEO of Hasbro Industries, concurs. "The amount of money spent doesn't guarantee a thing, and it doesn't cure all ills. Harvard Business School has some wonderful case studies about how to determine advertising levels. But when those students get in the real world, up against real competitors, it's not going to hurt them if they forgot some of those formulas."

"There's an enormous amount of baloney in this business," says Harry Washburn, a marketing consultant at Wallace and Washburn. "I'm not convinced that formulas work. Despite what everyone says, the most common formula for spending is 'outspend the competition'."

M. S. Garfield, of the marketing management consultants Garfield-Linn & Co in Chicago, points out the single clear correlation between advertisement spending and results. "The company that spends more as a percentage of sales will always realize a disproportionately greater share of the market and a greater return on sales. Every study confirms this."

A recent study funded by Cahners Publishing Company and based on earlier work by the Strategic Planning Institute bears this out. Valerie Kijewski, of SPI, points out that "While the process of formulating a marketing budget may at times appear unscientific, a set of rational decision rules can be identified as major determinants of what businesses actually spend." The report, "How Much to Spend on Advertising?" discusses a survey of mostly industrial firms. It found that "The average business in the sample devotes about one-third of its advertising budget to media and two-thirds to promotional efforts. This mix would be expected to vary depending on the business's strategic positioning as well as market objectives. However, there are many other variables that may affect marketing expenditures and productivity." Cahners' vice president of planning, Jerry Neth, agrees that "It will always be more of an art than a science."

From "Determining Ad Budgets" by Douglas M. Bailey, August 6, 1984, p. 14 ff. Reprinted with permission of *New England Business*.

it. Think about what *you* are doing and what you need to do to get it done. Then estimate increases or decreases from the average to set your budget.

Also, be particularly aware that the percentage of sales approach has one major built-in problem. If you expect declining sales or low sales for some reason, then your marketing expense allocation (based on a percentage of that declining or low figure) will also be declining or low. But, if advertising is supposed to increase sales, declining expense in the face of declining sales will simply exacerbate the problem. If you are aware of this counterproductive effect, you can make reasoned, appropriate adjustments to your expense projections as you go along.

The Unit of Sales Approach

If you can obtain or develop the data, this is a finer approach to setting your advertising budget. It assumes that you know, or can find out, about how much in advertising it takes to sell a unit of a given item. (You can build the data for later use as you gain experience.) This allows you to adjust your marketing expense based on what items you will be selling, rather than just looking at a percentage of aggregate sales.

If, for example, you were planning to sell $100,000 worth of goods in an industry in which the average percentage of advertising to sales was 5 percent, you would budget $5,000 (plus opening and any other adjustments you might make) using the percentage of sales approach. But suppose you believed that your product mix would be easier to sell than the product mix carried by most outlets in the industry average set. It might be more advantageous to you—in terms of cost and results—to consider the promotional costs of selling the specific items you plan to sell.

Say, for example, that your $100,000 of sales is expected to consist of 1,000 units of one product and 100 units of another. If it takes about $3 in advertising to sell a unit of the first product and $7 to sell a unit of the second, your budget would look as follows:

```
$3 × 1,000 = $3,000
$7 ×   100 = $  700
Total budget    $3,700 (plus opening ad costs and adjustments)
```

This approach will also tell you if your product mix is markedly different from that of the rest of your industry. If it is, it should not necessarily worry you. It is just something you ought to know and keep in mind as you go.

The Objective and Task Approach

This is definitely the hardest of the approaches to do. It assumes that you have highly specific marketing goals and that you have a pretty good idea of what it costs to sell units of whatever you are selling to specific groups of people. Because it focuses on what you are trying to do, it is more accurate and more controllable than the other methods.

Suppose, for example, you wanted to sell your first product to a student population. You already decided that your intended volume of product 1 sales is 1,000 units. You know also that selling these items to students is a new idea and is therefore likely to be more expensive than the normally expected cost of convincing the average prospect to buy the item. You estimate that the cost of selling a unit to a student in this first year will be closer to $4.50 than to the $3.00 for making each average sale. Rather than the $3,000 you budgeted under the unit of sales approach, you would expect to need $4,500 ($4.50 × 1,000 units) to achieve your goal.

Using the objective and task approach, then, involves estimating your promotional costs based on both unit sales by product and specific target segments. Thus, only after you have decided what the very specific sales goals are can you estimate what it will cost in marketing expenses to attain them. Using this approach effectively is probably way down the pike for you at this point.

Expanding Limited Funds

There is undoubtedly a realistic limit on how much you can devote to promotional expenses. Average-based planning is all well and good, but what if you cannot afford to spend even the 5 percent or the $3,700? You do two things. First, you prepare to cut back on your plans a little, hoping that sales and advertising are not tied as tightly as people led you to believe. At the same time you start to tap other sources of funds than your own. Obviously, you do not want to go to the bank to cover operating expenses. (They'd laugh you out of the place.) But there is money and help around, and it may be only as far away as your phone.

The place to start is with your suppliers and, through them, the manufacturers of whatever it is you sell. They may provide some direct advertising materials, generally point-of-purchase displays and the like, designed to induce impulse purchases. But more important are the co-op advertising programs they may run.

Cooperative advertising is the method by which suppliers and manufacturers assist you in selling their goods to the public. While each plan differs from all others in specifics, the basic idea is that the manufacturer will cover a percentage of your costs when you advertise the availability of his products in your store. You feature his products in your ads, and you get to place the ads at some fraction of the full cost. This is a great deal, and too many retailers fail to take advantage of it.

You need to ask your suppliers for information on such programs. You also need to be careful about complying with the terms of any co-op arrangements you may want to use. This can involve sending copies of the ads, relevant invoices, and your sales records for the manufacturers' products. This last may be required because the manufacturer probably bases the amount of co-op funds for which you are eligible on the amount of his goods you have sold. (He is not in this for his health either.)

Another way of stretching your advertising budget has to do with "per inquiry" advertising. You run an ad, generally on television at an off-hour, and you pay nothing for the air time. You do, however, pay some amount (agreed upon) for each inquiry/sale generated by that ad. Obviously, the station will run these ads when there do not happen to be any paying commercials around and when they do not have to run public service announcements. You have doubtless seen such ads. They are the ones that tell you to phone right now 1-800-555-1234. ("But wait! There's more ... !") As noted earlier, with late-night spots coming into vogue, this may be a dying commercial form.

Allocating the Funds You Have

Once you have a budget and have estimated how much you can add by the above methods, you have to deal with allocating your funds along two separate parameters. First, you have to decide what approaches you are going to use. Second, you have to spread your dollars over the year or period for which you budgeted.

Media allocations will initially be made by your sense of what seems reasonable and appropriate. A key consideration is "cost per thousand" (CPM) people reached. For the general population, this is simply the circulation or viewing or listening "reach" of the particular media outlet divided by the dollars you must spend on a unit of time or space.

For your purposes, however, that is not a fine enough calculation. You may well not care at all how many teenaged kids see a given magazine. You may be interested only in the number of business executives it reaches. *Your* effective CPM, then, is the number of relevant executives divided by the cost. Thus, a superficially inexpensive medium may be rather expensive for you when compared with an initially more expensive, but more targeted outlet. CPM calculations provide a reasonable standard of comparison in making allocation decisions.

Monthly allocations of your promotional budget should be tied to the patterns of sales in your industry. If your big season is late winter–early spring boat show sales, for example, you will want to structure your budget so that a large chunk of your promotion hits your market in February and March. If the Christmas season is your big thing, then you need to be absolutely positive that you will have enough budget left for major blitzes in November and early December.

Some help is available in this part of the allocation process. Your industry average data may well have included information on seasonal sales patterns. If so, use them as a working base. Then your question becomes one of the lag time, if any, between an action you take and any sales that result from that action. This part of the equation will come with experience and good monitoring.

One item that sounds small, but that often gets out of hand, is the problem of "advertising" in what is essentially a community service way. Companies are continually being asked to sponsor high school yearbook ads or place advertising in programs for football games or local productions or church functions. Unless the ad is likely to be really read by customers who are your targets, do not count this as part of your regular advertising. Count it more as creating general good will or, if appropriate, a charitable contribution.

Evaluating Your Efforts: Are You Getting Your Money's Worth?

The astounding fact is that many business owners don't know whether they are getting anything out of their promotional spending. It is just another expense of doing business, so they keep throwing money at it. The Advertising Research Foundation, for example, found that 4 of every 10 financial service providers—even large ones—do no research at all on the effectiveness of their ads. Most of the rest, they say, spend too little money and effort on tracking advertising effectiveness.[2] This is an approach that is wasteful of both money and effort—like sending salespeople out at $200 a call to see accounts that could, if landed, do $75 dollars in business. But it is easier than finding out what they are really doing.

You, however, have a distinct advantage. You are new and you are building your systems from scratch. You want to be sure that you can monitor your marketing spending so that you can adjust your programs as they prove (or disprove) their value or as conditions change. Happily, this need not be a difficult process.

You need to start with what you might want to know. Two main items are noted below. Please notice that much of the data will probably be wanted for other purposes as well so that there should be little or no additional cost in keeping marketing-related information.

1. Records of your promotional expenses by date, type, size (or length and time), medium, and outlet.
2. Records of sales by product and date so that you can compare sales of a featured product before and after a campaign or effort.

You can go still farther in tagging your advertising and promotions for later analysis. It need not be either expensive or complicated. If you use coupons, for example, it is a simple matter to code your coupons to tell you the source from which your customer got the coupon. If you use radio advertising on a number of stations, you could offer a small discount to people mentioning a certain code word. The word could be different for each station, and your clerks could simply keep a running tally by code word. Here again, creativity can substitute for large supplies of funds.

Such approaches will help conserve funds by telling you where and what kinds of efforts are really doing the job for you. Obviously, if something is not working, drop it. It is perfectly all right to consider your first periods as semi-experimental—as long as you learn as you go and fine-tune your approaches and your allocations as you go along.

SUMMARY

The selling of your company and its products or services may well be one of the most critical factors contributing to its long-term survival. It is difficult, not because of any inherent complexity, but rather because of the plethora of choices that exist. Key factors in making these choices are the notions of fit with your intended customer, consistency with the image you are developing of your company, and a stress on the benefits of the things you are selling to your customer.

Your objectives in promotion are, sequentially, to create awareness, to induce trial, and to foster repurchase. You have a wide array of tools to use in accomplishing these objectives. You can use straight advertising, telling people about your store, service, or products, or you can use various promotional techniques. These include giveaways, samples, and coupons, among other approaches. You can use various print media, ranging from inexpensive leaflets, to direct mail, newspapers, and magazines. You also have at your disposal radio and television as means of reaching your target customers. You may combine these approaches with publicity techniques and/ or with personal selling. In certain businesses, these last are the most effective approaches to the market.

Your choices among approaches and media should be guided by appropriateness and "fit" with your consumer and your image. Effective cost per thousand people reached should also be a key consideration in choosing where to place your advertising dollars. Your budget may be stretched by using various available cooperative advertising programs and/or through per-inquiry advertising, if these are consistent with your image and your market.

Budgeting your promotional expenses can be done in three main ways: Percentage of sales, units of sales, and objective and task. Percentage of sales as an approach is easiest, but has serious drawbacks. As a starting point, this method might serve until you gain the experience to move to one of the more sophisticated methods. Even in the early stages, however, adjustments should be made for opening ad campaign expenses and any other deviations from the industry average that seem warranted.

Your budget must be allocated among programs and media and over your budget period. Both these allocations should be considered somewhat flexible and subject to adjustment as you learn more about your particular business patterns. A good opening approach to time-related allocation is to lead intended sales by a small amount of time.

Keeping careful records of sales and advertising and promotional activities is the only way to ensure that your dollars are working for you. It is also the only way to gain the insight necessary to adjust your programs to do the most work for the lowest cost. If you begin with systems that capture the necessary data, you will be a long way down the road toward building marketing effectiveness.

FOR YOU TO CONSIDER

1. What are two key concepts you should keep in mind while developing your marketing programs? How should you use these as you develop your more specific marketing, advertising, and promotion programs?
2. What are the three sequential objectives of advertising and promotion? How does the third differ from the first two?
3. Compare the merits of newspaper and magazine advertising for a hotel in a resort area. For a clothing store in a suburban mall.
4. Discuss the advantages and disadvantages of direct mail as a means of reaching people and of generating sales.
5. Discuss the advantages of radio advertising versus television advertising.
6. Discuss some of the techniques of generating publicity. Why is this approach to getting out the word worth discussing?
7. How should you approach determining your first promotional budget? Why did you choose this approach over the other possible approaches?
8. What are two ways of making your basic advertising budget stretch farther? Discuss a business for which one or both might be appropriate. Discuss one business for which both are clearly inappropriate.
9. What is "CPM"? How should you adjust the figure quoted to you for CPM by a magazine space salesperson?
10. How should you approach allocating your budget among programs, media, and parts of the year (or budget period)?

NOTES

1. *Wall Street Journal* (February 9, 1984):29.

2. Bill Abrams, "Financial Service Advertisers Seen Neglecting Ad Research," *Wall Street Journal* (August 18, 1983):25.

FOR FURTHER READING

Bank of America, "Advertising Small Business." *Small Business Reporter,* 1982.

Small Business Administration publications:

> *Advertising Guidelines for Small Retail Firms.* SBA MA 4.015.
> *Developing New Accounts.* SBA MA 4.010.
> *Do You Know the Results of Your Advertising?* SBA MA 4.020.
> *Improving Personal Selling in Small Retail Stores.* SBA MA 4.014.
> *Measuring Sales Force Performance.* SBA MA 4.003.
> *Plan Your Advertising Budget.* SBA MA 4.018.
> *Profitable Community Relations for Small Business.* SBA 045-000-00033-8.
> *Signs in Your Business.* SBA MA 4.016.
> *Tips on Getting More for Your Marketing Dollar.* SBA MA 4.008.

12. How Much Do You Charge?

As you have no doubt divined by now, pricing is one of the critical aspects of your business planning. The price and pricing structure you choose will affect how you market, who will buy your goods or services, and how much profit you make. In some industries, the price at which you must sell may determine the materials and processes you use and your manufacturing methods. No matter how you slice it, the prices you charge, times the volumes you sell at those prices, is the amount of revenue that your company will have to work with on an ongoing basis.

Because of the importance and potential complexity of pricing issues, this entire chapter is devoted to an examination of pricing. It also includes a major section on costing, simply because much of pricing is based, at least loosely, on cost factors and issues.

There are some things that this chapter specifically does *not* do. While it is possible to build elegant, dynamic pricing models—indeed, some people and firms devote their entire careers to them—we assume that you just want to

262

FEATURE 12.1

Reilly's Machine Products

Reilly's Machine Products sells screws to industrial users. The screws are standard items. As long as Reilly's tolerances and general quality are up to the industry average for screws of a given specification, their products are interchangeable with those of other screw manufacturers. His price will have to be about what theirs is (pricing by what the competition is doing).

If, by some strange chance, Reilly could differentiate his screw products, he could move out of the pack. This will be difficult, since his product is made to be an adjunct to other products. Differentiation of the product itself, then, is unlikely. There may be potential for differentiating by service level. This would require Reilly to analyze how the industry operates and where better or different approaches to servicing customers might be viewed as worth some extra money to the customer. As you can see, in some industries, a great deal rests on seeing industry weaknesses and being inventive about meeting unmet needs.

Please note that it does not matter what it costs Reilly to make the screws. Unless he has managed differentiation, the users do not care about his costs. They are seeking the best price. If he cannot meet or beat the industry cost structure, he's going to be out of business soon.

---

get the job done efficiently and effectively. Thus, this chapter avoids major model-building, focusing instead on pricing basics. This discussion also does not address competitive bidding situations. This topic really requires a book in itself, combining probability and statistical methods with strategy considerations and cost issues.

INFLUENCES ON PRICING

At the most basic level, there are only three ways to price a product or service. You can price on the basis of your cost. You can price on the basis of what the competition is doing. Or, you can price on the basis of what you believe the market will bear. A number of factors will influence your choice of basic strategy.

1. **Your industry.** How your industry prices is critical to your choice. Are prices generally uniform across firms for a given item? If so, the basis of competition in the industry is probably price. And, as we noted earlier (Chapter 5), the only way to buck this practice is through significant product differentiation. Do prices in the industry cover a broad range for a

product or service type? Does there appear to be no pricing standard whatever? Either of these situations gives you a great deal more room to maneuver.

2. **Your product or service.** If your product or service is just like everybody else's, then you are restricted in how you price it. If you are, somehow, different, you have more choice in pricing.

3. **Your image of your business.** When we described the pricing continuum in Chapter 5, we pointed out that your position along that continuum would affect how you would do business. Thus, your vision of the kind of operation you want to run will, and should, affect your basic pricing strategy.

These factors combine to provide the limits on your pricing decisions and directions toward your choice of overall strategy. You can see how they interact in Features 12.1 and 12.2.

Reilly's problem is that his product is, almost by definition, just like everyone else's screws. They have to fit the same holes and the same tolerances in order to be useful to his customers. He does not have much opportunity for product differentiation because any advance he might make in

---

FEATURE 12.2
Charlisa's Boutique

Charlisa's is a large, beautifully appointed shop on the right side of the best shopping street in the city. It carries only top-of-the-line designer apparel and furnishings for women. There is at least one sales person for every customer. Regulars have their own special "assistants." Prices are outrageous. Even the wealthy say so, but they shop there anyway. Charlisa is clearly pricing based on what the market will bear. (Pick a number, any number ....)

Charlisa's market is really buying something in addition to the articles of clothing she sells. They are buying cachet, prestige, and the right to talk about "my salesgirl" at various parties. They know that everyone in town recognizes Charlisa's large, but tasteful, personalized labels in her coats. These are prominent when a coat is folded and slipped over a chair or hung on a hanger. They also know that the quality of her garments is the best that can be found and that any difficulties will be taken care of promptly and discreetly.

In short, they are buying service and other benefits in addition to the coat. They are buying assurance of quality and the recognition factor. And they apparently are willing to pay more than three times average department store prices to get them.

design would have to be great enough to cause all his customers to redesign their products to accommodate his "improved" product. This is rather unlikely, given his business.

He may have some ability to differentiate his company by service level. If, for example, the industry experiences delivery problems, Reilly might be able to charge a premium price by simply guaranteeing delivery within x days. He might achieve a similar level of differentiation and price by servicing small orders that the industry may not generally care to handle.

Charlisa's Boutique is at the other end of the spectrum. She has created and developed her products and service level so that she really has no competitors in the area. Without competitors, she can price at whatever she believes the market will bear. As long as she maintains close contact with what her clientele is really willing to pay and with what they are interested in buying, her operation will probably prosper.

Her only other major risk is that someone else will see the size of her market and choose to compete in the same ways. Her questions then would have to revolve around whether the market is large enough for two and whether her "name" and reputation/history will be enough to carry her through. Cutting price will not really be an option for her, given the nature of the operation she has created.

While most businesses are not as extreme as the two described above, the same factors affect them all: your industry pricing pattern, your particular place in the industry, and your image of your business. Your first pricing task, then, is to determine where your business fits in the range of basic strategies.

THE SPECIAL CASE OF PRICING NEW PRODUCTS

If you have a truly new product, your company immediately catapults into the "what the market will bear" category. "Truly new," in this case, means some product with no effective substitutes and no direct competition. Such a product is difficult to come by. (It also helps if people are likely to need or want it.) Such products are special cases in which you have two major strategy options. Your choice will depend partly on how easy it will be for others to copy your product and partly on personal preference and long-term goals.

Skimming

This strategy assumes either that your product is difficult to copy, or that you do not care whether it is copied. You expect to build "the name" in the business, and expect to retain it even when competition develops.

Using this strategy, you price your new product high, expecting relatively low-volume sales. Meanwhile, you are making large profit per unit. After you have exhausted potential sales (or momentum) in the top layer of your market, you bring out a variant on your original product. You either price the variant lower (Polaroid), or cut price on the original (Hewlett-Packard). In either case, you pick up the next price level of your market.

Polaroid is the classic example of this pricing strategy. It brings out a new advance in its instant picture technology in a high-priced camera, as it did with the Sonar focusing in the SX-70. When the company has sold its target volume at this level (or when the company sees its sales in that price range slowing significantly), it brings out the same feature or almost the same feature in a less expensive camera. It moves the technology down the price scale until it is as low as it can go. At the lowest levels, the camera is sold as virtually a vehicle to sell film (on which Polaroid makes a large profit and which is the only usable film for its cameras).

Penetration

The alternative approach to pricing a new product is to price it low to ensure that as many people as possible have one of yours before anyone else has one to offer. This approach also may have the effect, in some industries, of letting you produce in volumes large enough to realize economies of scale in manufacturing.

This approach, obviously, works best for products to which customers build commitments, incorporating them into designs of larger assemblies or simply growing fond of a certain feature or type. Operating systems for personal computers fall into this category. It also works well for products for which you expect the add-ons or continuing sales to provide the bulk of your profit. (Kodak's answer to the Polaroid was priced this way; Kodak intended to make its money from the sales of its special film. The Gillette Safety Razor originated virtually as an attempt to sell blades.)

Before you try either of these strategies with confidence, be sure that you really have a unique product and you really are in the "what the market will bear" category. Failing to do this, particularly if you choose the skimming strategy, could be disastrous.

COSTING: DETERMINING YOUR COSTS

As you can see, unless you are in the "pick a number" category, either your pricing structure or your ability to compete in your business depends on your cost structure.

If you are in a price-sensitive market, and you are unable to create or capitalize on some differentiating factor(s) (as was Reilly in our earlier example), what your competitors are charging will determine either your profit or your business existence. In such a circumstance, your costs are all-important. Your question is simply whether or not you can make the product (and your desired profit) at the going price and at the volume you will be able to produce. You are really working the pricing sequence backwards. It is useful, however, to know—in advance of sinking your money into production capacity—whether your operation is likely to live.

If your industry is such that you expect to price largely on the basis of your costs, you will be working the pricing sequence frontwards, figuring your costs plus profit at your intended volume to arrive at price. Clearly, it would be useful to know what those costs are likely to be. In either case, your costs are important, if only to enable you to figure out what your profit will be.

Cost Behavior

Costs come in two main varieties: fixed and variable. There is also an in-between category called, depending on your point of view, semi-fixed or step-function variable. Fixed costs are those that you will incur by virtue of the fact that you are open for business. They exist whether or not you sell any of what you are trying to sell during the period. What is a fixed cost depends, to some extent, on the business. While labor costs are generally considered to be variable costs, a restaurant, for example, must have a chef in order for the place to open. That chef should probably be considered a fixed cost. Generally, however, fixed costs are costs such as lease and rental costs for your equipment and premises, the cost of heating the place, base charges for your telephone, and similar expenses.

Variable costs, on the other hand, are those that depend on the volume of business you do. The cost of materials used to make your product, for example, depends on the amount used per unit times the number of units you produce. If it costs $1 worth of material to make each of your items, it will take $3 worth of that material to make three of them. The same is true for the labor that is directly involved in making the product (your direct labor costs). The notion is that if you do no business—even if you are open for business—you will incur no variable costs.

Unfortunately for all of us, unless you hire workers on a straight piece-work basis, you cannot hire one widget's worth of labor. You have to buy some standard amount of time from a person, an hour or a day or a week. In real life, then, even labor cost works by steps. The difficulty with such step-function costs is that you can produce only x widgets using one worker (or one unit of worker time). To make one more than x, you will need a second worker. That second worker will be there whether he makes one widget or x widgets. His cost is fixed once you agree to take him on for that period. This is a cost that functions in steps, a step-function variable cost.

Machinery and equipment costs (fixed costs) also generally function in this

FEATURE 12.3
Maxwell's Restaurant

One of the more difficult problems of any business is to determine exactly how much its product costs. In the restaurant business, the problem is particularly acute because menu items are so numerous and varied. Moreover, a number of people contribute to the actual assembly of each meal. Leonard Coleman, owner of Maxwell's Restaurant had always wanted "to get a grip on my total costs and eliminate the guesswork." Operating alone while actually running the restaurant, however, the task was just too large. Then he got help from a team of students from Virginia Polytechnic Institute.

The students were part of a Small Business Administration program that puts students into small companies as unpaid consultants. While the results an owner gets depend on the particular students assigned, if the work is good, the results can be invaluable. The Maxwell's team "did a really exceptional job," says Coleman. He still keeps their two inch thick report handy for reference.

Coleman claims that their main contribution was in the costing area. They costed each menu item right down to the salt and pepper. The next time Coleman redid his menus, he changed the prices of 12 entrees to reflect the pricing the students did for him. He now knows, for example, that his chef's salad should have only a penny's worth of bacon bits, rather than the two that had been used. He can use the students' costs to control his operation better and to make it more uniform and more profitable.

This is not to say that Coleman agreed to everything the students suggested. "Some of their suggestions were very textbookish," he says. He has also not yet installed a washer and dryer to escape his $300 a week laundry charges. But on the whole, the students did a fine job. The SBA agreed, judging the Maxwells' work the best of all the projects done in 1982.

———

From Teri Agins, "Unpaid Student Consultants Assist Firms Under SBA Plan," *The Wall Street Journal* (July 23, 1984): 19.

---

fashion. Once a machine reaches its capacity, to increase production by even one unit, you will need another machine. It thus becomes very expensive to produce that one extra widget. The full cost of the additional equipment must be absorbed by the $x + 1$ units. If, however, you can sell all or almost all of the output from the additional machine or the additional worker, it may be to your advantage to go ahead and make the addition.

Suppose that you lease a machine for $1,000 a year that will turn out 1,000 casings a year. Based on machine cost alone, your cost is $1 per casing. You know that you could sell 1,100 casings—but, since your current machine is at its capacity, you will need to lease another machine to do the extra production. If you lease the additional machine at $1,000 a year and make 1,100 casings, your machine-only cost per casing would be $1.82—almost double your original cost per casing. If, on the other hand, you could make and sell 1,900 casings, your unit cost would be $1.05.

Just as variable costs are rarely completely variable, most fixed costs are rarely entirely fixed. Two factors account for variability. The first is the units in which you can buy or contract for these costs. The second and major factor is the time period you are considering.

Let's take a look at a space lease, generally considered to be one of the more "fixed" of the fixed costs. Assume your lease is for five years—relatively long-term. If it turns out that you contracted for too much space, your lease may permit you to sublease part of your premises. Voila! The fixed five-year cost just became smaller. If your company is headed for total disaster, and you are convinced that the cost of your space is what is putting you under, you can usually either sublet or buy out of the lease entirely. You have just made a "fixed cost" disappear entirely. And you are still in business. By considering ways, over time, to change "fixed" costs, you can usually "unfix" those costs. The lease cost may be fixed for this month, but you could probably change that number within a longer period.

Other strategies for reducing fixed costs include subcontracting certain parts of your operation (and selling off the equipment that is creating the "fixed" depreciation expense) and buying, rather than building subassemblies for your products. The point here is that, in the long run, all costs are variable. The question is how inventive you become at making them so—if you need to do so at all.

Breakeven

The "breakeven point" for a company is that point at which the income minus the expenses equals zero. In formula, it is defined as follows:

$$\frac{\text{fixed costs}}{\text{sale price} - \text{variable cost}} = \text{Number of units you need to break even}$$

A breakeven chart is shown in Figure 12.1 on the next page.

Let's assume, for a moment, that you are planning to make lucite boxes as your business. You will only make one size. All your revenue will thus come from this one item. Each box will cost you $1.50 to make, counting material and labor and the specialized equipment use that goes into it. The total remaining expenses of your business are $25,000.

You plan to sell each box at $2.00. In order for your revenues to equal, exactly, your total costs—that is, for you to break even—you will have to sell

Figure 12.1   Breakeven chart—graphic view

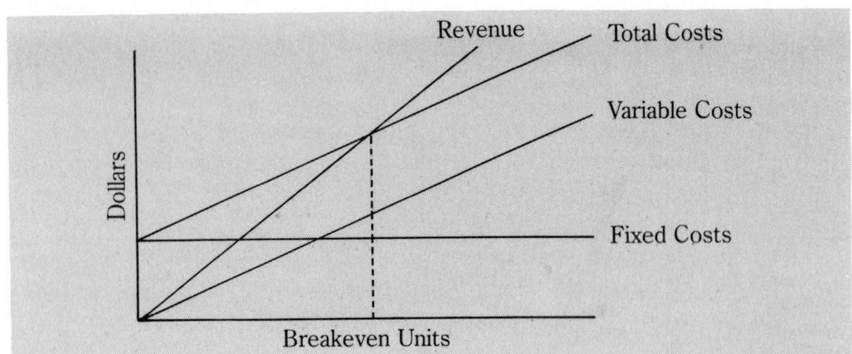

at least 50,000 boxes. ($2.00 – $1.50 = .50 contribution to covering fixed costs of each box sold at that price. $25,000 / .50 = 50,000 boxes.)

As you can see, the breakeven point depends on volume and price, each of which will be discussed in the following section. For the moment, however, just consider what the breakeven does for you. Even without the price, you can develop a total cost line based on the unit volume. This, in itself, is useful. It lets you see the difference in cost that you could achieve by reducing your fixed cost or by changing your variable costs. While the breakeven approach is limited (its limitations are discussed in Chapter 14), it is useful for pricing decisions and should not be ignored.

PRICE/VOLUME CONSIDERATIONS

The price of an item often influences whether or not you, as a consumer, buy it. If you have a range of choices in a product type, the price often influences which specific item you will buy. As a seller, you have to contend with the ability of your customers to do precisely the same things.

Price Affects Volume, Which Affects Breakeven

Recognizing that the price you set will influence the volume you sell is the critical recognition in your pricing strategy. It underlies all pricing strategies, as well as the pricing continuum we discussed earlier. It is what lets Charlisa's Boutique thrive. She simply sells small volumes at giant profit per item. Reilly's, on the other hand, sells large volumes at a small profit per item.

Generally, the strategy you choose will tend toward one approach or the other. Unless you have a particular competitive edge, however, it is generally wise to avoid the real extremes. Your job is to find the point at which price times volume less cost equals maximum profit.

Because price and volume are interrelated, this maximum profit point is not necessarily the highest price point. Suppose, for example, you make a product that costs $10 per unit to make (variable cost). The fixed costs of running your business for the year amount to $50,000. The most you expect to be able to sell at the test price levels are shown in the "volume expected" row in Table 12.1.

Table 12.1   Price/volume tradeoffs and effects

	At $20/Unit	*At $30/Unit*	*At $40/Unit*
Volume expected (units)	10,000	6,000	2,000
Total sales	$200,000	$180,000	$80,000
Variable cost ($10/unit)	$100,000	$ 60,000	$ 20,000
Fixed cost	$ 50,000	$ 50,000	$ 50,000
Net profit	$ 50,000	$ 70,000	$ 10,000
Breakeven (units)	5,000	2,500	1,667

Under the conditions set up in Table 12.1, you will maximize your profit at the $30 price. (Note, by the way, how rapidly the breakeven point drops. That is because the fixed costs are being underwritten by progressively higher "contribution margins"—the difference between sale price per unit and variable cost per unit.)

Estimating Volume

This is the most difficult part of your pricing calculations. It is probably wise to start with the amount you can produce or move through your store without moving up a step on the semi-fixed costs. See what your profit would look like if you priced at about what the competition now gets. How do your profit figures look?

Your next step should probably be to see what would happen if you were to raise the price a bit. Would the amount you could sell drop? How much? Could you recapture the volume with more selling costs? (Do not forget to add the cost of this extra effort to the fixed cost portion of your calculation.) Now, what would your profit figure look like?

Suppose, on the other hand, that you decided to buy additional equipment and drop the price. How much could you sell, do you think, at this new price? Is it worth it to you in profit?

The difficulty is, obviously, that you really have to estimate volume and price together. Essentially, you have to play with the numbers until you find a set that makes sense to you. Just do not forget to add or subtract costs as they move in and out of your tests. Also, do not forget that the prices and volumes you eventually settle on will have to make sense *in your market.*

OTHER APPROACHES TO PRICING

Many industries have nice, standard ways of setting prices. Most retail establishments, for example, tend to price merchandise at twice their cost. Restaurants often triple or quadruple food cost. Many crafts operations triple or quadruple materials costs (which is essentially the same thing).

These approaches have the advantage of being very simple. They generally assume that you can make and sell or simply sell as many units as you want. You then control your profit level by varying the volume of what you make and sell.

In certain circumstances, however, this "as many as you want" foundation will not work for you. If, for example, you can get only x pounds a month of some critical material, your production will be limited to however many of your product you can make with those x pounds. If, on the other hand, there are only a few workers available in your area who can make the product or perform the services you need, your output is limited to what that number of people can do for you. In either of these situations, a purely cost-based approach to your pricing will not really reflect the constraints that exist in production. Moreover, you may not be able to make the amount of profit you need at the limited volume level.

Please note that the key limitation on your volume in these instances is not the willingness of your market to buy. It is, rather, the ability to produce. The constraint is a production constraint of some sort. Under these circumstances, you might want to try a pricing structure that views your entire operation as dependent on the constrained resource. You essentially "load" the other costs of your operation into the cost of the constraining resource and price on the basis of the amount of the resource you can acquire.

Let's consider an example. Jonathan Hogan is a designer and builder of fine furniture. He is operating on his own. His sales appeals are the unique character of his designs and the quality of his workmanship. His obvious constraint is labor. Only he can perform much of the work that results in a Hogan chair or table. And he, like the rest of us, has only 24 hours in a day and seven days in a week.

Hogan generally works 10-hour days, five days a week. He thus has a total of 50 hours of time available. He knows, however, that he will not be able to spend all of this time in the shop, actually working on pieces. He also has to market the pieces and see to the other business/promotion parts of the operation. His best estimate is that he will be able to spend about 30 hours a week actually working on pieces for sale.

He knows that the material for an average piece costs him $500 and takes him 60 hours to design, build, and finish. The expenses of running his business will be $25,000 per year. He expects his personal expenses to total about $20,000. He would like to make at least $5,000 beyond his basic expenses. He has a number of options for pricing.

Number of hours available; $30 \times 50 = 1,500$
Number of pieces that can be made and sold in a year: $1,500 / 60 = 25$

Markup on materials cost

At four times materials cost: $\$500 \times 4 = \$2,000$ per average piece
$\$2,000 \times 25$ pieces $= \$50,000$

Sales	$50,000
Materials	12,500
Gross margin	37,500
Total business expenses	25,000
Profit before tax	$12,500

As you can see, using this approach, Hogan will not be able to cover all his personal expenses. He will certainly not be able to squeeze out enough to give him the $5,000 extra he set out after. Using this approach to pricing, in order to make his goal, he would have to produce and sell almost 34 pieces this year. To do this, he would have to work 2,040 hours in his shop. If he is right about the time consumed by his non-production business work, he will have to put in more than an additional 10-hour day per week to get what he needs.

Under this scenario, it should be noted that Hogan is charging only $5 an hour for his time. ($12,500 / 2,500 hours) Not a bad deal for the buyer!

Cost plus profit

Sales	(plug)
Materials	$12,500
Total business expenses	25,000
Profit	$25,000

Sales $= (\$25,000 + \$25,000 + \$12,500) = \$62,000$
Units $= (\$25,000 + \$25,000 + \$12,500) / 25 = \$2,500$ unit price

Pricing this way definitely gets Hogan the money he needs or wants out of the business. This price is higher than the one developed using the standard markup on materials method. Hogan has to consider whether his market will pay the $500 difference for a genuine Hogan. (They probably will, since he is in a "what the market will bear" kind of market.)

But he still has a problem. He does not make and sell "average" pieces. In fact, one of the things he sells is the uniqueness of each piece. How can he price each piece so that he makes enough to cover everything (if not more) by the year's end?

If you think about what he is really doing here, you will discover that the entire process hinges on his time and, particularly, the part of it he can actually spend in the shop. He could price on the basis of his labor hours. This would give him the flexibility to price each proposed piece by how long he expected it would take him to design and build. His pricing plan would look something like this:

Pricing based on labor hours

Total available shop hours	1,500
Business costs	$25,000
Desired profit	$25,000
Total costs	$50,000 + materials

$50,000 / 1500 = $33.33 price per estimated hour + materials

Therefore, for a simple piece expected to take 40 hours, the price would be:

Materials	$ 500
Other ($33.33 × 40)	$ 1,333
Total	$ 1,833

A more complex or larger piece expected to require 100 hours would be priced as follows:

Materials	$ 500
Other ($33.33 × 100)	$ 3,333
Total	$ 3,833

There are any number of variants on this approach. Hogan could, for example, fix a "salary" for himself. he could even choose two different payment rates, one for his general business work (at which he is just a practitioner) and a second for his shop work (at which he is an expert). The bottom line is that this general approach provides him with the flexibility to price according to the use of his most constrained resource, his own time. (It also gives him the kinds of information required to figure out whether it is worthwhile for him to concentrate on the design work, substituting outside labor for parts of the construction process, the business functions, or both.)

The dangers in this approach to pricing lie in inaccurate estimates of the use of the constrained resource—in this case, Hogan's time—and a poor estimate of the overall amount of time that he can be in the shop (his volume). Of course, these dangers will affect any pricing scheme. They are simply more obvious in this approach because the critical factor has been elevated to the controlling position.

PRICING MULTIPLE PRODUCTS

While the constrained resource approach to pricing will work for a job-shop type of operation like Hogan's, the problem of how to approach the pricing of multiple products still remains for many kinds of companies. Consider this case.

Dana Jamison is developing a company that will produce two major products. The first is a new kind of knitting machine. The second is a line of crafts canvasses and other needlework fabrics. She sells the machines to small crafts operations. She sells the fabrics as a wholesaler to retail crafts stores. How should she approach pricing the two products?

The issue is clear. Until this point, we have been looking at the fixed costs of a business as a single piece, to be allocated equally over all the units that will be produced. If a company produces more than one product, particularly if the products are as different as Jamison's two, the lump sum approach will probably yield irrational prices. In most businesses, this can create significant damage, not only in the market, but also in the way that the company evaluates the worth of its products. Table 12.2 shows her fixed costs and the variable costs of producing a unit of each product.

The underlying problem is how to divide (allocate) costs among products or

Table 12.2   Jamison Needlework: fixed and variable costs

VARIABLE COST OF:

Knitting machines (unit)		*Fabrics (100 square yards)*	
Labor	$25.00	Labor	$ 3.50
Material	25.00	Material	1.50
Factory overhead	10.00	Factory overhead	5.00
Total	$60.00	Total	$10.00

Fixed Costs	
Space costs	$18,000
Salaried staff	37,000
Other general and administrative (G&A)	20,000
Total	$75,000

product lines. There are numerous ways to approach this issue. There is no one right way, but, rather, a number of potentially reasonable ways of allocating any set of costs. Be aware, however, that the choices you make will have significant effects on the prices you eventually come to and also on the "profit" you recognize as coming from a given product or product line. You can see some of these differences in the allocation schemes for Jamison's company.

Suppose Jamison were to assume that each product was "responsible" for half of each fixed cost. She expected to sell 1,000 of the machines this year and 100,000 square yards of the fabrics. The total costs she would develop would appear as they do in Table 12.3.

Table 12.3   Jamison Needlework: Approach 1

	Machines	*Fabrics*
Numbers of units to be sold	1,000	1,000
Variable cost per unit	$ 60	$ 10
Total variable costs	$60,000	$10,000
Cost allocations		
Space	$ 9,000	$ 9,000
Salaries	18,500	18,500
G & A	10,000	10,000
TOTAL COST	$97,500	$47,500
COST PER UNIT	$ 97.50	$ 47.50
PRICE PER UNIT (Assuming 10 percent over and above costs)	$107.25	$ 52.25

Using the same volumes and aggregate cost projections, but allocating them differently can produce startlingly different results, as can readily be seen in Table 12.4. There, for example, her costing reflects the fact that storing the large machines and their parts actually takes up two-thirds of the space that the company uses. In addition, since the fabrics are sold mainly by telephone and at trade shows, fully 80 percent of the personnel expenses really belong to the machine segment of the business.

The idea is to reflect the reality as well as you possibly can. Thus, the "right" decisions about allocations for your company must grow out of your knowledge of your market and your specific operating structure. Such issues will, however, make major differences in your approach to pricing, which, in turn, will affect your success at sales and marketing.

Table 12.4   Jamison Needlework: Approach 2

	Machines	*Fabrics*
Total variable costs:	$ 60,000	$10,000
Cost allocations:		
Space	$ 12,000	$ 6,000
Salaries	29,600	7,400
G & A	10,000	10,000
TOTAL COST	$111,600	$33,400
COST PER UNIT	$ 111.60	$ 33.40
PRICE PER UNIT (Assuming 10 percent over and above costs)	$ 122.76	$ 36.74

Think hard about each cost item you will need to allocate among more than one product. Each cost or cost category should be addressed separately. Before deciding on the approach to use for a specific cost, ask yourself about how the cost you are allocating arises. Is it volume-based? Is the cost based on utilization of space, manpower, or some other input that will give you a valid basis for allocation? Most costs that are legitimate business expenses are generated in some way that relates them to what you produce. Use those linkages. Only for those costs that have no such simplifying basis—for example, executive salaries, corporate jet planes, charitable contributions—should you use the standard "percentage of sales" or even split or numbers of units approaches. Even when using these, your objective is to choose the one that seems to you to make the most basic sense.

ILLEGAL APPROACHES TO PRICING

In addition to the exigencies of the marketplace, you face another series of limitations on your pricing freedom—the government. There are a number of practices in which you are forbidden to engage. Most of them are, or at least were originally, designed to protect small business owners from the giants, so you are unlikely to want to engage in those practices anyway. They would be likely to prove fatal for a small new company.

Price-Fixing

You may not collude with others in your industry to set a general price on your product or service. In industries in which there is a strong price leader and severe competition, this is very difficult to enforce, simply because the market itself produces an almost uniform price level. What has to be proved is the collusion, not merely the uniformity of price.

A case in point is what was going on in the airline industry in the early 1980s. As deregulation phased in, major airfare wars broke out throughout the industry. Carriers matched each others' prices. The only time the issue of price-fixing arose was when an executive of American Airlines and one from Braniff actually spoke on the telephone about the fare war (and were imprudent enough to be taped).

Differential Pricing

You may not simply pick a price based on whether you like the customer. Your pricing structure has to be uniform across all customers. You may, of course, offer discounts for large orders or for early payment, but you have to offer these to all your customers, not just a select few.

Predatory Pricing

A seller cannot cut prices below costs for the sole purpose of forcing another company out of business. This is good for you because, given the probable level of your financing as a new company, you would be the first to go. When you become the giant in your industry, you will just have to live with this limitation.

If you have discovered a significantly cheaper way to do whatever it is that you do, you can, of course, take advantage of your advantage. The giants can follow your price down. They just cannot engineer losses on a product, knowing that they have more financial clout than you do.

SUMMARY

As you can see, pricing is a highly complex set of issues, involving your market, your production capacities, your strategic approach to your market, and your costs. The order in which those factors need to be considered, and the weight you assign to each, depends largely on the business you are in.

There are three basic approaches to pricing: what the competition is doing, what your costs are, and what the market will bear. If your industry requires that you price an undifferentiable product at the going price, your only question is whether you can make a profit at that price. Your pricing decisions have been made for you. If you do have pricing decisions to make, your costs come into play as a factor to be considered, rather than as an absolute constraint on the business.

In addition to cost considerations, volume estimates are also critical factors in developing your pricing structure. Generally, as you move up the price scale for your type of product, your volume will decrease. This price/volume relationship has significant effects on your breakeven point (the point at which sales revenue minus all costs is zero) and on your profit level. it is not always the case that you maximize profit at the highest possible price.

Many kinds of businesses have accepted approaches to pricing that have the advantage of being simple and the disadvantage of being inflexible and unable to adjust for special circumstances. It is wise to test any accepted approach in your industry against a more complex pricing method, if for no other reason than to confirm that the accepted method makes sense for you.

A cost-based pricing method generally begins with a division of your costs into fixed and variable components; these are, respectively, those costs you will incur through being in business regardless of your sales level, and those related to the production of a unit of your product. Often, a profit factor is added and considered a "cost" for pricing purposes. The total of your costs, divided by the number of units you expect to sell gives you a cost-based price. A pricing structure based on your constraining resource is a variant on the cost-based approach.

If you are intending to make or sell more than one product, pricing by any method that involves your costs also involves allocating fixed costs among products. Here, an understanding of how each cost is generated is most useful, as is common sense and some thought about what allocation basis best reflects reality.

As should be clear, pricing is part art and part analysis. The key notion is that, once you develop a tentative price structure by one of these methods, you carefully consider whether what you are seeing makes sense to you. Ask yourself questions. Try out a number of approaches and methods. But never lose sight of the fact that you will not be operating in a vacuum. Your competitors and your market are the final arbiters of how good your pricing method is (or was).

FOR YOU TO CONSIDER

1. What are the three basic approaches to setting prices? Name two kinds of businesses in which each approach might be appropriate.
2. What is "skimming" in pricing strategy?
3. What is a "fixed cost"? Consider the statement that "In the long run, all costs are variable."
4. What is a "semi-fixed cost" or a "step-function variable cost"? In what circumstances might the existence of such costs be important to a company?

5. Why is it true that you do not necessarily maximize profit at the highest possible price?
6. What is the "breakeven point"? What does knowing it do for you?
7. What is the standard approach to pricing in most retail business? What are the advantages and disadvantages of this approach?
8. Why might you want to make a constrained resource the basis for your pricing structure? How do you do it?
9. Why might you need to allocate costs among products? How should you go about doing such allocations?
10. Discuss two major legal constraints on how you go about setting prices for your products. Why do such legal restrictions exist?

FOR FURTHER READING

Monroe, Kent. *Pricing*. New York: McGraw-Hill, 1979.
Tucker, Spencer A. *Pricing for Higher Profit*. New York: McGraw-Hill, 1966.

Small Business Administration publications:

A Pricing Checklist for Small Retailers. SBA MA 4.013.
Pricing for Small Manufacturers. SBA MA 1.003.
Profit Pricing and Costing of Services. SBA MA 1.020.
Simple Breakeven Analysis for Small Stores. SBA MA 1.019.
What is the Best Selling Price. SBA MA 1.002.

CASES FOR PART 5

SALLY JONES AND "NEIGHBORS"

Sally and Janice knew that a key part of planning for their new restaurant was advertising for opening day and for the period immediately after that. They decided to plan this campaign early and carefully, since it was critical and would undoubtedly be costly, relative to their normal advertising costs.

From their industry average research, they had found that most restaurants spent between 1 and 3 percent of sales on their advertising. Their data indicated that restaurants of their proposed size could gross about $150,000 to $200,000 per year. For planning purposes, they decided to begin with the lower sales estimate. This implied an advertising budget of $3,000 to $4,000 for their first full year of operation. They then began to collect information on advertising rates for the various newspapers and radio stations in their service area. These are shown in the following exhibits.

Table 1   Advertising rates: print media, Pittsburg and Mount Lebanon, Pa.

OPEN, PER INCH	Black and White	Color	Circulation (metro.)
Pgh. Press (P.M.)	$ 81.27	$1,180.00	243,680
Pgh. Post Gazette (A.M.)	65.10	850.00	147,183
Sunday	132.72	1,770.00	509,452
QUARTER PAGE			
Mt. Leb. Almanac (WK)	199.78	60.00	29,702

Source: Standard Rate and Data Services, Inc. (Wilmette, Illinois, 1984).

Table 2   Advertising rates: spot radio, Pittsburgh area, selected stations

1 MIN. HIGH:	WPNT–FM (Easy)	WTAE–AM (Adult)	WTAE/WTKN–FM (Talk)
A.M. drive—til 10	$ 90	$270	$450
Daytime—10–3	110	123	205
P.M. drive—3–8	100	129	215
Night and weekend	75	84	140
30 SECONDS			
A.M. drive	—	246	360
Daytime	—	98	164
P.M. drive	—	103	172
Night and weekend	—	67	112

Source: Standard Rate and Data Services, Inc. (Wilmette, Illinois, 1984).

The partners realized that their signs, logo, and menus would also be important parts of their overall public image. They therefore decided to approach this as an advertising/marketing/promotion problem as well.

It was clear to them, as Sally's professors used to remind her, that advertising needed to say something and to fit the image of what they were really trying to sell. For "Neighbors," the two women decided, the key things to tell the world would be the quality of the food and the peace of the atmosphere. They reminded each other again and again that their primary target market was the housewife—who would also bring her family in the evenings. Their issues were whether these themes would sell to that group and how to make their major points succinctly and compellingly.

1. Develop an advertising expenditure approach for Sally and Janice. Be prepared to support your choices and allocations of dollars.
2. Are there any approaches to advertising and selling "Neighbors" that the two friends are missing? If so, how would you go about developing and exploiting the sources/methods/approaches you identified?
3. Sketch (don't worry about it being "pretty") and/or write the copy for the ads you would use for your opening blitz. If you absolutely cannot sketch, at least block out layouts. At the same time, develop ideas for a logo and menu design.

•   •   •

The final major area that needed to be addressed before the friends really got down to the final numbers and revenue and cost estimates was the pricing structure for "Neighbors." While there were a number of possible ways to approach this issue, they decided to start with the average check size that their customers were used to paying for lunch and for dinner. They kept in mind that theirs would be a "homey," everyday—or, at least, drop-in-often—kind of place, rather than a place for serious celebrations or significant events.

From their own experiences, they determined that their market would support a $5–$6 lunch check (without wine) and a $9–$11 dinner check (also excluding wine or beer). In order to make the place work, however, they also knew that there should be a mix of item prices on their menu. They didn't want to keep out groups of women, one or two of whom would rather spend less. They planned to add a children's menu at night to cushion the blow for Dad and Mom. Their entire thrust was to make it relatively painless for their customers to eat at "Neighbors" often.

They began by working industry average data backwards to figure out how much their food had to cost to enable them to come to these average check prices. The Robert Morris figures showed that small restaurants averaged a cost of goods sold (food cost) of 44.4 percent. The Dun & Bradstreet ratio for all restaurants was 53.5 percent. To be on the safe side, they decided to split the difference, figuring a food cost of 49.0 percent. This meant that their average lunch should cost them $2.50–$3.00 to make.

Using various books on restaurant management, they began working on a formula pricing method for a plain omelette.

3 eggs (@ 1.20/doz.)	$ .40
Croissant	.60*
Butter and jam, etc.	.20
Salad (2 oz. lettuce, 1 oz. dressing, .2 oz. tomato)	.70
Total food cost	$1.90
10% waste/shrinkage	.19
Total probable cost	$2.09
Minimum selling price	(2.09/.49) $4.27

*Would be priced in this way separately.

Assuming that they would charge $.80 for unlimited good coffee, and the next nearest rounded-up price for the food, the check for the omelette and coffee would come to $5.30—right in their lunch range.

They decided that this pricing approach looked good. They therefore developed the pricing/costing/portion size sheet shown as Figure 1. They then decided—with a great deal of trepidation—to see whether "Neighbors" could break even. At this point, they could only use very preliminary numbers, but they figured at least they would have some idea of whether they were in the right ballpark. They figured that they could fill their tables, on average, twice each lunchtime and one and a half times each dinnertime.

Figure 1   Menu pricing and costing form—"Neighbors"

Ingredient	Portion Size	Unit Cost (cooked)	Portion Cost

Preparation comments and/or methods	Cost
	+ *10% Shrinkage*
	Total cost
	Selling price
	− *Total cost*
	Gross margin $ and (%)

To be on the safe side, however, they bracketed their estimate on the downside by also looking at what would happen to "Neighbors" if they could only turn 1.3 times at lunch and once at dinners. They assumed that their non-food costs would total about $175,000 per year. Their gross margin had been set at 51 percent in their pricing calculations.

1. What do you think about how Sally and Janice developed their pricing strategy? Can you think of any modifications or changes you would recommend to them?
2. How flexible is their pricing methodology? Is this "good"?
3. What factor(s) will be absolutely critical to their operation in light of their pricing methodology?
4. Given the current set of assumptions, will "Neighbors" break even at the lower table-turn estimate? Assuming their total non-food cost estimate is roughly accurate, how much in sales volume will it take for them to break even?

ROB KING AND "KING FINANCIAL"

Rob King knew that he would have to leave his job at Consolidated before he began to actually solicit clients for King Financial. It was this aspect, his quitting, that had most upset Ginny. Not to quit, however, would leave him open to serious charges of conflict of interest. This could lead to serious legal and professional consequences that would be bad for the family and bad for King Financial (more like "fatal," in fact).

In searching for some middle ground, Rob hit upon two ideas that he believed might help set him up for King Financial. First, he would get out into the community more, moving into activities and organizations in which new entrepreneurs might be involved or interested. Second, he would start writing and speaking at every possible opportunity. He considered offering a local paper a column on small business financing, but he decided that it would be too close to home. He didn't want to alert Helm to what was going on before he was completely ready.

His next step was to determine what issues on the next few city council agendas might have effects on the small business community in the area. He then began to study these potential effects and to develop positions on the issues that would support the interests of small businesses. Positions developed and speeches written, he arranged to comment on selected proposed ordinances at the meetings—a feat which, oddly enough, could be accomplished in his city merely by telling the appropriate officials of his desire to be heard on the issue. He took great care not to knock the banks or to take any position contrary to the interests or policies of Consolidated. He figured he could do that later, if necessary—after he quit.

His first council appearance was set for the following month. He began to attend meetings immediately to get the lay of the land and to find out who showed up and how meetings generally went. He also began to drag Ginny off to school board and PTA meetings on the general theory that any additional people who knew him and whom he knew certainly could not hurt. The image he wanted to project was one of a comfortable, thriving family man on the move. "I'm in commercial lending at Consolidated," began to appear frequently in his conversations. After meetings he would get out his index cards and add the names, businesses, and anything else he could remember about the people he met and their families. His goal was to have a thousand cards by the time he was ready to open his "office."

In addition to his campaign to become known in the right circles for the right things, Rob also began to keep a list of all small businesses (proprietorships and partnerships) that filed with the city. He had a cousin of his monitoring new corporate filings at the state level.

Rob knew that this approach would take time, but that might not be all bad. It would give everyone time to get used to the new Rob King, business owner. Interestingly enough, Rob had noticed that since he had decided to go ahead with his plans for King Financial, he felt less threatened by Helm and by Consolidated National. He felt less angry and generally less distressed about going to work in the mornings. His secret seemed to calm him. It probably did not hurt to know that, if he were fired, he had a backup plan. A firing would only shift his time schedule—and it might induce Ginny's wholehearted support.

While he waited to begin actual operations, he designed what he intended to be his opening gun, a brochure describing himself and his services. It would, of course, be printed on classy paper, befitting his new image. He intended to have a professional do the typesetting and printing. He planned to mail this one-page item to every person he knew—either business-related or personal (including his index card deck). He figured that practically anyone might know someone who could use his services and that, therefore, anyone was worth the 22-cent mailing cost. We have reproduced a draft of his brochure in Figures 1 and 2.

1. Comment on Rob King's approach to finding his potential clients and to determining the size of his potential market. Are the companies that he is finding the ones that he targeted in his basic business definition? If not, what do you suggest he do?
2. Comment on Rob King's personal publicity campaign. Do you think it will accomplish his goals for it?
3. Comment on the brochure that Rob King proposes to circulate when he leaves Consolidated. What do you believe King intends for it to accomplish? Will it do those things? If there are things about it that you do not like, what improvements or alternatives would you propose to Rob King?

•   •   •

Figure 1   Draft statement of experience (for inclusion in brochure)

Robert J. King, president and founder of King Financial, has spent the last 10 years in commercial lending at Consolidated National Bank. During this time, he was responsible for working with loan clients in preparing their loan applications and for monitoring the performance of bank borrowers.

Prior to his experience at Consolidated, Mr. King served in the finance department of Acme General, Inc., a manufacturing company concentrating in the manufacture of widgets for industrial markets. He was responsible for analysis of capital asset acquisition proposals and for general cost and financing analyses.

Mr. King, a certified public accountant, served the accounting firm of Snyder and Roe for three years as an auditor. He holds a BSBA and an MBA, specializing in finance, from State University.

Figure 2   Draft brochure for King Financial (tri-fold)

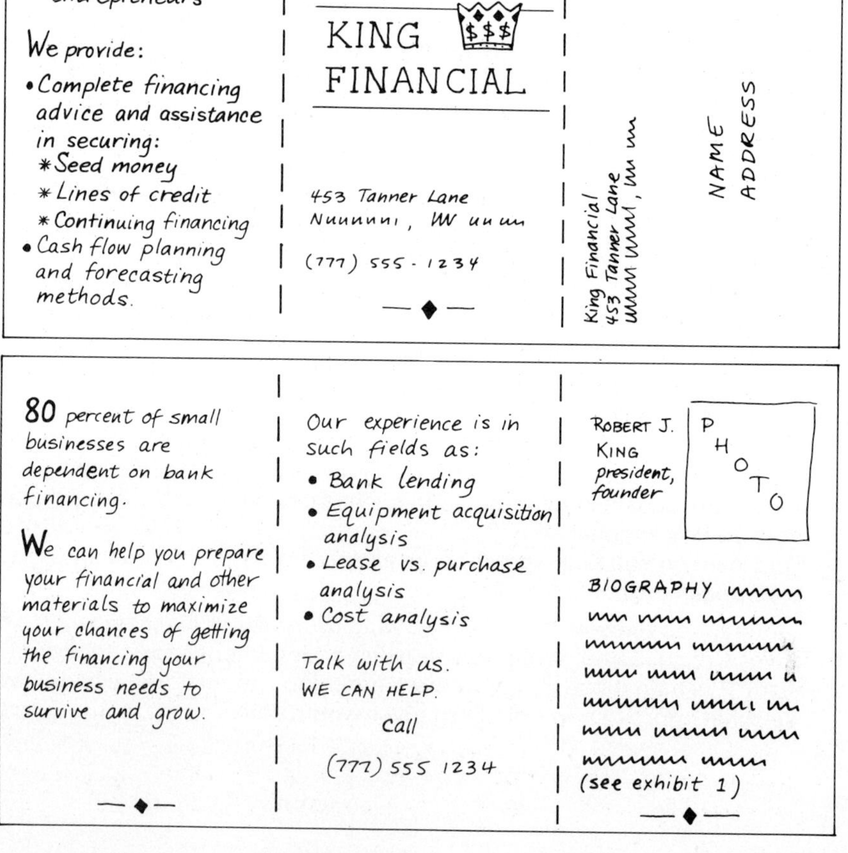

Rob King also had to determine a general pricing scheme for his services. As he had learned early in his research, people seemed to equate cost with quality in the consulting business. His particular market, however, was more prone than most consulting markets to consider cost an obstacle—particularly since King was planning to assist in the initial or early financing of businesses. He thus had to walk a very fine line between being too expensive for his clientele and appearing to be too cheap to be any good.

He had a number of options about how to price his services. He was playing with the notion of taking his fee on a contingency basis—that is, he would be paid a percentage of the financing that he helped his clients secure. He wondered whether this would be a good approach for him. He also considered a fee structure that gave him more if a financing went through than if it did not. He would charge a per diem rate in any case for consulting work not directly related to a particular financing.

In terms of developing that per diem rate, he belived that the market would have to be his main guideline. He expected his costs to be low in relation to any reasonable pricing scheme. The standard approach for large consulting operations, he knew, was one-third, one-third, one-third—the first for salaries, the second for overhead, and the third for profit to what was generally a partnership. These structures often resulted in fully loaded rates for partner-level consultants of upwards of $1,500 a day. His clients would not be able to afford him at those rates, even had they wanted to.

He then turned to a survey of per diem rates for independent consulting firms compiled in "The Professional Consultant," a newsletter published by Howard L. Shenson, Inc. Shenson's group surveyed a random sample of all independent consultants and found per diem rates ranging from $376 (in arts and cultural consulting) to $688 in scientific fields. He was pleased to note that consultants in finance were far from the bottom at $555 a day. He wondered how his prospective clients would react to a rate in that range.

He knew that he had to reach a decision soon, so that he could begin to figure out whether he would make any money at his new consulting practice.

1. How do you believe Rob King should go about making his choice of a pricing mechanism and a per diem rate for his services?
2. Comment on the possibilities and drawbacks inherent in the contingency approach to pricing for King's financing clients.
3. How does Rob King's situation differ from the groups with which he has been comparing himself? How are the situations similar? Do you believe that Rob King should emphasize the differences or the similarities in his pricing scheme?

DANIELLE MACKIE AND "DANIELLE DESIGNS IN CERAMICS"

Danielle Mackie also had a number of options about how to sell and publicize her work. She was not quite sure where her market was likely to be, if she decided to sell her work out of her own shop/studio. She of course visualized the rich and famous flocking (quietly and tastefully) to her elegant showroom, drawn by a full-color ad in the *New Yorker* magazine. But a quick check of the *New Yorker's* rates disabused her of that notion. They would want $8,900 for even a third of a page of 4-color, coated-stock advertisement. Even a third of a page (by 1 column width) in black and white would set her back $4,420 for a single insertion. She was clearly not ready for the *New Yorker* crowd (half a million in circulation) just yet. Only 190,000 of them are near enough to come to my place anyway, she sighed. (She counted the northeast and middle Atlantic states.)

More realistically, Mackie considered her selling options. She could sell her "bulk" pieces to wholesalers, directly to retailers, or to the general public. While she could probably combine sales to the general public with either wholesaler or retailer sales, she doubted that she could sell to both wholesalers and retailers without causing some distress among her buyers.

She could move her creative work on her own out of her studio and at shows or she could move it through established galleries. If she worked with galleries, she could either sell directly or work on consignment. Here, too, she figured that she could combine some direct customer sales and some trade show sales with either program. She could not, probably, operate differently with different galleries in the same general area.

Danni realized, as she thought about her situation, that three very distinct business roles were involved in her choices about how to move her goods. First, there was the role of the creative artist (or of the production artist). In this role, her tasks would be those she had envisioned from the start—coming up with the ideas, bringing her technical and artistic skills to bear on her materials, and ensuring the quality and consistency of her output.

If she decided to work with galleries, on either a straight sale or a consignment basis, she would be taking on the role of a wholesaler. She would be selling to the gallery owners. Initially, the sale would be to gain her gallery space—a tough sell, given the needs of the owners for rapid turnover. If her pieces sold well, she would become more of an order-taker. In either case, however, she would have to take time away from what she considered her real work to accomplish her ends. This would also be true if she decided to sell to large stores directly.

It would be even more time-consuming for her if she took on the role of retailer—either on direct sales to the public or mail order sales. In this role, she would have to handle advertising and publicity, the actual selling process, and the record-keeping associated with retail sales to the public. This role, too, would require a significant chunk of her time. At least, she thought, my education gave me some notion as to how to go about these things!

When she considered selling only out of her workshop/studio—whichever one she eventually chose—she realized that that approach would never work. According to data from National Decision Systems of California, the data producers for *Standard Rates and Data,* the Albany-Schenectady-Troy area ranked in the 50s in terms of populations and households among television areas, but only 160th in terms of average household income. It ranked only 147th in terms of retail sales per household. Oddly enough, relative expenditures in home furnishings stores were high, with the area ranking 54th. Looking at this data convinced Mackie that, to the extent she sold out of her place of work, she would be seeking mainly non-local people. She began to view sales out of her studio as adjunct to her real business. She was not really prepared to give up entirely the ego boosts and the sheer joy of talking with others about her work and about ceramics in general.

Danielle Mackie knew, as well, that her choice about how she would do business and the roles that she would take on would influence her choices about marketing her goods and about pricing them. She decided to consider the marketing effects first.

She already knew that her sole support could not come from her local population, but if she decided to open a studio shop she would hope to garner *some* business through it. The local paper, however, would probably not be a good place to advertise. While the populations of the area colleges, including Albany, Rensselaer, and Skidmore, might be good bets in terms of aesthetic sensibilities, she doubted that most students (and faculty members, for that matter) would be able to afford her serious pieces. Space in college papers and literary magazines was cheap, however, and she thought she might try selling some of her production pieces in this way. (She made a note about remembering to include her right to do this in any contract she made with a wholesaler or a store buyer.)

Posters in appropriate places might also work in this market. Particularly if she preceded her poster placement effort with some publicity. She was pretty sure that she could generate some interest from local papers in the beginnings of a new professional artist, a former museum staff member. This publicity would pave the way for her with town merchants, hotels, and other places likely to be pickup points for her brochure. (She made another note about the approach to and costs of developing a slick, small brochure. She realized that this wouldn't hurt, no matter which selling approach or approaches she chose.)

She also considered test marketing one or two of her simpler, "creative" pieces in mail order sales. She could buy space in the crafts magazines, she knew, for not terribly much money. A sixth of a page in *Crafts Magazine* (black and white) would cost her $959 and would reach almost 500,000 people—all interested in crafts. She could go with *Popular Ceramics*, getting a full page for $525 and an extra color for an extra $180. While this magazine presumably reached a more targeted audience—people interested in ceramics—the publisher had provided no circulation data to *Standard Rates and Data*, so Danni couldn't be sure of what she would be buying.

Mail order appealed to her for a number of reasons. First, it could be home-based. Second, she could produce pieces only in response to orders. She would not have to create a stock to keep on hand. Third, she got to keep the entire sales price—and perhaps even make a bit of money on the packing and shipping process. She would, however, have to handle the additional work and the advertising and order fulfillment costs. Obviously, she would choose pieces for her test—"limited editions, signed by the artist"—that would pack and ship well.

She knew she was going to be selling production pieces through larger stores. In fact, she had already committed to produce three pieces in bulk for autumn delivery to a number of stores. She knew that the relevant buyers frequented the art and crafts fairs and shows, so she doubted that this segment of her work would require additional time and/or sales effort. Of course, she had to keep coming up with good bulk-production pieces that would interest these buyers. And she would have to prove herself capable of producing to spec and on time—consistently. But this was what they were paying her for, why she wanted to make ceramics her business. It did not concern her particularly.

It was the gallery business that was her greatest concern in the wholesale area. She had to decide— before she went to the owners for their round of discussion—what her policies would be about how to relate to the galleries. The key issue was whether she would only sell her work outright to the gallery owner or whether she would accept a consignment arrangement. Under a straight sale arrangement, a sale was a sale. Accepting consignment meant that she would have to keep up with the sales of her pieces at every gallery she worked with on a monthly basis, collecting her money, checking displays, and changing and/or replacing stock as necessary. Consignment, on the other hand, might get her broader visibility in galleries, since the owner was taking less risk in carrying her pieces. Like artists, gallery owners were usually strapped for cash.

From a financial perspective, this choice was also important. The various distribution methods each carried different cost implications—entirely beyond the costs she had already considered. The average (or range of) amount that Mackie would receive using each different distribution channel is listed below. Within ranges, the precise figure would depend on the demand for Mackie's work, on the volume she would be producing and selling, and on how good a negotiator she was.

	Percent of Retail Selling Price
Retail reseller	50
Wholesale distributor	33.3
Consignment seller	60–70
Sales representative	70–95
Art shows/crafts fairs—entry fee	($25–$100) 70–95

After the shock of seeing this wide range of numbers, she realized that each level of the distribution channel was simply taking its share for services rendered. Her question, then, was largely which distribution roles, if any, she wanted to perform. Given this new insight, she decided to price her work so that she could make a living as an artist and production potter. She figured that this would be fair, no matter which distribution method she chose, since providing other distribution services would take time from her work and reduce her ability to produce. She would, essentially, be trading off larger production (volume) against higher profits per unit for herself on fewer units.

Her problem at the moment was that she had already made some sales. It was not the sales of her "creative" pieces that concerned her, though. She had already quoted a price to the buyers for larger stores who wanted her production pieces. She was now stuck with that price, at least for this round of sales, and she wondered whether she was likely to make any money on what had been intended to be her bread-and-butter work. In addition to this short-term issue, she had to develop a pricing structure that would make it easy for

1. Danni herself to eat and pay her bills.
2. Retailers to sell her pieces to final customers at twice what it had cost them.
3. Final customers to purchase and own her pieces.

She wrote up a very rough estimate of what her costs and her time would be for making an average production piece and for an average creative piece. She then listed her estimated costs of acquiring equipment, making renovations and improvements in her place, and supporting a studio. These estimates are shown in Table 1. Her estimates for materials costs are shown in Table 2.

Danielle knew that artists, craftspeople, consultants, and others who worked alone and had no clear guidelines tended to grossly underprice the value of their labor. She did not want to fall into that trap. She figured that her labor as an artist should bring in more than her labor as a slide cataloguer, but she also knew that this was unlikely to be reasonable before her work became known and desired. She thus began with the notion of replacing her current $23,000 salary in her labor charges for the year. She would not try to recoup the costs of the benefit package she had at the museum.

She had timed her work prior to her first crafts show in anticipation of needing to know how long it took her to make her pieces. Once her clay was properly prepared, her average time for throwing, trimming, and glazing her production decorative pitcher was 30 minutes, not including the actual firing times. Her fluted bowl took 15 minutes; her urn, 40 minutes; and her vase, 20 minutes. Her smaller pieces of creative work took an average of six hours, the medium-sized ones, eight, and her large or particularly complex pieces could take up to two days of solid work once the concept was clear to her.

She also knew that she would be unlikely to be able to work at her craft for eight hours a day, seven days a week—even if she wanted to. There would be the inevitable tasks involved with running a business. She would have to bill and handle collections, pay her suppliers, generally keep track of and account for things, and do whatever marketing and/or selling and/or promotion her choice of distribution channel implied. If she ran the business only through wholesalers, she expected that the details of the business would account for at least four hours a week. Under these circumstances, assuming a normal 40-hour work week, Danielle Mackie had, at maximum, 34 hours of salable time.

Danni also wanted to make some clear profit beyond the value of her labor, simply because of the level of risk associated with what she was doing. She thought that 10 percent of her sales (before taxes) would be a nice return. That was about what she could get (at the time) from investing her money in a money market fund at very little risk.

At the crafts show, she had offered her production pieces for sale to retail buyers at:

Pitcher	$40
Bowl	$20
Urn	$35
Vase	$25

Her orders, all three of which were taken at the show, were for (in total):

Vases	50
Pitchers	30
Urns	100

Also at the show, she had sold several pieces of her serious, signed work. The smallest and simplest had sold for $100 and the most complex, intricate piece she had brought had sold for $300. Other prices had ranged between. She had met no major resistance regarding her asking prices. Upon reflection, this fact worried her a bit. Was she charging too little?

With all this information before her, Danielle Mackie sat down to figure out what kind of shape she was in and how she ought to conduct her business.

1. It is clear that Danni is waffling around, trying to avoid decisions that are not immediately necessary. We both know that this may leave her in grave danger of drifting into disaster. Please help her out by structuring an approach or a mix of approaches to marketing her wares. Please include in your description of what you recommend to her
   a. The role(s) she is taking on in the distribution process.
   b. The costs she is assuming and those she is avoiding.
   c. The reasons you have made your recommendations.
   Try to convince her that you are right and are only trying to help her reach what you believe to be her goals.
2. What kind of shape is Danni in? Did she sell her bulk pieces for too little? Is she selling her "creative" pieces for too little? Assuming that she will be able to adjust her prices in her next round of selling (however you recommended she go about that process), what should her pricing structure look like?

Table 1   Estimated equipment and operating costs

Equipment	$1,750
Renovations and improvements	3,500
Racks, shelves	500
Electricity	400 per month
Rent (including living space)	900 per month
Show entry fees (seasonal)	100 per month (average)
Telephone, postage	60 per month
Promotion (seasonal)	100 per month (average)

Table 2   Estimated materials costs

Clays	$15 (50 pounds)
Glazes	$20 (enough for 150 pounds of clay)

Average piece expected to require 4–5 pounds of clay.

ED JAMES AND "OAK TREE BOOKS"

Once he ironed out his approach to the actual operations of his bookstore, Ed James began to consider how to let people know he was going to be in the market and what, specifically, he should tell people about his store. He already knew a few things that he would be unlikely to be able to do. A lifetime of frequenting bookstores had convinced him about some things he knew he didn't want to do.

What worried him most, perhaps, was being—or being perceived by the public as—"just another bookstore." He really wanted to provide something out of the ordinary, if not unique. He also knew he would *have* to do this to survive, since he would not be able to offer discounts on his books. His competitive edge(s) had to be based in something other than price.

The book industry had a fairly straightforward price structure. Discounts to retailers were offered on the basis of volume purchased. Since he planned to operate a single, independent store, he knew that his volume would not justify the really large discounts. Without such discounts, he would be unable to offer discounts to his customers, as a general rule. He expected to price his books at the suggested retail price—the one printed on the dust jacket or on the book itself. With a chain operation and a discounter already in the neighborhood, he'd certainly need something to entice potential book buyers into his store.

Ed also knew that his name and advertising would have to carry his special message clearly enough so that potential patrons would recognize his uniqueness immediately. The name of his store would clearly be critical to his success in this respect. But he foresaw a problem. He intended to sell in two virtually separate markets. In fact, he was trying to find space that would permit him to run two virtually separate shops, one within the other. In short, he needed a name that would work for children and for adults-as-parents, yet that would not discourage browsing and purchasing by adults-as-readers.

He had thought of a number of possible names for the place. He was really looking for one name with two parts—one for general books and one for the younger set. He definitely did not want to even think about his second shop as a "kiddie corner," since he believed that it constituted looking down on or talking down to the youngsters. From his teaching experience, he knew that this would be a fatal flaw in his plans. He wanted youngsters to want to come to his store. Some of his potential names are shown below:

> The Tree (and Acorn)
> Journeys (and Horizons)
> The Book Cellar

He was not overjoyed by any of these, so he put the issue aside in hopes that a better notion would come to him soon.

Selling his bookstore, whatever he chose to call it, would be a critical task for Ed James. He knew that people are confronted with books frequently, particularly the paperback variety that are sold in any supermarket or drug store. Buying books in such outlets was certainly easier and more convenient than coming to his store for a book. Youngsters of school age were also inundated with books, generally the kind that they *had* to read, as opposed to *wanted* to read. His advertising and any promotions he sponsored would have to overcome these edges in his two markets.

What Ed James really needed was something to draw people into his shop. He knew that "sidelines" were also key to bookstore survival and profitability, but he didn't want to carry the standard run of cutesy mugs and bookmarks. Magazines, apparently another profitable sideline, would not help, because it would not solve his problem of how to get customers to choose his store over more standard outlets. Everyone, it seemed, sold magazines.

He decided to give serious consideration to a small line of stationery and wrapping papers. He knew that it was difficult to find really nice note papers and unique wrapping papers. The "paper" aspects would fit with books, and, if the papers became a major item, he could expand the line and add a professional wrapping service to his repertoire easily at a later date. He knew of at least one such service operating at fantastic profits in New York City. He knew of no such independent service in his area.

Once his service mix was decided, Ed James began to develop a marketing and promotional plan for his store. He had decided on Oak Tree Books and Fine Papers (and Acorn) as his business name. He visualized his advertising material as framed by the side and outstretched branches of a tree for his adult material. He could inset an acorn to contain his specials or promotional items for the younger set. His bags for adult books would carry the tree motif and those for youngsters' books would show the acorn.

James also recognized the need to promote the educational value and services of the "Acorn" part of his operation. He hit upon the idea of an opening spelling bee for youngsters 12 and under. Entries, he figured, could be brought or mailed to the store. No purchase would be required. The contest would take place in the section reserved for Acorn in the shop itself. The prizes would be, of course, gift certificates at the store and, for the winners and runners-up, appropriately curley-cued parchment certificates. He would find teachers and/or administrators from the local schools to serve as judges.

He then set about determining where to place whatever advertising he would be able to do. He considered it appropriate that he do his advertising in print media, given the nature of his products. "Also," he added to himself, "It's all I'm likely to be able to afford." He collected information on advertising rates in the *Washington Post* and in three local papers (weeklies); this is shown in Table 1.

Table 1   Advertising rates and data: black and white print media, Washington, D.C., and Montgomery County, Maryland

	Daily	Sunday	"Book World"	Circulation
Washington Post				1,400,000
Per column inch				
1 insertion	$212.00	$275.00	$160.00	
3–12 insertions	195.00	240.00		
13–299 insertions	191.00	236.00		
Zone Edition:	*Thursdays*			
Montgomery County	$47.50			150,700
Maryland Weekly	82.50			307,700
Rockville Sentinel	*Fridays*			14,801
1 column × 5.25 inches	$ 63.00			
× 7 inches	83.00			
× 9 inches	108.00			
2 columns × 3 inches	72.00			
3 columns × 3.5 inches	106.00			
× 5.25 inches	189.00			
Gaithersburg Gazette	*Wednesdays*			48,175
Per column inch	$ 13.44			
Olney Courier Gazette				8,775
Per column inch	$ 6.12			

Combination rate: Gaithersburg and Olney: $15.12 per column inch.

Source: Standard Rate and Data Services, Inc (Wilmette, Illinois, 1984).

1. Comment on Ed James' choice of name and marketing approach for his bookstore. How do they "fit" with his intended customers? Can you improve on his approach? If so, how? Why do you believe this is an improvement?

2. Comment on James' intention to hold a spelling bee as part of his kickoff for his store. What benefits would this provide for Ed? Estimate the cost of such a promotion. How should he announce, advertise, and promote the competition, assuming you believe he should do it? If you believe he should not do it, explain why and offer an alternative approach to generating awareness of and interest in Acorn.

3. Develop an advertising plan and budget for the bookstore. Design his grand opening ad(s), paying special attention to the ad copy for each piece. If you prefer a format different from the one proposed by Ed James, design your own format, explaining why you believe yours to be better than his.

PART 6
SETTING UP
THE SCORECARD

13. Accounting and Financial Ratios: Using Numbers to Tell You Things

"In dealing with accountants, Levin tells his readers, never ask whether you can do this or that. The correct question, he states firmly, is "*How* can we do this?"

Robert R. Dince, *Fortune*

This section completes the basic information you will need in order to have a hope of developing a business that works—that is, unless you just want to start one and see how it all comes out. This latter approach often works, but, when it doesn't, it can be very expensive and very depressing for the owner/founder. The real point of this section—indeed, of the entire book—is that you can work out most of the bugs in advance, without risking your money. You can do this only if you know what to do and what you are looking for.

In prior chapters, you estimated the size and shape of your market. You decided the structure and staffing of your company. You determined its product mix and developed a tentative pricing structure. You have done just about everything for your nascent company, except one thing. You haven't determined whether it will fly.

In business terms, "flying" means whether or not a company will be able to make it financially. Even if your main objective is not "making lots of money," your business has to take in more money than it pays out—unless, of course, what you really want to do is give money away. If the latter is your objective, there are easier ways of accomplishing it than developing a business to do it.

Defining businesses as financial creatures, however, means that you have to understand at least the basics of how the numbers work in your business in order to determine whether or how well yours will fly. While earlier chapters walked through rough estimates of some of the major items (startup funds in

298

Chapter 7, for example), you have never had an opportunity to test the numbers of your developed business plan. This section gives you that chance.

Somewhere along the way, many people have become convinced that numbers, particularly accounting numbers, are very difficult to understand and to work with. One of the reasons, in fact, that this section is so far into this book is to permit people to work out their businesses before they are confronted with the need for looking at all of the numbers in one place.

The response to numbers is unfortunate. They are more useful than frightening—once you know what they can and cannot be used for. In fact, you have probably already seen places where more numbers would have been helpful to you. This section is designed to walk you through the numbers you are likely to need to understand and to show you how to use them to make your business work better (or at all).

This chapter is about basic financial statements and ratios. It is not intended to make you an instant expert or to permit you to replace your accountant. It has two main purposes. First, it is to enable you to ask useful and relevant questions of your accountant about your business. This helps both you and your accountant. Second, it is to enable you to use the data that your accountant produces to develop and run your business better.

Numbers are logical and, therefore, simple, once you pick up the underlying rationales and assumptions. Some of us even find them fun to play with, believe it or not. If you approach this section with an open mind, you may find that you are one of us—a closet numbers-nut. But first, a word about the underlying principles of accounting is in order.

A NOTE ABOUT ACCOUNTING PRINCIPLES

In general, accountants are conservative. This does not refer to the notion that many of them dress in three-piece, pin-striped suits, but rather that they generally seek the most conservative statement of accounting data. Assets are generally stated at the lower of their cost to you or their market value, for example.

This practice makes a certain amount of sense, given the basic purpose of financial statements. They are designed to tell other people—originally, potential investors—about your company. One of the basic functions of accountants is to ensure that the statements for which they are responsible are not misleading to those people. Thus, one of the key items in an auditor's opinion is that a company's data fairly reflects its operations and that it is consistent with prior years' data.

This general approach makes sense, given the period in which modern accounting developed. Much of current practice developed in response to the excesses that brought about the great stock market crash of 1929. During the

FEATURE 13.1
Ignorance Is Not Bliss

Ruth Clark began her temporary help company without a business plan and with very little background in business. Like many new small business owners, she concentrated on selling—and forgot that her job continued far beyond that.

The problem finally surfaced in the fourth quarter of '78 when she realized that her bookkeeper had embezzled $100,000. "I didn't know balance sheets," says Clark, "but I always kept on top of my billings. When I saw only $85,000 of the $200,000 I billed coming in, I knew something was wrong." An investigation showed that the bookkeeper had deposited corporate checks in his personal account.

Adapted from Carole Gould, "A Temp In Time," *Savvy* (May 1984):65.

period prior to the crash, the information put out by many companies was anything but clear and informative. Investors were often induced to buy companies that were not really there at all. The response to the disasters of the crash and the ensuing Great Depression included the development of standard accounting principles (the Generally Accepted Accounting Principles, or GAAP you hear accounting types talking about) and a significant change in the role of the accountant. While changes are always being made as new situations and requirements arise, this basic role, and those basic principles, are still accepted today.

This origin shapes many of the definitions of accounting items described in this chapter. When you get to thinking about why definitions are used that clearly do not accord with the reality you know, consider that what the accountants are really trying to do is attempting to build statements that are generally understandable (consistent in approach) and that do not mislead through overstatement (conservative).

Before looking closely at each of the two major financial statements, a look at the third basic accounting principle is warranted. This principle is "matching." The problem is that operating companies tend to do just that—operate. They are constantly buying things and selling things. The question for accountants, then, is how to "stop the motion" for reporting purposes.

They use one of two accounting methods. The cash method is handled just as is your checkbook. This essentially avoids the issue of stopping the flow of transactions. It does not attempt to stop the flow. It reports what the flow looks like at a given time. A sale, for example, is revenue to the business when the cash comes in. A purchase is made when the cash goes out. It is very simple—too simple, in fact, to show consistently and fairly the results of most kinds of businesses. The only kinds of companies that can use this method (according to the accountants and the Internal Revenue Service) are those that do not have inventories—consulting companies, physician practices, and similar businesses. If you think about this as we discuss some balance sheet items, you will understand quickly why this is true.

The second, and, obviously, more widely used in business, is the accrual method. This method uses "matching" as the means of showing business operations fairly and consistently. It shows the year's (period's) results as a function of sales for the period. A sale is a sale when a buyer takes the product (usually), rather than when it is paid for in cash. All costs and related items are figured on the basis of either the period of time itself (rent, for example) or the number and type of units sold. As you will see, this approach standardizes the results that a business reports to facilitate easy and reasonably accurate period-to-period comparisons.

With a basic understanding of the impetus and principles behind modern accounting, you can often anticipate what approach accounting will take to a particular item or issue. Start with the underlying purpose of building a financial statement and consider how you would figure or value the item within the parameters of consistency, conservatism, and matching. Odds are, your conclusion will be correct. You can test yourself on some of the items below.

THE FINANCIAL STATEMENTS: WHAT YOU WILL BE LOOKING AT

The basic financial statements for any business are the balance sheet and the income statement (or statement of profit and loss, or P&L). They are interlocking reports in that they reflect various aspects of the same business and in that actions to some items on one statement affect items on the other.

The **balance sheet** reflects the financial condition of a business at a specific time. The usual simile is a "snapshot" of a flowing stream. The balance sheet of an operating company is unlikely to be the same on two consecutive business days because transactions to certain accounts occur so often as to be effectively continual. The balance sheet is "current events." The **income statement**, on the other hand, reflects the results of the operation of a business over a period of time—a quarter, a year. It is "history."

Both statements usually provide material for comparison. The balance sheet usually provides comparative data for the same date of the preceding year. The income statement usually provides comparative results for the preceding period (year) or for the same period of the preceding year (for example, first quarter results compared with the results of last year's first quarter).

Taken together, these statements—if understood and used properly—can provide the basis for an understanding of how a company is doing and how it accomplishes what it does. This is why banks and other lenders (and equity investors who have no personal commitment to the entrepreneur or the business) are particularly interested in the financial statements and/or projected financial statements for your business. And if this fact alone is not sufficient to convince you to pay attention to your numbers, it may be added that financials and projected, or pro-forma, financials can flag and pinpoint problems and potential problems rather effectively—before they become full-fledged disasters. Businesses run on money, and the financials track what is happening to or is likely to happen to the money.

The Balance Sheet

The basis for the balance sheet is the idea that a firm's assets must be supported by something—its liabilities and the accumulated equity of its investors. That is, what the business owns must have been acquired using money—either borrowed money (liabilities), or invested and earned money (equity). Thus, the basic balance sheet equation is:

$$\text{Assets} = \text{liabilities} + \text{net worth}$$

The balance sheet shown in Table 13.1 is structured to make it easy to see this balance.

As you can see, the balance sheet is broken into subcategories. The underlying concept is that the term of the funding should roughly match the life of the assets it supports. Long-term funding—debt or equity, for example—should support long-term assets such as buildings or equipment. The statement is structured so that a user can check this matching. Current items are those that will be (or can be) used up (assets) or paid off (liabilities) within one period, generally a year. Other items are expected to take longer to be used up or paid off. *The bottom lines must be equal.*

While most items on the balance sheet are self-explanatory, some are not. In some cases, the methods of arriving at the balance sheet number also need some explanation.

Accounts receivable.   Accounts receivable are those debts owed to you by your customers. However, in most companies there is always a customer or two that does not pay up. These are your "bad debts." The asset figure is always shown as net of an allowance for this bad debt (conservative). For example, your flower shop's books show that all your customers together owe you $3,000. If, however, you know that the Greenes, who owe you $500 for party flowers, have left town, leaving no forwarding address, you would probably assume that that was one $500 you were never going to see. Your

Table 13.1 Generic balance sheet

Company A
Balance Sheet
as of December 31, 19xx

ASSETS	LIABILITIES AND NET WORTH
Current assets	*Current liabilities*
Cash and marketable securities	Accounts payable
Accounts receivable (net)	Accrued expenses
Inventory	Current portion long-term debt
Other current assets	Other current liabilities
Total current assets	*Total current liabilities*
Fixed assets	*Long-term liabilities*
Land	Long-term debt
Plant and equipment (cost)	Capital lease obligations
Less: accumulated depreciation	
Net book value plant and equipment	
Total fixed assets	*Total long-term liabilities*
Other assets	
Trademarks, patents	
Capitalized organization costs	*Contingencies*
Goodwill	
Total other assets	*Net worth*
TOTAL ASSETS	TOTAL LIABILITIES & NET WORTH

balance sheet accounts receivable figure would be $2,500, shown as follows:

Accounts receivable	$3,000
(allowance for bad debts)	500
Net accounts receivable	$2,500

While the allowance for bad debt is largely a matter of management estimate, prior actual experience (your own or the industry's) and accounting guidelines limit the ability of management to "adjust" the asset figures at will.

Inventory.   Inventory is the material that you will use to make whatever it is you make and sell or the finished goods that you will sell to your customers. Inventory is always stated at the lower of its cost to you or its market value (conservative). The problem is, what is its "cost"?

Inventory presents the classic problem of businesses not holding still for evaluation. Obviously, if you deal in large, readily identifiable items like nuclear generators, for example, you have no problem. You can track each specific unit through your company. But, for the rest of us, the "what is cost?"

...very real. Consider trying to track bolts, of which your company uses ...nds a month. Each, it is hoped, is indistinguishable from its fellows. But ...ice you paid for this month's shipment is higher than the price on an identical lot purchased last month. All the while, your production people have been using bolts from the common bin. What is the cost of the bolts left in the bin at balance sheet time?

Accountants have developed a pair of conventions to deal with this problem. Either of these two methods can be used: Last-In-First-Out (LIFO) or First-In-First-Out (FIFO). Graphically, they can be shown as below, imagining inventory as a stack of essentially identical things onto which new items are placed and out of which items are pulled for sale or for use in manufacture.

Figure 13.1   LIFO and FIFO inventory costing methods

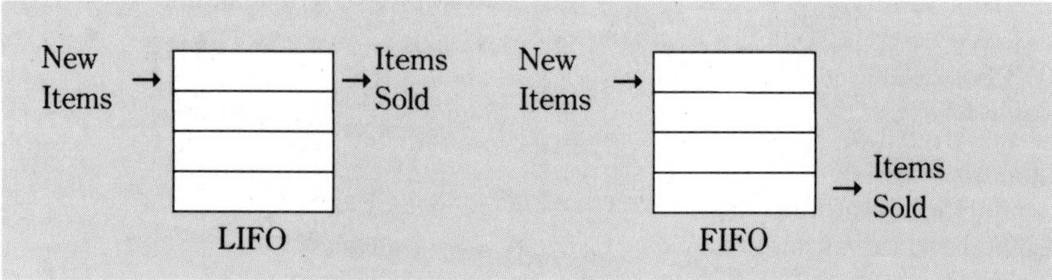

Please note that our bolts are indistinguishable one from another. The choice of inventory costing method does *not* alter the physical movement of the bolts at all. Your production person pulls a random assortment just the way she always did. These are accounting conventions, designed to help financial statement users understand what they are looking at and to keep you from having to tag each and every bolt that you use.

Your choice of inventory costing method is semi-permanent. Changes must be noted and explained (to Internal Revenue) and may not be frequent. The reason for this level of control should be obvious, given the effects of the different methods on the financial statements. If costs are rising, for example, and you were using FIFO, your assets would look larger than they would under LIFO, and the cost of the items you sell will look lower. If you used LIFO, the reverse would be true.

In Feature 13.2, you can see the effect. If you take the same inventory stack and apply each different method for "pulling" inventory, your ending inventory figures will also differ. Assuming inflation, the ending inventory figure that you get using FIFO will be larger than it would be if you used LIFO. Use of FIFO, then, will make your total assets look larger than they would look had you used the LIFO method.

Note that nothing is actually different. But permitting you to switch inventory costing methods at will would also permit you to "adjust" your total

FEATURE 13.2
LIFO vs. FIFO Inventory Valuation

Lot 3	1000 at $1.50 Each
Lot 2	1000 at $1.25 Each
Lot 1	1000 at $1 Each

Jeanne's Cosmetics stocks a certain kind of lipstick that sells very well. At the beginning of her year, she got an extra-special deal on a closeout lot, buying 1,000 units at $1 each. Later in the year, she paid regular price for a 1000-unit lot—$1.25 a piece. The price increased toward the end of the year meant that she had to pay $1.50 each for the lipsticks for her last lot. Her hypothetical inventory "stack" looked like the one shown above.

During the year, she sold 2,500 of the lipsticks. Her year-end inventory figure would look as follows, depending on her choice of inventory valuation method:

	Using LIFO:	*Using FIFO:*
Total purchases:	$3,750	$3,750
Sold from inventory:		
lot 1	500 (500 units)	1,000 (1,000 units)
lot 2	1,250 (1,000 units)	1,250 (1,000 units)
lot 3	1,500 (1,000 units)	750 (500 units)
TOTAL SOLD	$3,250	$3,000
YEAR-END LIPSTICK INVENTORY	$ 500	$1,000

asset figure (and other items that will be discussed later in this chapter). It would invite an unacceptable level of game-playing with the numbers (not conservative), not to mention making comparison with prior periods impossible (not consistent).

Fixed assets.   Fixed assets consist of property, plant, and equipment, referred to as "fixed" because they generallly stay where you put (or found) them and because they are tangible property. With the exception of land, which does not depreciate, fixed assets are shown at historical cost (what you originally paid for them) less accumulated depreciation. (Depreciation will be discussed later in this chapter.) Land is shown at its historical cost.

The principle of "matching" is at work in fixed asset accounting. A fixed asset is purchased to be used by the business over a number of years. Clearly, the first year in which you use it should not bear the entire cost of it. The cost is, therefore, spread (through the mechanism of depreciation) over the years during which the asset is expected to bring benefit to the company and during which the business is "using up" the value of the asset. Since land is not "used up" in most businesses, it does not depreciate. (In resource-based companies—mining or drilling, for example—land, or the particular resource used, is "used up." In these kinds of companies, "depletion" is the depreciation-equivalent approach.)

Please note that this entire process has nothing whatever to do with the real market values of the assets. It is related only to matching the original cost of the asset to its period of use. Real market value becomes an issue only when the sale of an asset is contemplated or in determining a residual or salvage value for the asset (what you expect to be able to sell it for on the market) should you contemplate selling the asset after its "useful life" in your business is, for accounting purposes, over. (The company that buys your old asset, interestingly enough, also gets to depreciate its cost to them over a new "economic useful life.")

Other assets, such as patents and trademarks, are depreciated or "amortized" in the same way and for the same reasons as are fixed assets. They are simply a good deal less tangible and don't "wear out" in the same way. Two of these items deserve special mention. First, it is common to amortize the costs of organizing and starting a corporation. The same notion applies as it does to fixed asset accounting. Does the expense benefit a number of years of the business? If yes, you can probably amortize the cost.

The second item is "goodwill." Goodwill is *not* that warm feeling experienced by your customers when they think of your product/service/company. It is a very specific accounting concept. "Goodwill" arises *only* when your company purchases another company for more than the book value of the purchased company. The difference between the "value" and the purchase price is "goodwill." The accountants apparently believe that you are not stupid and, since you paid more than value for a company, you must have been purchasing something intangible, but of value. Voilá—"goodwill." You cannot pick a number representing the value to your company of your or your customers' warm feeling and put it on your balance sheet as an asset.

Accrued expenses.   Accrued expenses arise from the matching function of accrual accounting. They result when your payment period for an expense does not coincide with your balance sheet date. Since the balance sheet is intended to show all obligations of a company at a specific time, the debt for the part of the period that has already passed must be shown. It is shown as an "accrual." This indicates that you already owe the money, but that you have not yet been required to pay it out, usually because of schedule differences.

A prime example of this might be payroll. Assume that you normally pay your staff on Friday for this week. Your balance sheet date, however, is on a Wednesday this year. At the point of your balance sheet, you technically owe your staff for three days of work. Your payroll expense for those three days will appear on your balance sheet as an accrual. Other expenses that are often accrued in this way are rent or lease costs and interest expense. (Note: the only way in which interest on your debt appears on your balance sheet will be as an accrual when warranted.)

Current portion of long-term debt.   The current portion of long-term debt is the part of your debt that will be due and payable within the upcoming period. Each year, as you pay off the current portion, the upcoming period's current portion is deducted from your long-term debt number and becomes the new "current portion."

Both the current portion and the long-term debt number include only the principal amounts. This is your debt. Interest is viewed as an expense, a fee for your use of the money, rather than as part of the debt itself.

Contingencies.   Contingencies are generally any items that could cost the company money in the future, depending on some outcome beyond the control of the company itself. They are usually items under litigation—suits that the company may win or lose. Accountants and securities analysts properly believe that to evaluate a company fairly, one needs to know what major (material) judgments might be made against the company. The notes to this item will generally describe the pending case and provide a lawyer's opinion of its chances. It is unlikely that you will have contingencies on your balance sheet in your early business days, if ever.

Net worth.   Net worth (or equity or shareholders' equity) is the amount that the owners of the company actually own. It consists of the original investment plus any additional investments plus the accumulated retained results of operations. This last piece is often called "retained earnings" and consists of the accumulated profits and losses of the business reduced by the amount of dividends that it has paid to owners. This is not a pot of money just lying around waiting for someone to use it (as in, "We'll pay for it out of retained earnings."). By balance sheet definition, it is already invested in something on the asset side—securities, equipment, even cash. What people who say this really mean is that they intend to convert one kind of asset (cash or securities) to pay for whatever it was they were talking about.

The Income Statement

The income statement is a fairly straightforward document designed to show the amount of money brought into a company and its uses in the operation of the company—the revenue and expenses of the company over the year (or period). It ends in the famous "bottom line"—profit or loss. The principle of matching expenses to the associated revenue rules the income statement and is particularly clear in the discussion of cost-of-goods-sold (COGS) below. A very simple income statement is shown in Table 13.2.

As with the balance sheet, comments on the meanings of income statement items have been provided only where the meaning is not clear.

Cost-of-goods-sold (COGS or CGS).   For many companies, COGS is one of the most critical items in either financial statement. It includes the direct costs to you of making your product for sale or acquiring and readying it for sale. It includes direct materials costs, direct labor costs, and the factory overhead that is directly attributable to making the product—for example, the direct supervision of production workers.

COGS is *not* the cost to you of producing or purchasing however many items you produced or purchased this year. It includes only the cost to you of producing or purchasing the number of items you *sold* this year. (As it says, "cost-of-goods-*sold*"). If you overproduced or overbought, the excess is in inventory (see balance sheet). If you underproduced or underbought, you will have drawn down inventory.

COGS is the other point in the financial statements at which your choice of

Table 13.2   Generic income statement

Company A
Income Statement
Year Ending December 31, 19xx

Net sales
(Less) Cost-of-goods-sold (COGS)
(Equals) gross margin (gross profit)

Operating expenses
  Selling, general and administrative expenses (SG&A)
  Interest
  Depreciation
(Less) Total operating expenses

(Plus or minus) extraordinary items

(Equals) net income before federal tax
(Less) federal tax
(Equals) net income after federal tax

(Less) dividends distributed
(Equals) amount added to retained earnings or net worth

---

inventory costing method has direct impact. It controls the "cost" of the goods being taken out of inventory and sold. When you "pull" inventory items off that hypothetical stack discussed earlier, the "cost" of those items (the ones you are selling out of inventory) becomes part of your COGS. In periods of rising prices, your COGS will be higher using LIFO than they would be using FIFO since you are pulling from the top of the stack (more costly units), rather than from the bottom (the less expensive, or older, units). (Keep in mind that, in reality, nothing changes about the way you actually use your inventory.) Since COGS is subtracted from "net sales" as part of the way to your profit figure, LIFO inventory costing will reduce the amount of income you show. It will therefore reduce your taxes.

Depreciation.   Depreciation is another item that needs some special consideration. As was noted in the discussion of balance sheet fixed assets, depreciation is the charge made against operations for the use of assets used in producing revenues for the business. In general, you have already paid for the asset, either through borrowing or using internally generated funds. Therefore, depreciation is an "expense" for which no money is actually paid out of the company. It is a "non-cash expense." It reduces your tax without costing you money directly. It is thus added back to net income when you want to consider how much cash the business generates. (Cash is discussed at length in Chapter 14.)

The specifics of available depreciation methods change with changes in the tax code. At present (1984) an accelerated cost recovery system (ACRS) is in effect. Your accountant will know the available options. At base, however, there are two general approaches to depreciation, straight-line and accelerated. Under the straight-line method, the cost of the asset is spread evenly over its economic useful life, the period over which the asset can be expected to be used to benefit the business. (There are guidelines to help determine the economic useful life of a type of asset.) Accelerated methods weight the amount of depreciation taken in the earlier years of the life of the asset. This means that, toward the end of its useful life, relatively less depreciation is taken.

Please note that the total amount of depreciation you can take does *not* change with the method. It is limited by the original cost to you of the asset. The economic useful life also does not change depending on the method. What changes is the timing of cash moving out of the business to pay taxes. Depreciation is an "expense," even though money is not actually paid out to cover it. As an "expense," it affects the bottom line.

It should also be noted that an asset does not generally collapse when its economic useful life is over. If you are still using it in the business, you simply carry it on your balance sheet at zero net book value. You may no longer charge depreciation for it because you will have already recovered your entire original cost.

Extraordinary items.   Extraordinary items are precisely that—items that are not in the course of the operations of the business. If a company lost a lawsuit shown in "contingencies," for example, the cost of the settlement or judgment would be shown as an extraordinary item. This allows statement users to separate the effects of such items from the regular business of the company.

Please also reconsider something that was noted earlier, in Chapter 6. Dividends are taken out of after-tax earnings. As mentioned then, these dividends are taxed again as part of the taxable income of the recipient.

FINANCIAL RATIOS:
HOW ACCOUNTING INFORMATION CAN HELP YOU

At this point, an eminently reasonable question is: Why are we telling you all this? Isn't that why you hired an accountant? Well, yes and no. Your accountant is there to help you, but not to make decisions about your company. As you have seen, building financial statements requires a number of decisions regarding methods and approaches that your accountant should not make alone. To assist in making those decisions, you will need to have some understanding of the options and implications associated with each. While we do not suggest that you hang over your accountant's shoulder while the statements are being prepared, we do recommend that you remain part of the process. Remember, it's your company.

But even beyond this decision-making issue, your accountant is unlikely to be around to do all the analysis you will want of the numbers he has developed—unless you have a full-time accountant. The numbers your accountant develops are useful to you. Properly arranged and considered, they can tell you what is going on in your company, point out the likely future path of the company, flag and highlight future or existing problems, and help find and test solutions to those problems. While this undoubtedly sounds overblown, this section will show you how it's done. You, too, will become a believer—and a user of your financial data. It works.

Financial Ratios

In your business, how well the business is performing (given its purpose and your intentions for it), may well be vital, rather than a matter of idle curiosity. The numbers in your financial statements or pro formas can help you to figure it out. "Figuring it out" is stressed because, as you have probably already

FEATURE 13.3
Lest We Forget—Hidden Expense Items

Part of the cost of doing business in a given place is the tax structure of the state and locality. A sometimes major, but often overlooked, part of that tax structure has to do with the tax to cover unemployment insurance. This is levied on a value of payroll basis and it varies from state to state. In 1984, the national high for unemployment fund contributions was in Alaska, where employers paid $642 per employee to both the federal and state government. The low was in Texas, with an average contribution of only $119 per employee.

Not only do employers foot the bill for regular contributions to the funds, but your state may have had to borrow money from the federal government to cover its obligations to workers during the recent recession. If this is the case, and if your state government has not repaid the loans promptly, you are probably also paying for their failure to do so. The federal government is levying penalty charges on their unrepaid funds. For Illinois, Wisconsin, and Pennsylvania, for example, the penalty charges turn a federal unemployment tax cost of $56 per worker into a tax of $112 per worker.

Once considered a "nuisance tax," the employer costs of both federal and state unemployment insurance are rapidly moving from annoyance to real pain.

Adapted from Eugene Carlson, "Regions," *The Wall Street Journal* (March 13, 1984):33 and (December 4, 1984):31.

seen, the raw numbers themselves are not particularly informative. The problem is that nothing in the business stands still for very long.

Consider, for example, a company that showed a net profit of $10,000 last year and $11,000 this year. They are making more money in absolute dollars, but is this performance "good"? Are they really doing better this year than last? Since performance really consists of inputs as well as outputs (how much was committed to or flowed through the business, as well as the amount the business produced), a single line item figure cannot really help owners to understand what has occurred. But if the net profit figure is compared with something else, say the sales figure, then some information emerges. You will have created a ratio that nets out the effect of changes in the absolute size of the numbers and looks at the relationship between the two pieces of financial data.

Now the profit figure can begin to tell you something. Suppose that sales for the company mentioned above had been $100,000 in the first year and $150,000 in the second. The ratio of profit to sales (return on sales = net profit/sales) would be 10 percent and 7.3 percent, respectively. The company has made relatively less in profit for every dollar made in sales. They are definitely not doing better—despite the increase in the absolute size of the profit figure.

As you can see, the key to making the numbers tell you what you want to know is to focus on relationships and to compare the resulting ratios. The two standard types of comparisons are internal (within a company over time) and external (across similar businesses in a given year, over time, or both).

A standard approach to internal comparisons is the common size statement, an example of which is shown in Table 13.3. These take the key number (sales for income statements and assets for balance sheets) and show all other items as percentages of the key number. In the following example you can see immediately where the problem lies. While other items fluctuate slightly from year to year, salary expense is growing out of proportion to sales and eating significantly into the bottom line. (This may not be a "problem" if the figure results from some change in strategy or approach intended by the owner. More likely, however, it is a signal that the owner needs to recognize and address the issue.)

Comparison of financial ratio data across companies presents a somewhat more complex problem. The technique is well-accepted in business—which is why companies and industry associations produce the industry average ratio data you have already used in your planning process. But, as is true of any comparison, care must be taken to ensure that you are not comparing apples with oranges. Firms in different industries are likely to have differing ratio profiles. This makes a great deal of sense, since a set of financial ratios reflects the operations and characteristics of a firm or an industry and industries operate differently from one another. It may also be true, for similar reasons, that firms of different size within an industry or an industry segment have major differences in financial characteristics.

The critical notion in developing and using intercompany comparisons of financial ratio data is to try, insofar as possible, to compare only what is comparable. Some businesspeople (generally those who don't like the

Table 13.3   *Hypothetical common size income statement*

	Year 1	Year 2	Year 3
Sales	100.0%	100.0%	100.0%
Cost-of-goods-sold	62.1	61.9	62.2
Gross margin	37.9	38.1	37.8
Space, utilities	10.0	10.1	10.3
Salaries	12.0	14.0	16.0
Other	5.9	5.8	5.6
Net income	10.0%	8.2%	5.9%

results) claim that no comparisons are possible since each company is different from all others. That approach leaves you with no sense of how you're doing or where you stand.

A middle ground makes more sense—and provides you with some value from the work and results of others. Your question should always be, "Will this comparison add to my perspective about my results or projections, or will it just add to the general confusion?" If it is likely to add perspective, try it. But always keep in mind the specific differences among the companies you are comparing and how those operating differences will affect (have affected) the financial ratio results. This way, the process of considering how well your ratio comparisons fit becomes almost as enlightening as the ratio comparison results themselves.

What Ratios Can Do to Help You

Although a ratio could be constructed mathematically from any two numbers, the idea is to develop ratios that illuminate important relationships within a business. This section outlines the four main categories of ratios, the broad issues that each addresses, and some standard ratios from each category. You will recognize some of them from your earlier work. This is not intended as an exhaustive list. It is representative of the kinds of questions that can be addressed using financial ratio analysis.

Profitability ratios. Profitability ratios deal with the issue of how much a company made (profit or return) in relation to some data element representing what it took to make that amount (sales or some kind of investment). These ratios are the best-known category, since everyone these days is talking about "return."

1. Return on sales (ROS) = profit / sales
2. Return on assets (ROA) = profit / total assets
3. Return on equity (ROE) = profit / net worth or equity

The one you want to consider in a particular instance depends on the specific question you are trying to address. For example, if you want to find out whether it is worth your while to put your money into a company (equity investment), you want to consider what the return on that equity will be (has been). Your passbook savings account at the bank returns 5.25 percent.

Liquidity ratios. Liquidity ratios consider the ability of a company to cover its short-term obligations, given its short-term assets. As you recall, the balance sheet is structured to highlight current assets and liabilities. This emphasis exists because a company cannot stay in business unless it can pay its bills. (The next chapter discusses this at length.) This category of ratios is designed to assess how likely it is that a company will be able to convert its current assets into cash to cover its current liabilities. As you can see, the ratios address successive layers of speed with which a given asset can be converted for use in this manner.

1. Current ratio = current assets / current liabilities
2. Quick ratio = cash and accounts receivable / current liabilities
3. Acid test ratio = cash (and securities) / current liabilities

The objective for a company is to strike a balance between high and low liquidity. While low liquidity ratios can signal impending disaster (possible inability to pay the bills on time), high ones can indicate that a company could be using its assets more productively (an example may be keeping money in low- or no-interest accounts when that money could be used to expand a business that is returning 20 percent on investments in assets). What is "high" or "low" depends on the industry in which you are working and on the distribution of the assets among actual balance sheet accounts.

Leverage ratios.   Leverage ratios examine the proportion of the business owned by the owners against the proportion of the long-term financing provided by lenders. It is one way of considering the exposure of the business to the outside pressures of lenders. The various ratios consider different definitions of what "the business" is.

1. Debt / equity
2. Debt to total capitalization = debt / (debt + equity)
3. Debt / total assets

Here again, the trick is to find the appropriate balance between using "other people's money" effectively and taking on too much debt. As usual, acceptable levels of leverage vary among industries.

Activity or turnover ratios.   Activity or turnover ratios generally relate an income statement item to an asset item. The idea is to consider whether the level of asset is appropriate to the level of operations that the asset is supposed to support. The asset turnover ratio, for example, asks how many dollars in sales is produced by each dollar invested in assets in a given company. The underlying question is whether that level of asset investment is adequate (or excessive). (You consider this latter question by comparing the company ratio with those of other similar companies or with industry averages, as discussed earlier.)

There are many possibilities for developing useful ratios in this category. You are constrained only by your ability to make use of the ratio once you have developed it. Only three of the most commonly used are shown below.

1. Asset turnover ratio = sales / total assets
2. Inventory turnover = cost-of-goods-sold / average inventory
3. Days in accounts receivable = net accounts receivable / (sales/360)

What Do You Do With These Ratios?

In the final analysis, financial ratios permit you to focus on relevant areas of a business, help you to ask the key questions, and provide you with information with which to make judgments. Very rarely does financial ratio analysis provide a definitive answer to the underlying question of what to do next. That is fair. The decision making is your job. Financial ratio analysis can provide you with the information you need to do it well.

Once you have developed the ratios for your business, you have a set of numbers *all reflecting the operations and condition of a single company.* When you compare them with prior results or with results from similar companies, you will find areas of significant difference. This is where you will want to concentrate your analytic effort.

Your first move should be to consider why these differences might exist, whether there might be a legitimate reason for the divergence. If you are working with your own numbers, have you made some change in the way the business operates that would affect the numbers in the ways you see? If you are working with averages, does (will) your company operate in a manner different from the norm in ways that would cause the differences that you see? Also keep in mind that, as a new company, your figures are quite likely to diverge from an average composed of data for companies that are already at normal operating levels. How these differences affect the ratios should therefore be a major consideration.

If there is no logical reason for your ratios to differ as significantly as they do, you will need to move to step two. You use the fact that your ratio-set reflects a single company to construct chains of interlocking ratios. This chaining will help you to pinpoint the problem or potential problem. Once you have the problem targeted, you can decide what to do about it. (One of the most difficult things about any consulting assignment is to figure out what the problem is. It is often not what the client tells you it is. But once you have it in your sights, the solution is not usually difficult to see. The trick is in solving the right problem.)

A simple example can show you how the chaining approach works. Suppose that you are Company A. You are working with a set of comparable industry average data. You cannot see any logical reason for the difference in asset turnover ratios that you see below.

	Company A	*Industry Average*
Asset turnover	1.3	2.5

Clearly, something is out of line. Your question is "What?" Here you need to remember that a ratio is constructed of at least two elements. To get to the next level, you can begin to examine each of the elements using other ratios. Suppose you then find:

	Company A	Industry Average
Return on sales (percent)	6.4	6.2
Return on assets (percent)	8.3	15.2

The deviation is obviously in the asset figures. Your next level of analysis involves chasing the issue back through other ratios to pinpoint the problem asset areas. You can use such ratios as the fixed asset turnover ratio (Is our investment in plant and equipment relatively high?), inventory turnover (Are we carrying too much inventory for our sales level?), and days in receivables (Are we failing to collect what people owe us?). You always want to be checking for significant deviations and for logical reasons for why they should exist.

Keep in mind that it is not necessarily "bad" to deviate from the average. In addition to the possibility that strategic choices have dictated a different operating approach, it is always possible that there are perfectly reasonable explanations for the divergence from average. If, for example, Company A has just completed a major plant expansion and its sales have not yet caught up with its asset growth, the figures above would be quite reasonable. (The fixed asset turnover ratio would also be very low.) Comparison of this year's ratios with prior years of Company A's results would probably show a sharp change for this year if such an expansion had occurred.

Please note that the use of ratios here was not to find "The Answer." It was to discover whether there was a problem and, if so, where that problem lay. If, in the example above, the high asset amount was, in fact, a problem (there was no logical explanation for it in the operations of the business), you, as owner, would have a number of choices regarding how to deal with the problem. The ratio analysis would have told you that you have a relatively high asset investment, but how you might go about reducing it would depend on your further analysis and your personal preferences.

The flexibility of the financial ratio analysis approach is the real reason that it is such a valuable tool for business owners. It permits you to pinpoint difficulties and to examine the size and scope of such difficulties. While it does not prescribe a solution, it permits you to consider the potential effects of your proposed solutions on the full range of your financial operations and position.

Such testing can be done through running the ratios backwards—for example, what would my financial statements look like if I reduced my asset levels to be more consistent with industry averages? How much in asset investment would be freed by such a course? Alternatively, you can project a new set of financial data and compare your new business configuration with the averages. (For these kinds of iterative activities, use of a computer may be most helpful.) Under no circumstances forget, however, that your business may not operate in the same way as the average business in your industry. Before slavishly following the average, then, give careful consideration to why your numbers or your best projections differ. You may have a better way of doing things. You may be part of a new wave in your industry.

As you can see, financial ratio analysis is as much art as science. However, it is an extremely useful technique for a business owner to have in her tool kit. Despite its unfamiliarity, it becomes easy with use. And you will find that you will use it a great deal because it is so flexible and effective.

SUMMARY

Accounting statements are logical approaches to telling others (and yourself) about how your company is doing. The two most basic financial statements are the balance sheet and the income statement (or P&L). The balance sheet is a statement of what the company owns and of its obligations. It also shows who really owns how much of the company (you and other investors through equity, or the bank through long-term debt). It is a picture of the company at a specific point in its life, reflecting its condition only on the day of the statement (the balance sheet date).

The income statement, on the other hand, reflects the results of operations for an entire accounting period. It is history. It shows sales and expenses for the period, and it comes down to the famous "bottom line," the net profit figure for the period.

Pro formas are the projected statements for a new company or for the upcoming year of an operating company. They show best estimates of how the results of the next period(s) of operations will look. They look exactly like actual financial statements, except that they include only projections. (See Chapter 15 for how to develop them.)

As promised, accounting treatment of your business need not be an area for anxiety—even if you do not really like to play with numbers. If you remember the underlying principles of accounting—conservatism, consistency, and matching—you can figure out almost anything you need to know to understand and work with your statements. We reiterate: do not run right out and fire your accountant. Understanding is one thing. Expertise is in an entirely different matter.

Working with your accounting data using financial ratio analysis is a simple, flexible approach to finding out what is going on in a company (including yours). It is an essentially comparative approach in which relationships between significant pieces of accounting data are considered. This basis in relationships permits you to net out the effects of size in looking at financial data.

A critical item to remember when working with financial ratio analysis is that deviating from an average is not necessarily "bad." Differences may stem from differing operating strategies or from short-term special circumstances. Therefore, before you play follow-the-leader, decide whether that is really what you want to do. The averages are there as guides, not as straight jackets.

FOR YOU TO CONSIDER:

1. What does a balance sheet do?
2. What does an income statement do?
3. What are the three basic accounting principles, and what does each mean?
4. How is "current asset" defined? Why is it important to separate "current" items from non-current items for balance sheet purposes?
5. What are the two main inventory valuation options, and how does your choice affect your balance sheet and your income statement?
6. What is "goodwill"?
7. What is "depreciation"? What is it intended to accomplish from an accounting point of view?
8. What is "cost-of-goods-sold"? How is it linked to your inventory number?
9. What is "retained earnings"?
10. What is a financial ratio? Why would a business owner want to construct one?
11. What is a "common size income statement"? Why would you use one?
12. List the four major categories of financial ratios. Describe briefly the kind of question(s) each is designed to address.
13. Describe how and why you can "chain" financial ratios.
14. Discuss how financial ratio analysis provides answers to questions regarding what to do when you discover a potential problem in your business.

FOR FURTHER READING:

Bank of America. "Understanding Financial Statements." *Small Business Reporter* 109 (1980).

Fess, Philip E., and Carl S. Warren. *Accounting Principles*. 14th ed. Cincinnati, Ohio: South-Western Publishing, 1984.

Needles, Belverd E., Jr., Henry R. Anderson, and James C. Caldwell. *Principles of Accounting.* 2nd ed. Boston: Houghton Mifflin and Company, 1984.

U.S. Internal Revenue Service. *Tax Guide For Small Business.* Publication no. 33. Washington, D.C.: U.S. Government Printing Office, annual.

Small Business Administration publications:

Basic Budgets for Profit Planning. SBA MA 1.004.
Check List for Profit Watching. SBA MA 1.018.
Guides for Profit Planning. SBA 045-000-00137-7.
Keep Pointed Toward Profit. SBA MA 1.003.
Ratio Analysis for Small Business. SBA 045-000-00150-4.
The Profit Plan. SBA 045-000-00192-0.

14. Cash Flow: You Can't Pay 'Em With Promises

An MBA student was doing some course research on the causes of business failure. He interviewed a veteran owner of small companies. The young man held his breath, waiting for the real scoop. "Well, Son," the old-timer said. "The main cause of business failures is lack of cash."

Everyone has heard stories of companies that are profitable but that still go out of business because of financial failures. Particularly recently, everyone has also heard of companies that are losing money, yet staying afloat. In case you were wondering how these things could happen, the answer is simple— cash flow. Companies that cannot arrange the flows of their cash properly go out of business—even if they make money on an accounting basis. Those that can—profitable or not—remain in operation.

"So why," you ask, "did you tell us all about accounting in the last chapter if it is not really the bottom line for my new business?" There are two major reasons. First, you have to know about accounting because it is one way that investors and bankers look at your company. Without the standard pro forma financial statements in your business proposal, it is virtually certain that you will get neither loan financing nor equity (from anyone other than your friends and relatives). Also, it is required by the federal and other governments that you use accounting rules for tax purposes. Essentially, you have no choice. And, if you have to use accounting, you might as well understand it.

Second, and more important, the way accounting looks at your business allows you to learn some things about how your business operates and how you can make it operate better. As we showed in the last chapter, you can use your accounting information as a tool to plan and control your business, making it take you where you want to go. Understanding and using financial results and projections lets you drive a car rather than simply ride in the back seat.

Despite all this, the financial statement approach to your business is not the only way—nor the only *important* way—of looking at your company. It really ignores one critical aspect—cash. And cash is the basis of business. In this chapter, therefore, we will examine how cash differs from accounting results, how you can focus on the cash aspects of your business, and why you might want to do so. As noted earlier, the next chapter will discuss how to make projections of both cash and accounting data.

CASH DRAWBACKS TO ACCRUAL ACCOUNTING

One of the major strengths of accounting is also a major drawback from the perspective of a business owner. Accounting, for most firms, is committed to the accrual approach. Under this approach, the expenses of one period are matched to the sales of the same period. This is a strength in that you can thus see results in some standardized way. It is a weakness in that you cannot really track the cash coming into your company or the cash leaving it in any easy way using only the financial statements. As you will see, this is a critical issue for your business.

The essential problem is that accrual accounting reorganizes the timing of business transactions. It ignores the timing of when your company actually has to come up with the cash. Moreover, the principle of matching also dictates that certain things that cost you real money are not viewed as "expenses." Others, which do not cost you money at that time *are* viewed as "expenses."

As a business owner, your major task is survival. And you cannot survive if you cannot pay the bills. As the old-timer pointed out, without the cash, you're out of business. You can only pay 'em with promises for so long before creditors get upset and/or angry enough to shut you down.

WHAT IS "CASH"?

It seems almost silly to consider defining something as basic to life as "cash." After all, everyone knows that it is what jingles or crackles in your pockets, what you pay your bus fare with, or buy a loaf of bread with at the super-market. But the key, in business terms, to an accurate definition of "cash" is that you can spend it now, if you want to, or you can let it crackle in your pocket a while longer. You are in control of what happens to it. Even if you owe people money, you are the one who decides who to pay and when. Money is only really cash to you during the period over which you can control what happens to it.

Cash has another characteristic implied in the general definition. It is acceptable by anyone, anywhere (in the country) for purchase of goods or for payment of debts. It even says so on paper money: "Legal tender for all debts public or private." Some businesses prefer payment in cash and discriminate against non-cash purchases. Service stations, at present, are charging differential prices that favor cash purchases.

While there are (illegal) tax reasons for preferring cash to credit purchases, there are real business reasons for the preference as well. Every step that a business takes away from cold, hard cash exposes it to additional risk. Bank credit card payments and checks on local banks (with proper I.D.) are not "cash." While they are close (taking a day or two to be turned into cash), there are the possibilities of stolen cards, fraudulent checks, or checks against insufficient funds. While competitive positioning often requires it, there is no legal requirement that anyone accept payment in other than real, immediate cash.

Timing Differences

Using the definition of "cash" given above, you can see that most business receipts, these days, are not cash when they are accepted in return for goods or services. Similarly, it is likely that you will not have paid real, hard cash for most of your purchases when you take physical possession of them or when you agree to take them. Accountants, however, view these transactions as "sales" and "purchases," respectively. This "goods on various types of credit" system creates one of the more universal differences between accounting statements and statements that track cash.

Most companies face such timing differences in three main areas: credit sales, credit purchases, and fixed asset purchases. The severity of the difficulties created by these differences, of course, varies with the type of company and the company's dependence on transactions in these three areas. A closer look at the credit issues will clarify the problem that this creates for business owners intent on survival.

Credit sales and purchases.   When a customer purchases something from you on credit, the accountants recognize a "sale." They immediately also book an "account receivable," indicating that someone owes you money in the short term—theoretically, whatever your normal terms of trade credit are. The balance sheet recognizes that no cash has changed hands, simply by making no transactions to the "cash" accounts. When (and if) the customer pays you for the purchase, the accountants take the amount out of "accounts receivable" and add the amount to the "cash" account. At the point at which the debt is actually paid, nothing happens to the "sales" accounts on the income statement.

PROFILE

Ruth Clark: A Quarter of a Million in Receivables

Ruth Clark is a black woman who decided to capitalize on the fact that large corporations were seeking minority enterprises with which to do business. Her temporary services business began in 1973 with $3,900 and in 1983 had sales of over $2 million. She almost went out of business in 1974, despite a first-year gross of $350,000.

Her problem was cash. Despite receivables from Fortune 500 companies, she had no cash with which to meet payroll. "My kind of business is not easily financed," Clark notes. "My business has no hard assets to back up a loan."

She wound up using factors, companies willing to make loans against receivables. Because of the riskiness of the business and because she had no other options, Clark paid 21 percent for cash when the prime interest rate was only 6 percent. Not only are they expensive, but they also often view repayment of loans differently from banks. As Clark found, factors will often add delinquency charges to the balance after an account was 35 days late. Banks, on the other hand, will generally let accounts go until they are 90 days overdue.

Clark is finally able to use bank financing—a line of credit. "But I still have problems meeting payroll. A quarter-million in outstanding receivables does me no good when I have to pay temps $30,000 each week."

Adapted from Carole Gould, "A Temp In Time," *Savvy* (May, 1984): 64–66.

When you buy something from a supplier on credit, you take the goods, and the accountants add the amount to the inventory accounts. At the same time, they create an "account payable," indicating that you owe someone a short-term trade debt. Only when you pay up is the "cash" account touched. Then the payable is wiped out and a transaction is made to the cash account. (Please note that the balance sheet will balance at all times by these methods.)

An example of the transactions to balance sheet accounts is shown in Table 14.1 on the following page.

But what happens in real life is a very different story. If you are the seller, you have sent off some goods or provided some services—and received nothing tangible in return. You cannot spend the "receivable" you have created. You have created an asset, but no cash. (Note: A receivable is an asset. You can sell or "factor" your good receivables. In some industries, doing so is a sure sign that you have hit rock bottom. In other industries, notably the apparel manufacturing business, such transactions are a fairly standard way of business life. The "factors"—people who buy receivables—

Table 14.1   Balance sheet transactions for credit purchase

BASE CASE—Before any transactions:

Assets		*Liabilities*	
Cash	100	Accounts payable	0
Inventory	100		

STEP ONE—You add inventory on trade credit:

Assets		*Liabilities*	
Cash	100	Accounts payable	100
Inventory	200		
Changes to totals	+ 100		+ 100

STEP TWO—You pay your supplier:

Assets		*Liabilities*	
Cash	0	Accounts payable	0
Inventory	200		
New changes to totals	0		0

generally get to choose the receivables they will buy. They obviously pay less than the face value of the debts, making their money on the differential.)

Suppose that you are waiting around for one of your customers to pay off when one of your suppliers demands his payment from you. There you sit, without the cash to pay him. Your accounting statements show "sales" more than sufficient to cover your "expenses," but you are still fresh out of cash. What now?

You have a couple of options. You can try out your powers of persuasion on either your debtor(s) or your creditor(s) or both. You can go right over to your bank for a short-term loan. If you cannot convince any of the above to come through for you, your creditors—or any one of your creditors with which you have an overdue account—can take you to court for the beginning of the end. Interesting options, are they not?

What you have here is a potential, built-in timing differential. Because of the normal terms of trade and the various manufacturing lag times, it is probable that, in many businesses, payment for purchases will be due before payments from customers appear. And some payments will be due whether or not you are waiting for a pile of receivables to become cash. Somehow, a business owner must figure out ways of ensuring that when the bills are due, they can be paid. How this is done is discussed later in this chapter.

Fixed asset acquisitions.   You have undoubtedly already come across the third potential timing difference in your preliminary planning. Unfortunately, the people who are prepared to sell you your plant and equipment are likely to want to be paid for their property. You have to figure out how to get them their money before anyone can even begin to pay you for your products or services.

You have the same options in dealing with this problem as you had in dealing with the shorter term issue described above. Essentially, you can bring in real cash money faster (either through customer deposits or through adding investors), or you can ask your bank for a loan. Most new entrepreneurs take this latter route, adding loan payments to their burden of fixed costs.

In the startup phase of a business, this problem of paying for equipment is so common that it is almost not seen as a timing problem. If you cannot solve it, you simply do not open up. Therefore, it is almost not a "business problem." But the same set of issues will arise at any time you need to add or replace major pieces of plant or equipment.

The asset acquisition problem is definitely a cash-related problem since, if you had the cash, there would be no problem. Thus, the same approach can be applied. Your job, or part of it at least, will be to ensure that the cash is available when you are going to need it.

Differences in "What Counts"

The accounting/cash issue goes even beyond the issue of timing. Here, the accounting approach to fixed assets described in the last chapter is what creates the difficulty.

Consider the problem. Before Day One of your new operation, you have to come up with sizable amounts of cash to acquire your equipment (not to mention your site). To the extent that you have to or choose to purchase, rather than rent, you are making capital expenditures. According to accounting rules, you cannot consider the cost of these acquisitions to be "expenses" of your first year. Yet, you have to pay for them the first year.

Assuming that you or your associates or investors have the cash, you can choose to pay for the item outright. (We have already discussed the pros and cons of this approach in Chapter 9. This is simply a demonstration.)

Assuming further that the asset you buy is a five-year asset and that you use the straight-line method of depreciation (10%, 20%, 20%, 20%, 20%, 10% is the closest to straight-line depreciation you can get under the Accelerated Cost Recovery System), your accounting statements would show the fixed asset accounting shown in Table 14.2, part A.

Your other major option for paying for the equipment is to use debt, as shown in part C of Table 14.2. This improves the cash picture somewhat, but it carries some problems of its own. The accountants do not consider the part of your debt payment that is principal as an "expense." The only "expense" associated with debt, as was noted earlier, is the interest cost. This leads to yet another potentially major difference between accounting results and cash

Table 14.2 Cash flow vs. accrual accounting in fixed asset purchases

A. BALANCE SHEET RESULTS—EITHER METHOD OF PURCHASE

	Year					
Balance sheet	*1*	*2*	*3*	*4*	*5*	*6*
Historical cost	$10,000	10,000	10,000	10,000	10,000	10,000
Accumulated depreciation	1,000	3,000	5,000	7,000	9,000	10,000
Net book value	9,000	7,000	5,000	3,000	1,000	0

B. RESULTS USING CASH TO PURCHASE

Income statement expenses:

Depreciation	$ 1,000	2,000	2,000	2,000	2,000	1,000

Cash activities:

Outflow of cash	$10,000	—	—	—	—	—

C. RESULTS USING DEBT TO PURCHASE

Income statement expenses:

Depreciation	$ 1,000	2,000	2,000	2,000	2,000	1,000
Interest		1,047	681	255	—	—	—
Sum:	$ 2,047	2,681	2,255	2,000	2,000	1,000

Cash activities:

Outflows: downpayment	$ 2,000	—	—	—	—	—
Total loan payments	3,328	3,328	3,328	—	—	—
Sum:	$ 5,328	3,328	3,328	—	—	—

flows. Table 14.2C assumes that you financed that $10,000 asset at 15 percent for three years. You paid the first $2,000 yourself.

The point here is simply to show you how different the accounting results can be from what you see as your daily operating reality. The difficulties engendered by confusing the two sets of data are illustrated in the following example.

The Great Breakeven Confusion

The story goes that a neophyte business owner found himself a recent business school grad to do his accounting and assorted other number work. The owner was worried about whether he would make or lose money, given his assumptions about how many items he would sell. The whiz kid came up with the answer: a breakeven analysis.

Now a breakeven analysis is a very useful tool—when confined to its place and when everyone understands what it is intended to do. Its value is discussed in Chapter 12. Essentially, the purpose of a breakeven is to tell you at what sales level you will begin to make a profit in a given year. This, of course, is exactly the question that the owner asked the accountant.

The breakeven analysis separates the direct costs of making a single unit of whatever from the fixed costs of running the business. It then asks you to subtract the variable unit cost from the selling price to get a "contribution margin"—the "contribution to fixed costs." You then divide the contribution margin per unit into the amount of fixed cost you have to cover, and, voila!—you know how many units you have to sell to come out with exactly zero profit. Beyond that sales level, all contributions to fixed costs are "profit," since all the fixed costs have already been covered and accounted for. The breakeven is shown graphically on page 270.

Our owner, overjoyed to have a reliable tool, immediately began to use his breakeven as a management guide. He promptly went out and began to sell. His entire focus became getting enough units out his door to make his breakeven number.

The hitch . . . He failed to consider actually collecting the money from his customers. In his zeal to get the product out the door, he extended his trade credit terms. His suppliers did not do the same for him. Not surprisingly, one end-of-month he found that he had surpassed his sales breakeven, piled up a raft of accounts receivable (most of them probably good), and could not figure out how to cover his payroll, let alone his other bills.

The moral of this story should be clear. While a breakeven figure is a useful, probably necessary number to have in the back of your head (and somewhere on paper), it is not the only, nor necessarily the best, game in town. It is particularly useful in making pricing decisions, as we noted earlier, but it fails to take into account the cash issues discussed in this chapter. Given that failure, its use as a tool for operating management is severely limited.

Cash is the reality. Without it, your company will not have a long future. Guaranteed. The rest of this chapter is dedicated to showing you ways to think about and manage your business with a cash orientation.

MANAGING CASH INFLOWS

The obvious reason for thinking about managing cash inflows is that, unless the cash flows in, there's nothing to flow out. And if there's nothing to flow out . . . So we start with the inflows.

If you keep in mind that money is cash to your business only when you can control it, the basic issue is clear. You need to figure out how to get your customers to pay you for the goods or services they buy faster than they do now. The best solution would be to not grant credit of any kind, but for most businesses, that is an unrealistic approach.

A second-best approach is to begin to see your credit terms as a marketing device (which they are). You originally chose your terms of trade based, no doubt, on what everyone else in the industry was doing. And that is fine—for a start. You need to remain aware, however, that those terms are not cast in concrete. And that just because everyone is doing it does not make it the best deal for you.

Terms of Trade

What would happen to your sales if you shortened your credit terms? Do you believe that your customers would desert you in droves? Or is your product good enough to support a slight difference from the terms of the rest of the industry? (Another question that you need to ask yourself is whether a "sale" is really useful to you if you do not see the cash until months later.)

We can take a look at the cash budget for a hypothetical manufacturing company to see the potential effects of making such a change. In Table 14.3, only the first six months are shown, but the general notion is clear. This company purchases materials in the month it uses them in manufacturing. It pays its suppliers in the same month. The owner has assumed that the goods will be sold in the month following the month they are made. Its customers pay 45–60 days after the sale. Materials cost is 60 percent of the eventual sale price. The second section, B, of Table 14.3 shows what would occur if the owner shortened her trade terms to 30 days. She assumed that she would lose 10 percent of her business by doing so.

As you can see in Table 14.3, two things occurred. First, the time period before her cumulative cash turned positive was shortened from Month 7 to Month 4. If she had been funding the shortfall in cash with a loan, she would have just saved a quarter's worth of interest cost. Second, the amount of the shortfall that she would have to cover has decreased significantly. The original projection required her to cover shortfalls of $14,000. Under the revised scenario, she is short by only $6,400. This may mean less borrowing or less strain on her personal funds or less of the company given to investors, depending on how she chooses to finance the cash shortages.

This is one instance in which slightly smaller may prove to be a whole lot better. The standard small company preoccupation with increasing sales, sometimes at the expense of sound cash flows, can be dangerous to your business health.

But you have other options in managing your cash inflows. You might consider offering a small discount for customers who pay earlier than is absolutely required. (You will have many options to take such discounts from your suppliers. This will be discussed further in the "outflows" section of this chapter.)

In the example shown in Table 14.4, we have gone back to the original projection. The owner here offered a 2 percent discount to customers who

Table 14.3 Cash budgets for differing terms of trade

A. CASH BUDGET—XYZ MFG. CORP.: PROJECTED CASH BUDGET

		Month				
	1	*2*	*3*	*4*	*5*	*6*
Cash inflows	$		10,000	10,000	10,000	10,000
Outflows for:						
Purchases	$ 6,000	6,000	6,000	6,000	6,000	6,000
Other	$ 1,000	1,000	1,000	1,000	1,000	1,000
Net cash	$(7,000)	(7,000)	3,000	3,000	3,000	3,000
Cumulative cash	$(7,000)	(14,000)	(11,000)	(8,000)	(5,000)	(2,000)

B. CASH BUDGET—XYZ MFG. CORP.: REVISED PROJECTED CASH BUDGET—NET 30 DAYS

	1	*2*	*3*	*4*	*5*	*6*
Cash inflows	$	9,000	9,000	9,000	9,000	9,000
Outflows for:						
Purchases	$ 5,400	5,400	5,400	5,400	5,400	5,400
Other	$ 1,000	1,000	1,000	1,000	1,000	1,000
Net cash	$(6,400)	2,600	2,600	2,600	2,600	2,600
Cumulative cash	$(6,400)	(3,800)	(1,200)	1,400	4,000	6,600

paid within 30 days. This is a "trade discount." (A more normal trade discount is 2 percent if paid within 10 days, or total amount due within 30 days. We are exaggerating to demonstrate effects.) She assumes that 50 percent of her customers will take her up on her offer.

Clearly, this strategy is somewhat effective at reducing the size and duration of the cash shortfalls, but not as effective as the prior method. Your choice should recognize that terms of trade are largely a marketing considera-

Table 14.4 XYZ Mfg. Corp.: Projected cash budget with 2 percent trade discount

		Month				
	1	*2*	*3*	*4*	*5*	*6*
Cash inflows	$	4,900	9,900	9,900	9,900	9,900
Outflows for:						
Purchases	$ 6,000	6,000	6,000	6,000	6,000	6,000
Other	$ 1,000	1,000	1,000	1,000	1,000	1,000
Net cash	$(7,000)	(2,100)	2,900	2,900	2,900	2,900
Cumulative cash	$(7,000)	(9,100)	(6,200)	(3,300)	(400)	2,500

tion, and that your decisions should reflect your understanding of your market and your competitive strength.

Organizing Collections

Even if you do not choose to alter trade terms, there are often steps you can take to improve your cash inflow situation. All these methods begin with adequate record-keeping about who owes you how much and when such debts are due. This is known as "aging receivables." What you want is a handle on how much cash is *not* coming in and who is not paying. A simple table, as shown in Table 14.5, will suffice, at least for your early operations.

Table 14.5   Aging accounts receivable

	FOR JANUARY, 198X			
	1–30 Days	*31–45 Days*	*46–60 Days*	*61–90 Days*
Sandy's Supply	$5,000			
Jack's Marine	$	8,000		
Terry's Industries	$			10,000
...				
Total	$5,000	8,000	—	10,000

Your first move should probably be to get on the phone and call Terry to find out what the problem is. Sometimes, a call from the owner works wonders. Sometimes, there really is a problem that the customer has not been able to have taken care of and is consequently protesting by not paying. You may be able to take care of the problem and get your money. You may also, using this method, hear about operational or service problems that you will not hear of any other way.

If you see that large amounts of cash are not coming in, you might look for a structural problem in your collection operation. It is amazing how many companies have no structured approach to collections. In some others, the salespeople are supposed to do the collections. Now, how likely do you think it is that a person on commission is going to blow the next sale by bothering the customer about something as mundane as payment?

You can avoid many of these problems by setting your collections operation up properly from the beginning. Determine the point at which you will begin to call your delinquent accounts and when you will refuse to "sell" any more product to a slow- or non-payer. Determine the point at which you will turn the whole matter over to a collection agency (in which case you may get at least some of your money). Determine when a receivable will be written off as bad

FEATURE 14.1

Collecting From the Federal Government

It has been the unfortunate experience of many contractors to the federal government to find that getting the contract and doing the work has been only part of the battle. The real difficulties have often come in getting paid. This is also often true of work done for state governmental units.

The Federal Prompt Payment Act of 1982, however, has made the contractor's life significantly easier, and the federal example has been followed by more than half the states. This Act provides two approaches to getting the government to pay up—a carrot and a stick. The carrot is the ability of the contractor to offer a trade discount which the government is obliged to accept if the discount saves more than could be made at the current Treasury rate. The normal offer in 1984 was 2 percent discount for payment within 20 days.

The discount approach seems to work. A company that does 15 percent of its business with federal agencies reports that "We offer 2 percent for payment in 20 days, and the GPO (Government Printing Office) takes it all the time. They make payment like clockwork." Another contractor simply reports that "The Prompt Payment Act has had a decided effect."

The stick involves the requirement that the government pay interest on any balances over 45 days after invoicing. During the first half of 1983, such penalties cost the federal government only $518,000—a remarkably small amount in the opinions of those who backed the law. "No agency director wants to spend his or her resources on delinquent interest charges," says Kenton Pattie, who led the fight for the law.

Adapted from "News and Trends," *Inc.* magazine (March 1983): 46; and "Ideas You Can Use," *Inc.* magazine (March 1984): 112.

debt. Perhaps most important of all, determine who is responsible for collections. And make sure that that "someone" is not your sales staff. (In any case, your commission structure should be set up to pay only when the customer has paid up. In that way, your salespeople will be at least marginally interested in whether payment is ever actually received for "sales." You will also not be fronting the cash outflows for commissions.)

MANAGING CASH OUTFLOWS

In looking at the cash outflow side of the business, you can see that you have some of the advantages that you have to deal with from your customers. You get to choose when you will pay a supplier. The one thing that you want to be particularly careful about, particularly as a "new kid on the block," is to pay up within the agreed-upon time period. At this early point in your business career, one of the most important things is to establish a reputation for honesty and straight dealing. In most industries, particularly at the local level, word gets around fast. *Never* break your word—and a deal with a supplier is simply another form of your word. If something arises that makes it impossible for you to come through, extend the supplier the courtesy you would like. Call to explain and work out a new payment date *before* they chase you.

Within these limits, however, you can choose. And you should choose so as to maximize the amount of cash that you control and the period of time during which you maintain that control.

Most of your cash outflows are fairly static throughout a year. Blips generally come from such periodic payments as insurance (often a quarterly payment). For companies that rely on variable, part-time work forces, outflows to wages are also likely to fluctuate. There is a significant difference between the two types of outflow fluctuation, however. In the second instance, the increase in outflows is likely to be tied to or to presage an increase in sales that will (or does) translate into an increase in inflows. Insurance payments, on the other hand, will be due whether or not sales and inflows are likely to increase. You will have to plan on how to cover them, regardless of the state of your current sales.

By far, the area of your greatest flexibility in cash outflow planning is in the inventory and/or materials field. In this area, you decide how much to purchase at which times. You negotiate deals on how and when it is to be paid for. Given this situation, it is clear that purchasing and inventory planning and control are critical elements of cash flow management and planning.

Economic Order Quantity (EOQ)

While the economic order quantity has been discussed in Chapter 9, a brief review of the basic notion is warranted here. The formula assumes that inventory and purchasing procedures have a certain set of costs in your business. There is a cost to keeping excess inventory, a cost to placing an order, and a cost to tying up money in inventory or in borrowing money to pay for the inventory. The EOQ equation trades off all of these factors and gives you the best volume of a given item to purchase at one time, given the sales volume of that item in your company.

If your purchasing pattern and list of inventory items fit the requirements for effective use of EOQ, this section is a good place to reconsider its use. The formula

$$EOQ = \sqrt{\frac{2 \times \text{Annual use} \times \text{cost of purchasing}}{\text{Unit cost} \times \text{inventory carrying cost}}}$$

shows you the numbers that will minimize your overall inventory costs. It may not be feasible for you to come up with the amount of cash that the equations recommend at the outset. Most new small businesses are consistently strapped for cash. But the EOQ approach to inventory management does provide a goal toward which you should manage your cash flows. Part of the reason for considering the trade terms and collections approaches outlined earlier is to provide the cash necessary to take advantage of inventory purchasing breaks.

Trade Discounts

As mentioned earlier in this chapter, trade discounts are one of the means by which sellers induce their customers to pay earlier than absolutely required. This improves the cash flow of the seller and offers the buyer a bit of a price break. To determine whether you should take the trade discounts offered, you first need to determine whether you will have enough cash early enough to pay early without causing you to miss other payment dates. Your cash budget (which will be discussed at length in the next chapter) will tell you this immediately.

If you find that you could take the discount, if you chose to do so, you can figure out easily what not taking the discount will cost you. Assume that you have terms of 2/10 net 30 on a payable of $1,000. That means that you could pay $980 on day 10, or $1,000 on day 30. You are essentially paying $20 for the privilege of using the $980 for an extra 20 days. This is 2.04 percent for one eighteenth of a year, or more than 36 percent a year. If your supplier will really let the debt go unpaid for 60 days, the annualized cost drops to slightly less than 15 percent.

As you can see, failure to take trade discounts can be a very expensive way to finance your business. The attraction for smaller companies in letting discount deadlines pass is that it doesn't *look* expensive (2 percent) and it is an easy way to finance for firms that cannot or do not choose to qualify for bank credit lines. Given the expense, however, one of the primary goals of your cash flow management program should be to take advantage of every available trade credit deal offered.

CASH DEFICITS

As was noted early in this book, most new companies find themselves behind in the cash game even before opening. This is, of course, because they have to cover, somehow, the costs of the startup—equipment, deposits, initial inventories and/or raw materials, etc. These costs are generally handled in the initial debt and equity financings for the new company.

Many companies, and those in certain fields in particular, also face deficits of operating cash in their first few months or in some seasonal pattern. The kinds of companies at greatest risk of such cash deficits are those with a long lead time between acquisition of raw materials, eventual sale, and actual customer payment, and those with a seasonal pattern (and a short season). In the former category, an extreme example would be a maker of scotch or bourbon, both of which need to be aged for significant periods of time before they can be sold. In the latter category, one might find boat sales operations and garden (or winter sports) shops. For the bourbon maker, the deficit would probably be a front-end problem. Once she could begin to sell the product, the problem would disappear. For the seasonal operation, however, the problem will most likely recur on an annual basis.

There are a number of possible ways to deal with such cash shortfalls—if you know that they are coming (and when and how big they will be). Your cash budget will be of great help in identifying when and how much. The rest is your job—one of your main jobs, in fact.

The neatest approach to funding cash deficits is, obviously, to have money left over from your previous "up" cycle. This is often difficult, particularly for the new firm that has had no prior cycles, and for the company that is growing at such a pace that its cash needs keep outstripping its prior surplusses. (If you are thinking about being one of the latter types, you might consider whether you want to grow that rapidly. It might be cheaper and might leave you in better control of operations to slow down so that you could fund your growth needs for cash internally.)

Another nice way to handle this snag is to work out deals with your suppliers. Quite often, suppliers will make special credit arrangements if you are likely to become a good customer. Often, special extended payment arrangements can be made for such things as initial inventory purchases. In some of the more seasonal industries, suppliers have already developed programs to help their customers over the real cash flow humps. The only way to find out is to ask—and ask others operating in your industry.

(Please note that, in some industries, the rule for new businesses is cash on the barrelhead until you prove yourself. As is to be expected, this tends to occur more in businesses in which the inventory is perishable, such as restaurants, than in businesses in which the creditors could theoretically recover something against the inventory if the deal goes sour.)

Another standard approach, particularly to funding a seasonal shortfall in cash, is to arrange a line of credit with your bank. If you qualify, this will permit you to handle your required outflows, take available trade discounts, and operate until your own cash flow turns positive on a monthly basis. This kind of credit normally requires that the outstanding balance be at zero for at least one month in each year.

Requirements for qualifying for this kind of credit arrangement tend to be tight, since credit issued in this way is generally unsecured credit. That means

FEATURE 14.2

Risky Christmas Tree Business Can Bring Growers Big Profits

"The Christmas tree business works like this: You put money into planting, pruning and protecting trees for six or seven years—and no money comes in. After that, you have trees to harvest and sell if weather, bugs and disease haven't destroyed them. If you mess up in one or two years, you have nothing," says Aaron Shannon, a grower. "But, if all goes well, you make a bundle."

Shannon has been expanding his business since the 1960's. He now has 1.2 million trees growing. But he has had to borrow to do it. He now carries $850,000 worth of debt at 15 percent. This year, if all goes as planned, he will reduce that figure to $250,000. Later in the year, however, he will have to borrow another $400,000 to cover his operating needs. "You're only paid once a year in this business," he notes.

Growers invest about $5,000 an acre in the trees, between planting and the time they are cut. Trees are generally sold for about twice the cost of raising them. Granting credit to purchasers is particularly risky since, after Christmas, the trees are essentially worthless. Shannon tries to collect before Christmas Day, while giving customers time to sell some of the trees first. To hedge a bit, he requires a 20 percent non-refundable deposit with orders and does not give credit to new customers without good credit references.

Adapted from Sanford L. Jacobs, "Small Business," *The Wall Street Journal* (December 13, 1984): 37.

that the bank generally does not arrange for collateral. Rather, the bank assumes that the company is "good for" the money, or that the total company is more than adequate to cover all outstanding debt. In any case, such revolving credit arrangements are worth talking over with your banker if your business pattern fits the seasonal profile.

CASH SURPLUSSES

Believe it or not, some companies actually generate cash surplusses at certain times in their years. A tax preparation operation, for example, will be cash-rich in May and June. Proper management of such cash surplusses—and those that exist for far shorter time periods—can actually increase the amount of cash that you have.

Investing relatively small cash surplusses for relatively short periods is an option that has been given us by the new competition in the banking industry.

The critical items in deciding to invest surplus cash include: knowing how much cash will be "surplus" for how long, and determining an adequate cash cushion for the business, "just in case." Your cash budget will assist in making the former determination. Your assessment of what is reasonably likely to go wrong and your own personal comfort levels will determine what is an "adequate" cushion for your business at the time you are considering investing.

Competition also makes it wise to shop around for a bank that will handle business of the size and duration you are considering. In general, minimum times are about 21 days, minimum amounts, $10,000. Please keep in mind that the banker with whom you are planning to develop a long-term relationship may not approve of your use of another bank. If this is the case, he may make a deal. If not, you need to weigh your potential dollar gain against the damaging of this relationship. Whether any of this is worth your trouble obviously depends on the cash cycle of your business and the going interest rates in the economy.

SUMMARY

Cash is what really makes businesses operate. Without it, you cannot pay your bills and you are out of the game. With it, you have greatly increased your flexibility in the marketplace.

Cash in the business can be defined as spendable money over which you have control. Defined this way, most business is done on a non-cash basis. Checks and credit cards are not cash, although they can be turned into cash fairly rapidly. A large part of your job as owner/manager is arranging the flows of cash into and out of your business so that you will always be able to pay your bills and other obligations as they come due.

A cash orientation differs from an accounting orientation in that cash focuses on the real movements of money. It differs specifically because of timing differences between transactions and because certain things that require cash payments are not considered "expenses" for accounting purposes and vice-versa.

To some degree, you can manage the inflows of cash into your business by defining or changing the credit terms of trade under which you do business. You can do this by shortening the period within which customers are expected to pay, by offering a small discount for early payment, and/or by tightening up your collections policies and operations.

You can also do some managing of your cash outflows. You can arrange the timing of required payments to coincide with your expected inflows. You can do your purchasing more scientifically with economic order quantities. You can reduce overall costs by taking advantage of trade discounts offered to you.

When shortfalls are anticipated, you can arrange in advance to cover them, using various kinds of trade credit or a line of credit from your bank. Should your business be one that generates periodic cash surplusses, the surplusses can be invested. The return from such short-term investments can make managing your cash even sweeter.

The key to managing your cash effectively lies in the projected cash budget. This document is one of the basic pieces of your financial control network and will be discussed at length in the next chapter.

FOR YOU TO CONSIDER

1. Why can some companies that are losing money continue to operate? Why do some companies that show profits fail?
2. What is "cash"? Is a check cash? Why or why not?
3. In what two basic ways does a cash orientation differ from the one used in accrual accounting? Give at least one example in each of the two categories you cited.
4. What is one of your major jobs as owner/manager in assuring the survival of your company?
5. Why is a breakeven not particularly useful as a tool for operating management?
6. What are "terms of trade"? How can you use them in cash flow management?
7. Why are collections functions so important to your business? Discuss two major pitfalls in organizing your collections function. How can you avoid them?
8. Why are purchasing and inventory control vital functions in managing your cash outflows? What options do you usually have in these areas?
9. How can you cover short-term cash deficits (other than failing to pay all or some of your bills)?
10. Why might a company have a cash surplus at given times of its year? What can it do to make some use of the surplus cash?

FOR FURTHER READING

Bank of America. "Cash Flow/Cash Management." *Small Business Reporter* (1982).

Small Business Administration publications:

Cash Flow in a Small Plant. SBA MA 1.006.
Consumer Credit. SBA 045-000-00179-2.
Credit and Collections. SBA MA 1.007.
Credit and Collections for Small Stores. SBA 045-000-00169-5.
Credit and Collections: Policy and Procedures. SBA 045-000-00180-6.
Sound Cash Management and Borrowing. SBA MA 1.016.

15. Projections: Will This Business Really Fly?

The size of the market for No. 1 gauge model trains did not discourage the Millers of Bangor Train Factory, Inc. In fact, they didn't even bother to research it. Both brothers were inexperienced in their industry and it showed quickly. The company showed a loss of just under $50,000 last year. They will not meet their 1984 sales forecast. The problem, says Duane Miller, is not with the market, it's just that the company is still an amateur in projecting sales.

Frank E. James, *Wall Street Journal*

Now you have everything you need to enable you to put together the documents that let you see whether your proposed business will really work (and what modifications it might need if the initial answer is "no"). These same documents will get your banker to talk to you as if you knew what you were doing—and might get you a loan. These same documents can help you convince investors to invest in your business and show Uncle Harry that, yes, you really are serious about this. These same documents will serve as your scorecard for your first year of business operation. You will be getting a great deal of mileage out of what will eventually be three thin sheets of paper.

But don't let the size fool you. Those three sheets will synthesize all the work you have done to date to make your business a success. That's why we are spending an entire chapter on them.

This chapter will give you a graphic demonstration of why we spent the last two chapters talking about accounting, financial ratio analysis, and cash flow tracking and management. Using these tools, you will be able to put your entire company into "numbers" so that you (and whoever else is interested) can take a look, modify as necessary (or desirable), and make the thing work. Or you may discover that there is no acceptable way for you to make it work. All this without risking any of your money.

The key tools are the financial statements, cash budgets, and financial ratios discussed in the previous chapters, and techniques for projecting your probable business results under differing circumstances. This chapter is about your projections. It discusses how to do them, what to do with them once you develop them, and how to make their flexibility useful to you in planning and restructuring. It also begins the discussion (continued in Chapter 18) of how these documents are used as the basic control mechanisms of your business.

THE STATEMENTS AS PERSONAL DECISION AIDS

The three pieces of paper are: pro forma income statement, pro forma balance sheet, and cash budget. One year projections are the bare minimum that you should prepare. Remember that the basic questions are yours. Can the business work the way I have designed it? Will I make enough money to satisfy the personal financial objective(s) I set up so long ago? Are the operations of the business likely to meet whatever other objectives I defined for it?

Remember, too, that you are likely to be the one who will be damaged most if your company folds. Your bank, banker, and shareholders are also likely to participate in a fall, if there is one. But you're the one who is the front person for this operation. You're the planner and the one who is responsible for execution. You're the one who needs the answers that the projections can give you. Treat them as personal decision aids, therefore, rather than requirements of some "outside" forces. Under these circumstances, it is generally wise to do a bit more than is absolutely necessary. If you are seeking financing from a bank or other financial institution, or equity money from anyone other than Aunt Tillie or your buddy Jim, you will be required to present at least three years' worth of projected results for your company before anyone will talk with you.

If you have access to a personal computer, now might be the time to use it. The spreadsheet-type programs can be invaluable in helping you to build (and adjust and test and play with) these projections. However, a word of caution: Do consider whether the results make sense to you and are likely to make sense to your banker.

One of the better stories about spreadsheets has to do with the prospective business owner who carefully set up his first year's data and his assumptions and let the computer run up a five-year projection. The pieces of paper looked very professional and very neat. The only problem was that he didn't really look at the results. They showed mounting losses and total disaster by year three. He proudly presented his projections to his banker—with predictable results. In addition to providing a rather sad joke for the entire small business lending group, this would-be entrepreneur had blown his credibility with this bank forever.

So a bit of care is definitely in order—whether you turn a computer loose on your numbers or do them by hand. Think about what the numbers are telling you and what they will tell your banker. After all, that's really the purpose of running numbers. They tell you things you need to know. If you know these things first, you can make corrections and adjustments. If your banker sees them first, you may well have neither a banker nor a business.

MAKING PROJECTIONS

Making projections for your business involves a major leap of faith. What you are really doing is synthesizing everything you have learned about how businesses in your industry operate and applying that synthesis to your vision of your own company. In addition, you are putting it down on paper, where its very permanence makes the whole process even more frightening. Finally, you are probably going to be showing your projections to other people, adding the risk of semi-public humiliation to the list of potential personal disasters. Nobody said it would be easy.

That is the downside to making projections. You need to consider, however, the downside to *not* making projections, to not making that leap of faith in yourself and your nascent company. The one we have discussed already is the fact that, if you need money to start the company, you will not get it without written projections.

More important in the long run is controlling and containing the element of surprise. For most small business owners, except the most steadfast pessimists in the crowd, surprises tend to be of the unpleasant sort: your sales are not bursting your premises at the seams, your suppliers raise their prices or change their order quantities, and so on. Surprise! You're in trouble. The thing that you are aiming for in making projections is "no surprises." A good, flexible set of projections lets you preview the future, seeing some surprises in advance and knowing the limits of your company under various sets of circumstances. On the whole, making projections for your company is smarter than letting things happen to you. But it takes effort and not a little intestinal fortitude to make that first set of projections. You need to grit your teeth and do it. Believe it or not, it gets easier as you get into the process.

Because of the work you have already done in taking your company this far, you have most of the data you need to begin to make your formal projections. You have some industry sales/cost/operating information left over from your initial foray into market research (Chapter 4). You have a great number of your own cost estimates for such items as your space costs, your inventory costs, and your personnel costs. Essentially, you have the whole thing. It is simply scattered about in little pieces. Your job now is simply to put it together in the right form and to play with the results.

It helps to try to detach yourself from the numbers you are looking at. You know that you can make this business work in one way or another. You have been doing reality checks throughout the building process to this point. It is unlikely that you will discover a total bust in this quantification process. It is more likely that you will find some modifications you want to make, ways of making a pretty good approach even better. And keep firmly fixed in mind that you do not have to show your projections to anyone until you are satisfied with them.

PRO FORMA FINANCIAL STATEMENTS

As noted in Chapter 13, "pro forma" is simply a fancy term for your projections as they are displayed in projected financial statements. Pro formas look exactly like regular financial statements, except that the data is projected, rather than actual. This is noted at the top of the statements and confirmed by the dates. This being the case, all you have to do is follow the forms.

Once again, the process is logical. What you are trying to do is to show how your business will begin and how it will operate over its first few years. You will need to consider both its financial condition (balance sheet) and its probable operating results (income statement).

Opening Balance Sheet

The easiest place to start is with the opening balance sheet. This document is intended to show what your business will own and what it will owe on the day it opens its doors. Label it, date it, and create a form by listing all the balance sheet categories in order, assets first, down the left-hand side of a piece of paper. Proper accounting paper makes life easier because columns are already created for you, but any old piece of paper will do. We have provided a sample worksheet for you as Figure 15.1.

Next, get out all the numbers you have developed and collected in the course of your work on this project. List the cost to you of all the capital equipment that you will have to buy to start your company—that is, all the items you intend to use for more than one year. Group items together into categories defined by their economic useful lives or accelerated cost recovery system "lives" and add up the categories. This number is the "net property, plant, and equipment" item for your opening balance sheet. Enter it in the appropriate space. You're on your way.

Next, consider all the other assets of the business except cash. Obviously, you will not yet have any receivables because you have not yet made any

Figure 15.1   Pro forma balance sheet worksheet

	PRO FORMA BALANCE SHEET		
Company name:			
Item:	*As of Opening Date:* ____	*As of Year-End Year One Date:* ____	*As of Year-End Year Two Date:* ____
ASSETS:			
Current Assets:			
Cash and marketable securities			
Accounts receivable			
Inventory			
Prepaid expenses			
Total current assets			
Fixed Assets:			
Land			
Plant and equipment: Cost			
Accumulated depreciation			
Net book value			
Total fixed assets			
Other Assets:			
Patents and trademarks			
Goodwill			
Total other assets			
Total Assets			
LIABILITIES:			
Current Liabilities			
Accounts payable			
Accrued expenses			
Current portion LTD			
Total current liabilities			
Long-Term Liabilities			
Long-term debt			
Capital lease obligations			
Total long-term liabilities			
Contingencies			
Equity or Net Worth			
Total Liabilities and Equity			

sales. But you will have your initial inventories. List the items and amounts that you will have to buy to open for business. Be sure that you haven't forgotten something small, but vital, like business stationery or paper bags. Group these items into categories based on how you buy them and how you intend to keep track of them. Put the sum in the appropriate place on the balance sheet form.

You will also probably have some "deposits." You will pay one on your phone(s) and, possibly, one on your lease. These are assets, because someone is holding your money for a specified period. In some businesses, this can be a large number. Whether these are added to the "current" section or the "other" section of your asset list depends on when you can expect to see your money. Put it wherever it is appropriate.

Now you can move to the liabilities part of your opening balance sheet. Are any of your suppliers likely to be willing to extend trade credit to you for your initial purchases? If so, the amount you will owe them for this opening inventory is your opening accounts payable figure. Enter it.

If you are planning to take a long-term loan from the bank, you will need to split the loan into two parts, the part that will be due within the year and the rest. Remember that the balance sheet only notes the principal amounts, so you will have to separate principal from interest as well. The principal amount due during the first year should be noted in the "current portion" line. The remaining principal is "long-term debt." Deal with any debts you expect to owe Uncle John and/or your friends in the same manner.

You also know how much money you are planning on putting into the business. Add to this any money being put in by partners or coming in from the sale of shares of the company. Add up all this "equity" and put it in the line for "net worth" or "equity" or whatever you have chosen to call it.

If you now add up the liability portion, you will get your "total liabilities and net worth." In accord with the basic balance sheet equation, $A = L + NW$, you also have the total asset figure. This figure, less the sum of all the assets you already listed, will leave you with a "leftover" amount (we hope). This amount is "cash." In other words, "cash" is the "plug" figure in this opening balance sheet. You should also have this much in the bank on the day you open. In other words, it should all balance.

You now have a pro forma opening balance sheet. This is your starting financial position.

First Year Income Statement

To see whether your company is going to do favorable or unfavorable things to this initial position, you will need a first year income statement. We have provided a blank worksheet for you as Figure 15.2.

The key estimate for your opening income statement is your estimate of

Figure 15.2   Pro forma income statement worksheet

<table>
<tr><td colspan="4" align="center">INCOME STATEMENT
Company: ________________________

Years ending 12/31/______</td></tr>
<tr><td>Item</td><td align="center">198X</td><td align="center">198X + 1</td><td align="center">198X + 2</td></tr>
<tr><td>Net sales</td><td></td><td></td><td></td></tr>
<tr><td>Cost-of-goods-sold</td><td></td><td></td><td></td></tr>
<tr><td>Gross margin (profit)</td><td></td><td></td><td></td></tr>
<tr><td>EXPENSES:</td><td></td><td></td><td></td></tr>
<tr><td>Salaries and benefits</td><td></td><td></td><td></td></tr>
<tr><td>Rent or lease</td><td></td><td></td><td></td></tr>
<tr><td>Utilities</td><td></td><td></td><td></td></tr>
<tr><td>Phone</td><td></td><td></td><td></td></tr>
<tr><td>Supplies</td><td></td><td></td><td></td></tr>
<tr><td>Advertising</td><td></td><td></td><td></td></tr>
<tr><td>Travel and entertainment</td><td></td><td></td><td></td></tr>
<tr><td>Insurance</td><td></td><td></td><td></td></tr>
<tr><td>Interest</td><td></td><td></td><td></td></tr>
<tr><td>Depreciation</td><td></td><td></td><td></td></tr>
<tr><td>____________</td><td></td><td></td><td></td></tr>
<tr><td>Total expenses</td><td></td><td></td><td></td></tr>
<tr><td>Net income before
   federal taxes</td><td></td><td></td><td></td></tr>
<tr><td>Federal tax</td><td></td><td></td><td></td></tr>
<tr><td>Net income after tax</td><td></td><td></td><td></td></tr>
</table>

sales. Almost everything will eventually turn on the accuracy of this estimate. Therefore, you will probably want to "bracket" this estimate—develop sets of numbers for slightly lower and higher sales estimates to determine the range of likely results. (This "bracketing" technique was described earlier in Chapter 4.)

Sales estimates.   To make your best estimate, you will need all the industry data you collected earlier. Now you will tailor it to fit your particular business operation. The first thing you will probably look at, if you are a retail operation, is the average sales per square foot for your type of company. Then you start asking yourself questions. Is the mix of merchandise you plan to sell about average for your industry? If not, how will your particular mix affect the sales-per-square-foot figure? Will your products be more or less expensive relative to the space required to display them than the average?

When you have considered all the relevant issues you can think of, adjust the industry average figure to reflect your expected average sales per square foot and multiply by the square footage of your place. Be sure that you know whether the estimates you are using as a basis include or exclude storage and other non-selling space. Match your estimating basis to the one in your starting figures. This will give you a good beginning estimate of total sales in an average year.

But also keep firmly fixed in mind that your first year is extremely unlikely to be "average." How "unaverage" it is likely to be will depend on the kind of business you are running and where you have chosen to locate, among other factors. Were you starting the Christmas tree business we described in the last chapter, for example, you could not possibly expect to have your sales in Year One look like those of a grower who had been operating for seven years. When you get the initial sales estimate, then, adjust it further to reflect what you expect to be a realistic first year for a business of your type, and, more specifically, for your particular business.

When you come to this best estimate, subject it to a "reasonability" test. Consider what the sales volume in this estimate represents in terms of the total market size you estimated earlier, when you were first exploring this market. If your best sales estimate for your first year is 10 percent of the market, is that reasonable for you to expect? Is 50 percent of the total market? If your answer is "yes," you might ask yourself again why all these people are going to flock to your place, abandoning their current suppliers to do so. If your answer is "no," you might pare your best estimate down still further.

If you are planning a manufacturing operation, your constraint is not square footage, but rather the manufacturing capacity that the square footage represents. Probably a fair place for you to begin would be with the industry average asset turnover ratio or fixed asset turnover. Both of these consider the output in sales for a given amount of assets. Manufacturing tends to be an asset-based function. Make adjustments similar to those described above. When you review your projected sales figure for reasonableness, however, you will be considering both market share and manufacturing capacity. Make sure that you do not intend to sell more than you can produce.

In all cases, keep in mind that certain economic factors will affect your business. Different factors obviously affect different businesses in different ways. You need to use all the industry literature and the longer term progressions of historical average data to determine what factors will probably affect you, how they are likely to interact with your business, and why. Then cast your eye over the consensus economic forecasts (to be found in almost any business journal or magazine or newspaper) for your first few years in business. Make any necessary adjustments. Granted, the economists have not done very well over the last few years, but they currently have the only game in town. And any recognition that the state of the general economy has some effect on your business beats the calm assumption that your company will somehow exist in a vacuum.

If you are planning to enter a business that has no good parallels from which to use industry averages, or if you are intending to do business in some radical way that renders such parallels meaningless, you might try to estimate your sales by reversal. Essentially, you take that proportion of the total market that you estimated back in Chapter 4 as a reasonable proportion. You translate that estimate into a sales volume for your business, and then you see whether, when you have done all the rest of the cost estimates, you can make enough (or any) money in the business at that sales volume.

This approach to estimating sales is not as good as the direct approach because you have no outside reality check. You have already assumed a market share. Also, rather than being a true estimate of what the business should be able to do, you will have created a goal with no underlying justification for it in the operations of the business. If there really is no other way, however, it is better than nothing.

A final note on sales forecasts. There is great temptation to "hype" the sales forecasts so that the results will look good to your bank, your share-holders, and, after a while, to yourself. *Do not do it!* There are a number of reasons. If the original game is for the benefit of your bank, it probably will not work. Your banker has seen many business forecasts and the statements of numerous operating companies in your line of work. He is likely to spot the game pretty quickly, and then you've lost him.

And even if you win, you lose. Suppose you succeed in snowing him, but the actual first year results are lower than your "hyped" projections. Will you be able to pay him? What will he say the next time you need a loan and he compares your last set of projections with your actuals? On the whole, the game is not worth it.

More to the point, as we have emphasized, your first use of these documents is personal. You will be using them to determine whether you want to go ahead or to go ahead after you have made changes. If you start with anything less than your best estimate of your sales, you will be building in probable disaster. You will be making major decisions based on data you know is faulty. If you are going to do this, there is no real point in completing this exercise at all.

Other income statement estimates.   Putting together the rest of your pro forma income statement is fairly simple. Your cost-of-goods-sold is, as you will recall, the cost to you of making or buying whatever it is that you expect to sell. This includes the costs of materials and direct labor to make your product and the factory overhead used to produce it. Your gross margin is your sales less this cost-of-goods-sold.

You figured most of your expenses in earlier pieces of your work. In this section of your income statement goes all your costs associated with occupying your place of business, the depreciation on your plant and equipment, the salaries of your staff not totally involved in the manufacturing process, interest on your debts, professional fees, telephone costs, and any other expenses that your particular business might require. Your profit before taxes is your gross margin less the sum of these expenses.

To estimate your taxes, *do not* simply divide by two as you may have been doing in cases for years. Actually get the current tax rates for a small business with your level of profit and your legal structure. There is a sliding scale way down at the short end for corporations. If you are a proprietorship or a partnership, obviously, your individual tax rate(s) applies. Do not forget that state and local taxes also cost you money (expenses), as do the various payroll taxes (for social security and unemployment insurance). These rates—and perhaps the entire tax structure—are likely to change, but this will give you a rough estimate of your actual net income from the business. Incidentally, if you are politically inclined, this process will also probably give you some idea about which tax reforms you want to root for.

First Year Cash Budget

As we noted in the last chapter, you will have to be aware of when people are likely to pay you (in real money) and when you are going to have to come up with cash to pay others. Your first year cash budget will help you not only to figure out how to make it work, but also to figure out what your balance sheet is likely to look like after a year of operations. Therefore, the next document that you should begin to build is your cash budget. A sample is provided in Figure 15.3.

Cash inflows.   This document again focuses on your sales estimate as its starting point. Your first task here is breaking the annual sales figure you developed for your pro forma income statement into your sales pattern by months. (Do not simply divide your sales by 12. Nobody will believe that there are no seasonal fluctuations in most kinds of businesses.) Here, the data gleaned from industry data and figures can be most helpful. Some thought about how people use and purchase whatever you are selling will also help.

Once you have the projected sales by month, you bring your credit terms into play. Figure out how much cash will come in in the month of a sale, how much the following month, etc. In general, you can count sales through bank credit cards as "cash" since they are paid almost immediately. The same is true of local checks. The "charge cards," like American Express, often take longer to pay off, depending on your arrangements with them. Your objective is to figure out how much cash you will have to spend and how much you will have in accounts receivable at the end of each month. The cash is the critical

Figure 15.3 Pro forma cash budget worksheet—for year one, monthly

Item				Month			
	−2	−1	0	1	2	3	4
CASH INFLOWS:							
"Sales"							
Cash sales							
Collections							
Other							
Total cash inflows							
CASH OUTFLOWS:							
Purchases							
Rent							
Salaries & benefits							
Phone							
Utilities							
Advertising							
Insurance							
Taxes							
Other							
Debt service:							
Interest							
Principal							
Total cash outflows							
Net cash for month							
Cumulative cash							

part for this document. The receivables figure will be critical to your year-end balance sheet.

Cash outflows. Most of this part is easy. To a great extent, your outflows are nice and regular. Simply list them. Do not forget such things as taxes, however. You will need to pay federal quarterly estimated income taxes, some employee-related taxes (withholding plus your contribution), and whatever your own state requires.

Two types of outflows, however, one large and one small, are tied to your sales estimates and cash inflow estimates. The small one is the direct cost to you of accepting credit cards. Needless to say, the banks are not in the credit card business solely to make your life safer. They charge fees for their services. There is a set-up fee, and there is a charge to you on amounts charged on cards in your store. These charges work on a sliding scale by volume. Once again, being small will get you a higher percentage charge. Bank cards charge up to 5 percent. The charge cards can charge up to 7 percent, but they will often arrange a lower charge if you do not need your cash as quickly—that's 10 days or more, rather than an almost instantaneous turnaround. Not months and months. Do not forget these costs. Five percent of 50 percent can wipe out the profit you thought you had.

The real outflow estimating problem for most businesses is, of course, the purchasing of inventories and materials. Some businesses have standard inventory-buying periods. Toy stores, for example, or apparel retailers, have very clear patterns. If you are in such an industry, your problem is figuring out how to finance the cost of large chunks of inventory. You have little choice about when to purchase.

In other businesses, however, you can determine your economic order quantity. Then, working with your sales forecast by months, you can back through your manufacturing or ordering time to get to when you have to buy the items. You then work forward, using the terms of trade of your various suppliers to arrive at when you will have to come up with the cash. Those amounts in the relevant months are the figures that should be entered on the "purchases" line of your cash budget.

Startup costs.   A classic oversight of not-yet-entrepreneurs is neglect of startup costs as cash outflows. This simply makes a major funding problem vanish into thin air. This would not be a bad trick—except that those costs do not really go away because you haven't accounted for them. Startup costs are simply another set of cash outflows that have to be covered. Thinking about the timing of these costs, however, may give you some pause.

By definition, startup costs are generally incurred before or at the very time of your opening. The nature of the preparations that you will have to make to open will dictate the timing. But consider the fact that you cannot pay to renovate a place on which you are not yet paying rent. The point here is that you may actually have to come up with lease or rental payments, for example, a full month or two before you can open for business. The health spa back in Chapter 3 would be an example of that kind of business. If you are in manufacturing, your problems could be getting your equipment installed and/ or the lead time required before you can turn purchased raw materials into goods that you can sell. In some companies, the constraint may be training the staff, in which case you will be paying some salaries before the operation can generate any income at all. It is a rare company that can just open its doors one fine day.

You will probably cover these costs out of your own funds and/or through loans, but they have to be covered. And both pieces of the transactions to your company's cash—the outflows to wherever and the inflows from loans or investments—should appear on your initial cash budget. If necessary, show your first year as having 13 or 14 months, but pick up all the cash outlays that will be required by your new business.

Year-End, Year One Balance Sheet

Using the three statements you have already developed, you can now add the next column to your pro forma balance sheet table, showing your financial position after your first year of operation. Some pieces are self-evident. Your new net book value of your property, plant, and equipment, for example, will simply be its cost (your opening figure) less the depreciation you took on your income statement. This, of course, assumes that you have neither added nor gotten rid of any equipment. Assuming no new loans, your new long-term debt number will be the opening amount less the principal amount that will be due next year. The new current portion will be that due-next-year amount. (The "current portion" shown in your opening statement will have been paid off.)

Getting your new net worth figure is a two-step process. First, add to your opening figure any investments that have been made in the company since opening. Next, go to your pro forma income statement for year one and pull the net-income-after-tax figure. Subtract out any dividends or partnership payments that will have been taken out of the company and add the remainder to the net worth figure. This new number represents the equity that there will be in your business at the end of your first year of operation.

Now you will make heavy use of your cash budget. From that document, you should know how much revenue will be outstanding in accounts receivable at year-end. You will also be able to see how much you owe in outstanding trade payables. Enter these figures on the appropriate lines.

Your cash budget will also help in getting to your new inventory figure. From it, you will know how much you will have purchased over the year. You also have already estimated what you will sell in the course of the year (income statement). Take the units sold and multiply by the purchase cost to you of the materials and/or components to get to an inventory cost-of-goods-sold. You probably could also use your backup calculations for your cost-of-goods-sold figure. You then simply start with the opening balance (your initial inventory), add the purchases, and subtract the inventory that will be sold to get to your ending balance—your new inventory figure.

To the extent that you will owe taxes that you have not yet been required to pay, you will also have an accrual on the liability side.

Your cash figure on the Year One balance sheet should be your initial cash balance, plus the change in cash over the year from your cash budget, plus the amount of depreciation you showed on your Year One pro forma income statement.

And that's it. You have the full set of projections for your first year in your prospective business. You can, of course, simply repeat this process to develop projections for the following years as well. It is quite true that one's projections get shakier as one gets farther out in time, but do not let that deter you from giving it a try. Do not get caught in the old increase-everything-by-10 percent-for-inflation game. It will not help in your decision-making process. The entire key to making useful projections (note that we did not say "precisely accurate projections") is to think about what you are doing and why you are doing it. It also helps to remember that just because you wrote it down does not make it "Truth" or unchangeable. In fact, the next phase of this walk-through begins to raise questions about what you might want to change.

RUNNING YOUR OWN RATIOS

Your very first move upon completing your first set of projections should be to look at the bottom line and at the cash throwoff of the business. Remembering that this is the first year of the business, you want to consider whether the numbers you see make you feel pretty good or absolutely awful. If the answer is "positively rotten," stop for a moment to think about why. Have your objectives changed somewhat since you started this plan-building process? Is the poor result simply a function of the fact that the business is really just starting? Is the result really poor, or were your expectations a bit unrealistic? You have developed the projections for your ideal company. Will you be able to modify? Or is this an all-or-nothing proposition for you?

The real point here is that the process of projection calls for a dispassionate attitude, and the process of analysis requires the same approach. Running a successful business, on the other hand, requires that you be happy and satisfied (to a reasonable degree). You, and your feelings about the business and its probable results, are the only things that can determine that satisfaction level. It is not an analytic or dispassionate decision. Rather, it is a highly emotional one. The numbers you are playing with represent the business. How you feel about them should be separated from your analytic conclusions, but should be a very major part of the decisions you are about to make.

While we can ask you to stop and consider the emotional aspects, we cannot help you to define them. That is something that is yours alone to do. But we can show you how to approach the analytic parts. And here, once again, the industry average data you collected is going to be very useful to you. It will serve as a reality check for your projections and as a generator of items and approaches for you to consider.

Your first analytic step must be to cast your projected data into the forms in which you can compare it with the results of your business peers—or as close as you can get. This means that you will have to calculate common size statements and develop the standard set of financial ratios using your pro forma income statement, your year-end balance sheet, and the operating data that you used to develop them.

Next, lay the best industry averages you have come up with right next to your projected ratios. Run down the set and note where there are major differences. A dash of ice water: A giant difference in a direction normally considered "good" should not (as yet) produce cheers. You should, rather, begin to consider whether there's something major you forgot. (I particularly recall the student who managed to show massive first year profitibility in her personnel agency plans by the simple expedient of not planning to pay her clerical/secretarial staff.) Only after you have convinced yourself that nothing major has been left out should a very cautious grin be permitted.

Once you have pinpointed the differences between your projected ratios and those of the industry, you have to consider why they exist. Some may well be simply a function of your newness. Your asset turnover, for example, is likely to be out of line for two reasons. First, your equipment is newer, therefore less depreciated, therefore carried on your books at a higher relative value than that of your average competitor. At the same time, your sales have probably not yet hit their full potential. This kind of difference is probably nothing to be concerned about.

If, on the other hand, your inventory turnover ratio deviates significantly from the average, you might want to consider some of your proposed business policies. Are you planning on doing business in some way different from the norm in your industry? Would this difference in business operations account for the difference in the ratios? If not, you might consider whether they might know something that you do not yet know. Perhaps you have underestimated the amount of stock you will need (if your ratio is very high). Alternatively, you may be planning to carry too much inventory (if your ratio is very low). In either case, you might want to consider modifying your approach and reworking your numbers. Note that, if you were unhappy with your prospective profitability, reducing the size of your inventory would probably help.

Each deviation should cause you to think about *why* the deviation exists and whether you can or choose to do anything about it. If you want to test what would probably occur if you made a particular change in your intended business practice, you can simply plug in the new estimates and rework your numbers. (This is where an electronic spreadsheet can be really useful.) Since the projections are not set in concrete, you can simply shift back to your original projections if you do not like the results.

After you get a set of projections that you like and that make sense to you in terms of how the industry operates, please go back and reread the objectives you set out for this business and for yourself. They come into play here. Since it is very easy to get lost in the numbers, particularly when you are testing options in this manner, you need to compare the business that you finally finish projecting with the vision you had at the outset.

Granted, the reality will never be as glamorous or as exciting as was the vision. Too much hard work has already gone into your project. Your question is whether the resulting business is acceptable to you and likely to meet your major, basic objectives. If your answer is "yes," trot right on down to your banker. You're ready to talk with her. If your answer is "no," you might try another round of adjustment and modification. Failing that, put the project away. Another day you will want to analyze what went wrong and how your next business idea can be structured to work out better.

SUMMARY

The process of developing projections of the probable activities and condition of a soon-to-be-opened business provides the only way to get any real idea of whether the business will survive and provide a profit to its owner. The projections themselves are also required (for the same reason) by any institution or unrelated individual likely to consider lending to or investing in the company. Projected balance sheets, income statements, and cash budgets should all be available, for decision making by both the entrepreneur and potential lenders and investors. Three-year projections are the minimum requirement of most banks.

The numbers entered in these three documents should be your best estimates of what reality will be like. They should draw on all your research and your general knowledge. The specific data can be drawn from the work you have done in earlier sections of your planning. Since nobody needs to see your projections until you are satisfied with them, you can modify and adjust the numbers until you have a business that makes sense to you.

This does not mean that you should deliberately create unreality. That is likely to simply create very expensive later disaster. You can, however, alter the operations and, therefore, the resulting financial picture of the business until you find a set of approaches and business principles that work for you and your proposed business.

Keep in mind, however, that "working," in this context, encompasses a great deal more than simply making the numbers work out to something that looks successful. You will be living with this company. You have to be comfortable (if not wildly enthusiastic) about the way it will do business. In short, the working model needs to meet your objectives. If it does not do so, it is unlikely to fly. At least, not for you.

FOR YOU TO CONSIDER:

1. What is a "pro forma"?
2. What three documents will your banker be looking for from you when you come in to ask him for a loan with which to start your prospective business?
3. Aside from the fact that your banker will be looking for them, why should you develop all these projections?
4. How would you estimate first year sales for a clothing store? For a roofing company?
5. How can you test the reasonableness of your sales estimates?
6. If your proposed business has no good parallels from which to draw industry data, what is an alternative method for estimating sales? Why is this method only an alternative?
7. Assume you manufacture widgets. How would you figure out when you will need to pay for purchases of the metal housings that are a major component part of your widgets?
8. Why should you not "hype" your sales estimates or "pad" your expense estimates?
9. How should startup costs be handled in your projections?
10. How can industry average ratio data be useful to you in developing your projections?
11. Why is it important to reconsider your business in terms of earlier written objectives after or as you try to make the numbers work out?

CASES FOR PART 6

SALLY JONES AND "NEIGHBORS"

As Sally and Janice got even farther into their planning process, they began to assemble much better and more specific cost estimates of what it would cost for them to start and run "Neighbors." They found a storefront location in a community shopping area (not an enclosed mall) that was right near their homes. The shopping center contained a supermarket with gourmet tendencies, a jewelry store, a dress shop, a dry cleaner, a physicians' office, and a small office building. Homes in the immediate area were selling for $100,000 to $250,000. They could lease the storefront for five years for about $1800 per month.

Table 1   Estimated specific costs (annual) for "Neighbors"

Insurance	$ 4,500
Lease	21,600
Advertising	9,000
Utilities	11,250
Payroll (including benefits)	$116,500

Table 2   Industry ratios—asset size < $1 million—1982 data, Robert Morris Associates

Net sales	100.0%	Total assets	100.0%
Cost of sales	44.4	Inventory	7.3
Gross profit	55.6	Total current assets	25.3
Operating expenses	51.0	Net fixed assets	57.5
All other expenses (net)	2.0		
Profit before taxes	2.6%	Current matur. L-T-debt	6.6
		Accounts payable	11.8
		Total current liabilities	40.1
		Long-term debt	30.3
		Net worth	26.6
Current ratio	.6		
Fixed worth	2.4		
Debt/worth	2.7		
NPBT/total assets (ROA)	6.6		
Sales/total assets	3.4		
Sales/fixed assets	6.1		
Lease/sales	5.0		
Depreciation/sales	3.1		
Officers' Compensation/sales	5.4		

Source: Robert Morris Associates, *Annual Statement Studies* (Philadelphia: 1983).

The space was not currently set up as a restaurant, and Sally and Janice were considering adding a bar, since a liquor license had come onto the market recently. While they made up their minds about it, they had taken an option on it. (Licenses were very hard to come by in the area, and if they had let it pass, it would have been gone in a matter of days.) The option had cost them only $500, since the license itself would be easily salable any time.

They spent a day with a $300-a-day restaurant consultant who had looked over the place and who estimated that the renovations they wanted would cost roughly $250,000. That included equipment and decorations. If they wanted new equipment—which the consultant did not recommend— it would cost about $30,000 more. She also told them that a place like the one they were developing should gross about $400,000 in sales a year and should make them a 5 percent pretax profit. It would cost them $750 to incorporate a Subchapter S company and another $750 to have an accountant set up their books.

They had already collected numerous sets of financial ratios for the restaurant business. They chose the ones that looked most useful and set them out separately. This data, and their other estimates, are shown in Tables 1–4.

Table 3   Industry ratios—all respondents—1983 data, Dun & Bradstreet

Net sales	100.0%	Total assets	100.0%
Cost of sales	N.A.	Inventory	7.5
Gross profit	46.4	Total current assets	30.7
Operating expenses	N.A.	Net fixed assets	44.1
All other expenses (net)	N.A.		
Profit before taxes	N.A.	Current matur. L-T-debt	N.A.
Profit after taxes	4.4%	Accounts payable	7.4
		Total current liabilities	28.5
		Long-term debt	23.5
		Net worth	47.9

Current ratio	1.0
Fixed/worth	.9
Debt/worth	0.5
NPBT/total assets (ROA)	8.7%
Sales/total assets	3.1
Sales/fixed assets	7.2
Lease/sales	N.A.
Depreciation/sales	N.A.
Officers' Compensation/sales	N.A.
Return on net worth (ROE)	22.1%
Return on sales (ROS)	4.1%

Source: Dun & Bradstreet, *Key Business Ratios,* Business Economics Division (New York: 1983).

Table 4   Income statement ratios—100-Seat restaurant—*Small Business Reporter,* 1981

	Ranges
Sales	100%
Cost of sales	33–43%
Gross profit	57–67
Operating Expenses	
Controllable:	
Payroll	23–33
Employee benefits	3– 5
Direct oper. expenses	3.5– 9
Music, entertainment	0.1– 1.3
Advert. and promo.	0.8– 3
Utilities	3– 5
Admin. and general	3– 6
Repairs and maintenance	1– 2
Occupation expenses:	
Rent, property tax, insurance	6–11
Interest	0.3– 1
Franchise royalties (if any)	3– 7
Income before depreciation	12–19
Depreciation	0.7– 5
Net profit before income tax	5–15

Source: Bank of America, "Restaurants," *Small Business Reporter* (1981).

They knew, now, that they would have to sell equity in their company and borrow at least half of their startup costs from a bank. Don and Jim had talked to some friends in the banking industry who thought they could borrow on personal guarantees and the assets of the business up to $150,000. The term would be for five years at a fixed rate of 13 percent—if, of course, the final numbers on the restaurant looked reasonable. The bank would not accept used equipment as part of such a package.

1. Develop a pro forma income statement and balance sheet for "Neighbors." Make any assumptions that you need to make, but be sure to state each assumption clearly.
2. Given the more accurate estimates of costs, what will it take "Neighbors" to break even? Can they do it at the volume levels they estimated earlier?

• • •

Sally and Janice realized that they would also need at least one year of monthly cash projections in order for a banker to take them seriously.

1. Develop a cash flow statement for "Neighbors" for the first year by

months. Use the same data and assumptions that you used to build their income statement and balance sheet. Be sure to include its startup costs as cash outflows. Determine how much Sally and Janice will have to borrow (and when) to make "Neighbors" work.

2. Assume you are the banker to whom Sally and Janice bring the financial projections you just developed for them. Are you likely to give them the loan that they seek? If yes, under what terms and conditions? If not, why not?

ROB KING AND "KING FINANCIAL"

Rob King had just about decided to go ahead with his plans to begin King Financial. His first sets of remarks to the city council had been well received. He had been quoted in the *Gazette*—correctly, even. His name/information index card file was growing by leaps and bounds. He had joined one of the athletic clubs in the city (one that did not require nominations and votes for entry) so that he would have a convenient and properly plush place to bring clients and prospective clients for lunch or for a drink. He was getting ready to take the plunge. But there was one nagging problem. Could he make money at this game? He had put off testing these waters for as long as possible. He finally had to get his numbers together and take a look.

King had tentatively decided on pricing his services at $500 per day. He had also decided to operate on a straight per diem basis for all his work, except when he and a client agreed upon a fixed price for a specific project. In situations in which a fixed price was called for, King intended to estimate the time required to perform the work involved and price at his standard per diem rate times the number of days he expected to have to put in to accomplish the tasks required.

With this set of decisions out of the way, he could concentrate on figuring out how much he was going to make at his consulting business. He was aware that the key to making money in this field was "billability," or "billable hours," the amount of time that could actually be billed to one client or another. He also knew that larger consulting companies figured that their consultants should be billable 75–80 percent of the time, at minimum. If he intended to work a standard 40-hour week, this would mean that only eight hours of his week could be spent on marketing his services and on taking care of administrative matters. He knew that this approach probably wouldn't work for him.

Data from the *Professional Consultant* survey told him that the average consultant spends 4.2 days in an average 31-day month on marketing, 3.1 days on practice management, and 1.6 days on professional development. Counting weekend days and other days taken off for vacations and such, the average consultant spent 12.5 days on actual billable client work. This struck him as a more reasonable estimate of what he would be able to do. This, he knew, was average. He recognized that his billability would be particularly low since he was just beginning to practice. He would have to spend even more productive time on marketing than the average.

He also began to consider his expenses and the amounts he needed to get out of his practice to enable him to actually enter the field. However strong his dislike of his current job, he did have the responsibilities of a wife, children, and a mortgage to contend with. He was very much afraid that Ginny may have been right all along. He determined that he would find a way to make his strengthening dream come true.

He began to look at his personal requirements as well as at his expected business expenses. He would be giving up his nice, steady $40,000-a-year salary—plus such fringe benefits as family health insurance, life insurance, and paid vacations. Bank employees also got reduced rates on certain bank services such as installment loans and credit card fees, and interest rates. His personal expenses included $750 a month for his mortgage (including taxes), $275 for his car (fairly new, including payment, gas, and repairs), $350 for food, and an average of $190 a month for utilities (including the family phone). He was paying down credit card debt at the rate of $100 a month.

He expected his business expenses would include:

Startup:	Phone installation and deposit	$ 325
	Answering machine	130
	Club memberships	450
	Stationery and business cards	600
	Initial mailing (incl. postage)	550
	File cabinets	150
	Filing fee	10
	Accounting set-up	200
	Computer and equipment	3,000
Ongoing:	Telephone (business)	$ 70
	Travel (local) and entertainment	250

He figured that about one-eighth of his house would be deductible as a business expense, since the house was his principal business address. He could buy secretarial services at about $10 an hour. He figured that three days of consulting would produce about a day's worth of typing. This average included sales and administrative paperwork. He expected to spend about $20 a month on copying. He also expected to pay his accountant friend $200 a quarter to check over his quarterly financial statements. Additional insurance would cost, he estimated, $150 a quarter.

In an effort to remain professional about these estimates, Rob King also collected the data shown in Tables 1 and 2.

With great trepidation, he undertook the figuring out of his potential earnings from King Financial.

1. Given Rob King's plans as you understand them, what costs, if any, has he left out of his calculations?

2. Using his numbers *only*, and making your best estimate of his billability, prepare a pro forma income statement for Rob King's first year in business. Based on your results, what do you recommend that he do?
3. Revise the pro forma you developed to reflect your best estimate of his costs and revenues. Based on these results, what do you recommend he do?
4. Given his planned pricing structure, how far wrong does your estimate of billable hours have to be before Rob King cannot cover his basic necessities?
5. Discuss, briefly, the effect you would expect of raising his price by 20 percent. Of lowering it by 20 percent.

Table 1 Selected elements of overhead for consulting practices

TOTAL OVERHEAD	100.0%		
Clerical	10.1%	Insurance	1.8%
Office rent	3.2	Stationery, supplies	1.2
Telephone, postage	5.6	Legal, accounting	1.5
Automobile	4.5	Administration	10.3
Personnel, tax, benefits	21.1	Marketing	24.6
Average pretax income:	All consultants	$50,122	
	Finance	59,345	

Source: Howard Shenson, *The Professional Consultant* (Woodland Hills, California: 1982).

Table 2 Selected financial ratios for consulting companies, 1982–3

	Robert Morris Associates	Dun & Bradstreet
Return on sales	4.8%	8.5%
Cash as a percentage of assets	11.1	20.7
Long-term debt as % of assets	12.6	10.3
Depreciation as % of sales	1.8	—
Accounts payable as % of sales	—	3.4
Days in receivables	50.7 days	39.7 days
Officers' salaries as % sales	13.3	—

Source: Robert Morris Associates, *Annual Statement Studies* (Philadelphia: 1983); Dun & Bradstreet, *Key Business Ratios,* Business Economics Division (New York: 1982–83).

DANIELLE MACKIE AND "DANIELLE DESIGNS IN CERAMICS"

The next step for Danielle Mackie was to develop her pro forma financial statements. She had decided that, at the beginning at least, she would sell in only two ways. First, she would show at selected art shows and crafts fairs. This would require that she have some inventory of her "creative" pieces and that she have samples of her current or proposed production pieces for examination by the wholesalers and/or retail resellers. It would also help her to design and build some traveling display racks or shelves so that she would look professional and would not be operating from a bare table. She would also have to develop a slick brochure and acquire business cards to help her attract the gallery owners who would be her second sales target.

Her second sales method would be to sell directly to galleries. She would not operate on consignment, since the time involved in tracking consignment arrangements might be excessive. She had also, by now, heard some of the horror stories of artists who never saw any money or whose work mysteriously disappeared while on consignment. While she believed that adequate record-keeping, close tracking, and good contracts could prevent much of this activity, she frankly did not want to have to worry about it. Once she made a sale, she wanted to have made a final sale.

To do this properly, Mackie believed that she would need a professionally done photographic portfolio of her work to date and the work she had available for sale. She figured that if she bought the right portfolio, she could tailor her presentations to the price level of the particular gallery simply by changing the pictures she carried into the presentation. Using this method, she would only have to carry samples of her work to meetings with or presentations to gallery owners. This would save not only hassle, but also avoid possible breakage.

She estimated that her cards, business stationery (including invoices), and brochure would cost about $1,000. She expected the initial photographic work for the brochure and the portfolio to cost about $1,500. She decided to lease the farmhouse for both living and work. That way, if she wanted to sell out of the studio any time within the next five years, she would have that option. The monthly cost was $900 (including her living space in the house). Including the required electrical upgrade, venting, insulation, fire extinguishers, and other requirements, she expected the costs of renovation to be about $3,500.

Her major equipment purchases would consist of a 5– to 10–cubic foot kiln that would cost about $1,000 and an electric wheel for about $750. She already had most of the hand tools that she would require.

She expected to hire no help during the first year of her operation and to make pieces that averaged four to five pounds of clay each. $20 worth of glaze would normally cover about 150 pounds of clay pieces. The clay itself, as she had noted earlier, would cost her about $15 for 50 pounds. Her kiln would hold roughly 30 pounds of pieces if she packed it carefully using every available corner. (She made a note about the possibility of adding some very small pieces to her production line, simply to use the space better.) Mainly because of her kiln and her wheel, she expected her monthly bills for electricity to average at least $400. Leaving the light on in the bedroom wouldn't even make a dent, she thought ruefully.

In developing her pro formas, she assumed that she could get a loan from a bank or from her father (when she finally told him about her plans) for $10,000 for three years at 14 percent. Her intended sales volumes in dollars, including the effects of any discounts she had to offer bulk buyers, were as follows, based on the pricing scheme she had developed earlier.

Production pieces:	Pitchers	$20,000
	Vases	10,500
	Bowls	10,000
	Urns	17,500
Creative pieces:	Small (or simple)	$ 1,500
	Medium	1,000
	Large (or complex)	5,000
Total		$65,500

She also decided that her standard terms of sale would require payment within 30 days. She would offer a 2 percent discount to bulk buyers for payment within 10 days, and her contracts would specify a 1 percent per month interest charge on payments from 45 days after the sale. Freight and shipping would be charged to the customer at cost. (Prices quoted FOB factory/studio.) Danni made a note to talk with Harald, the lawyer, about developing standard contracts. She also added his expected fees for the year (along with those of an accountant/tax preparer) to her budget— $2,000 for professional services. She had structured her company as a sole proprietorship.

1. Prepare a pro forma balance sheet and income statement for Mackie's first year of operation. Use her assumptions and make whatever additional assumptions are reasonable and necessary. Specify your assumptions.
2. Prepare a pro forma cash budget for Mackie, using the same rules as in 1.
3. Assume the role of consultant to Danielle Mackie. Prepare a report on and an analysis of the pro formas you just developed. Be sure to comment on her sales projection(s), potential areas for reducing costs, and the advisability of going into the ceramics business as she has structured it. If you have negative comments on her intentions and/or approaches, suggest alternatives to her.

ED JAMES AND "OAK TREE BOOKS"

Ed James knew he had put it off for as long as he possibly could—he finally had to develop the numbers that would tell him whether he was likely to make any money running Oak Tree Books (and Acorn). He also needed to face, once and for all, the magnitude of the amount of money he would have

Table 1   Percentage of total sales in bookstores by month

	Average	**High**	**Low**
July, 1979	6.4%	8.0%	5.0%
August	7.2	8.9	5.5
September	6.9	9.5	5.8
October	8.4	10.5	6.6
November	9.0	10.7	7.1
December	17.5	20.4	12.6
January, 1980	7.6	10.4	6.3
February	7.0	8.9	5.9
March	7.4	8.9	6.2
April	7.4	8.7	5.7
May	7.4	9.2	6.2
June	7.3	8.9	6.1

Source: *ABA Bookstore Financial Profile 1981* (American Booksellers' Association, New York: 1981).

to raise to start and to cover his first year of operations. He knew that this step might be tantamount to the death of his dream. He also knew that he had to do it if he was going to get the financing from anyone—probably including Aunt Hattie, who was rather hard-headed when it came to business deals. "That's probably how she got so wealthy," Ed grinned.

Again, he assembled all the financially based information he had accumulated in his earlier planning phases, shown in Tables 1, 2, 3, and 4. He reviewed his plans to date, focusing particularly on those plans that were likely to make his costs, revenues, and cash flows different from the "average" bookstore in his size range.

Table 2   Assets and liabilities of retail book and stationery stores (1982–3)

	D&B	**RMA**		**D&B**	**RMA**
Cash	13.3%	7.3%	Accounts payable	15.0%	25.7%
Accounts receivable	3.8	18.3			
Inventory	57.3	47.4	Current maturities	1.6	5.0
Total current	77.9%	74.2%	Total current	29.4%	50.4%
Fixed assets	14.2%	20.4%	Long-term debt	9.5%	16.5%
			Net worth	61.0%	30.9%
Total assets	100.0%	100.0%	Total liabilities & NW	100.0%	100.0%

Source: Dun & Bradstreet, *Key Business Ratios,* Business Economics Division (New York: 1982–83); and Robert Morris Associates, *Annual Statement Studies* (Philadelphia: 1983).

Table 3   Common size income statement for bookstore $150,000– $300,000 sales

	Average	Median
Sales	100.0%	100.0%
Cost-of-goods-sold	62.9	63.2
Gross margin	38.1	36.7
Payroll expense	17.0	16.9
Occupancy (incl. utilities)	6.7	6.2
Advertising	1.7	1.6
Telephone	.4	.5
Professional services	.4	.6
Depreciation	1.0	1.0
Travel and entertainment	.4	.9
Insurance	.4	.7
Credit card service charges	.3	.5 (10–11%) of sls
Dues and subscriptions	.2	—
Misc. office expenses and postage	.6	.7
Taxes	.3	.5
All other	1.3	1.5
Total operating expense	30.7%	32.3%
Operating income	7.4	4.1
Other income	.6	.7
Other expense	.7	.8
Net income before tax	7.3%	3.5%
Allowance for unreported owners' income	3.1	
Adjusted net profit	4.2%	

Source: *ABA Bookstore Financial Profile 1981* (American Booksellers Association, New York: 1982).

He expected to remain a small bookstore, having sales of about $150,000–$200,000. He expected his seasonal pattern to differ slightly from the industry average because of his emphasis on children's books and related activities. The two non-school summer months were likely to be even lower than the industry's, and his pickup in sales would probably come in September, rather than October. The Christmas peak would remain, he was sure.

He knew, for example, that his costs for equipment were likely to be higher than average simply because of the extra furnishings—chairs, tables, and the like—that he intended to put in Acorn. He was also consider-

Table 4   Estimated startup capital

ASSUMES: Sales $125,000   3x inventory turnover
1,750 square feet   33% gross margin

Beginning inventory	$27,900
Three months' rent	1,530
Furniture, fixtures	3,000
Prepaid insurance, utilities, fees	1,000
Leasehold improvements	2,500
Initial advertising	500
Cash reserve	2,000
Total	$38,430

Source: Small Business Administration, "Bookstores," in *The State of Small Business: A Report of the President* (Washington, D.C.: U.S. Government Printing Office).

ing a second cash register for Acorn so that he could see better what was making money for him. His rent, too, was likely to be higher than average because of his choice of area and location. Personnel costs also might be higher since he intended to hire and retain more specialized staff for his store. While he knew that all these "over averages" would have to be balanced with "under averages" somewhere, he feared that the big loser would be his earnings or the store's profitability. He did not relish either result.

He locked himself in his office, spread out his data, plans, and other paraphernalia, took a few deep breaths, and plunged in.

1. Develop an opening balance sheet for Oak Tree Books (and Acorn). Assume that Ed James will be able to borrow up to half the total capitalization of the bookstore at 12 percent for five years. What is the minimum amount of equity he is likely to have to come up with? What, in your opinion, are the chances of his coming up with the amount you estimated (assuming Aunt Hattie is still in good shape)?
2. Develop a first year income statement for Oak Tree Books (and Acorn). State your assumptions clearly. Is Ed James likely to make money at his bookstore? (Remember that, as a sole proprietorship, his payment comes only in the form of pretax net income from the business.) Will Oak Tree meet his original goal of replacing his income from The Academy?
3. Develop a first year cash budget for Oak Tree Books (and Acorn). State any assumptions you make in preparing this statement. Will Ed James have to borrow any additional funds to cover cash deficits during the year? If so, how much will he need? When will he need it? Will he be able to repay?

4. Given the statements you have just developed, should Ed proceed to establish Oak Tree Books (and Acorn) as he envisions it? Is he likely to be able to get the loan(s) he will need? If you said that he should not open as proposed, recommend alternative approaches to structuring a bookstore for him. Explain your recommendations. Will he buy them? Why or why not?

PART 7

IF YOU'D RATHER NOT START FROM SCRATCH ...

CHAPTER 16
Buying a Going Concern

CHAPTER 17
Starting a Franchised Operation

16. Buying a Going Concern

The initial, overwhelming advantage that you bring to a business that is not living up to its potential is objectivity. ... As obvious as these opportunities [for improvement] seem to you, it's important to understand that they are probably either unnoticed or intentionally ignored by the present owner.

Kenneth J. Albert, *Straight Talk About Small Business*

This chapter and the next present alternatives to building your own company from the ground up. This chapter discusses purchasing a company outright. The next chapter considers buying a franchise—essentially a compromise between buying and building. Both chapters are intended to help new entrepreneurs explore all their options for getting into businesses of their own.

It is widely believed, particularly by people who have never done it, that buying a business is a great deal easier than building one. In some cases, this may even be true. The buyer, however, is likely to spend at least as much money, probably more, for a going concern than she would to build a similar operation. If the financial risk is as high, it seems only rational to give the expenditure at least as much careful scrutiny and consideration. Unfortunately, far too many purchasers do not see it this way—often with disastrous (and expensive) results.

The purpose of this chapter is to alert prospective purchasers to some of the potential difficulties and particular advantages in buying businesses. It also raises the basic issues about how to investigate and evaluate a going concern, how to make financial comparisons between buying and building, how to value a company, and how to negotiate with the current owner. Often in this chapter, you are reminded to reread the objectives you devised for yourself at the beginning of your busines planning process. However enticing

FEATURE 16.1
How Not to Buy a Business—A (Very) Short Story

Anne Webster, 60, is a hypothetical retired kindergarten teacher who wanted to start a small business to bring in some money and to use, rather than waste, her newly freed time. Understandably, she had had it with little kids, so the idea of buying a day-care center was distasteful. She knew, however, that she wanted a service business, and one in which she could continue to help people.

Doing essentially no research, Webster began to read the "business opportunities" section of her local newspaper. She eventually bought a small nursing home on the outskirts of her city. She could cover most of the cost because she had recently inherited some money from a cousin and because she had saved a sizable sum over her years as a teacher.

After taking over, she quickly discovered all the things she did not know about the business. The industry was heavily regulated by the state. She soon concluded that it was almost impossible to make any money legally in the home. On principle, she refused to participate in illegal or shady activities.

Perhaps because of her discoveries about how one made money in this business in this area, she found herself wary of, if not outright repelled by, many of her new colleagues. She also discovered, much to her surprise, that she did not like the old folks who peopled her home and who would be her responsibility. She stayed away from the home as much as possible, and away from industry gatherings.

In short order, therefore, she was in trouble. The staff, which she had not changed, really required an owner's supervision. The new suppliers (which she had changed when she discovered their ways of doing business with the former owner) were not playing by her rules. She was not meeting all the regulatory requirements. She hated her new life and work. Clearly, helping people did not, for her at least, include all people in all ways.

She also found that, because of the regulated nature of the industry, it was difficult to find a new buyer whom she thought might be appropriate. She was either stuck with the place, or would be forced into a significant loss. And she had wondered why she could buy her new business at such a bargain price!

an existing establishment may look, a prospective purchaser must remember that, if an operation cannot meet the basic objectives set for it, it will probably be a failure in the eyes of the new owner—and also a good candidate for failure in fact.

A perfect set-up for a small business failure is contained in the hypothetical, but typical, case of Anne Webster, described in Feature 16.1.

Webster deserved essentially what she got. She ignored virtually every rule of starting (or buying) a business. She entered an unfamiliar field. Thus, the regulatory aspects of her new business took her by surprise. She did not spend time talking with prospective colleagues, customers, or suppliers. Discussions with these people might have told her about the level of questionable legal practice in this field in her area. She might also have discovered that she did not like being around the very people who would be her customers. It is probable that she would have learned, in advance, that her employees would need her personal supervision to maintain the quality of care and service that she wanted and needed to provide.

The morals of this tale are: look (very carefully) before you leap, and be at least minimally happy about the business you are buying into. In short, buying a business, as opposed to building a business, does not get you out of all the work we have already discussed. Buying, in fact, *adds* a number of issues for research and consideration, rather than subtracting some.

BROAD ISSUES IN BUYING A GOING CONCERN

Despite some disadvantages, buying a business can be a very attractive option, depending on you and on the particular business. The first prime attraction is that it *is* a going concern. The startup problems are over, or at least minimized. The building of reputation and clientele have been done. Relationships with suppliers already exist for the company. Sites have been selected, and the physical assets required for the business are already in place. Actual time between decision and getting in may be shorter. It is possible that the going concern may be cheaper than the startup. Sounds like sheer joy, right?

But these same things that may be advantages can also be the greatest drawbacks to buying a particular business. Is the reputation of the business the one that you want for your business? Is the current clientele the one you want for your operation? If not, making the changes you desire can be almost impossible. "Your people" may stay away simply because they know that "your people" never shop in that particular store. Changing an existing reputation may be more difficult than building a new reputation from scratch.

Considering the purchase of your business is really a process of tradeoffs. You can bet that you will not find a business for sale in your price range that is precisely what you would have built. You are the only one who can say what you are willing to give up in trade for the advantages offered by a particular business that is for sale. If you have not done your homework, however, you will probably be giving up a great deal more than you would if you had taken the time to think in detail about that particular purchase.

FINDING A BUSINESS TO CONSIDER

Once you have decided that you might be willing to consider buying a business rather than building it, there are a number of ways to get information about businesses that are or may be for sale. The first step is probably to check out the print media in your area. The regional edition of the *Wall Street Journal* has numerous listings for businesses for sale. Your local newspaper probably does too, assuming you are in an area in which enough businesses turn over. Many areas now have local business tabloids—for example, the *Washington Business Journal*—which will also have "businesses for sale" listings.

In addition to published sources, there are numerous ways of finding businesses for sale. Most directly, many areas have sprouted numbers of "business brokers." These services try to get buyers together with sellers. They can be very helpful about what kinds of businesses are available. Many

FEATURE 16.2
Business Brokers With an Entrepreneurial Twist

For a startup cost of $5,000, Max B. Steingart has a company that he expects to collect $2—$3 million a year—and net him 25 percent of that in profit. He helps other entrepreneurs to sell businesses and to find businesses to purchase. The company, Business Owners Multiple Listing Service (BOMLS), is national and is selling businesses at the rate of 200 a month.

The business works very simply. A seller lists his business with BOMLS for a $75, one-time fee. The business is added to the directory, which goes to about 11,000 subscribers, including venture capitalists, corporations, and other entrepreneurs. The subscribers pay $45 for a three-month subscription. The subscription price includes a directory covering about 5,800 listings and two monthly updates.

Sellers gain because they will not pay brokerage fees, which come to as much as 10 percent of the sale price. Buyers gain because they have more detailed listings of potential purchases and, thus, waste less time and effort in pursuing companies that turn out to be entirely inappropriate—or being caught by regular brokers, many of whom, according to Steingart, place ads simply to flush out potential clients.

"We face no well-organized competition," says Steingart. A twice-weekly ad in the *Wall Street Journal* produces 400 calls a week. The company lists firms in all industries that range in size from very small to multi-million-dollar.

Adapted from "Matching Buyers and Sellers," *Venture* (September 1983): 9.

are sincerely interested in your success, but remember that they essentially work for the sellers, much as realtors work for the sellers. Their bread and butter comes from selling companies. Some even appear to be more interested in moving the real estate that the companies are sitting on than they are in moving the companies themselves. Check out the reputation of your business broker, if you intend to use one, as carefully as you check out any service with which you intend to do business. Such a check should include discussions with former customers of the broker and a call to your local Better Business Bureau office.

You have two other major sources at your disposal. First, assuming that you have been doing research and general investigation of the industry you are interested in, you already know many people in the field. Talk to these people about businesses that are potentially for sale. Often suppliers know which of their client firms are on the market. Sometimes, they know before an actual decision to sell has been made.

Your banker is also an excellent source of information about companies that may be for sale. He or she is probably on the grapevine of the local business community. If an owner is interested in selling, his banker is likely to be one of the first to know. Also, since bankers often know of entrepreneurs seeking businesses to purchase, non-clients often report businesses for sale. If you have maintained or developed a good relationship with this adviser, your banker may be your best source of information about businesses for sale.

EVALUATING A BUSINESS FOR PURCHASE

It is assumed that you are seeking a certain type of company, one related to a specific field that interests you. If you start with a specific, well-considered interest, you are less likely to purchase something utterly wrong for you than if you just look to see "what's there." Keep firmly fixed in mind that in the heat of a "buy" decision, it is easy to overlook numerous things that you should not overlook. A firm handle on what you wanted when you started out is essential to keeping on track.

As you cull through the output of all your sources, you should focus on a number of initial considerations. First, and most obviously, there is the price. While an initial price quote is really a beginning point for negotiations, it is probably in the range that the present owner intends to get. Do not expect to negotiate $2 million down to $500,000. It is a poor bet and therefore a waste of your time to pursue.

A second major item that should catch your attention is the location of the business that is for sale. You will have already done a significant amount of location research in the "build-your-own" sections of your work. You know, therefore, what characteristics a location will require to facilitate the success

FEATURE 16.3
Beating the Odds—The Bowens

In 1976, Lenora and Stuart Bowen bought the Williamsville Inn in western Massachusetts. Neither partner had any restaurant experience. Neither owned a business at the time of the purchase. Neither knew a great deal about western Massachusetts. Both were Boston-based. Their market research consisted of visits to a number of successful country inns and discussions with people in the inn business. They took restaurant management courses.

The company they bought consisted of a deteriorating 1797-vintage building and a dying restaurant business. Their job was to rejuvenate both the building and the operation—accomplish a turnaround. The building required extensive renovations and the restaurant operation needed major overhaul. They offered only a minimal business plan to their bank, financing their buy through a home mortgage—very unusual and very lucky.

They decided to build on the ambiance the previous owner had begun to create, and to establish a reputation for high-quality food. This required improving the basic menu and overseeing an almost complete turnover of existing staff. From the beginning, Lenora took over as chef herself.

Within four years they were attracting customers from as far away as New York. But they wanted to return to a city and to move from the seasonal operation of the inn to a year-round business. They sold the inn for two and a half times what they had paid for it.

Printed with permission of Lenora Bowen.

of a business of the type you want to own. Obviously, at this point, you will have only a general area to consider, a section of a city or town, for example. But if the place seems unlikely to you because of your prior research, you might be wise to stop considering that particular business. The same is true if you just do not want to be wherever that particular business is.

There is a certain allure, to some people, in buying a business in an unknown, far-away town. They seem to view it as a first step to developing a whole new life, a new personality, a new outlook, etc. In general, this is not a recommended approach to starting a business. You immediately lose your support system as well as the information network you have built in your area. More to the point, you do not know the area or where the inhabitants go to get whatever it is you will be selling. In short, you will place yourself at a severe disadvantage. If you must move, get a job until you can survey the new territory and build new lines of communication in your field of interest. It will be time well spent.

First Steps: Getting Information

Once you have concluded that the business that is (or may be) for sale meets your initial tests and is worth looking into, there are a number of things that can be done before the discussions between you and the current owner become serious. First, if the business is "seeable"—a retail operation or a restaurant, for example—pay it an anonymous visit. If possible, do some business there. You want to pay particular attention to the specifics of the physical location, the clientele, the general feeling of the place and its employees, and the day-to-day approach to operations.

Two very different perspectives are required at this stage, and throughout the purchase process. The first perspective is very cool and detached. You will need to be able to evaluate what you are seeing with the eye of a horse-trader. In short, the first perspective is highly objective. The second, on the other hand, requires you to monitor emotional responses and bring your imagination to bear on what you are seeing. These two perspectives must interact so that you get both a clear idea of what you are considering purchasing and a good sense of what you could do with it if, in fact, you bought it. This is very difficult. If often helps to have someone(s) with whom to visit potential purchases and with whom to discuss the reality. It would also be useful if this person could temper, but not stop, your flights of imagination.

An initial visit to a potential purchase provides opportunity for both perspectives. The objective look is described above. After the visual inventory, however, back away and simply visualize yourself as owner/manager of this particular place. Do you feel out of place? Do you feel as if you've come home? How would you feel about going to work there for 10 or 12 hours a day, six or seven days a week? If you feel uncomfortable, try to figure out why. Then consider whether you would be able to change these factors as owner.

Obviously, what you will do to change the place is critical to your purchase decision. It is also one of the trickier aspects of the decision. As noted earlier, some things are likely to be unchangeable. The regulatory environment that Anne Webster found, for example, is a given, unchangeable by a single entrepreneur. Other potential changes may be prohibitively expensive and/or take too long to accomplish. As you do your first survey of the place, then, try to view what exists as a working base. Consider the purchase price in terms of paying for that base. Imagine a modified future, but try not to imagine a palace built on the foundation of a two-room hut.

If you are still interested in continuing after looking at the place, begin talking to people. In this case, "people" includes practically anyone who knows anything about your industry or this particular business. You want the broadest mix of opinion and information you can get. Talk with whoever told you about the sale. Talk with your banker. Talk, particularly, with competitors, suppliers, and customers of the potential purchase. Talk with owners of other businesses in the area. (But keep in mind that the information you get should be viewed with a clear sense of its source. Everyone probably has some axe to grind. Take it all in and sort it out later.)

In this round of talk, you should be particularly interested in four main kinds of information:

1. Perceived trends in the area in which the business is located
2. Perceived changes in the business itself
3. The role of the present owner/manager in the operation
4. Why the owner is selling

Trends in the environment.   There are more "war stories" around than you would believe about new owners who bought businesses on busy intersections only to find that the highway was rerouted six months later. Such changes are not planned and implemented overnight in secrecy. Any purchaser who buys into such a situation really deserves what he gets—simply for not doing the homework.

If a change in traffic patterns or physical structures is in the works, it will be public information. The owners of neighboring businesses will know. They will undoubtedly enjoy a new ear to talk to about it. Give them every opportunity to tell you. Such changes are also usually debated in the branches and agencies of the local government, city council and/or planning commission. Check the records. *Do not skip this step.* You do not want to buy a drive-in where suddenly nobody is driving by.

Building projects or ongoing shifts in population also often have significant effects on the viability of area businesses. Consider owning an artists' supply store in a city neighborhood that is undergoing "gentrification." Your market will soon be centered elsewhere. Are your customers likely to travel long distances to shop at your store? Or consider buying an ethnic grocery in an area in which the ethnic mix is changing rapidly. Will your customers come back to "the old neighborhood" simply to shop at your place? How much will you have to change the place in order to stay in business? Can it be done? Do you want to do it?

While this sounds like a retail/restaurant-oriented issue, it often arises for wholesale or supply operations that are tied to specific industries as well. When the textile mills left New England years ago, they took with them numerous suppliers. Those suppliers who did not move had nobody to supply. The same is now occurring as shoe manufacturers shift to more rural areas in search of available and relatively cheap labor.

In either case, people in your industry will know what is in process. You have probably already heard about some of this in your general background data-gathering discussions. Talk about it some more in relation to the specific business you are considering purchasing.

Changes in the business.   Has the business you are looking at changed in the last few years? Do people seem to think that it has changed? Since you deal with people, their perceptions are often more important than any reality. A mattress manufacturer that used to be considered top-of-the-line has been demoted, in public and trade opinion, to an also-ran. In this instance, the problem stemmed from a batch of bad mattresses that got through quality control a few years ago. It is entirely immaterial, however, whether the mattresses they make changed in any way. Public and trade perceptions of their product are all that count. The company still has difficulty finding distributors. Similarly, a restaurant that has a declining reputation is likely to resist attempts to reverse the trend.

Reputation counts. And you need to know the direction of change of the reputation of the business you are considering purchasing. You can find this out only by listening to what people who use the business, supply the business, or compete with the business are saying.

As you can see, there are really two kinds of information you are collecting. The first is hard data, reality that can be checked in some document. The second is soft data, reflecting how people feel about and react to what is happening. The weight you give to each kind of data will vary, depending on the business you are considering, the specific information itself, and the source(s). To make a good decision, you need to be able to separate the realities from the opinions and to determine the appropriate relative weights. Do not discount mere opinion, however, since your buyers are people and people are often notoriously illogical about those with whom they do business.

The role of the current owner.   Often a small business works or does not work almost solely because of the specific personality/expertise/contacts of the current owner. Unless you arrange a lengthy lead-in/training period and unless the two of you work really well together, his or her relevant attributes may not be transferable to you. They are not the "sellable" part of the business.

Professional practices are prime examples of this kind of business. A person often continues to do business with a professional largely because of the personal relationship that has developed between provider and client. This relationship is not automatically transferable. Moreover, some former clients resent the attempt to transfer their loyalties in this manner. A restaurant may face this problem if the owner is also the chef—noted for his particular flavorings or sauces or whatever. A garage may face this problem if the owner is believed to have a "way with cars." In short, almost any business can consist largely of the attributes of the owner.

A similar problem may also be presented by a key employee who is tied personally to the owner, but not necessarily to you. You would have to ensure that this key person remains with the firm and consider what the company would be like without him.

Assessing the weight of this factor is often difficult. Start by trying to visualize the operation without the current owner. Next, visualize yourself as owner, doing the key things that the current owner does. Can you do them? Will you feel comfortable doing them? Will the people with whom you have been talking accept you in that role?

As you talk with people in the industry who surround your prospective purchase, listen "between the lines" for insights about why those who do business with this company do so. If their underlying reasons for maintaining relationships with your potential purchase really reduce to "the owner," look very carefully at the deal. You may be considering buying the assets of a business, without being able to buy what others see as the *real* asset of the business. A possible alternative to walking away from the deal is to attempt to arrange a management or consulting contract with the current owner for a year or two following the purchase. This may assist in transferring the untransferable.

Reason(s) for selling out.   Another critical question is why the current owner is getting out. If she is 80 years old, has no offspring or relations in the business, and has been running the place for 40 years, she's probably just tired. If, on the other hand, she seems strong, healthy, smart, and young, why she is leaving may be important. Does she know something that you do not yet know?

Obviously, if she has concluded that she cannot make a living with the present square footage (or something equally vital), she is not going to tell you about it at your first meeting. But it is quite likely that one of your other sources will. Listen. Ask both the owner and your other sources. If the reasons do not make sense, view the entire deal with increased skepticism.

Using Your Advisers in Research

If, after doing your original research and the informal research just described, you are still interested in pursuing this business purchase opportunity, this is the time to do your specific research and to bring in your advisory team, particularly your lawyer and accountant. You have a specific location before you. You need to develop data about your potential market in that location and for that amount of space. All the criteria you developed earlier (Chapter 9) should be applied, as should such long-term considerations as potential for expansion.

To help you assess markets and market shares, you will have the records (if any) of the existing business. The owner may have also made projections.

Do keep in mind, however, that the owner's projections are likely to be biased. After all, he *is* trying to sell the business. If the owner's claims and projections seem too unlikely given what you already know about the broader market, this will tell you something about how he is likely to do business with you. A word to the wise being sufficient, be on your guard.

While you are checking the market, turn your lawyer loose on their contractural arrangements and your accountant on their financial statements, tax returns, and records. While small businesses are notorious for poor record- and file-keeping, the basic documentation should be available and in reasonable order. If you are not permitted to see and have your advisers

FEATURE 16.4
Financial Statements of Companies for Sale

It is well known, and eminently reasonable, that small, closely held companies understate the profitability of their businesses to reduce their income tax bills. This practice makes it difficult for prospective purchasers to assess the true potential of the businesses they are considering. A buyer cannot even be sure that current owners will tell the truth off the record. The "buyer" may be an Internal Revenue Service agent using what the IRS terms "an appropriate and necessary technique to uncover fraudulent activity."

The best way around some of the subterfuge is to rework, or recast, the data shown in the financial statements to reflect the probable profitability of the business had it been run as a profit center of a large corporation. Deductions for such items as company cars used personally by the owner and first-class travel are backed out. The cost of professional management is substituted for the owner's salary. In short, potential buyers try to figure out what they are really getting.

Geneva Corp., a business broker and company-valuation specialist, surveyed 500 of its clients in 1984. They found that 20 of these paid their owners compensation of more than a million dollars. Highest paid was the owner of a company that imprints messages on advertising specialties—$1.8 million (excluding retirement benefits).

Geneva recast the statements in the manner described above. "It is almost impossible to buy a private company without recasting," says Richard Rodnick, Geneva's president, "Because the owner is understating profits." The process more than doubled the average earnings of the group. "The book figures were about 43% of what we feel are their real profit," Rodnick says.

Adapted from Sanford Jacobs, "Private Firms' Finances," *The Wall Street Journal* (June 11, 1984): 27; and Kevin Farrell, "Should IRS Agents Pose As Buyers?", *Venture* (August 1984): 160.

evaluate these records, it is probably time to reconsider this particular purchase. The same is true if the records are very sketchy or in worse shape than one would expect.

Assuming that you have access to a useful set of documents, your lawyer should be looking at what parts of the business are transferable (sometimes leases, for example, are not). Your accountant will be looking for the obvious things. Note, however, that for tax reasons, small business owners routinely minimize the profits they show. Your accountant will probably rework the financial statements (if the current owner's accountant has not already done so) to reflect what the business is probably really earning. A 1984 study by Geneva Corp., of Santa Ana, California,[1] showed that probable real profits were more than twice the reported profits. Be particularly aware of recastings of the owner's salary and such items as company cars, club memberships, and the like. For purposes of making the sale, the incentive is to *overstate* such items.

If both your lawyer and your accountant are satisfied that the business is in reasonable shape (and, of course, if you are still interested), you now move toward making a deal.

NEGOTIATING A DEAL

As noted earlier, making a deal to buy (or sell) a business is a process of negotiation. It is not quite like selling a piece of equipment, however. Often, the seller thinks about his company as his creation, his baby. Thus, any negotiation over selling can be expected to have an emotional element. On the other side of the table, you are trying to be objective, but you really want this business. Both sides are "involved" in a way different from a transaction involving, say, a loaf of bread.

The incentives for each side are clear. The creation factor tends to make the company more valuable in the eyes of the seller. He or she is also probably selling out in order to retire comfortably or to build or buy a new venture. In either case, the seller views the company as the major salable asset to use in accomplishing that end. This leads to a high asking price.

You, on the other hand, are seeking a low price. You see what you will need to add to the business or to change in the business in order to make it the business you really want to own and run. You also have limited financial resources, out of which you need, not only to make the purchase and changes, but also to provide initial operating funds and a cash cushion.

While you want a low price, and the seller wants a high price, you should remember that you both want to make a deal, if possible. Therefore, your joint goal is to walk away from the table with an arrangement that everyone feels reasonably good about. You do not need a former owner (who has been

PROFILE

"I Liked It So Much, I Bought the Company."

Victor Kiam's wife really did buy him a Remington Micro-Screen Shaver before he bought the company. She pointed out that he had never even shaved with an electric device. He noted that "I was in the bra-and-girdle business once and I didn't know anything about that beforehand either." But he did try it and he did buy the company.

What he bought was a quality product with a good name—and $30 million in losses over the previous three years. His first moves were to cut costs so that he could cut his prices. He wanted his product within reach of more people. In his first week, he cut 79 executives and $2 million off the payroll. He consolidated manufacturing and removed costly, but non-functional features and succeeded in bringing the price of his least expensive shaver down from $34.95 to $19.95. Only then did he begin the famous advertising campaign quoted above.

In less than five years, Kiam doubled company sales and raised Remington's market share from 19 percent to 40 percent. His work force has doubled as well. Only one of the 400 new employees is a non-production person. The company is now exporting, selling more than one third of its production overseas. Diversification is also in the works for Kiam's Remington. The Center for Entrepreneurial Management refers to Remington as "one of the leading entrepreneurial companies in America."

Adapted from brochures of the Center for Entrepreneurial Management and Chief Executive Officers Club of New York, 1984.

in this business for x number of years) running around telling everyone about how terrible you are to deal with. And he will do it, if he believes that you pushed him to the wall or took unfair advantage of some circumstance.

It is also true that, since this is a negotiation, there needs to be some give and take in order for everyone to feel good about the outcome. I have run negotiation exercises for a number of years. Every so often, one group of "buyers" or "sellers" has its initial position accepted. They then feel miserable, convinced that the initial position must have been too generous to the other side. (It usually was.) Even in a short exercise, this provokes a remarkable amount of bitterness and anger. Thus, even if you like the opening number, negotiate!

Valuing the Business

As you can see, "value" is in the eye of the beholder. Although some make distinctions between "value" and "price," there are enough different ways of determining the "value" of a company to raise serious questions about such a distinction. In the final analysis, we believe that in a purchase/sale situation, the value of a business is what the buyer and the seller agree it is—the price.

Part of the key to negotiating well is understanding where your opponent is coming from. In a business purchase, this involves not only knowing as much as you can about that owner in particular, but also knowing her probable range of price flexibility. Understanding the major approaches to valuing the business can help. Using them, you will then have some notion of how the seller's numbers have been developed. Knowing that, you can often move the discussion from an emotional toward a more rational basis.

Understanding the approaches to valuation can also provide you with a reasonable range for your own offers. While your maximum price will be influenced by such factors as how much you want this particular business, having a handle on where your maximum is in the "reasonable" range is often helpful. An understanding of the basic approaches will also provide you with logical support for your own proposed purchase price. The claim that your position is grounded in reality will not only help you in the actual process of negotiating, but it will also make you feel a great deal more confident and competent. Both senses are critical to successful negotiation.

Asset valuation approaches.   There are two basic approaches to valuing a business for sale or purchase. The first group of approaches is based on the value of the assets of the company. They assume that a business is no more than a collection of assets. At the most extreme variation, an asset valuation approach assumes that the value of the business is what its assets could be sold for in a liquidation, less the amount of obligations that would have to be paid off. This liquidation value will provide the lowest possible estimate of "value" for the company.

To use this approach, your lawyer will have to tell you what is legally transferable, and the costs, if any, of making transfer arrangements. You begin with the balance sheet and immediately exclude all assets with no cash value to you—for example, the cash surrender value of life insurance, or goodwill.

You also must make sure that all the assets shown on the balance sheet are, in fact, there and in the condition that you would expect. Since you are interested in the market, rather than the "book" values of these assets, a physical inventory is absolutely necessary. It is also probably worthwhile to call in a specialist in your industry to participate in this valuation process. This is particularly important if your purchase involves a great deal of specialized equipment. If physical structures are involved, it is wise to call a professional engineer and inspector. Your lawyer will tell you what documents and representations you will need.

You then have to consider which assets you are interested in purchasing and which liabilities you will assume. You then add up the "values" you believe to be reasonable for the assets, subtract the relevant liabilities, and that is your proposed price.

As you can see, depending on which assets are in and how you price those assets, the asset valuation approach will produce a range of "values" for the company. They will range upward from the liquidation value noted earlier. While a liquidation value will probably be insulting to the seller as an opening offer, some asset-based valuation is often the opening offer for the potential buyer.

Stream-of-earnings approaches.   The second general approach to valuing a business is a stream-of-earnings approach. Rather than simply assessing the values of the assets of a business, this set of approaches considers the value of the assets when used in concert to produce profits for the business. Stream-of-earnings approaches generally produce higher ranges of "values" than do the asset approaches. They are, therefore, generally the method underlying the asking price of the seller.

The general method is to develop earnings projections for the business as it is now operated. You also need to determine what level of investment return you realistically want to get out of the business. You then figure out the "value," based on this projection and the required return, using the following formula:

$$\frac{\text{Average annual projected earnings}}{\text{Required investment return or capitalization rate}} = \text{"value" or proposed price}$$

Obviously, stream-of-earnings approaches will also yield a range of "values" for the business, depending on the earnings estimate and the risk/return assessment. In general, however, they generate larger "values" for the business.

The stream-of-earnings approaches raise two major issues for you as buyer that the asset-based approach does not. First, you must be careful to use projected earnings for the business *as it is now.* If you build into this estimate the effects of changes you intend to make, you will be offering to pay the present owner for the improvements and the work that you intend to put in after you take over. Thus, you will have to make a separate set of projections, solely for valuation purposes. This will be in addition to the projections you have already made of what you believe you can make of the business as you intend to run it—the ones that convinced you that you want to buy this company.

Second, a stream-of-earnings approach requires that you split the amount of money that you want the business to produce for you into two pieces: some direct payment for your work in the business, and a return on funds invested. The formula above is concerned only with the return on invested funds. If you were evaluating this business as one of a number of investment opportunities, you would consider that return rate as a function of the level of risk. A greater risk should produce greater return. Look at the business in that way.

If the business is risky, set your required return higher. This will produce a lower "value" for the business. Because of the inherent risk in small businesses, the capitalization rate often used in the formula for a small business is 0.25 (25 percent). Another way of considering this number is to note that at a 25 percent capitalization rate, the earnings from the business, after you have been compensated for your work, should return the entire amount you originally invested in four years.

Given the range of "values" you could develop for any specific business, it seems absurd to argue that there is some "true value" for that business. This is one of the reasons that the negotiations are so interesting and so vital.

It is highly recommended that you walk into your negotiations with a range of values (potential prices) already developed. Determine and be prepared to support your opening offer. But most of all, know clearly a firm upper bound—the absolute most that this business is worth *to you*. If you cannot meet or beat that price, walk away. There will be other businesses to purchase. Your biggest risk in the negotiation lies in getting caught up in the "I have to buy something *now*" fever. Proper prior planning can help.

Financing the Deal

Once you have agreed upon a price, you have to deal with the terms of sale and with all the paperwork and agreements necessary to conclude the agreement formally. Your lawyer should be involved in the negotiation and intimately involved in drawing up (or, at very least, reviewing) any legal agreements that you will be expected to sign. Your accountant, too, should be involved in negotiating terms. Do not exclude these advisers simply because their time costs you money. In the longer run, they are likely to save you a great deal more than their cost in time, energy, and later difficulties.

One factor that is often part of the price negotiation for a small business is the method of financing the purchase. Unless you are independently wealthy, or you have heavy backers, this will be one of your prime concerns. Obviously, there is your equity contribution (and those of anyone you could convince to join you), but what then?

Sometimes, the fact that you are looking at a going concern is helpful at the banks. You can show some solid history and a base from which to work. You will have to sell both the history and the validity of your proposed changes to the banker. Many of the same caveats apply here that were discussed in the section on financing startups. If your banker will not make a loan for a deal that looks really good to you and to your advisers, you might want to rethink. Ask why. Find out what the banker sees that you do not. It is still not too late to discover that you are about to make a mistake. If you still think you are right, try other banks and other methods.

Among the other possible methods of financing the deal might be financing from the seller. Often, sellers can and will make a loan to the business, or to you, backed by the business, essentially taking their payments over a longer period, rather than all up front. This is often a better deal for the seller, since it spreads his tax liability for the gains over a longer period as well. Sellers, naturally, also charge interest on such transactions, so that, in the long run, they see more cash.

This approach to financing has at least two advantages. First, there is the obvious one. You get to buy the company—a benefit to you both. But what may be equally important is the fact that the current owner will maintain at least a marginal interest in the success of your venture. After all, he has a stake in it. Particularly if you are not yet comfortable in the field or the area, even this level of interest can be of enormous help. But do be wary of a current owner who is prepared to give you the moon when no banker will lend you a nickel. The business may be in worse shape than you think. The seller may figure that any money is better than absolutely no money for the business.

Should you find yourself facing higher prices than you expected when you started looking for a business to buy, you are not alone. Business brokers nationwide report that the sale prices for businesses are rising rapidly. The hottest properties, say the brokers, include liquor stores, mail-order merchandisers and wholesale distributors. Many buyers, they report, are "scared of retail" and "sick of working with the public." In less demand than in recent years are video stores, ice cream parlors, and automated laundries. The brokers also note that the practice of seller financing, mentioned earlier, is increasing—good news for financially strapped potential buyers.[2]

SUMMARY

Buying a small business is a viable alternative to starting one from scratch for many would-be small business owners. The advantages include almost immediate startup, fewer startup difficulties, and the confidence that comes with having a head start. The disadvantages include the fact that you will be running someone else's creation. Certain factors that you may not like may also be virtually fixed. You have a working base, but, in some respects, it may operate as a straitjacket. Also, since small business records are often poor and sometimes distorted, you are buying something of a pig in a poke.

Buying a going concern does not exempt you from doing the kinds of research and analysis that you would do for a startup. You still need to assess the trends in the industry and in your market. You still need to consider pricing, equipment, and operations costs. With a purchase, however, you are doing much of this work against an existing background. You are comparing what you would have done with what you have a chance to purchase. You are the only one who can make the necessary tradeoffs. For this purpose, keep your written objectives both in your mind and near at hand.

In addition to the standard kinds of analysis, you need to study your prospective purchase with great care, using your own powers and those of your major advisers. You need to do informal research on the business, talking to as many people as possible who come into contact with it. You need to scrutinize its financial records and situation and potential changes in its physical environs. In short, buying is inevitably as much work as building. It is not the lazy person's alternative.

Once you find a business that seems interesting even after you have taken a close look, you get to develop an offering price and a negotiating range. You can use either an asset-based approach to valuing the company or a stream-of-earnings method. The former views the business as a collection of assets and generally produces a low "value" for the business. The stream-of-earnings method requires you to project the company's earnings and determine your desired rate of investment return. These methods focus on what the assets will produce when used in the business. They will usually underlie the seller's asking price.

The final step in concluding a purchase deal is arranging the financing and the terms of the sale. In many cases, the former small business owner will finance part of the purchase by making a loan to the business. Making this kind of loan is one way of sweetening the deal for the former owner, because it spreads his gains for tax purposes. Your lawyer and accountant should be heavily involved in this phase of the deal-making, making sure that your way is smoothed as much as possible for the long term.

FOR YOU TO CONSIDER

1. What are some advantages and some disadvantages of buying, as opposed to building, a business?
2. List three potential sources of information about businesses that are for sale.
3. What should be your first step upon hearing or reading of a business that interests you and is in the right general area? Why?
4. Why should you spend so much time just listening to people, rather than concentrating solely on the hard data? What should you be listening for in particular?
5. What kinds of signals might alert you to rethink your interest in this particular company? Why?
6. What is the value of a company?
7. What is the asset approach to valuing a company? What is its underlying assumption? When and why might you want to use it?
8. What is the stream-of-earnings approach to valuing a company? What is

its underlying assumption? When and why might you want to use it?

9. Will the fact that you are buying a going concern help you in getting bank loans for initial financing? Why or why not?

10. Why might the seller help to finance your purchase? What two main benefits might his willingness to do this provide for you?

NOTES

1. Sanford Jacobs, "Private Firms' Finances," *Wall Street Journal* (June 11, 1984):27.
2. "Business Bulletin," *Wall Street Journal* (December 13, 1984):1.

17. Starting a Franchised Operation

"Before switching to Pepsi from Coke last summer,
Burger King Corp. spent more than two years
examining data from the soft drink industry and
doing its own market research. At one point, it
sent employees on an undercover mission to Jack-
in-the-Box franchises to clock how much time was
wasted informing customers who asked for Coke
that the chain serves Pepsi instead."

John Koten, *Wall Street Journal*

As noted earlier, starting a franchise is yet another way of getting into a business of your own. In many ways, buying a franchise is an interesting compromise among buying a going concern, building your own company from scratch, and working for a major corporation. In this compromise lie the advantages and disadvantages of buying a franchise. In the end, of course, the keys to making the decision lie in your personality and your reasons for wanting your own business in the first place—your original objectives.

This chapter will explore the world of franchising. It will thus complete your tour of options for getting into your own company. In addition to discussing the major advantages and disadvantages of the approach, it will explore ways of finding and researching franchise opportunities. It will also raise some of the standard (and substandard) contractual issues and cost issues.

One of the critical notes that we will raise often is that each franchise is different from every other franchise. While we have tried to address the more common features of what is generally considered to be "franchising," we cannot possibly have mentioned every feature of every program. Do not assume, therefore, that if you like the general arrangement outlined here, almost any franchise will do. You might be in for a rude awakening.

GENERAL NOTES ON FRANCHISING

Franchising is big business in the United States today, and it is getting to be bigger every year. In 1984 sales of franchised goods and service were expected to exceed $457 billion. It was also expected that the number of franchised establishments would reach 462,000, employing about 5.3 million people (including part-timers and working owners).[1] Franchising has invaded most sectors of the economy, from campgrounds to construction to dentistry.

Franchising is a very broad term, covering two major types of arrangement between the franchisor and the person who deals with the actual customers. The first is known as "product and tradename" franchising. These arrangements are largely distribution arrangements, under which a company doing business with customers becomes associated with the products of specific manufacturers. Your local Chevy dealership is this kind of franchise. The dealer has the right to sell GM Chevy products and to advertise with the Chevy name.

The second kind of franchise arrangement is known as the "business format" franchise. This is the type of arrangement under which the franchisor and the franchisees become involved in total relationships, often including the colors of the walls of the place of business. This is the smaller, but faster-growing segment of the franchising industry. These are the kinds of franchises that are currently generating interest among entrepreneurial types. We have, therefore, restricted this discussion to business format franchising.

In 1983, business format franchising was a fairly concentrated business. Fifty-seven large franchisors controlled 49 percent of all franchising sales and 53 percent of all franchised establishments. That is more than 142,000 outlets and $49 billion. Fourteen of these giants were in the restaurant business (for example, McDonald's). Twelve were in automotive services and supplies (Midas, AAmco). This left more than 1,700 other franchising companies to split up the remainder.

In addition to the large number of smaller franchisors now operating, more companies are beginning or moving into franchising every year. In 1983, while 141 franchisors either failed or stopped doing business as franchisors, more than 350 new companies entered the market. As you can see, among the smaller franchisors, there is a great deal of coming and going. This should reinforce our continual advice to be very clear about what you are getting into and about the company with which you are planning to do business.

WHAT A BUSINESS FORMAT FRANCHISE
CAN DO FOR YOU

Buying a new business format franchise essentially permits you, as franchisee, to replicate a successful business in the area in which you have the

Figure 17.1   Advertisements for franchise opportunities

franchise. You use the successful name. You benefit from the franchisor's large-scale advertising. You will use the successful trademarks. You will use the same ingredients and/or supplies. You will benefit from the quantity purchasing discounts of the franchisor. You will use the methods of operation that the franchisor has already found successful and is continually refining.

You will not be able to experiment with your own creations (unless you have signed on with one of the newer, more flexible franchisors, some of whom permit small areas of difference). You will not generally be able to arrange and decorate to your taste. In short, you will not generally be able to operate your business as you see fit, altering a bit here and there. You also may be limited in potential expansion.

At its most basic, a franchise permits you to use trade names and sell products or services. Most franchisors, however, also offer services designed to help their franchisees to succeed in their franchises. This makes a great deal of sense when you consider that the franchisee is the one who usually gets the goods to the ultimate customer. Failing franchises cost the company market share, in addition to making it look bad.

The remainder of this section looks at some of the more standard services that you can expect from a serious franchisor. If having to deal with all these services and all this "assistance" turns you off, franchising may not be for you. It is almost always part of the deal.

An Operating Area

In general, you are granted the franchise by a franchisor for a given area. The idea is that two franchisees of the same company should not be in direct competition with each other. You will be seeking the exclusive right to operate the *xx* franchise in your chosen area—or the area that is available.

Site Selection

Most of the larger franchising companies have sizable staffs that do nothing but seek and target appropriate sites for company outlets. At minimum, most serious franchisors have a great deal of data about the demographics of areas in which successful outlets operate. They also have data on the size and characteristics of appropriate sites.

Since they succeed or fail on the basis of your success (and the successes of your fellow franchisees), the franchisors have a vital interest in the selection of your site. In some cases, this vital interest extends to actually choosing your site for you. In other instances, the assistance is less coercive. In almost all cases, the franchisor will require approval of a site that you select.

Sometimes a franchisor will actually purchase the chosen site and lease it to you. Or, the franchisor may lease the property and sublease to you. In

Table 17.1   Franchising—by selected fields of business, 1984 (est.)

| | *Franchisee Owned Units* | *Franchisee Sales* | *Percent of Total* | |
Kind of business			*Units*	*Sales*
Total	374,152	$393,684,046	100.0%	100.0%
Educational products and services	6,643	593,231	1.8	.2
Fast food	51,755	28,786,765	13.8	7.3
Convenient stores	7,046	4,518,681	1.9	1.1
Business aids and services	46,681	7,855,098	12.5	2.0
Construction, home improvement, maintenance, and cleaning	18,221	1,968,383	4.9	.5

Source: U.S. Department of Commerce, *Franchising in the Economy* (Washington, D.C.: U.S. Government Printing Office: 1984).

other cases, you will lease directly from the site owner. In any case, try to make sure that your lease term coincides with the term of your franchise agreement. The last thing you need is to develop a successful unit and then have to renegotiate leases.

Site selection is rapidly becoming one of the critical problems in franchising in general. As the number of outlets grows, acceptable remaining sites are difficult to come by. Particularly in the fast-food business, where traffic is crucial, firms have even resorted to purchasing smaller franchisors simply for their real estate. Marriott, for example, bought Gino's Pizza to convert into locations for its Roy Rogers Roast Beef chain. Franchisors are also trying to adapt their operations to non-traditional sites—inside office buildings or in existing stores.[2] Given this scramble, you should welcome any assistance you can get.

Despite all the high-powered help that may be offered (or required), we suggest that you do your own research. In the early phases of your work—for example, in choosing an area and an industry—you will have collected a large amount of data that can be brought to bear on the site selection issue. Do not fail to use that information. Check the projections you have made against those of the franchisor. Not only will this process tell you something about how good the franchisor's "experts" are, but it will also give you a better handle on what to expect should you sign on for the particular franchise being offered.

Product Line Selection

Some franchisors permit some flexibility in product mix. Hallmark Card shop franchisees, for example, could choose additional product lines, providing they do not compete with anything in the Hallmark lines. Some of the newer fast-food franchisors leave room for regional/local variations. Fresher Cooker, for example, permits 20 percent of menu items to be geared to the local market.[3] Most franchisors, however, insist on uniformity. This provides them with a measure of quality control and with the knowledge that possibly inferior "additional" product lines will not impair their good names with the public. In some cases, uniformity is part of both the marketing and cost strategies. The public knows what to expect. At the same time, the franchisor ensures purchasing savings through requiring uniformity.

For the franchisee, having a standard product line removes the requirement of going through the selection process alone. Here, too, however, you might want to consider checking the franchisor's assumptions and projections against your own. You know this territory and its people. While you probably will not win an argument with the franchisor, you will at least have a better notion of what to expect if you open the franchise. If you do not expect the product mix to work in your situation, consider another franchise.

Set-Up and Training

One of the key functions of a major franchisor is to train franchisees. In general, training is formal, covering all aspects of running the franchise unit. McDonald's, for example, runs "Hamburger University," created for the sole purpose of such training.

Programs usually take one to six weeks and are generally at some central location. While the cost of the program itself is usually included in the franchise fee, the costs of transportation and living while training are often borne by the franchisee. Some franchisors offer small salaries or stipends to franchisees during the training period.

Many franchisors supplement their formal training programs with both on-the-job training and initial supervision. For the former, new franchisees often go to work in operating franchises to learn the ropes. In addition, some franchisors employ teams of supervisors or coordinators who will spend time with the new franchisee as he opens his new franchise.

Operating Methods

The heart and soul of a good franchisor's operation are the methods used to run the units. Thus, most franchisors develop detailed operations manuals for their franchisees. These manuals underlie much of the curricula in the training programs and form the structure of how the units are expected to be run on a day-to-day basis.

Such manuals—Ray Kroc of McDonald's called his "The Bible"—are a large part of the reason that little or no business experience is needed to own

---

FEATURE 17.1

Ray Kroc's Hamburger University

When we were planning to build a company store in Elk Grove Village, I insisted that it have a full basement instead of the usual partial basement. That was to be the first classroom for courses that would eventually become Hamburger University. There was a motel next to the Elk Grove store so it was convenient for out-of-town operators and managers to stay there while attending classes. They would sit at desk-arm chairs down among the potato sacks and listen to lectures. ... At noon the students would apply what they'd learned by doing practical work upstairs in the store. Our first class had eighteen students. We awarded them a Bachelor of Hamburgerology with a minor in french fries.

Hamburger University had meshed fully into our system by 1963.... Classes had grown to an average of twenty-five or thirty students, and we were holding eight to ten two-week sessions a year. Hamburger U was also helping to test and implement training procedures on new equipment....

From Ray Kroc, *Grinding It Out: The Making of McDonald's* (New York: Berkeley, 1977):125–126, 139.

---

and operate a successful franchise. (Where experience *is* needed is in choosing an appropriate and honest franchise.) These manuals are also generally tied by contract to your performance as a franchisee. Thus, if you fail to perform as the manual requires, your franchise may be terminated.

In addition to addressing such issues as work flow and portion control, a franchisor may specify a management information and control system for its units, tracking such things as employee productivity, materials usage, and inventory levels. At very least, the franchisor will require highly specific and detailed sales reports. These not only afford the franchisor market data in a uniform format, but they also let the franchisor know how well you are doing compared with similar units and compared with your plans. While these systems may be onerous for a unit owner, they generally provide any owner with all the information needed to manage effectively and to make informed decisions. Consider such accounting and information systems as potential plusses in your search for a good franchise.

Purchasing Effectiveness

As noted earlier, being part of a franchise operation gives you access to the volume buying strength of the entire organization. While it is illegal for a franchisor to demand that you buy only through the company, it is generally advantageous for you to do so. As Larry Kohler, an executive vice president at Burger King noted, "Just deciding to put three strips of bacon on a burger can have one heck of an effect on the supply of pork bellies."[4] Now *that's* purchasing power!

Occasionally, a franchisor in trouble will try to force its franchisees to accept lower quality goods than had been the norm. Pressure can be brought to bear. In a sensational recent incident, the associated franchisees of Arthur Treacher's Fish and Chips raised voices in the press about the company's shift to a different kind and quality of fish. The incidents led, among other consequences, to withholding of royalty fees from the franchisor and the breaking of franchise contracts.

Clearly, purchasing power arises from size and power generally. This can cause difficulties for unwary franchisees. Your protection lies in being very clear about what is in the contract and what is the general practice of your franchisor.

Financing

Franchisors make their money from selling franchises, from selling supplies, and from sales made by their units. They take fees for granting their franchise. They can be of significant assistance on the other side, however, in helping you to get the necessary startup funds together. They do this, in general, by providing support to approved, prospective franchisees at local banks.

You instantly look, to your banker, like a much safer bet when you walk through the door with a major franchisor behind you than when you walk in alone. Most large franchisors will provide data for your bankers on the growth and stability of the franchise as a whole. They will also usually provide their projections and other data for your unit in particular. Even if you like your projections better than theirs, therefore, use the ones with the letterhead at the bank—at least as adjunct to your own. One needs every legitimate edge one can get.

As you can see, working with a franchisor does not absolve you of the responsibility of developing a business plan to take to your bank in most cases. The partnership between you and the franchisor may simply make your job somewhat easier. We reiterate: Do your own projections whether or not the franchisor provides projections. It would be good for your banker to know that you have checked and can discuss any differences intelligently.

Some franchisors simply cut out the middleman, making long-term loans directly to franchisees. Check the rates. Shop around. If the franchisor to whom you are talking insists on being the financer, it is probably time to find another franchise. If they are really offering a good deal, and if your lawyer and your accountant agree that it is a good deal, take them up on it. If you mind permitting one organization that much control and influence over your business life, get your loan elsewhere.

FEATURE 17.2
Financing Help from a Franchisor

Donna and Mike Olesen were turned down for loan guarantees when they wanted to open a photo processing store. Working with their franchisor, Moto-Photo, the nation's largest franchisor of one-hour photo labs and Banc One, Ohio's largest bank, they worked out a deal.

Underlying the Olesens' deal was a joint program between the franchisor and the bank to give undercapitalized potential franchisors a chance. The company pre-screens applicants. "We largely depend on their judgment concerning the franchise, and whether a person has a good chance of success," says Bill Harrell of Banc One. Moto-Photo trains and reserves the right to revoke the franchise at the end of the training period.

The bank has taken the time to learn about the one-hour photo business and, consequently, can evaluate risk in context. Potential franchisees must offer downpayments of at least $35,000. A franchisee can qualify for a loan of $100–150,000, however, with equity (including equity in a home) of as little as $50,000. The bank is also using the program to broaden its loan portfolio outside Ohio.

What Moto-Photo got out of this arrangement was a larger supply of otherwise qualified potential franchisees to continue their expansion. What the Olesens got was their loan–five-and-a-half years at "prime plus two." It was guaranteed 90 percent by the SBA because of the bank's clout with that agency and 10 percent by Moto-Photo. Even with this backing, however, the Olesens' loan wasn't assured. "The hardest part," says Mike, "was making the right presentation for the bank."

Adapted from Jay Pridmore, "Franchises for the Masses," *Venture* (November 1984):184–6.

Equipment financing and financing for initial inventories are also provided by some franchisors. The same caveats apply as above.

As noted earlier, almost every franchise has at least one wrinkle that is different from all others. This outline of the general kinds of services offered (and/or required) is just that—general. Read, and have your advisers read, all the disclosure statements and all the contracts before you seriously consider signing anything. And, before you even get to that point, consider carefully whether owning a franchise is what you meant when you said you wanted to get into a business of your own.

FINDING A FRANCHISE

Assuming you have decided that owning a franchise is worth serious effort, your job becomes finding the right franchise for you and for your area. Some of the same methods apply here as applied to finding an independent business to purchase. In addition to such sources as your banker and the newspapers and journals, there are two associations of franchisors and innumerable books on the subject. Even the federal government publishes their *Franchise Opportunities Handbook* on an annual basis.

There is no lack of data about available franchises. In fact, unless you have done some homework and decided, at least, on the industry in which you want your franchise, you are likely to be swamped in all the information.

In addition to determining the industry in advance, you should probably also have a clear understanding of how much money you have and can raise by yourself. This, too, will help you narrow the list of potential prospects. In the fast-food franchising field alone, equity requirements range from less than $25,000 to $125,000. This is before you even go to the bank for a loan. There is no point in chasing a $125,000 rainbow if there is no way you could scrape together that much money.

A number of fast-food franchisors have recently embarked on programs to recruit minority, particularly black, franchisees. In such cases, even the largest, hardest line franchisors are being very flexible about equity. More important, some that usually do not offer financial assistance are doing so.[5]

In general, newer franchises will be less expensive to get into. Of course, they are also riskier because they have very short track records. Your tradeoff is relatively low front-end costs versus stability and predictability of earnings patterns. If you do consider a new franchise seriously, check especially carefully into the histories of the people running it. If they have numerous failures or non-successes behind them, you have every reason to question whether they really have anything to sell to you now.

As you cull through the potential franchises in your price range and in your area(s) of interest, please remember that your franchise unit will be your small business. If you cannot stand the thought of those "golden arches" overhead all day, every day, find another franchise. Seek one whose decor will not offend you and whose general atmosphere you expect to find congenial. (Unless, of course, you are simply making a financial investment and have no intention of ever going near the place.)

If no franchise "fits," you may want to go back to building from scratch or buying an independent operation. Do not buy a franchise you are unlikely to be happy with simply because people have always told you that starting a franchise is much easier than starting from scratch. Nothing is easy if you hate doing it.

INVESTIGATING A FRANCHISE

Obviously, your first move in finding out about a particular franchise is to write or call headquarters for information. You may get a packet of information or you may get a lot of forms to fill out about yourself, or both. This is your first lesson in franchising. Investigation is a mutual process. Most serious franchisors go through a painstaking process to ensure that you are right for them while you are doing the same thing in reverse.

The reasons should be obvious. Franchisees who fail or who are dissatisfied with their franchises make the company look bad. A few years ago, one of McDonald's proudest boasts was that none of its units had ever closed. In fact, if your franchisor does not take a detailed and lengthy look at you, you might begin to wonder about their entire program.

Sources of Information

But, assuming that you are likely to pass muster, how do you find out more about them? Essentially, you do the same thing that you would do to investigate an independent business that you were considering purchasing. You talk with anyone who might have any information for you. Above all, you talk with other franchisees of the company. Most will provide you with lists of their satisfied (local) franchisees. If at all possible, talk as well with some not on the list and, by phone, with some franchisees out of your area.

You are seeking information about how the company really does business. How long has each franchisee been in operation? Is each satisfied with his or her deal? Did the company really come through with whatever they promised? How useful was the training program? Most important, what is the main problem or problems that each is facing now? How is the company responding?

You get the picture. What you are looking for are indications of how truthful the company is, how helpful it is, and how well it responds to franchisee difficulties. If you talk with enough franchisees, a pattern is bound to emerge. Take this pattern more seriously than almost any other piece of information you find in your search process.

While you are in this round of talks, also get in touch with your Better Business Bureau to find out whether they have any negative reports about your prospective partner. The franchise associations listed at the end of this chapter may also be helpful. These organizations are dedicated to helping franchisees and to preserving the good name of franchising as a way of doing business. They will probably have information about your particular franchisor and large amounts of useful data and tips about franchising as well. On the whole, it will be two stamps well spent.

Disclosure

As franchising took off as a way of doing business, unscrupulous operators naturally joined in the fun. Partly as a response to abuses in the 1970s, the Federal Trade Commission issued rules for franchise disclosure in 1979. This

Table 17.2   Average sales per establishment, 1984 (est.)

	Franchisee-owned	*Company-owned*
Educational products and services	$ 89,000	$ 162,000
Fast food, restaurants	556,000	665,000
Convenience stores	641,000	766,000
Business aids and services	168,000	279,000
Construction, home improvement, maintenance, cleaning	109,000	1,526,000

Source: U.S. Department of Commerce, *Franchising in the Economy* (Washington, D.C.: U.S. Government Printing Office: 1984).

requires that a franchisor provide a prospective franchisee with broad information about the company at least 10 days before a contract is signed or 10 days before the franchisee makes any payment, whichever comes first.

Items that must be disclosed by the franchisor include:

- Identifying information about the franchisor
- Business experience of its key people
- Business experience of the franchisor
- Litigation history of people and company
- Bankruptcy history of people and company
- Description of the franchise
- Statement of total funds franchisee needs to start
- Statement of continuing payments required of franchisee
- List of persons with whom franchisee is required to or advised to do business (including any payments to the franchisor resulting from business done by the franchisee)
- Financial assistance available
- Restrictions on the franchisee's conduct of the business
- Required personal participation
- Termination, cancellation, and renewal information
- Statistical information about franchisees
- Financial data, including audited financial statements, of franchisor

among other information.[6] In addition to these federal requirements, at least 15 states also require disclosure and/or registration of franchise offers.

While it is comforting to be inundated with numbers and disclosure form information, be aware that *nobody verifies* the information contained in such statements. Believe it and sign at your own risk.

The message is, "Do your own research." If you turn up something that differs from what the disclosure statement says, be doubly on your guard. Ask the franchisor about the difference(s). If you are not satisfied, don't consider that franchise.

Pyramids: Look-Alikes to Beware of

Assuming you are serious about wanting to own and run a long-term, legitimate business, you should be aware of a variant on the franchising notion that is illegal in many places. It is the "pyramid" scheme. And it does not take much examination to separate the real franchises from them.

A pyramid is essentially a fast game in which the idea is to suck in new "distributors" or "franchisees." Each of these new people pays a fee to join up—just as in a real franchise. But the fees are the only real money-makers in the operation. The "distributor" who brings in the latest "investor" shares in the fee the new person pays. In fact, that's how he makes his money back. Since, as the game goes on, the area runs out of naive people, pyramids are generally self-limiting. Therefore, those last into the game are likely to be big losers. It is a lot like a chain letter (also illegal).

The process of selling "distributorships" in these kinds of operations differs markedly from the normal franchising process. While a legitimate franchisor will generally look you over very carefully, the pyramiders will usually subject you to a hard sell. Often, the signing-on process occurs at group meetings or "sales meetings," at which enthusiastic dealers will talk about their millions. There is usually little focus on the product(s), and less on product advertising and distribution methods.

Should you happen to walk into one of these situations, your job is to remain objective, not be swayed by all the enthusiasm and pressure. Do your research—on the product and the company. Aside from the illegality of some of these schemes, if they are holding mass meetings, you can bet that you will be getting in toward the end of the game. Remember that only the early entrants ever make any money out of them, since they generally can bring in the greatest numbers of "investors" and the structure usually divides new "investor" fees by level of the pyramid. Those at the top of the pyramid, the early joiners, get a piece of fees produced at all subsequent layers. And, should you care, numbers of innocent, if gullible, people usually lose a lot of money.

WHAT'S IN A FRANCHISE CONTRACT?

The opening statement here is our same old refrain. Read all contracts, leases, equipment purchase agreements, and financing arrangements, with extreme care. And make sure your lawyer reads them as well. The remainder of this section does not cancel that advice. Its only intent is to raise some of the points in many franchise contracts that have created difficulties in the past. Using this information, you can be particularly alert to the relevant clauses and evaluate them better.

Keep in mind that a franchise contract *is* a contract. It will come to you all printed and clean. This, along with the intimations of the franchisor, will work toward convincing you that the deal is a take-it-or-leave-it affair. But, as any good lawyer will tell you, contracts were made to be negotiated. If some clause is a particular problem for you, negotiate.

There will undoubtedly be some non-negotiable areas—we doubt, for example, that you could convince McDonald's that you should operate without the golden arches. You can probably figure out in advance what these items are and stay away from them. If your non-negotiable points coincide with their non-negotiable points, you will not have a deal. It is highly unlikely, however, that most franchisors have contracts that are as uniform as they would like you to believe. If you are offered a deal you almost like, then, it is certainly worth a shot at making it better.

Fixed Period of Agreement

Most franchise contracts are for fixed periods of time. The most common period is 10 years. The issue for you is what happens when the 10-year period is up. In the past, some franchisees have had to sit by and watch while their carefully built businesses were taken over by the franchisors.

This is not a common occurrence. In 1982, out of more than 352,000 franchisee-owned units, 11,415 franchises came up for renewal. More than 10,000 were renewed. Only 513 were not renewed at the option of the company.[7] While non-renewal is not standard operating procedure, it remains a major, and legitimate, fear.

You can protect yourself, to some extent, through the contract. First, examine with care any clauses relating to renewal. Try to limit the company's discretion, while preserving your own options to sell the unit back to the company. Under all circumstances, make sure that a formula for a buy-back is included as part of the contract. This will ensure that, if you have to sell your unit back, you will at least get a good price for it. Some states also regulate renewal clauses. Your lawyer will know whether your state is among them.

Keep in mind that, even if both you and the franchisor are overjoyed with your relationship, because of the limited period of the original contract, you will have to renegotiate the deal sometime. Some franchisors charge an additional franchise fee at that point. Find out the normal practice of your franchisor (if it has been operating long enough to have a normal renewal pattern). Failing that, you are on your own. An advantageous buy-back formula should add to your strength in this situation.

Termination

Understandably, most franchisors retain the right to terminate a contract if the franchisee is not performing as required. This ensures that your Big Mac will be uniform, coast-to-coast (and in foreign countries), and that the franchisors get the information and the fees due to them. In your contract, however, you want to spell out, as clearly as possible, the circumstances under which your contract can be terminated.

On the other side, you may want the right to terminate your contract if the franchisor is not living up to his end of the bargain. Make sure that conditions for this situation are also clear in the contract. In both cases, make sure that the buy-back formulae are tied into the transaction.

In 1982, 6,180 franchise agreements were terminated. More than a third of these were initiated by the franchisor. Almost half had to do with non-payment of royalties and other financial obligations.

Transfers

One of the joys of having your own business is that you can sell it or will it to your children. This right to transfer your business at your own option is usually limited by your franchise agreement. For the franchisor to refuse a requested transfer is rare. All but 42 of more than 3,080 transfer requests were approved in 1982. Some states also limit the franchisor's right to refuse a

Table 17.3 Average total investment and startup cash required, 1984

A. BY SELECTED INDUSTRY GROUPS	*Investment*	*Startup Cash*	*Total*
Educational products and services	$ 50,000	$20,000	$ 70,000
Restaurants, all types	285,000	75,000	360,000
Convenience stores	100,000	30,000	130,000
Construction, home improvements, maintenance, cleaning	35,000	15,000	45,000

B. SOME FIRMS WITHIN GROUPS	*Investment*	*Fee*	*Royalty*	*Advert.*	*Av. Sales Per Unit*
Ponderosa, Inc.	$705,000–780,000	$15,000	4%	—	$1,000,000
Sizzler Rest., Int'l	1,000,000	20,000	4%	5%	1–1.5 million
The Pewter Mug, Inc.	375,000	10,000	3%	—	850,000
Pepe's, Inc.	75,000–200,000	15,000	4%	2%	350,000
Athlete's Foot	60,000–70,000 inventory to 125,000 total	7,500	3%	—	375,000
Second Sole	60,000–125,000	10,000	3%	.5%	300,000
Postal Instant Press	67,000	35,000	6–8%	1%	225,000
Kwik Copy	75,000	36,000	5%	2%	N.A.

Source: *Part A data:* U.S. Department of Commerce, *Franchising in the Economy* (Washington, D.C.: U.S. Government Printing Office: 1984).
Part B data: "Franchise Facts," *Venture,* various dates.

legitimate transfer. Here, again, just make sure that you understand and can live with whatever arrangement you decide to sign.

Fees and Other Charges

The franchise agreement will generally require that the franchisee cover or provide for a number of different kinds of costs. Do not make the mistake of assuming that the franchise fee, or even the initial investment, is all you need to get in and stay in. In 1980, the total investment required of franchisees, for example, was two or three times the required startup cash. But there are additional financial requirements as well. Make sure yours are clearly spelled out in the agreement. Moreover, since there seem to be no standard terms in the industry, make sure you understand what your franchisor means by each cost/charge item.

The franchise fee.   This is your payment for the right to use the trademarks, and such, of the franchising company. It may include some territorial guarantee. It may include initial training.

Site evaluation fee.   This may be separate, or it may be included in the franchise fee.

Initial working capital.   Most franchisors will specify the amount they believe you will need to start the unit and to cover early operating costs. It is not a bad idea to have some cushion beyond their requirement, particularly if you believe their projections to be shaky. Consultation with other franchisees can help significantly here.

Equipment, construction, remodeling, fixtures, initial inventories, and other opening costs will also need to be handled. The same advice as above applies.

Service charges and royalties.   Many franchising companies charge you for such services as the use of their computerized accounting and management control systems or their market/product research. These charges may range from 3 to 12 percent of monthly gross sales. Obviously, franchises differ in how much and when paid, as well as in services offered.

Advertising costs.   Advertising costs may be included in the service charge category, or they may be a separate charge. These costs are essentially contributions to the national or regional advertising program that ensures your market. It also often supports a local advertising blitz to promote your new unit. These charges may be 1 to 2 percent of your monthly gross.

FEATURE 17.3

Supply Again Creates Franchisor/Franchisee Friction

William Glassner, Jr., attorney for the Nutri/System franchisees commented that: "My feeling on the franchise system is that it can be a license to steal as far as the franchisor is concerned." He recently concluded a negotiated settlement between his clients and the franchisor that will reduce by 28 percent the cost of the diet food they buy from the franchisor.

The courts have taken two basic positions on the relationship of franchisor supply to the anti-trust provisions of the law. First, franchisors can make such requirements of franchisees only if the product is "indigenous" to the franchise system. This was critical in a case involving Baskin-Robbins decided in 1982. The company could require its franchisees to buy the ice cream, since it formed the basis of the franchise. It could *not* require them to buy freezers, toppings, or other related items from the company.

Second, franchisors may not require purchases from specified vendors. This might constitute an illegal tie. They may, however, set specification for products which franchisees may then buy from any vendor providing an acceptable product—within the specifications.

Timothy Fine, general counsel for the National Alliance of Franchisees in Landover, Maryland, notes that there is now a new factor in the supply equation. "...[M]ore of the franchisors are being acquired by conglomerates and are pressuring the franchisees to purchase products manufactured by one or more of the divisions of the conglomerate."

The lawyers generally recommend a strong franchisee trade association as the best way to protect against undue pressure and to bargain with the franchisor as an alternative to expensive and time-consuming litigation.

Adapted from Lewis Beale, "Buy-Or-Else Franchising," *Venture* (August 1984):139.

Indirect charges. These may consist of markups by the franchisor on the supplies they sell to franchisees, and/or interest and other financing costs on equipment, inventory, and other items financed by the franchisor. As noted earlier, you will want to compare these franchisor charges with those of competitors on the open market.

Supply Arrangements

This area has been a frequent source of franchisor/franchisee friction, largely because it is rather difficult to pin down. Many franchisors are insistent in persuading their franchisees to buy from them, claiming, perhaps with some validity, that buying cheap alternative supplies impairs their good names. Such pressure can create additional expense for you, however.

Controlling the supply lines is also useful to a franchisor in keeping its franchisee in line in other ways. Some franchisees have reported that their decisions not to participate in promotions or to set prices other than those "suggested" by the franchisor have resulted in late deliveries of supplies and product.

In short, this is a very murky area. It is not really amenable to good contractual definition. Your prime guide here should be the experiences of other franchisees of your company. A great deal of existing friction in this area should serve as a loud alarm bell for you.

We repeat—skepticism is a very useful quality in a franchise purchaser, or a purchaser of any business. So are good market, site, product, and company research abilities. Use your lawyer on the contracts and your accountant on the franchisor's numbers and on their projections for your prospective unit. But do not neglect your own work. In the end, you are the one who will be laying your money and your time on the line.

SUMMARY

Buying a franchise is a cross between owning your own business and working for a large company. It is like owning in that you are responsible for the obligations of the business and you keep the profits. It is like employment in that the franchisor controls many important aspects of your business. These aspects can include decor, product line, operations, record keeping, and transfers of the business. The franchisor also usually provides assistance of the sort unavailable to independent business owners. The extent of control and the availability of assistance vary with the company. Because of this similarity to employment, you need to be very careful in considering whether owning a franchise will meet your personal goals for having a business of your own.

Despite the level of control exercised by the franchisor over startup and operations, you should not expect to do less work in buying a franchise than in buying or building your own company. While the franchisor has an interest in your success, it cannot possibly be as vital as *your* interest in your success. Check everything, particularly their assessments of your market, your site, and your product mix. Check, particularly, their reputation with their existing franchisees. Listen to those other franchisees. Check, also, the franchise company's disclosure statements. While these documents are required by law, they are not verified by anyone but you. Make sure what you find matches what they have told you. Clarify any discrepancies. Be aware that a good franchisor will be evaluating you, even as you are evaluating them.

Use and listen to your accountant and your lawyer in the financial analysis and contracting processes. Key issues in financial analysis are the stability of the franchisor and the projections for your operation. Key contract issues include the various circumstances under which the company can re-acquire your unit or can restrict you in transferring it to others. Be aware of all financial requirements and arrangements before you sign anything. In short, treat the purchase as the major financial obligation it is. The fact that the company offers to buy back the unit if you do not want it will not absolve you of most of the financial obligations you will have incurred.

This chapter advocates skepticism. While most franchisors are entirely honest and sincerely interested in building an ongoing business for themselves and with you, some are not. What you need to make sure of is that you are preparing to do business with one of the former. Your odds are good—particularly with a well-written contract.

FOR YOU TO CONSIDER

1. What is "business format franchising"? How does it differ from "tradename franchising"?
2. What is a good franchisor really selling?
3. List the advantages and disadvantages of buying a franchise as opposed to building or buying an independent business. Where do you stand on these issues?
4. Why is it a good idea to do your own market survey and market research when the franchisor is much bigger and will do it for you?
5. What are the easiest ways to cull through the giant lists of available franchises?
6. Once you have targeted one or two franchises in which you might be interested, how do you go about checking them out? What are some of the key items you need to find out?
7. What is a "disclosure statement"? Note some items that a disclosure statement must contain. What is the key thing to remember when you receive a disclosure statement from a franchisor? Why?
8. Why is it important to a franchisee that a franchise agreement is a time-limited document?
9. What are "royalties"?
10. Why is supply a major area of friction and litigation between franchisor and franchisee? How can you assure relative tranquility?

NOTES

1. U.S. Department of Commerce, Bureau of Industrial Economics, *Franchising in the Economy, 1982–84* (Washington, D.C.: U.S. Government Printing Office, January 1984).

2. Lee Kravitz, "Fast Food's Fast Movers," *Venture* (November 1984):46.
3. Ibid., 48.
4. John Koten, "Fast Food Firms' New Items Undergo Exhaustive Testing," *Wall Street Journal* (January 5, 1984):25.
5. "The Rush to Enlist Blacks in Fast-Food Franchises," *Business Week* (June 1984):54.
6. Bank of America, "Buying a Franchise," *Small Business Reporter,* 1981.
7. U.S. Department of Commerce, *Franchising 1982–4,* 11.

FOR FURTHER READING

Bank of America. "Buying a Franchise." *Small Business Reporter,* 1981.
U.S. Department of Commerce. *Franchise Opportunity Handbook.* Washington, D.C.: U.S. Government Printing Office, annual.
U.S. Department of Commerce. *Franchising in the Economy.* Washington, D.C.: U.S. Government Printing Office, bi-annual.

Readers may also write to the following franchise associations for additional material:

International Franchise Association
1025 Connecticut Ave., N.W.
Washington, D.C. 20036

National Franchise Coalition
P.O. Box 366
Fox Lake, Illinois 60020

CASES FOR PART 7

SALLY JONES AND "NEIGHBORS"

After considering the costs of startup for "Neighbors," Sally and Janice were extremely discouraged about ever opening their restaurant. In the period during which they had been doing research and talking about it, they had become very attached to the concept of "Neighbors" with themselves at the helm. To say the least, they were depressed. They believed they could still do it, but they thought there might be an easier way to get "Neighbors" going.

One afternoon, Janice came running over to Sally's, waving a copy of what turned out to be the *Pittsburgh Business Journal.* "They're selling our restaurant!" she cried. "Jim brought home this paper. He never does that. And there it was! It must be meant to be our place."

The ad simply said that a sole proprietor was interested in selling his 80-seat restaurant (with liquor license) in the South Hills, an area larger than, but including, their chosen area. The price mentioned was $150,000. That gave them an idea about the range. And it was less than their expected startup cost. They were, of course, forced to call and check further.

When they called the number in the ad, they got a secretary who answered the phone with "West Penn Security," and who said that Mr. Peters (presumably Jack) was over at the restaurant, "Jack's Place." She gave them the number.

They tracked down Mr. Peters at "Jack's Place" and in the conversation that followed, Sally and Janice told him about their attempts to start "Neighbors," and about their financial and time limitations. Jack Peters told them that "Jack's Place," the restaurant for sale, was in the commercial district of Dormont, a working-class area between their original intended market and the city of Pittsburgh. Jack also told them that he had been trying to run the place as a sideline, as an absentee owner. He noted that using a manager for this type of business was very difficult—and could be expensive. "It really needs you to be there," he added. They arranged to meet at "Jack's Place" on the following Friday for lunch.

After getting off the phone, Sally and Janice immediately got into Sally's car and headed for Dormont. They clocked it. The drive took 10 minutes. They found "Jack's Place" without any difficulty.

It was in a sort-of strip mall on the main street through Dormont. The street was also a main route from the suburbs to the city, used by many buses and commuters. The strip was set back from the street, and the space in between was a metered municipal parking lot.

The "mall" building was a wood frame structure, two stories high. "Jack's Place" shared it with an audio store, a convenience store, a discount drug store (these last two were parts of chain operations), a state alcoholic beverage outlet, and a few other retail shops. Upstairs seemed to house an answering service office, some medical professional offices, and a karate school (maybe, thought Sally, to supply the chiropractor).

The strip was directly across from the Dormont Public Library, half a block from town hall, two blocks from the post office. Nearby, an entire street had been rehabilitated. The area was surrounded by converted homes (now largely insurance, legal, and medical offices) and small apartment buildings with storefronts at street level. Off the main street were medium-sized, one-family homes. The nearest restaurant was four blocks away.

Sally and Janice did not go into "Jack's Place" or any of the other shops. They walked around a couple of times and spent a while just watching the people. The place looked to be in pretty good shape. The menu in the window of "Jack's" showed it to be a relatively low-priced sandwich-type place for lunch. Dinners also seemed moderately priced, to put it mildly, at about $7. The food was fairly standard. Few people actually went in or out—not unreasonable, since it was mid-afternoon.

The people who walked by seemed neat and well-, if inexpensively, dressed. The attractions seemed to be the drug store, the upstairs offices, and the library.

The two friends realized immediately that their original concept would have to be modified somewhat to fit into "Jack's" setting. But they wanted any shot at their restaurant—the sooner, the better. They would mention the meeting to their husbands, but they would actually meet Mr. Peters on their own, they decided.

They met Jack Peters at "Jack's Place" for lunch on Friday. Inside, the place was rather dark, partly because of the dark wood fixtures and panelling. A wood bar dominated the entranceway, running half the length of the left-hand wall. There were a few small tables to the right, but the main eating area was toward the back. All of the bar stools were occupied. About half the tables were also in use. They took a table in the back corner. After they were seated, they realized that they were facing Peters in the corner, rather than looking into the restaurant. The waitress was attentive, but that could be expected. This was the Boss. The drinks were rather weak, but the food wasn't bad.

Jack explained that he had gotten into the business almost three years ago because he had always wanted to own a restaurant/bar. He was not prepared to give up his regular business, however, because it was a real money-maker. He had purchased the equipment for "Jack's" used at a restaurant auction and had bought the furniture the same way. He had done the panelling himself and built the bar area himself. He was clearly particularly proud of the bar.

The problem with continuing ownership was staffing. As an absentee, he was almost wholly dependent on his manager (of which there had been six since he opened) and his bartender. Because of the various sideline activities of some of his bartenders, Jack was still not sure of the costs and revenues of the beverage side of his business. This, he said, was one of the reasons that the place was not as profitable as it should be. This could be corrected, he asserted, by on-the-spot management.

After lunch, Sally and Janice got the grand tour. The kitchen was clean and the equipment looked good. Jack noted that, of course, they'd want a professional to look over the equipment, etc., before any deal was finalized. Jack also provided financial statements (shown below as Tables 1 and 2), apologizing for the lack of a current balance sheet, but pointing out that, as a sole proprietor, he was not even required to file one for tax purposes.

Table 1 Balance sheet for "Jack's Place" as of 12/31/84

ASSETS		LIABILITIES AND NET WORTH	
Cash	$ 19,500	Accounts payable	$ 23,500
Inventories	15,200	Current portion LTD	15,600
Accounts receivable	9,500	Accrued expenses	8,300
Total current assets	$ 44,200	Total current liabilities	$ 47,400
Net plant and equipment	$118,000	Long-term debt	$120,900
Other assets (net)	$ 43,000	Owner's equity	$ 36,900
		Total Liabilities and	
Total assets	$205,200	*net Worth*	$205,200

Table 2 Income statements for "Jack's Place"—Years ending 12/31

	1983	**1984**	**1985 (9 Mos.)**
Revenue: food	$420,000	$454,300	$365,000
liquor	280,000	315,700	265,000
Total revenue	$700,000	$770,000	$630,000
Cost of sales: food	$140,000	$160,000	$137,000
liquor	140,000	163,400	140,000
Total sales	$280,000	$323,400	$277,000
Gross margin	$420,000	$446,600	$353,000
Operating expenses:			
Payroll (incl. benefits)	$231,000	$269,500	$213,600
Laundry, linen	7,000	7,700	6,400
Supplies	7,500	5,000	3,500
Menus, printing	4,500	1,000	600
Advertising	7,000	8,000	6,000
Management salary	35,000	38,500	32,000
Utilities	15,000	16,000	14,000
Depreciation	8,000	8,000	6,000
Interest	22,500	20,500	13,600
Insurance	7,000	7,700	6,300
Lease	36,000	37,800	30,000
Other (incl. services)	25,500	3,900	4,000
Total operating expenses	$406,000	$423,600	$336,000
Net profit before taxes	$ 14,000	$ 23,000	$ 17,000

Sally and Janice left, prepared to purchase, if an appropriate deal could be struck.

1. How would the purchase of "Jack's Place" alter Sally's and Janice's plans for their restaurant? Do you consider these significant changes?
2. What reasons are there for making this purchase—assuming an "appropriate" deal? What reasons are there for not making this purchase—even if there is an "appropriate" deal offered? Which do you believe is the stronger argument and why?
3. Even if you think that the purchase is a bad deal for Sally and Janice, develop a credible offer for Jack Peters to make to them. Develop also a credible offer for Sally and Janice to make to Peters for "Jack's Place." (Note: "Offer" here includes cost/price, and terms.)

ROB KING AND "KING FINANCIAL"

As the time for decision drew closer, Rob King's feet began to get colder and colder. He began to consider ways that he could hedge his bets—just a bit. He was disappointed that the bait he had dangled in front of so many of his new acquaintances had not resulted in a single request for help ("on the side") in preparing a financing plan or a business plan. He did seem to be gaining credibility, but the world of small companies was not yet beating a path to his door. Maybe Ginny had been right about staying in his job. He was beginning to feel that he was unlikely to ever get King Financial off the ground.

And Helm, his boss at Consolidated, seemed to be backing off a bit. Perhaps it was Rob's new attitude—or a figment of his imagination—but Helm seemed to have become almost human of late. He had smiled at Rob once or twice and some of the things Rob did were being well received. There might be some percentage in staying around the bank a little longer.

He began to think about the possibility of a franchised operation in business as either an alternative to starting his own company or as an adjunct to King Financial. Which he preferred seemed to depend upon how confident he felt about his ability to sell consulting services. Whether he liked either option seemed to depend on how his day at the bank had gone.

But a franchise seemed seductive. It promised a brand name to sell and a shift of some of the responsibility for both sales and product. Moreover, the actual operation of the business would be prescribed by the franchisor. The deal sounded better and better. If he could combine his own operation with the stability of a franchise, he might really be in business.

Since what King wanted was simply an assist, rather than a full-time franchise operation, he began to look at franchises for tax preparation operations. This approach, it seemed to him, had a number of built-in advantages. First, he was a CPA and, therefore, taxes were second nature to him. Second, he expected that tax preparation work for small business owners might lead to broader mandates to provide consulting work to their businesses. Finally, if his own work load from King Financial got to be too much, he could run the tax preparation operation as an absentee manager, using the franchisor control mechanisms to keep track of operations.

The more he thought about this approach, the more he liked it. Even Ginny seemed a bit warmer toward this idea than she had to the notion of King Financial as a free-standing entity.

He began to look at two franchise operations, both involved in tax preparation services. One required a franchise fee of $17,000; the other, a bigger "name" in the business, required only $2,000 of equity in the franchise. The more expensive franchise offered financial assistance of up to two-thirds of the fee and worked with franchisees in bookkeeping services and financial planning as well as tax preparation services. The less expensive franchise offered only tax preparation services.

1. Discuss the advantages and disadvantages to Rob King of buying a franchise and running it as his sole operation.
2. Discuss the advantages and disadvantages to Rob King of buying and running a franchise as an adjunct to King Financial.
3. How might the addition of the tax-preparation-only franchise affect King Financial? The addition of the tax-bookkeeping-planning service?
4. What would you recommend to Rob King? Why?

ED JAMES AND "OAK TREE BOOKS"

As he wrestled with his pro forma financial statements, Ed James began to think seriously about the possibility of opening a unit of a franchised bookstore chain. He knew that, although the largest current chains—B. Dalton, Waldenbooks, Crown—were wholly owned by the companies that operated them (by major conglomerates or general retailers, in fact), there were some companies that franchised bookstores.

The notion of a franchise offered some benefits to Ed James. First, the franchisor would teach him the mechanics of the book business, and of business in general. They would also offer a standard list of books so that Ed would not have to make any purchasing decisions. (He was not at all sure about his ability to choose books that the public would snap up.) Moreover, since the central office could purchase in bulk for all the outlets, his inventory costs were likely to be smaller. The advertising assistance and name recognition factors were also beginning to look attractive to James. While he recognized that he would still have to do pro formas and make presentations to the bank to obtain financing, he knew that the job would be much easier if his bookstore had been approved by a larger, recognized company.

There were, of course, significant drawbacks from Ed's point of view. First, while bookstores were not as rigidly standardized as, say, McDonald's, what he still thought of as Acorn would have to go. He would also be required to manage to their numbers—no specialized staff or expensive "help" services. He was not really prepared to give up the freedom to implement these approaches. A major concern was the idea that a franchisor might offer him an arrangement off in the backwoods somewhere when he really wanted to stay in the Washington area. He liked the vicarious excitement of living near the source of government.

With these thoughts in mind, Ed James began to explore the possibility of buying a franchise for a bookstore. Some of the offers were interesting. Of those he considered, the one that had the most potential in his opinion was one that simply offered to franchise the name and the management and operating systems. James would get to choose his own location, subject to a fairly loose approval process. The company would provide a four-week training program and all the forms required to set up the required reporting systems. The company would handle replenishing and renewing stock based on James' inventory and sales reports. Payment for inventory would be required within 30 days.

The costs to Ed James of buying this franchise would be $25,000 as the fee, plus 5 percent of gross sales as a royalty payment and 2 percent of gross sales for advertising. According to company estimates, a unit in an area like the one Ed had chosen would break even at about $300,000 in sales. They figured that initial inventory should be about $50,000, which they were prepared to finance over his first year in operation at 15 percent. They estimated that the cost of equipment, furniture, improvements, and fixtures would be about $30,000. They also recommended that their franchisees have at least $5,000 in extra cash available to meet any unforeseen needs. The company also offered to supply inventory at 35 percent gross margin.

Ed James sat down to evaluate this potential franchise as a serious option.

1. Leaving aside, for the moment, any financial considerations, do you believe that a bookstore franchise is a good idea for Ed James, given what you know of him and his plans? Why or why not?
2. Has Ed James done all the work that he needs to do to evaluate this franchise opportunity? If not, which bases has he not covered and how should he proceed to complete his research?
3. From a financial perspective, is this franchise a good deal for Ed James? (State any assumptions you made to arrive at your conclusion.) Why or why not?
4. Advise Ed James regarding whether he should purchase this franchise or build his own bookstore. Be sure to explain to him why you believe he should do what you recommend. You may need to persuade him.

PART 8
KEEPING SCORE

18. Keeping Control of Your Business

If we can know where we are and something about how we got there, we might see where we are trending—and if the outcomes which lie naturally in our course are unacceptable, to make timely change.

Abraham Lincoln

If you have been diligent about working your way through this book, by now you have a good structure for a working company. You know what, how, and how much it will sell. You know how it will operate and how much it will cost to operate. You know how much money you need to raise and where you will get it. You have the initial projections for your company, both financial and operational. In short, you are set to go.

This section is designed to assist you in the beginning and ongoing care and feeding of your new company. It is divided into two parts, reflecting the two different major management tasks you will face as your company becomes established. This chapter addresses issues and methods of control. Chapter 19 considers issues of longer term growth and planning.

A pervasive problem in many smaller companies is that the owner/manager is spread very thin. He or she opens the doors of the business and immediately becomes involved in firefighting, rather than in managing. The underlying assumption of these two chapters is that this syndrome need not be true for you.

The watchwords, slightly paraphrased from a popular saying in the U.S. Navy, are "Proper Prior Planning Prevents Particularly Poor Performance"— the "seven Ps." You have already done a great deal of planning. In this chapter we will consider how to make that planning prevent poor performance.

HOW DO YOU CONTROL A BUSINESS?

A clear sense that you are in control of the functioning of your company is a major factor in preventing feelings of stress and overreactions. Clearly, then,

414

a major goal, especially in your first few periods of operation, should be to achieve that sense of control.

In general, this feeling comes from real understanding of the relationships among facets of your business and from sound expectations of its performance and results. This, in turn, will be based on a good pre-opening planning and projection process (which you will already have done) and a good monitoring system. Given these pieces, you need only add structured spaces of time for analysis in order to be capable of control.

In many ways, it is easier to say what control is not than to describe what it is. It is not, for example, as we noted in Chapter 10, keeping watch over the shoulders of your employees at all times. It is not doing everything yourself because "If you want something done right, do it yourself." These practices are self-defeating, and, since you are only one person, quite likely to kill you with overwork and overworry.

Structuring a good control system and letting it work for you will be a major contributor to your success. Your system should produce all the information you need to keep tabs on what is going on in the business. It should provide enough detail to facilitate analysis, problem identification, and problem-solving. It should give you clear signals when you are heading into trouble. And it should show you where the trouble is likely to emerge.

Letting your control system work for you involves a number of steps. First, you have to describe what you want to happen (your plan). Then you have to capture the information that will tell you whether you are on the right track (your monitoring system). Finally, you have to assess what, if anything, you have to do to keep your company moving toward the goals you have set for it. This last step includes comparative analysis (actual to plan), problem definition, solution development, solution testing, and implementing the solutions you choose to adopt.

What you are really preparing to do is develop a continuous diagnostic system that will keep you informed about the relative health of your company. To do that competently, you will need some history and/or some norms, and a good description of the symptoms you are seeing. You also need to be able to recognize a symptom when it comes along. In the remainder of this chapter, you will walk through the diagnostic process. You will also see how to translate the diagnostic information that your system produces into prescriptions that have the potential for making your company better.

WHAT INFORMATION WILL YOU NEED?

In order to build an adequate control system to monitor the performance of your business, you will need a continuous flow of information about key areas of your operations. For a monitoring system to work for you, it must meet two

FEATURE 18.1
Control Becomes Critical to Nike

The president of Nike, Inc., Philip Knight, was noted for having kept a limosine-full of investment bankers waiting while he finished a run. No more. With falling net income and slowing growth, Nike's "laid-back" management approach is giving way to more attention to control and planning. "Certainly there's a need to have more formalized procedures," says Knight, agreeing with us, "But that doesn't mean a sledgehammer approach." He notes that "with a 5 percent increase in sales and a 5 percent cut in operating expenses, you restore margins and have a very, very healthy performance."

Achieving that performance is requiring changes at Nike. Knight plans no dramatic announcements, but has announced his goal as to "manage our existing business better over the next couple of years." Key changes are being made in the management structure of the company. Robert Woodell, hand-picked to succeed Knight as president, has been reassigned to work on longer range planning. Knight is again in control of day-to-day operations. This is a clear reflection of the fact that operations had gotten out of control.

Lack of operational control was reflected in the steep climb in inventories and the proliferation of products at Nike. Shoe inventory, for example, had reached 22 million pairs before controls and cutbacks took hold. As of 1984, these inventories were down to 15 million pairs. The goal is 12 million. Nike plans to reduce the total number of shoe models they make by 30 percent by 1986.

While changes in sales approach and strategy are also in the works, a clear goal at Nike is better control to enable them to meet more intense competition in the athletic shoe and apparel markets.

Adapted from Mike Tharp, "Easy-Going Nike Adopts Stricter Controls," *The Wall Street Journal* (November 6, 1984):31.

main criteria. First, it must capture all the data you are likely to need. Second, it must be simple and easy to work with. If you plan carefully and collect needed information *as it is being generated in the business,* both criteria will be met. Monitoring and control becomes a problem only when you try to recreate information from fragmentary or non-existent records.

Fortunately, developing methods of capturing the relevant data in useful formats is not difficult. As everyone knows, Uncle Sam generally requires that you have some documentation for claims made on tax returns. Systematizing your approach simply makes your life easier—at tax time and year-round.

But to think about such a system as merely a mechanism for supporting your tax claims is to lose much of its value. Monitoring current events, and especially monitoring them in relation to what you thought would occur, is a valuable tool for achieving control of your business. It also helps you to feel as if you are in control, an important sensation for a new entrepreneur.

DATA COLLECTION: TWO EXTREMES AND A GOLDEN MEAN

Monitoring/control systems tend to polarize new entrepreneurs. One common type is the shoebox variety data collector. A small-company classic is the owner/manager who walks into the bank with a shoebox full of canceled checks and another of invoices. While this owner theoretically has all of the relevant records, they cannot help in decision making or planning simply because they are not readily usable. To find any specific item becomes a matter of going through all the paper that the business has generated since its inception. To make sense of it is impossible because there is no structured way to look at the information that has been collected.

An alternative approach to data collection seems to be overkill. Entrepreneurs who believe in the overkill approach seem to believe that every piece of data is equally as important as all other pieces of data. They tend to build elaborate information and control systems. While often elegant, such systems tend to fall into disuse, simply because it is so annoying to keep them fed.

You want to try for some middle ground. The KISS principle should apply to all your data-related activities—"Keep It Simple, Stupid." You have better things to do than reorganizing your operations around your control system.

The critical rule for ensuring that you have the data you need, but not every piece of paper that has ever entered your door, is to know what you intend to use a piece of information for before you begin collecting it. This, obviously, is a function of proper prior planning. In practice, it means that you develop your analytic formats before you actually open your place of business—and that means *now.*

The key to building such a simple, maintainable system is to collect data as it comes in. This, too, depends on planning. You will need to find or develop forms that permit you to write things down once, rather than copying items three or four times into three or four different places. A sale, for example, would be recorded in your revenue records. But you would also want to show it in cash or receivable records, show the removal of the physical items in your inventory records, and also, perhaps, in some system you have developed for tracking the performance of your salespeople. Basic systems to do this for the more standard types of records are available for sale. They are generally driven by an accounting system. Your accountant may have a preference for one brand or another, so, before you commit to one, ask.

The basic notion, however, is the critical point. Your system should be simple enough for you to use on a day-to-day basis with little or no real inconvenience. It should produce only the data you need to help you to manage (control) your operation effectively. It should summarize that data so that you can see an appropriate level of detail on a regular (and frequent) basis. We guarantee that you will not spend an hour or so a day to simply create and maintain records. Even if you have the inclination, you will not have the time.

TWO MAIN AREAS YOU NEED TO ADDRESS

Out of your data collection and monitoring systems will grow your control systems. If you do not collect information about something, you will not be able to exercise control over it. It is therefore incumbent on you to determine, in advance, what specific items and/or processes you will need to control in order to make your business run smoothly, well, and in the right direction.

Financial Factors

Uncle Sam's requirements provide a useful starting point (and some impetus) for your consideration of an appropriate data collection system for your new company. A serious discussion with your accountant may also help. Sit down and think about what the tax people would want to focus on in your company. These items generally include your inventory (and cost-of-goods-sold), your sales and expenses, your depreciation expense, and anything that has to do with what you, personally, (or you and your partners) get out of the business. These are the first items that require documentation. With these documented and under control, that dreaded word, "audit," will portend mere annoyance, rather than serious trouble.

Tax-oriented information and controls are inherently accounting-based. For this kind of information, you already have formats that will collect the aggregate numbers—the financial statement formats. You will need to develop categories of revenues and expenses that are appropriate to your business and that will facilitate your periodic analysis. There are "charts of accounts" that will help you here (see your accountant), but again, be aware of the dangers of developing too much detail. You will get lost in it, rather than working with the factors that actually drive your business.

Operating Factors

If you use only financial data in your information system, however, you will be missing a number of the major items you need to know about how your business is doing. Consider the following scenario. You know you have orders backlogged. You are producing your widgets as fast as you can. You have not changed your sale price, and your inventory costs per widget sold are exactly where you expected them to be. But sales are down. What's wrong?

In truth, there may be a number of problems. But you can make it easier to find out where the problems lie by devising and collecting relevant data on the operating relationships in your business. Are your machines running below par? You could check that easily if you had been collecting information about the output of each per hour (or per day, or however). Are your workers not performing as they should? Data on productivity per labor hour (or day) is easy to develop for most businesses and can be extremely useful in diagnosing problems. Developing such data simply requires you to track how much time (labor hours or machine time or both) is put in and how much product (or service) comes out. Your data can be compared with industry averages, with data from the business censuses we mentioned in Chapter 4, and/or Bureau of Labor Statistics productivity data.

PROFILE
William G. Mays, Mays Chemical Company

Mr. William G. Mays is deliberately slowing the growth of his company this year to let his systems and controls catch up with his operations. "We'll be respectable at a million a month," he says, "but we've got to get our internal systems more in line with our size."

The problems at Mays Chemical became almost impossible to ignore. In fact, one of them nearly bankrupted the company. A clerk had jumbled $450,000 in invoices into a drawer and simply forgot about them for three weeks. Only when the cash flow dried up did Mays find that they had never been mailed. Still, the outflow payments to Mays' suppliers had to keep flowing. "It nearly exhausted our credit line," Mays commented.

Another slowing of inflows occurred when a $15,000 bill to a major chemical company went unpaid for 45 days. When Mays finally realized something was wrong, he called and found that it was awaiting the approval of a manager who was out of town. Another company official saw to it that Mays was then paid promptly.

Either of these difficulties could have been averted—or discovered sooner—had Mays been using a system that flagged late or out-of-pattern payments. Mays is working on just such a system. He now knows exactly how many days it has been since he received products for which he owes suppliers. He is working on tightening up the company's own billing procedures so that he can shorten the billing lag from the current two weeks. Until he gets his house in order, he is prepared to slow down.

Adapted from Heywood Klein, "Firm's Owner Learns Dangers of Growth Without Controls," *The Wall Street Journal* (August 15, 1983):19.

In developing the key operating relationships for your business, the same rules apply. The collection process should be simple, and you should see only the few relationships that are really important to the health of your business. This involves more thought on your part about what is really critical to your success and what data will reveal most starkly how well you are doing at maintaining those relationships. Once again, the difficult part comes before you actually start operating. If you structure your monitoring and control systems properly, your company will almost tell you where the problems lie and how to address whatever problems arise.

BUDGETING AS A TOOL OF CONTROL

Your budget, what we referred to earlier as your projection, is the standard against which you are running. While "budget" is commonly used to refer only to dollars, the kinds of budgets you will use in your monitoring and control systems may well contain operating factors as well. To reach the revenue projections in your pro formas, for example, you had to estimate unit sales. Your pro forma COGS number involved estimates about output per labor hour and materials usage per unit of output. For control purposes, you would want to track these budgeted operating factors as well as the financial results of these factors. Such a comprehensive system will permit you to see causes of problems as well as the problems themselves.

The underlying assumption is that you did a good job of estimating what the next period would be like. At all times, remember that you made this assumption. Do not lose sight of the (bare) possibility that you did a poor job of projecting and that your company is doing the best it can while you expected too much of it. (The trick is not to use this as a "cop-out," that is, a constant excuse for not meeting projections. While it is easier than analysis and change in the short run, it is a poor long-term approach to success.)

As you move to manage and control your business, your budgets become your yardsticks. You will be measuring how you actually did against how you expected to do. Where the two figures diverge significantly, your job becomes to figure out why, to fix the difficulty, and to get back on your planned track.

Because of the planning process that resulted in pro forma financial statements and your first year cash budget (Chapters 13–15), the financial side of your budgeting process is set to go. It simply needs to be reformatted to make it easier to use in monitoring your operations. Your next move is to examine the operating and cost assumptions you used to put together that set of documents. Out of that set of assumptions about how your business will operate, you will need to highlight those that are critical to meeting your projections. That way, you can monitor these factors separately. If you have chosen the right factors to track, they will probably give you warnings of approaching danger before your financial numbers react.

Your cash budget and your pro forma income statement are the documents

most amenable to a budgeting process, simply because sales and cash flow are
the active parts of a financial program. A balance sheet, on the other hand, is a
statement of condition, a result of activity. Using the active statements as
your basis, then, you can set up summary budget sheets that look like the one
shown in Figure 18.1.

Figure 18.1   Budget-to-actual comparison

	ABC COMPANY — First Year Operations					
	Month _____			*Year-to-Date*		
	Plan	*Actual*	*Difference* $ %	*Plan*	*Actual*	*Difference* $ %
Sales						
Cost-of-goods-sold						
Gross margin						
Wages and salaries						
Commissions						
Rent						
Utilities						
Telephone						
Interest						
Etc.						
Total operating expense						
Net income						
Operating ratios:						
Output/labor hours						
Machine hrs/unit produced						
Etc.						
Key financial ratios:						
Current ratio						
Days in receivables						
Etc.						
Cash flows:						
Inflows from x						
Inflows from y						
Total cash inflows						
Outflows to r						
Outflows to s						
Outflows to t						
Total cash outflows						

Your own schedule, of course, would include all the months along with a year-to-date set of columns. Your planned or budgeted data would be entered in the appropriate columns for the entire year. Each month, you would add a new column of "actual" data and update the year-to-date "actuals." Once the variances are calculated, you will be able to see the overall performance of the business relative to plan. You will also be able to see whether the variances are self-correcting (You simply estimated alternately high and low, or you are off by a month or so in timing.) You may find that variances are remaining high or increasing, in which case you may have a problem—perhaps more than one.

It is most likely that different items will show different patterns. Your business might simply be slower than you expected in getting off the ground, for example. This may be a simple timing problem. If you wait, actuals may well catch up with plan. At the same time, your cost-of-goods-sold may be well above your planned cost, and getting larger by the month. This will not self-correct. You need to correct it/manage it/control it. That's what they pay you the big bucks for. ...

The format we have recommended helps you in two ways. Not only does it let you know how you are doing for each period and the year to date, but it also gives you a structured way of assessing how much attention you need to devote to deviations from your plan. It does this by showing variances in two ways—dollars and percent. Essentially, it lets you choose not to spend time on small dollar amounts (even if they represent large percentages of the planned figure) or choose not to pin down variations that represent only tiny percentage deviations. Thus, it helps you to budget time as well as money.

As you can see in Table 18.1, despite the low sales in March, this company is running above-plan sales for the year to date. Utilities appear to have a self-correcting pattern, probably owing to the fact that, not surprisingly, the owner probably cannot predict the weather (heat) or the strength of sunlight (electricity). Commissions simply vary with the level of sales. The additional commission expense reflects the sales overage.

Two factors, however, require this owner's attention. They explain why his business is showing less profit (by 12.6 percent) than he planned. They are his cost-of-goods-sold and his telephone expense. The largest item explaining his variance from plan is in cost-of-goods-sold—$1,400. His projection shows that he expected COGS to be 50 percent of revenue. His plan, corrected for the extra sales, should have shown a COGS of $18,000. Instead, COGS is $18,900, or 52.5 percent of sales. His March COGS figure is fully 55 percent of sales. This combination of figures indicates that he faces a problem that is unlikely to disappear in and of itself. In fact, the problem appears to be worsening. Unless he takes steps to bring his cost of goods down, he can bet that his company will be below plan (budget) by year-end.

Table 18.1   Budget-to-actual comparison

ABC COMPANY

First Year Operations

	Month 3: March 198—				Year-to-Date			
	Plan	*Actual*	*Difference*		*Plan*	*Actual*	*Difference*	
			$	%			$	%
Sales	$10,000	9,000	(1,000)	(10.0)	$35,000	36,000	1,000	2.9
Cost-of-goods-sold	5,000	4,950	(50)	(1.0)	17,500	18,900	1,400	8.0
Gross margin	5,000	4,050	(950)	(19.0)	17,500	17,100	(400)	(2.3)
Wages and salaries	1,700	1,700	—	—	5,100	5,100	—	—
Commissions	500	450	(50)	(10.0)	1,750	1,800	50	2.9
Rent	1,200	1,200	—	—	3,600	3,600	—	—
Utilities	500	400	(100)	(10.0)	1,500	1,500	—	—
Telephone	200	400	200	100.0	600	700	100	16.7
Interest	90	90	—	—	270	270	—	—
Miscellaneous	110	—	(110)	(100.0)	300	300	—	—
Total operating expenses	$ 4,300	4,240	(60)	(1.4)	13,120	13,270	150	1.1
Net income	$ 700	(190)	(890)	(127.1)	4,380	3,830	(550)	(12.6)

Note: ( ) = Actual smaller than budget (plan). Obviously, this is positive when it relates to expenses, negative when it relates to revenues or net income.

Depending on how his company does business, the additional telephone expense may or may not be an incipient problem. The gross dollar amount is small at this point, so significant effort is not indicated. If making sales requires use of the phone in this company, then the increased telephone cost may be simply a reflection of the additional sales made by the company. If telephones are not involved in the selling process (as might be indicated from the generally low budgeted figure), the owner may have caught the beginnings of burgeoning employee abuse of company phones. This item will bear watching.

PROBLEM DEFINITION: WILL THE REAL PROBLEM PLEASE STAND UP ...?

Unfortunately, the answer is "no." Once you determine that there is some difficulty in a specific area, you have to track down the real problem(s) and dynamics to which your aggregated numbers are responding. Poor sales, for example, do not just happen. They are caused by some other problem— shoddy product, perhaps, or sloppy sales techniques, or inadequate production capacity, or poor purchasing, to name just a few potential causes. If your response is simply to chase more sales when the problem is really deeper, your efforts are doomed to failure. The key to solving a problem is first to define the right problem.

Defining the Problem

Defining the right problem is a function of the kind of analysis already discussed in Chapter 13. Once you notice a problem area or item appearing in your budget-to-actual figures, you need to decide whether it is worth chasing down. Assuming that you decide it is large enough or important enough, your next move should be to sit down and think through the related processes—the things in your business that combine to produce or influence the deviant number.

Next, consider how each of these influencing factors or processes would appear in your set of projections and results. Consider, in other words, what would also have to be true for the problem you are examining to be the real problem. For example, if "poor sales techniques" is what you believe to be the problem underlying your low sales, then you should find significant differences among your salespeople when measured by sales per sales call. If you believe the true problem to be "poor purchasing," then a comparison of the turnover rates of your products should help confirm this diagnosis. You might also look at how many times you had "stockouts," how often you could have sold more of a product except for the fact that you did not have any more to sell.

Peeling Onions: Multi-Level Approach to Problems

As you can imagine, the list could go on indefinitely—even at this level of analysis. And you will want to go at least another level deeper. Think of the problem that shows in your aggregate data as the outer skin of an onion. You can (and should) peel back successive layers until you reach a level of problem that has potential solutions. In a sense, you are playing your own four-year-old, seeking the "why" of every answer you give yourself. Unlike the average four-year-old, however, you will want to stop playing when there is an acceptable approach to a solution. Figure 18.2 shows the process of "peeling an onion."

Obviously, the example in Figure 18.2 does not exhaust the possibilities. Nor does it go to the limit in defining the problem. One could still, for example, ask why (or in what ways) the people are or the training is inadequate. The purpose here was simply to represent the process graphically. You can and should "peel your onions" way down.

Figure 18.2   *"Peeling an onion"—sales below plan*

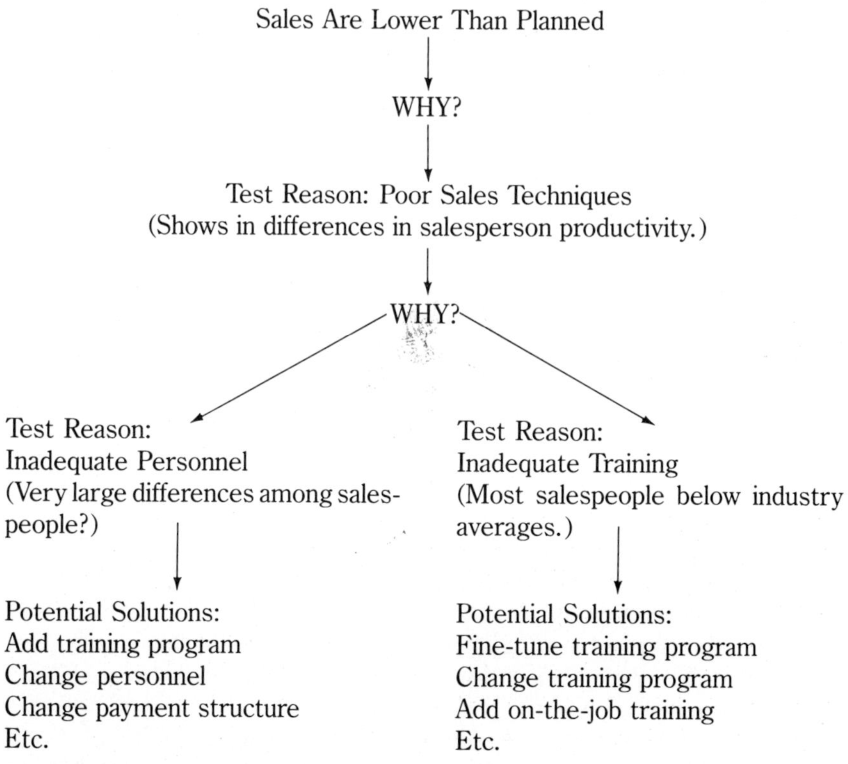

Using the Problem Definition Approach

Monitoring, control, and analysis are learned behaviors. As noted in the discussion of forecasting, you will get better with practice. Do not expect to have all the data you need all the time, for example. Your plan for data collection is unlikely to be complete the first time. It is better, in fact, to err on the side of collecting less. Your system will be less daunting, less cumbersome. Besides, when you discover a real need for a new piece of information, you can always add it to the collection routines. But do make the addition. If you needed it once, odds are you will need it again. Businesses are remarkably repetitive entities.

As you consider the data that your monitoring and feedback systems provide, you must consider two opposing cautions. On one hand, you need to listen to what your numbers are telling you. After all, you built the system to "talk" to you about what is going wrong. On the other hand, you do not want to jump in with a number of "quick fixes" when there is not yet really a problem or when a problem has not yet really taken shape.

You are looking for balance. This balance can be achieved only through exercises of your good judgment about your business. There is risk in acting too swiftly. There is risk in waiting too long to act. You must balance those risks, using the information you get from your system, rather than letting your system dictate to you. The greatest risk, however, comes from having no idea what is going on in your business, a risk you will avoid by developing a good monitoring system.

TESTING SOLUTIONS

In addition to the advantages of monitoring for control that have already been pointed out, the formats you will develop also offer you the ability to test solutions you believe might work in each particular situation. Remember in Chapter 12, when you tested various sales levels to determine how much you would have to sell in order to make a specific level of profit at a given price? Or in Chapter 9, when you tried out various methods of paying for your fixed equipment in order to find the best deal? What you did was to plug your revised estimates, reflecting the new conditions, into your financial schedules. You recalculated and considered whether you liked the expected results. You can do essentially the same thing to test solutions to the problems turned up by your monitoring system.

When you have seen a problem and defined it reasonably clearly, think about all the figures that affect the problem item and all those that are affected by it. If, for example, you determine that your low sales are caused by an inadequate staff, paid in an inappropriate manner, your list of items affected would include: sales, commissions, training costs, and recruiting and hiring costs. It could also include additional telephone costs (from qualifying leads and general business development) and decreased transportation expenses (from the same causes).

In short, if you are really going to test a solution, you have to take your best shot at all of those factors you expect to change as a result of the change you are making. Only if you include all probable changes in base data can you expect your system to feed you a fair picture of what is likely to happen to your business under the proposed conditions.

Your next step is to see whether the proposed change will make matters better enough to be worth the effort. This is another area in which your judgment will have to prevail. You are not only interested in whether your proposed solution ameliorates or removes the original problem, but you are also concerned about whether you will create a whole new set of problems by what you propose. (This is why you have to recalculate the whole set of statements each time. Sometimes problems are created where one least expects them. Assuming that you have the basic relationships right, the wholesale recalculation will catch them all.)

If you do not like the first solution, or if you think you can do better still, simply pose new questions, make new changes, and run all the numbers again until you find a solution that satisfies you. (Here, we could give another loud cheer for computerized spreadsheets. They make this process largely effortless.) As you can see, you really do not want to go through this process unless the problem is worth the effort. That is why your first step was to decide at what point (dollar or percentage) deviation from plan was large enough to create serious concern.

OPERATING CONTROLS

One of the key things to remember about using financial data to address business issues is that the numbers are intended to reflect and explain the operations of the business. Thus, to use these numbers as an effective control requires more than just moving numbers around or picking a number that looks good to you. Your number-based control system is intended to show you where you may need to make changes or modifications in the operation of your business, as well as to show you where you need to reduce costs or increase revenues. The tracking system for critical operating ratios discussed earlier in this chapter (page 419)—in conjunction with your financial projections and results—should give you a good handle on where you need to make adjustments in your operating procedures.

In fact, some operating controls are so basic to the success of a business that you will want to develop the physical controls before you give your monitoring and control system a chance to tell you that you should have done it. Quite naturally, these critical physical control areas include those that deal with the lifeblood of the business—inventory and cash. The inventory represents potential revenue to you (and actual money already spent). The importance of cash in your business has already been discussed at length (Chapter 14).

The interesting thing about both of these items, inventory and cash, is how easy they are to lose or to have removed, unless your inventory is extremely large or heavy. Thus, we recommend that you build physical control systems to protect yourself and your business in these areas. The idea is to preempt the opposition (those who want to steal from you or to feather their own nests at your expense) by making such activities difficult from the start. Since problems in these areas are so common, and so critical to your business survival and success, we do not recommend waiting until your number-based control systems tell you you have a problem.

Inventory Controls

Your inventory control system should provide a running total of how many you have at any given time of each item you stock or use. For tax and financial statement purposes, your inventory records should also show how much you paid for each unit and when each unit that is gone was sold or used. Your cash disbursements (outflows) will provide the cross-check here, as will your periodic inventory counts (physical inventory) and your balance sheet data.

In addition to the financially oriented controls, however, you will need to devise physical controls for your inventory, especially your highly movable and valuable inventory. Consider a jewelry store. It has alarm systems and various methods for ensuring that a "customer" cannot collect large amounts of stock on an open counter. Display cases are locked. There is invariably a safe in which the really expensive items are kept and in which nearly everything is locked away after hours. In addition, window displays are usually stripped of valuable items every night. It may be inconvenient, but it reduces risk of theft and, quite probably, reduces insurance expense. (In this business, such procedures may well be a condition of getting insurance.)

Granted, you may not have the next best thing to the Hope diamond in your shop, but your inventory is what makes money for your business just the same. If there are "leakages" in your inventory, not only do you have less to sell, but you also have the added cost of replacing the items lost. This kind of cost can really kill your business. And it is preventable—easily. There are numerous lessons to be learned from that jewelry shop.

Interestingly enough, recent research has shown that most inventory losses come from employee pilfering. If you have ever walked off with a box of paper clips from your office, you are part of the problem. And you know how the reasoning goes. "It's only a paper clip. What's the big deal?" Well, the one

Figure 18.3   *Sample inventory control sheet for manufacturing company*

Part No.	Item	Additions to Inventory		Removals from Inventory		
		#	Date	#	Date	Employee

paper clip, obviously, is not the big deal. But multiply that one box times the number of office workers in the place times two "removals" per year times $.70 per box, and you do have a major problem. Particularly for a small firm that is not yet on its feet. Besides, they are now your paper clips. . . .

It is difficult to think of the employees you just hired (and whom you really like) as "pilferers" or thieves. And, in the main, they probably do not think what they are doing is wrong. If thinking "theft prevention" is going to really disturb you, consider your efforts in this area as designed to reinforce their naturally good instincts. You are merely putting temptation out of the way. Your alternative is to simply absorb all losses.

Some businesses are, of course, more prone to pilfering problems than others. Although it has been done, it is rare for someone to walk off with an entire boat or a wrought iron railing, for example. Many bar owners and restaurant owners, on the other hand, have come to believe that bottles and beef (dressed) really do grow legs. They just seem to disappear. (Owners of these establishments have the additional problem of "freebies for friends." This, too, takes money from the business. It is also controllable.)

There are two major keys to controlling the problem in your company. First, limit access. Second, create paper trails.

Limiting access.   In some companies, limiting access to goods and supplies is as easy as putting a lock on a door or locking an already existing one. In other kinds of companies, access to some kinds of inventory by relatively large numbers of staff is almost a requirement. Despite the restrictions inherent in your kind of business, you can probably go a great deal farther toward limiting access to portable goods than you now think. If you are going to run a restaurant, for example, would it really cause serious dislocation if you locked most of your inventory away—providing that you or a trusted employee had a key and was on the premises during all business hours? What if you permitted access to a fixed amount of most items, the amount fixed by the projected utilization for the time period?

Manufacturing activities also sometimes require rapid access to stocks.

But would it hurt to put a control person inside a screened area to do the actual stock-picking (by part number) for any employee needing resupply? At the same time, that person could note who took how many of what parts. You would be not only limiting direct access to your stocks, but also creating a paper trail for your inventory items.

Paper trails.   An ideal control system would have at least two different checks on everything that touches your inventory—each of them written down by a different person. This could get cumbersome in practice, though, in many businesses. Here, too, however, you can probably get closer than you think with little distress. You simply begin to tie operating methods into your financial and other control and information systems.

There is a story told about a waitress in a small restaurant who had a group of "regulars," all of whom would seek her station. The owner was also the chef/cook. His was a marginal operation. One night, as things slowed down, he began to notice that while he was cooking steaks, his cashier was ringing up hamburgers. Upon investigation, he found that his in-demand waitress was calling out orders for steaks, while writing up checks for the cheaper meals.

This could easily have been prevented by the simple expedient of duplicate checks. One goes to the cook (and the cook works only from those checks). The other remains with the server and eventually goes to the customer, then to the cashier. Tracking the check numbers would further ensure that such waitress largesse went out of fashion. The extra paperwork is minimal. The savings could be significant.

Or consider the manufacturing operation we looked at earlier. If your parts person were writing down who took what when, you have an immediate cross-check with your other financial inventory figures. Your parts sheet for the day would show how many parts left inventory with whom on any given day. This could be matched to production records for the day. The difference between the parts supplied (plus those on hand at the beginning of the day) and those used should be the starting amount for the next day's production. You have an immediate cross-check for each production worker for each day and a running parts count to match with your purchasing and sales records.

The point here is that a system need not be elaborate, time-consuming, or very bothersome. It does need to provide means of checking back on what happened to your goods. After all, you make your money (and, therefore, your employees' wages) by selling those goods in one form or another. "Removals" or inventory with "legs" can put you and your company under.

Cash Controls

In addition to inventory and supplies, the easiest thing to lose is your real cash. Simply reducing the ability of employees to manipulate the inventory data will eliminate many of the games played with cash. A bartender, for example, intent on skimming a quarter a drink and making up the differences by altering the composition of the liquor used, will go elsewhere for a till into which to put his hand if he recognizes that he is unlikely to be able to beat your inventory control system. But there will always be dishonest folks around. It is one of your main jobs to make it hard for them to make you their mark.

Think about who in your organization gets to handle real cash. Also consider who signs the checks and does the payroll. Essentially, consider what happens to cash or negotiable items that come into your shop. Follow the paths. And try to figure out how you would do it if you wanted to steal from you. See how inventive you can be. Then, systematically close up all the holes you found by placing controls at key points in the processes.

Tackle the obvious places first. Most companies permit a bookkeeper or the accountant to write and sign checks up to a certain amount. Beyond that amount, two signatures (one of them should be yours) are required to write a good check. Be absolutely sure that your bank understands the arrangement. There will be no real control if your bank will pay the check anyway. (If I were intent on thievery, I would send through a one-signature check "by mistake," just to see what the bank did.)

Even if you have an outside group prepare your payroll, make frequent checks on the names of the people you are paying. One of the better games is to simply create a few new "employees" with the address of the thief. Keep track of who is responsible for adding employees to payroll. Better still, structure the process so that you have to sign off before any addition is made.

Another simple and easily preventable game works through the purchasing process. There are a number of variants, but the basic method is that invoices are written for more than the actual cost of the goods. The employee on your end takes part of the extra amounts as kickbacks. An alternative form involves purchasing goods at higher prices than you could get elsewhere, with the same end result. Yet a third approach involves paying invoices for goods that never existed at all. (A bigger "excess" to split.) Still another is to create a "company" that will invoice your company. The invoice is duly paid—to some employee at the "company's" address.

As you can see, there's gold in them thar hills. You can prevent some of these inventory-based scams by simply building a good inventory control and monitoring system. Costs well above plan should alert you immediately that something is wrong. Simple attention to your disbursements and to the companies with which you do business also goes a long distance in the right direction. Preventing the standard rip-offs is, thus, relatively simple. Beyond these, you have to examine your business with the eye of a criminal. How would you go about stealing from your company? This variant on setting a thief to catch a thief can save you large amounts of money and trouble.

SUMMARY

Good monitoring and control systems serve as your antennae in your organization. When you really can watch everything that happens, it is less critical than it will be as you grow. But control is a habit, and your ability in these areas will grow with practice. In addition, the early years of your business are the very ones during which an out-of-control period or a series of losses due to theft or pilferage can put you under. Consider your control systems, then, as cheap insurance mechanisms, contributing at least as much to your survival and success as your regular insurance policies.

As you build your monitoring and control systems, two main segments will emerge: financial controls and operational controls. The former are based in your accounting system. They produce the information required by Uncle Sam in addition to telling you how you are doing. To use this control mechanism, you will need your pro formas and your cash budget. What you are comparing your actual performance with is your expected performance—your budget.

The format suggested for these comparisons allows you to target areas in which your variance from plan is significant enough to cause you concern. Once you have targeted such areas, the method used to track the problem to its underlying causes is very similar to the process of financial ratio analysis. You can peel back the layers until you reach the core of the problem. This format and method also facilitate the testing of potential solutions by permitting you to see the probable effects of your proposed actions before you actually invest time, money, and the business in them. This is done by revising your base numbers to reflect the reorganized reality, and recalculating the statements to see whether the problem disappears and whether others spring up in their place as a result of the revision.

Operational controls include those that monitor the actual processes in your business. The major candidates for such scrutiny are the areas in which you can lose the most money most easily. For most companies, these are inventory-related areas and those having to do with the handling of money and checks. Fortunately, these are usually fairly easy to control, if you pay attention to them.

In any case, whatever control system you develop and implement must be relatively simple to administer (KISS!) and it must produce the data that you expect to need to do your analyses of what is really going on in your company. If it is not simple, you will not maintain it, nor will you use it. If it does not track the items that are important to you and to your business, there is little point to maintaining it. Your antennae will function well for you if you tune them properly and listen to what they are telling you.

FOR YOU TO CONSIDER:

1. Discuss the notion that control is structuring a good system and letting it work for you.
2. Why is it not an adequate control system to simply do everything yourself?
3. Where do you get the information that you will use as input to your monitoring and control systems?
4. What information do you want to collect? How do you decide?
5. What are the two critical attributes of a useful monitoring and control system? Why is each important?
6. How does a budget assist you in controlling your business? How do you use it effectively?
7. Why might you not want to jump into solving a problem the minute you see a variance from your planned performance? What steps should you take?
8. What are the two main kinds of controls that you can build into your business? What are the main differences between them? What is the purpose of each?
9. Why are inventory controls critical to most businesses? What are the key things that you are trying to accomplish through an inventory control system?
10. How would you approach controlling the movement of cash and checks through your company?

FOR FURTHER READING

Small Business Administration publications:

Analyze Your Records to Reduce Costs. SBA MA 1.011.
Budgeting in a Small Business Firm. SBA MA 1.015.
Cost Control. SBA Business Basics 1008.
Financial Control by Time-Absorption Analysis. SBA 045-000-00134-2.
Financial Recordkeeping for Small Stores. SBA 045-000-00142-3.
Keeping Records in Small Business. SBA MA 1.017.
Preventing Embezzlement. SBA MA 3.009.
Preventing Employee Pilferage. SBA MA 5.005.
Purchasing Management and Inventory Control for Small Business. SBA 045-000-00167-9.
Stock Control for Small Stores. SBA MA 3.005.

19. Beyond the Business Plan: The Future of Your Company

Control of the new operation is often not the only function to go by the boards once a company is actually open and running. Despite (or, perhaps, partly because of) the careful, lengthy planning that is required for startup, owners appear to believe that their initial business plan is all that they really need to develop. Planning, however, is a tool. And, like most other tools, it has to be kept sharp to be useful. Moreover, since planning projects the continuous operation of your business, it is easier, in the long run, to maintain a system than it is to build one each time you think you might need one.

There are a number of essential differences between the type of planning that we advocate here and the kind of planning that goes into your budgeting and day-to-day control systems. First and foremost, the kind of planning discussed in this chapter focuses on the longer range issues of seeing that your company gets from wherever it now is to the objectives you have set for it in the future. These longer range objectives will have been specified in your business plan. While your control system will be of prime importance to this process over the short term, a longer range component must be added to really get you where you want to go.

Second, because of the difference in time-frames, the focus of your planning will shift from the income/expense approach that we emphasized for your day-to-day control systems. Since the focus is the condition of the company, rather than its short-run performance (this month, or even this

434

year), balance sheet concerns become more important in your long-range approach.

Third, unless both you and your economic environment are unprecedentedly stable, the reality for your business will change over time. If your business plan is the only statement of objectives you ever make, you are entirely likely to wind up with a set of highly unrealistic objectives. These objectives will, therefore, be useless to you in piloting your company. A long-range planning process provides a structured approach to rational reassessment of such objectives.

To add this longer range component to your planning process, this chapter builds on the base that you will have already developed as you planned your operation originally and as you have developed control systems to monitor it. You will be using the same formats and the same principles. The objectives are essentially the same. You want to minimize surprises and maintain some ability to direct your company toward the goals you set for it. Drift is really the only alternative to planning. And, as you well know, drifting does not even necessarily get you downriver.

This chapter first discusses why most owners of smaller companies avoid structured planning. It presents an approach to planning that minimizes some of the fears and most of the excuses. It will also highlight key planning areas and issues, discussing some of the pressures for change and for inertia that often exist for owners. Finally, the chapter will address contingency planning. The ultimate route to "no surprises management" is, of course, to have structured your plans so that you have answers to questions that have not yet arisen.

It is the underlying thesis of this chapter, and this book, that while luck may give you a hand, the best you can hope for from that Lady is a good start or a good year. You are the one responsible for making your business a long-term success. A major key to succeeding, particularly with limited resources, lies in knowing exactly where you are going, how you intend to get there, and what you will do with every scrap at your disposal in order to maximize the benefit you can wring from it. Without a good, continuously updated plan, you are operating in the dark—with no map or compass.

WHY PEOPLE AVOID PLANNING

Aside from the fact that good planning is difficult, most people, including owners of small businesses, have multiple excuses for not doing it. If you let yourself think about it, you will recognize that they are really just excuses. This section will help you around or over some of the more common excuses by letting you consider what you are really saying when you use them to avoid potentially business-saving activity.

"I Don't Have the Time."

This is the old standby. It is usually trotted out after all other excuses have failed. We have put it up front to dispose of it early. That way, it will not always be there to fall back on.

The underlying statement in the "I don't have time" excuse is generally that events should control your activities rather than you controlling your activities. "Firefighting," responding to anything that comes along that looks like or is presented as a problem, simply chews up all the time there is. Of course, you are the person who decides whether a problem really demands your immediate attention. A bit of consideration will sometimes shift an item from "fire" status to an issue with a more reasonable time-frame. While sometimes there is a "fire" that has to be fought or that is worth fighting, remarkably often the "problem" is not really a problem at all—certainly not worth the level of attention it gets.

It is, of course, true that there is a great deal to do (all the time) and that there is invariably too little time in which to do it. As a business owner, however, not to mention as a responsible adult, your job is to determine what activities are most important to your life and to give priority to those activities. Each of us has only 24 hours in a day and seven days in a week. Few of us know how many weeks we have. If you choose talking to an employee about football or watching television over planning for your business success, you are making a serious statement about your priorities. Examine such statements with great care.

Not only can a good planning system give you the means to discriminate between real problems and minor "glitches," but it can also give structure to your considered set of priorities. It can help you foresee potential "fires" and avoid them. In short, not planning virtually guarantees a continuous stream of "fires" that "have" to be fought. You never get on top of your operations if you operate that way. Eventually, you really *don't* have the time to do anything else. While planning does take time, its net effect is usually to *give* you more time. And it helps you use your time better.

"I Can't Do Anything About It Anyway."

This is the second-best excuse for not planning in your business. Here you are, poor owner of a tiny, new company, pitted against giants in your industry and against events in the world economic situation. What can poor, tiny you do about any of the forces that buffet your business? Since the obvious answer is "nothing," you simply drift along wherever these overwhelming tides push you.

If you really believed all that, you would never have bothered to start your business in the first place. The giants were part of your initial analysis. World events, to the extent that they might affect your business, were also taken into account. Why, suddenly, should you be so helpless against them? Why, in fact, are they suddenly ranged against you?

The feeling is understandable. Being very small and new at your game is an overwhelming feeling. You have taken a big risk, and "they" will get you for it. The more you let these feelings take over, however, the less in control of your business and your life you will feel (and, in fact, be).

Planning can help in two main ways. First, it can help you to see the areas that you can control—and help you to maintain control in those areas. Second, it can help you avoid the clashes between you and those titan forces out there by letting you see in advance what they are likely to do, what the effect is likely to be on you, and how you can either minimize those effects or actually make positive steps because of them. If you went into an industry of giants in the first place, presumably you did so because you saw some niche in which you could compete. Planning can keep you in touch with what is happening to that niche and alert you to new niches into which you might move.

If you really believe that you cannot deal with the forces to which you are subject, you should probably go back to a 9 to 5 job. In that situation, at least someone is giving you a nice, steady paycheck for confronting forces you cannot deal with. But you do not really believe that, or you would not be here.

"But They'll Find Out!"

Another key excuse that owners of small businesses tend to favor is that if they write their plans down on paper they may fall into "the wrong hands." Competitors will discover the plans and thwart them. On the whole, they continue, it is better not to write them down anywhere. Since a proper planning system requires that one write down plans and goals, they conclude that planning as a whole must be a bad idea.

In real life, you know how much you can learn about your competitors without resorting to stealing their planning documents. Your initial research was largely directed toward this end. Unless you keep your entire place of business closed, people will be able to find out a good deal about how you operate, regardless of what you do about planning. Moreover, unless you have targeted some specific item—the piece of property at the corner of Main and State, for example—why should you care?

We are not suggesting that you tape these papers to your windows or mail out copies. If you are particularly paranoid, you can always lock your planning documents in a safe or a safe deposit box at your bank. We are suggesting, however, that the level of others' interest in your business planning is probably greatly exaggerated in your own mind. Either they, too, are worried about the giants, or you really pose no threat to them.

For most small companies, the game is in the execution, rather than in the concept. As an oriental military philosopher once noted, "Weak leadership can wreck the soundest strategy; forceful execution of even a poor plan can often bring victory." If you really have a "secret formula," it is reasonable to take special care of it. But if, like most of us, your plans do not depend on exclusivity, there is absolutely no validity in the "they might find out" excuse for not planning.

One Real Reason for Not Planning

What most entrepreneurs really seem to be trying to avoid is the commitment to performance associated with planning. This syndrome was discussed in Chapter 2 in relation to setting personal and business objectives. Committing to your goals and objectives is scary and difficult. This is doubly true once you actually get your operation going.

You can minimize the difficulty of doing this by the simple expedient of not showing your early planning efforts to anyone else. (We discussed this approach when talking about developing your initial plans for your business plan as well.) While it is often useful to solicit opinions from key (and trusted) staff members, it is not absolutely necessary to developing adequate plans. If you skip that step in your early planning cycles, you will have the benefit of plans without the potential embarrassment of having others know you did not meet plan. (On the other hand, they will find it hard to believe you when you announce that you are precisely on track....) If the one you are trying to hoodwink is yourself, however, you may well be in trouble already.

STRUCTURING PLANNING TIME AND THE PLANS THEMSELVES

As you begin operations, you will be under real time pressures. There will be real "fires" for you to fight. This is why it is so easy to convince yourself that you really have no time to give to planning. The answer is to make the time to plan. It is a vital function. And you are the only one who can do it for your business.

Time and Place for Planning

Start by considering how your average week shapes up. If your busiest time is Friday afternoon, obviously do not try to put aside planning time on Fridays—unless, of course, you are trying to *prove* that you have no time to plan. Choose a time in which you are likely to be able to create relative calm and quiet. You want time during which you can think clearly and well. Therefore, if you never really get going until noon, Saturday morning from six to noon is probably not a good time either. You know yourself best. Give yourself some good time. Most owners choose an evening or a weekend morning at least once a month.

Your second step is to make this time inviolable. Announce that you do not want to hear about anything unless the place is really, physically burning down and the fire department is on the way. Choose a place that is conducive to work and thought. If nobody is in the office during the time period you have chosen, that may be a good place. If, on the other hand, you are bound to find some "fire" to distract you at the office, find someplace else. Closet yourself in your study and send the kids to the zoo. Borrow a friend's workshop. In short, set yourself up to do some uninterrupted thinking.

What you want with you are your original personal and business objectives and the financial planning documents you developed for your startup—your business plan. You will also want any output from your control systems that show your operation since its startup. At the very beginning of this business plan process, you determined areas that were absolutely critical to your success. Those critical success factors and the key ratios you highlighted in Chapters 15 and 18 should help you to direct your planning efforts toward the areas that are most important to you.

A Format for Developing Objectives

Once alone with your materials, it is a good idea to structure an approach to thinking about your business plans. A variant on the approach shown in Figure 19.1 will be simple, but will also let you see interrelationships among parts of your business and will ensure that you do not forget a crucial piece of the operation.

This format is flexible, permitting you to focus on whatever seems appropriate given what is going on in your business at the time. If you structure the form so that all areas and critical ratios are included, however, you will at least have to determine, at each planning session, not to focus on a particular item.

The format is also flexible about the time-frame you can consider. You might choose to use different periods from those shown here. You might choose to extend the horizon, creating spaces for five- and 10- year plans and objectives. You can also, obviously, vary the emphasis that you place on any time period. It is recommended, however, that you balance short-term concerns (next month, this quarter) with some view of the more distant future. This will serve as a counterweight to the naturally short-term focus of your day-to-day affairs. You will also be able to see clearly how your shorter term plans will move you toward your longer term objectives.

Using this format, each box can be used either for a numerical statement of an objective—for example, "increase sales by 5 percent—or a description of what needs to be done by that time—"develop new training program for sales staff." In order to be most useful to you, however, it is best to make as many as possible of your goals and objectives numerical. This makes them specific and measurable—easy to see when you make them or miss them in the period you have given yourself. The key notion, however you do it, involves

Figure 19.1   Format for continuing business planning

Business Area:	Next Month	Current Quarter	This Year	Long Term
Sales	Stay on plan	Increase model 7240 5% (units)	Increase total by 5% ($)	$1 mill/ mo. by '88
Production		Reduce scrap by 10%	Reduce unit labor $ by 5%	
etc. ...				
Critical Ratios: Inventory Turnover			4x by Y.E.	5x by '88
Output/Labor Hours			Increase by 5%: 20 to 21	
Return on Sales		14% pretax	15% pretax	18% by '88
etc. ...				

developing specific written objectives that recognize the various segments and functions of your business and that are related to specific time periods.

For each key objective, you will want to develop a brief statement of how you will accomplish that objective. If, for example, you want 5 percent more in sales, you would first specify whether you are going to count in units or in dollars. Then you would note what product line(s) these extra sales should come from. Finally, you would add that you expect to get them through a special dealer promotion or by adding a new territory and a new salesperson, or however you plan to do it.

Adding the Financial Component to Planning

Obviously, each of your goals and plans will have certain financial implications for your business. Your next step is to consider those implications and fold them into your plans and budgets.

Bring out your budgets and your pro formas and go through them, adjusting all of your projections to reflect your new or revised goals. If you have not already done so, your planning session is also a good time to compare your projections with the emerging reality (see Chapter 18). At your planning sessions, you can thus also make any necessary budgeting adjustments—and, at the same time, assess whether some particular area or item requires special planning or a new approach to control. You could then incorporate such items into your objectives for the current period.

Feedback

After your initial planning session (first month), it is also a good idea to review previous plans to see how well you have done, or are doing, in meeting them. If you have missed, or are off track, try to figure out why. Was there something wrong with your execution of your plan? Can you correct it? Was your plan a poor one in the first place? Can you make it better or more workable in your next round? Did something truly beyond your control intervene in an entirely unpredictable way, making your plan impossible?

The dangers here, depending on your personality, lie in making some unpredictable reverse "your fault" or in making a real planning or execution failure the result of "something beyond your control." Of course, you are the only one who will know, but if you are going to take the time to plan at all, you should not make the process a sham. Though you have the time to spend, you do not have the time to waste.

A Planning/Budgeting Cycle

While you want to continually adjust and fine-tune your plans and budgets, you really do not want to go through an entire revision or update each month. You do not have the time, nor is there a great deal to be gained from that level of effort. In some rational way, therefore, you have to differentiate among months and develop a cycle of reviews, updates, and full-blown revisions or extensions.

You have a working base already in your business plan: your long-range objectives and first year budgets and pro formas. While technically both your plans and your budgets began on the day you started operations, the reality of how they were developed differs from the technicality. In fact, as you worked through this process, your plans preceded your budgets. This is quite reasonable, since what you will spend and make are dependent on how you plan to go about bringing it off. The planning/budgeting cycle you develop should reflect this reality.

Consider the key points in your operating year. Are there real beginning points? In the toy business, for example, a real beginning might be the preparation for the New York Toy Fair. For a tax preparation service, the beginning might be January 1. No matter what your business, there will be some point in each year at which you take a deep breath and start all over again. That is the beginning of your operating cycle. At that point, your plans and budgets need to be ready to go.

For your plans and budgets to be ready to go, you need to have prepared them before that point in your year. You will need, therefore, to begin your planning phase early enough so that you have a comfortable amount of time in which to do your major annual planning *and* develop your next year's budgets and pro formas. There is danger in backing up too far, however. If you start too early, your budgets, particularly, are likely to be in need of revision before you really even start them.

The planning part of your planning/budgeting cycle tends to take longer than the budgeting part for two main reasons. First, while your budgets generally only cover a year, your plans should have a longer range component. The plan for the upcoming year, for example, should be viewed as a step toward a three- or five- or 10-year objective. Both the annual and the longer range plans should be specified in your planning cycle.

Second, the planning part of your planning/budgeting cycle is probably the best time for you to draw your staff into the goals and objectives for your business. Ask them for input into the plan development process. It need not be formal input. It can, in fact, be as informal as talking with your sales staff around the water fountain about how they think your products are moving in Peoria and elsewhere. However you do it, keep in mind that your employees are usually one step (at least) closer than you are to the real processes of your business. Their information can help you find the main problems and challenges or identify the main issues. Besides, it cannot hurt to ask. And it makes them feel more a real part of your operation.

In fact, if you want to tie the performance of your employees into your compensation and/or review systems, getting their formal input to your plans is a vital link in the chain. This part of your planning cycle would, thus, also be part of your management-by-objectives program (discussed in Chapter 10). Unless you do this, they will, quite properly, cry foul when you tell them that they will not get that raise because they did not meet the goals set for them. It has been shown time and again that such a "management-by-objectives" system only works when employees have some part in determining the goals that they will be required to meet. In any case, collecting information from the field and the shop floor tends to make the planning process a relatively lengthy one.

Budgeting, on the other hand, is relatively quick, once you know what the plan looks like. You simply repeat the processes you followed in building your initial budgets (Chapter 15). Obviously, as you did earlier, you may have to consider the financial tradeoffs among different ways of accomplishing some of your goals. Similarly, parts of your plan may have to be revised because of financial constraints that appear during the budgeting process. Leave time before the start of your operating year for such eventualities. Also, if you have set up a management-by-objectives-based compensation system, leave time to run both final plans and budgets past your key employees. After all, they are the ones who will make your plans and budgets work in the end.

REORIENTING PLANNING/BUDGETING FOCUS

As has been noted earlier in this book, most entrepreneurs tend to consider income statement items as their prime points for planning. This tends to foster a short-term approach to planning and budgeting since your income statement is inherently single-year and historical. Using an income statement focus for planning means, in short, that if you cannot see results within the year under scrutiny, you will not feel as if you are making long-term progress.

A balance sheet, on the other hand, reflects the financial condition of an ongoing business entity. It can be continuously improved. It highlights the underlying financial relationships in your business in a manner that cannot be matched by data on the income statement. Do you own, for example, an increasing share of your company? Have you improved the flexibility of the company through improved liquidity? Is the growth of assets or the growth of net worth adequate to let you know that you are moving toward your original goals? Using the balance sheet as a major planning focus is the only way to address such questions. Thus, including balance sheet considerations in your planning process permits you greater breadth and flexibility.

Neither statement should be ignored. Each obviously has value in the planning process. What we are dealing with here is a question of emphasis. The normal small business focus on "sales" and "return on sales" is important, but not at the expense, say, of carrying massive inventories to ensure that you will always have anything a customer might want. A planning and budgeting process that makes liberal use of balance sheet information ensures that there will be little danger of such a strategy being implemented.

As was noted earlier, think of the balance sheet as a directory of sources of cash and uses of cash. Make a specific part of your planning process a review of whether you believe that you are using your resources as well as possible. Do you, for example, really need all the equipment you have? Could you use your resources better by subcontracting a task and selling off the related equipment, using the cash in some more productive way in the business? Whatever the specific options available to your company, if your utilization is not what you consider to be optimum, you can change how you are using those resources over the next planning cycle or two. You will probably find that you save at least as much money in controlling resource use as you add to annual profit through sales increase planning.

MAJOR PLANNING ISSUES FOR NEW COMPANIES

Growth

There appears to be an ethic in small business circles these days that to succeed, you must grow. This is myth. In very few circumstances is it really true that you grow or you die. Perhaps the only current example is the personal computer software business. Here competition is creating a situation in which growth is required to support ever-increasing advertising and marketing costs required by a rapidly expanding market for personal computers. Under more normal circumstances, growth is an option—a choice, not a necessity.

That myth out of the way, growth becomes a planning issue. Do you want to grow? How do you want to do it? Is it feasible for you to do it that way? If you decide you want to remain at your present size, however, you cannot simply coast. No-growth has its own planning requirements. If your choice is not growth or death, it is certainly improvement or stagnation.

Growth is expensive if accomplished in the more standard ways. As you did when you put together the plans and the financing for your basic company, so do you have to operate when planning your growth. Your banker will expect, however, that you supply some of the startup funds for the expansion out of the earnings of the business. He will assume that if you cannot do so, your enterprise is not ready for growth or does not deserve to grow. He will be right.

The first requirement for growth, then, is that your existing business base be stable. It is neither wise nor likely for you to try to expand an operation as an alternative to going under. Two partners in a boat-building company tried to do just that. After a year of trying and failing to sell a single boat, while manufacturing and showing a number of them to dealers, they decided to expand into a retail operation to sell their boats. Their assumption was that the problem lay not in their boats, but in the vision of the people to whom they wanted to sell their boats. Despite the clear warnings of the distributors through whom boats were sold about what people would buy, these two went ahead and sank more money into backing their very own sinking ship. It was a classic example of not listening to what your market is telling you quite clearly. It was, as they found, a dangerous assumption. Their extension turned out to be throwing good money after bad.

The next requirement is a good plan for your growth or expansion. Try to grow in manageable increments. Working in small enough jumps permits you to move cautiously, using relatively small amounts of money and incorporating your size additions into your management control systems smoothly. Incorporating large chunks of new business often produces terminal indigestion, as has been the case with many successful companies that accomplished too many takeovers in too short a period.

In some circumstances, your growth will have to be too fast. This is bet-your-company time. In these circumstances, you just have to go ahead and do your best, hoping that you were right about growth in the first place. Fortunately, such circumstances are rare, even among large corporations. IBM did it in the mid-sixties when they brought out a new line of computers.

FEATURE 19.1
Diversification: It Doesn't Always Work

Frank Sands graduated from the Harvard Business School and into the family business—the $3 million operation of Sands, Taylor and Wood, makers of one product—King Arthur Flour. It was a successful old company. Within five years, Sands had managed to turn it into a $45 million company that was near bankruptcy. "The problem was me," he'll tell you straight out. But he has learned that bigger isn't necessarily better.

Within months of taking over the company, Sands began a buying binge. He bought a bakery ingredients supply company. He bought a manufacturer of fillings and toppings for bakery products. He bought another bakery supply manufacturer. He bought a maker of frozen bread dough. He also expanded some of the businesses he was buying, taking on the supply of 200 Dunkin Donuts shops across New England. Essentially, it appeared that since Frank Sands knew flour, he also could handle the other businesses—from dough to distribution.

As the losses began, Sands moved his family to rural Vermont. In attempts to regain control of the company, he brought in outside management and actually listened to them. "It was a nightmare," recalls William Walsh, brought in as the financial expert. "Most commodity vendors demanded prompt payment. Most assumed I was lying and would never pay them."

Frank Sands began the great sell-off, slowly shrinking the company back to its original core—the unbleached flour for which King Arthur was famous. "We're now reaffirming the qualities that distinguish us from the others," says Sands. It is back in the $3.5 million sales range, but it is profitable and has increased its area market share significantly.

Adapted from John Persinos, "The Once and Future King," *Inc.* magazine (March 1984): 54ff; and Sally Jacobs, "Profile," *New England Business* (May 7, 1984):92.

Citibank did it more recently when it moved into retail banking with a vengeance and with thousands of automatic teller machines (ATMs). The intent in both cases was to preempt the competition, forcing users to commit to one system before any similar systems got up and running. The odds on having to make such a move with your company are slim. If you think you really must, think again. If you still believe it to be true, we wish you luck.

Once you have decided to grow and figured out reasonable and financeable growth increments, your next step is to decide how to do it. Your choices are limited only by the nature of your business and your ingenuity. If yours is a manufacturing business, your issues include whether it is more advantageous to split your production between two or more sites or to move your entire operation to a single larger site. Alternatively, you might license your process and product in return for royalties, or subcontract your excess production requirements. The various choices have differing impacts on how much equipment you will have to duplicate or trade up and how much inventory you will have to add. An often unnoticed, but major, consideration is that additional management time, effort, and, possibly personnel will be required by your choices.

If yours is a retail business, you have similar options and tradeoffs regarding site, but an additional option exists if your strength lies in your operating methods. You might consider franchising your operation, making extra money from royalties rather than from actual operation. This option will provide you with exposure for your name and with extra money while adding little direct risk to you. The obvious key is that you have something to franchise that others think is worth buying into.

Diversification

Diversification is a special form of growth. Many of the financing issues are, of course, the same. Some other parts of your decision process will be distinctly different. The major underlying issue, assuming that you want to grow by diversification, is whether your diversification should be "related" or "unrelated." In English, the question is whether your new product should be similar to your old one(s) or very different.

The two schools of thought have been arguing for years. Those who favor related diversification point out the greater ease of managing and integrating the new product(s) into your existing operation. They also add that related diversifications can be home-grown fairly easily. Those who view unrelated diversification as a good idea point to the management approach of the conglomerates. They note that most unrelated diversification is done through purchases of existing businesses, complete with managements that know what they are doing. They add that if your industry is dying, related diversification is unlikely to save your company. Both sides have points, of course, or the argument would have long since been won. If you are considering growth by diversification, however, consider each set of points carefully.

Not Growing, but Doing Better Anyway

As we said, growth is an option, rarely a necessity. In some situations, not growing beyond a certain point is a positive decision. Examples of such businesses might be consulting companies whose owners refuse to let them get beyond their personal quality control limits or owners of crafts operations who believe that they should be personally involved in any project that will carry their names. The personal goals of other owners might involve using

FEATURE 19.2
But Some Diversifications Do...

Eastpak bags and packs are now a big-selling item in many stores. They represent a successful diversification of Eastern Canvas Products, originally mainly a military supplier of duffel bags, canteen covers and similar items. The company was begun by Monte Goldman in 1960. Its business was done on a low-bid basis. In 1976, Monte's son, Mark, joined the business and helped all that change.

Mark saw potential in commercial products for a largely student market. Monte let him give it a try—and decided to back Mark's vision with money and changes in the way the company did business. "I had to convince him we were doing something different," said Mark of his attempts to convince his dad that the company should spend money on fancy labels and packaging. "We had to build a brand name for people to associate quality with Eastpak—not just price."

The risks for the company were considerable. The new products cost $10,000 each to develop. The company was operating in an unfamiliar market. It would need an entirely different approach to sales, using a sales force rather than a bidding process. But the Goldmans already had capital and ties with their existing suppliers. They also had the employees with design skills. Most important of all, they were prepared to take some risk. To combat an industry-wide delivery problem, for example, Mark Goldman built Eastpak inventory so that he could guarantee shipment within a few days. The cost to Eastpak was $50,000. The response from customers? "This has amazed me."

In 1976, when Mark joined the company, it had $10 million in revenue. In 1983, volume was $21 million. $7 million of this revenue came from Eastpak.

Adapted from Johnnie Roberts, "Pentagon Supplier Finds Niche Selling Knapsacks to Students," *The Wall Street Journal* (September 17, 1984):31.

the business as a working base for other activities. In those cases, growth in the business might be either not required for, or detrimental to, the real objective.

Whatever the reason for the no-growth choice, it does not get you off the planning and control hooks. You can always improve operations in ways that accord with your goals or that bring in more profit without aggressive growth. These improvements also require planning and good goal-setting.

In these situations, you want to consider your planning process as a guide to places for potential improvement. You can even make it a game to squeeze out an extra percent in profit by, say, using your materials better or targeting your sales calls better. You are perfecting your control techniques, not trying to extend them to new or broader fields.

FEATURE 19.3
Slower Growth Is OK, Too

My view was that long-term profitable growth was more important than short-term market share. My theory is that you start out with a set of principles and beliefs, and from those you begin to develop business strategies that are consistent. My purpose in building a business is to create something that will live beyond me...so I needed to stick with some fundamental principles. They became both conditions of and constraints to our growth. We couldn't take on too broad a market, for example, because how, then, could we be perceived as product leaders? Trying to do too many things might require us to grow faster than our principles would allow us to grow.

Here's 3Com. It went public in the worst time in years, and its stock went up; it's acknowledged as being a very well-managed company; and it's growing at 300% a year, or whatever. And so you say, "Well, didn't you miss? You could have grown at 500% a year." Yeah, yeah...but I'm not embarrassed to go to my investors and say that we grew from $4.7 million to $16.7 million this year...and we had 15% operating profit in doing so. Maybe there's some lost opportunity, but I find it hard to believe that it's worth the risk.

I don't want to take the [all-or-nothing] risk as an entrepreneur. I just don't think it's worth it. The reason I don't is that a more conservative, lower-flying, more controlled growth, more wait-and-see approach has a higher probability of success. I believe it will get you there in the end.

From "Growing Steady" by Tom Richman. Reprinted with permission, *Inc.* magazine, September, 1984. Copyright © 1984 by *Inc.* Publishing Company, 38 Commercial Wharf, Boston, MA 02110.

The real point here is that once you actually open your doors, your work has just begun. Assuming that you are like most people, unless you set goals for yourself, you will get sloppy and stagnate. If you let that happen to your business, you may wake up one day and find it in major difficulty. Without the appropriate operating, planning, and control systems, you will not know until it is too late. Continual adjustment and fine-tuning of your operation—whether geared toward growth or not—at least ensures a marginal amount of feedback. You may also simply enjoy a bit of tinkering.

CONTINGENCY PLANNING

Whether you are planning for growth, for diversification, or for steady-state operations, a significant part of your planning energy should be directed toward developing plans for what to do when the assumptions underlying your initial plan are not working out—contingency planning. What do you do if...?

We began discussion of this broad topic under a number of previous headings. It was discussed as early as the initial market survey when we suggested that you see what would happen to your estimates if you were off x percent in either direction. The same "bracketing" technique was applied to critical estimates in developing your pro forma financial statements. Contingency planning is simply a broader version of the same approach applied to what you expect to happen to your business as a whole.

Start by looking at your planning format (Figure 19.1). Target the critical pieces of the plan. Then think the unthinkable. What can go wrong? For each way you have found that your plan can go awry or be sidetracked, determine how likely you believe that scenario is. For each scenario you think has good potential for wrecking your main plan, develop a counterplan. When you have run through this process for the major and reasonably likely plan-destroyers, you have a set of contingency plans.

Assume, for example, that your goal for the remainder of this year is to increase sales of your widgets by 5 percent. The manufacturers to whom you sell your widgets are not expected to grow this year, so your sales increase will have to be taken from other widget manufacturers. Your plan is to offer a special introductory volume price to orders of more than a thousand widgets. Since you have a backlog of unshipped widgets, you can also promise delivery within a week anywhere in the country.

Your intent is to shift some large widget buyers from the competition to your new widget line. If you can pull it off, this strategy will not only increase your sales, but also will decrease your shipping costs and generally ease your paper flow. Since your large accounts are also your better payers, you expect this strategy to improve your collections pattern as well.

This looks like a pretty solid plan. Now you get to work on it. What can go wrong? The two items below are only two possibilities. If this were really your business, you could undoubtedly be more creative.

First: Are you really expecting your competitors to sit still for this? Since you are so small, you may have some hope that your 5 percent increase is such a miniscule amount for them that they will not even notice you are taking sales from them. Possible, but how likely? What if your competitors, or only one or two of them, match your price and delivery promises? You have a number of options, each with advantages and disadvantages.

1. You can take current orders and end the promotion as soon as you gracefully can.
2. You can keep the promotion going on the grounds that you are showing better results in lower costs and improved collections. This will work if these effects occur and your special prices are not too low.
3. You could reduce your price still further. This is an option if you believe that you are better able financially to take the required level of drain than are your competitors.

4. If you believed that it was a real selling point and if you knew that your competitors had no finished goods inventory, you could offer even faster delivery times. This would work only until you worked off your own excess inventory.

Second: Your slow payers may consolidate their orders and still not pay on time. Under this scenario, you would not really be gaining sales, but rather shifting them. Moreover, rather than shortening your receivables, they would lengthen. You believe this to be a good possibility. Should this occur, you might:

1. Fill current orders and end the promotion as soon as possible.
2. Tighten your collections process and put some teeth in it by planning liberal use of a collection agency and your lawyer.
3. Modify the qualifications for your "special offer" to exclude the potential problems. You might, perhaps, limit the promotion to new customers of your "new" line. Or you might refuse to permit customers with outstanding receivables to participate. You would, of course, check any such limitations with your lawyer.

Please note that this last option shows an added benefit to contingency planning. By thinking through how your plan is likely to be thwarted or derailed, you might come upon ways to improve the original plan to make derailment less likely. Since planning is basically a process of making successive improvements, contingency planning fits right into the process.

As you can see, the basic idea is to be prepared for a next move no matter what happens. Obviously, you will not always have anticipated the specific difficulty with whatever plan you are following, but contingency planning becomes a habit of mind. After a number of structured passes through your plans, you will automatically begin to think in strategic alternatives. One of your basic planning considerations will become maximizing options, a notion that underlies contingency planning. In short, once you start doing contingency planning, you will enjoy a sense of readiness for anything that you will find difficult to give up. It will give you the confidence to test your limits and to strengthen your company. That level of confidence is especially important in developing a successful enterprise.

SUMMARY

One of the problems consistently associated with small business failures is the lack of planning of so many entrepreneurs. Even those who develop good initial business plans (because their financing plans required them) often stop all planning activities once they actually open up shop. The standard excuses include: lack of time, lack of effective control over the forces that influence the

FEATURE 19.4
And If You Want to Sell Your Business...

Their dad started the business 50 years earlier in the back yard. The two sons recently sold it off to a conglomerate for an estimated $75–100 million.

There are excellent reasons for wanting to sell a company. Sometimes, in fact, an eventual sale may be the purpose in building the company in the first place. In the case of Lender's Bagel Bakery's sale to Kraft, the sale was an emotional struggle. "It's not easy to back out of something that has been such a dominant part of your life."

The decision for Murray and Marvin Lender came when they realized that their seven-day, ten-hour-a-day work style would handicap the business and/or strain their personal lives beyond repair. "We're just not smart enough to develop a professional management style," says Murray. "We decided, based on that, that we're probably better off getting out. Better off personally, better off for our families, better off for the business, the product and the employees. There's no question that at one point or another the growth of the company would have [been] curtailed because it was much too personalized."

"I have a philosophy about business," Murray continues. "I don't think you *can* contain the growth of something if there's a potential in the marketplace without receding. You either move ahead or go backward. If you don't develop it, someone else will." The Lenders have found someone who can capitalize on that market potential for them—using the Lender name. After all, who better than the foremost cream-cheese maker?

The family will keep two retail outlets, operating under the name of H. Lender and Sons. "We will still have something with the Lender name on it."

From "The Lender's Bagel Leaves Family Phase with Sale to Kraft" by William Donovan, September 3, 1984, p. 63. Reprinted with permission of *New England Business*.

business, and the "need" for secrecy. Often the real reasons include plain laziness and the difficulty of committing to performance goals.

Another real problem, addressed in this chapter, is the lack of understanding about how to plan. The first key step in planning for an ongoing operation is making the time to plan on a regular basis in a quiet, comfortable place. The second step is to structure a format that helps you consider all the aspects of your business, setting specific, quantifiable, measurable, and time-bounded goals in each major area. The final step in plan development is to feed your new or adjusted plan into your pro forma financial statements and your budgeting documents.

It is helpful also to develop a planning/budgeting cycle based on your real operating year. In this process, planning should lead budgeting. Particularly if you tie compensation to meeting goals, your key employees should participate to some degree in your planning process. Both planning and budgeting should be complete by the time your year begins (whether or not it matches your tax year).

Key planning issues for new, smaller companies are often issues of growth and diversification. Taking steps to accomplish either is a matter of choice. Should you choose to pursue either course, the key to success is in the planning. You will want to move slowly, adding in manageable increments so that your systems are not overwhelmed. Your planning process for such inclusions should cover how you intend to finance them and how you intend to integrate them into your basic business.

Finally, planning in an ongoing business includes contingency planning. This is the process by which you anticipate major potential problems and develop your responses before the problems actually arise. If you are really good (and lucky), you may never have to adopt a contingency plan. If, however, you ever face one of those problems you anticipated in the planning phase, the speed of your response and the flexibility of your position will dazzle the opposition.

FOR YOU TO CONSIDER

1. Why should owners of small businesses bother to plan once they get their shows on the road? Discuss two reasons why they so often do not do so.
2. Discuss one way of minimizing the problem of committing to performance goals.
3. Define "firefighting" and discuss its effect on planning.
4. Why are the right time and place so important to good planning? How do you arrange such times and places?
5. What are two critical characteristics of a useful goal or objective? Why?
6. Why do you need to do monthly planning and reviews if you have structured an annual planning/budgeting cycle?
7. How might your compensation program affect and be affected by your planning process?
8. Why should you ensure that balance sheet information is considered in your planning process?
9. Discuss growth as a planning issue for small businesses.
10. What is contingency planning, and why is it important in small company planning?

CASES FOR PART 8

SALLY JONES AND "NEIGHBORS"

Sally and Janice knew that the key to managing any restaurant, particularly one like "Jack's Place," with a history of employee pilferage, would hinge on their ability to develop a system to control three main areas of the business: food inventory, beverage inventory, and cash. While final decisions had not been made about whether to buy "Jack's Place," the women knew that a well-designed system could be operated in any restaurant with the basic characteristics of the one they wanted to operate. They decided to at least outline the requirements and possible pitfalls of a working control system for their prospective restaurant.

They knew that to be really effective, the various parts of their control system would have to interlock. That is, they thought that a discrepancy in one area ought to sound figurative warning bells in other parts of the system. Such interlocks would make pilferage inherently more difficult, since more than one system would have to be altered to cover any potential problem. They realized that the point of interlock should be their financial records, but they were unsure as to how to structure a report that would give them the data they would need to tell whether they had a problem. With this background, they decided to tackle the three areas one at a time.

Beverage inventory. One or the other of them would have to be the person to place orders with wholesalers and to count incoming deliveries. Also, it was common practice in their business to require that their bartender retain empties for later counts and cross-checks. Physical counts of beverage inventories were done as often as once a week. Beyond this, the two did not know how controls could be placed on their beverage inventory. They did know that losses in this area had brought down many an eating and drinking place.

Food inventories. Here too, the two women knew how to handle the ordering and physical movement of food. Early in their planning, they had determined that one of them would handle ordering and deliveries. Their menu pricing would be pegged to a controlled portion size, but as yet they had developed no method for ensuring that portion sizes were, in fact, controlled. They were also concerned about waiting staff giving away free meals or charging less than the menu price using any of a number of fairly standard dodges.

Cash. Sally and Janice expected that most of their business would be done on a cash basis. This would prove very tempting to any non-owner cashier. While each owner expected to take a tour at the cash register, they knew that another person would often be handling the cash. They intended, of course, to get a cash register that would do an internal tally of the amount of cash that should be in it each day. They also intended to implement a check control system to keep a tally of the food ordered and billed for by their service staff (including the bar checks). They wondered whether these steps would be adequate to protect the cash moving through their restaurant.

1. Are there any areas of Sally's and Janice's restaurant that will need special controls that the two have not targeted? If you think there are, what are they, and why do you believe them to be critical?
2. Invent a simple way to circumvent each of the specific controls mentioned by Sally and Janice in each of the three relevant areas. Develop additional approaches for Sally and Janice to maintaining control of their beverage and food inventories and cash that would prevent you from doing what you just "planned."
3. Develop and/or explain how the control that you and Sally and Janice have developed will tie into the accounting and financial systems of the restaurant. Define the minimum amount of data that the owners would have to look at to determine whether or not they had a pilferage or theft problem in these key areas.

ROB KING AND "KING FINANCIAL"

Rob King was still committed to going ahead with King Financial. He knew, from his years in business and his research in small business, that keeping track of his operation would be critical to its success. He therefore decided to build the controls and data collection mechanisms for King Financial even before he opened its doors.

Rob knew that certain things would be critical to staying in business and to expanding. He also wanted to be able to tell when it would become reasonable for him to hire additional consultants and to begin to have real clerical personnel. At some point, he would also need a proper office and a receptionist. He had seen and heard about too many companies that had gone down the tubes because they added people and cost before the business itself was able to support them. He had vowed that that, at least, would not be his downfall.

Thus, he began to list the items that he would need to keep track of in order to hear what his business data was telling him. He had already arranged to have another professional look at his financial results on a quarterly basis, and to assist in budget-to-actual comparisons, so what he was after now would really be approaches to tracking operational data. His list of important items to track looked as follows:

1. Billable hours. This would be the cornerstone item that would tell him how well he was doing at selling his services.
2. Business development time. This, along with the billable hours, would tell him how well his sales efforts were producing work for the company.
3. Consulting time to secretarial/clerical time. He would need to track this because his expense estimates were based on a 3:1 ratio here. If this ratio

did not hold true, he would have to adjust his cost estimates. Moreover, this figure, coupled with his billable hours, would tell him immediately when it would be cost-effective to hire a typist on a full-time basis.

4. Work turned away. He knew that it would be prudent to shift work not in his specialty to another independent consultant. If enough of such work came in any particular specialty area, however, it might be prudent to add a person with that specialty. Thus, requests for project assistance had to be tracked—even if they did not result in direct work for King Financial.

While Rob King did not particularly want to build an empire, he definitely wanted to grow. He had figured out that the best way to make money in consulting was on the markup of employee work—where the one-third/one-third/one-third approach could come into play more. He also certainly would not mind becoming big enough to show Helm a thing or two about success. Thus, while growth was not an immediate requirement, he wanted to be ready when King Financial was ready.

1. Develop a set of forms that Rob King could use to track the operational components of his business. Be very clear about what each form is intended to do and why each form is necessary.
2. For each form you developed, describe how it will interlock with financial data shown on the company's financial statements.
3. What should Rob be looking for in each form or form summary that will tell him when King Financial is ready to grow?

DANIELLE MACKIE AND "DANIELLE DESIGNS IN CERAMICS"

As Danielle Mackie got more deeply involved with the details of her prospective business life, she realized that constant worrying about these details would detract from her performance as an artist. It would divert her mind from the work itself, and it would steal time away from her production and creative efforts. This could not be permitted to happen. She knew that the only way to avoid the constant worry was to develop a system that took care of most of the critical details virtually automatically—and still let her know when there was likely to be a problem.

She would, of course, track her performance against her monthly projections and budgets, just as they taught her in her administration courses. But she knew that she would need additional control and monitoring systems, particularly for the time when she would hire employees. She figured that that change in her work would be difficult enough without having to design and implement new systems. She wanted them to be second nature to her by the time expansion became an issue.

She was aware of some of the things she would need to watch carefully—and more frequently and in greater detail than her monthly financial review would permit. The first cluster of issues centered on her raw materials inventories and her use thereof. The materials themselves represented a major out-of-pocket cost for her. She had both to maintain adequate supplies and to track their use. Appropriate use of these materials would depend on at least three factors: first, the care with which she apportioned and used them; second, the dried pieces that she determined were not up to her aesthetic or quality standards; and, third, the proportion of worked pieces that were broken in the firing process. In short—care, quality, and scrap. She needed to design a simple tracking system that would tell her whether she was using too much material for the level of actual salable work produced. This same system also ought to tell her when she needed to reorder material. She wanted to be able to include in the system any new employees that she might hire in the future.

A second major cost category for Danni would be the cost of electricity. This would be tied to her use of the kiln and the wheel. Her main concern was the efficient use of the capacity of her admittedly small kiln, since the cost of firing a load would be high. She needed a simple way of tracking kiln utilization and loads in relation to her salable production. She would also want to be able to track the efficiency of any employee in this area.

Finally, while she had estimated the amounts of time she would spend on each piece and each function in her business, her estimates did not make her feel particularly comfortable. She needed to know when items or processes or functions were taking longer or shorter than her estimates. In addition to the obvious pricing implications of this tracking system, Danielle expected to use it as a means of encouraging self-discipline. When she hired employees, she also wanted to be able to see how they were spending their time in the production process.

She also was considering the (successful) future of her business. She knew that there would come a point at which it would make sense to take on an assistant and/or to pay a sales representative to market her pieces. However, she had little idea how to tell when those points arrived or were approaching. Like her parents, though, Danni believed in being prepared for impending change. Therefore, she was trying to develop an approach to deciding when to make such additions and changes in her business.

1. Has Danielle Mackie left out any areas in which you believe she really needs continuous monitoring systems? If so, list them and explain why you believe each of them should be added to her list.
2. Design simple monitoring systems for:
    a. Her inventory and production
    b. Her electricity and capacity utilization
    c. Her time/function issue
    d. Any other items you listed in 1, above
   In each case, describe how your system is to be used, why it is likely to work, and how Mackie will know whether she has or is approaching a problem.
3. Given the monitoring systems you just developed, how should Danielle

Mackie know when she needs to add staff and/or dispense with her own marketing duties? In which order might she take these actions, given what you know about Danielle and her proposed business? Why do you think so?

ED JAMES AND "OAK TREE BOOKS"

Ed James knew that the absolutely critical thing to keep track of in the bookstore business was inventory. It was the largest single expense of the business, and it also drove turnover, which produced profit for the store. He had to develop a system that would work if he was going to succeed in this business.

The inventory control practices of the industry in general left a great deal to be desired. In his research, Ed found that more than half the independent bookstore owners used an "eyeball" method of inventory control—not a control at all, to Ed's mind. Other bookstores tracked sales by making notations about what was sold or by removing control tags or slips from books as they were sold. Still others did periodic physical inventories of books on hand. Less than 10 percent of independent stores used any type of computerized inventory control method. Ed theorized that the reason had to do with the initial expense of the equipment and the costs of (and, perhaps, abilities involved in) getting a good system into operation.

Ed knew what he wanted his inventory control system to do, but he was perplexed about how to go about getting it done. First, he obviously needed to know how much he had sold and how specific titles or items were selling so that he could maintain adequate, appropriate stock. Because of "shrinkage" (the 1.5 percent lost to thieves, errors, and miscounts), he would naturally run periodic physical inventories. Second, he wanted to tag his sales by groups so that he could see, for example, whether his line of wrapping papers or note papers was paying its way and making money for him. He was particularly interested in developing a system that would tell him how Acorn was doing in relation to its costs to him. Finally, he wanted to use his inventory control system to fine-tune his purchasing so that he could keep turnover high and minimize his investment in inventories.

Ed realized that he was going into what was largely a cash business. Bookstores in his projected size range did, on average, more than 80 percent of their business on a cash basis. He also knew that it would be impractical for him to be the only staff member with access to the cash register—particularly since he was still considering a separate register for Acorn. After all, he thought, he planned to be open some 60 hours a week, and it would be virtually impossible for him to be there every minute of every hour. That meant that at least one other person would have access to the cash drawers. That meant, to Ed James, that he'd better develop some approach to controlling the cash that came into and went out of the store itself. "It's not that I don't trust that nice white-haired retired teacher I'm going to hire," he commented. "But why create temptations? And, besides, what about the part-time youngsters who will be helping in Acorn?"

As part of his control system, Ed intended to use the kind of registers that provided a continuous internal tape, duplicating the transactions on the tape that was normally torn off and given to the customer. He knew that he should tie his cash control system into his inventory control system and also into his method for handling bank deposits and reconciliations. He was unsure, however, about how they should fit and about what would be a simple yet effective approach to the entire cash issue.

1. Develop an inventory control approach for Ed James that will fulfill his requirements. Describe how your approach meets each stated requirement. Does he need for his inventory control system to accomplish anything other than those things he has stated as needs? If so, what should he add, and how would you suggest he add them to the system you just outlined?
2. Develop an approach to controlling the actual cash coming into Oak Tree Books (and Acorn). How does your recommended approach meet Ed's needs for his bookstore?
3. Aside from standard financial statement analysis and the two control systems you developed earlier, does Ed James need to implement any other major controls? If so, what are they, and what should he do about them?

APPENDIXES

A   Suggested Business Plan Outline

B   Using Microcomputers in Your
    Small Business

Appendix A. Business Plan Outline

PREFACE

1. What do you want your lifestyle to be like in ten years?
2. What do you want to get out of your business?
3. What do you expect to have to put into your business?
4. How does your choice of business fit these desires?

I. The Business
   A. What will your business do? What are its objectives?
   B. What are the critical success factors in this field?
   C. What major policies will make your business a success?
   D. What is your general strategic approach to making it work?

II. Legal Form and Organization
   A. What will be the legal form of the business?
   1. Why did you choose this form?
   2. Tax implications of your choice of form?
   3. Financial and management participation in your business?
   B. How will the business be organized?
   1. Organization charts (initial, Years 3, 5)
   2. For the major positions in your company:
   a. What kind(s) of skills, characteristics do you need?
   b. How will you find, attract, retain such people?

III. Your Market
   A. Target
   1. How large is your target market and how is it defined?
   2. How many competitors? Who are the main ones? Why?
   3. What will be your competitive edge?
   B. Selling your product/service
   1. How will you attract your target market?
   2. How will your product/service reach them?
   C. What volumes do you need to make your business work?
   1. What unit and dollar sales is this for Years 1, 3, 5?

2. What is your pricing policy and how will it support its aims?
3. What share of relevant market does this level represent?

IV. Operations
    A. Production
        1. Equipment requirements, including cost, replacement, maintenance, depreciation
        2. Space and utility requirements (initial, Years 3, 5)
        3. Technological and production factors (if appropriate)
        4. Direct costs of production
    B. Budgets and control
        1. Opening and Year 1 balance sheet
        2. Detailed pro forma income statements (Years 1, 3, 5)
        3. Monthly cash budget (Year 1)

V. Financing
    A. How much money do you need to begin and operate this business?
    B. When do you need it? Where will you get it? Cost?
    C. Additional major financing: when needed? from where?

VI. Evaluation
    A. Frequency and criteria for evaluation? Cost? Use of results?
    B. Contingency plans: What will you do when your results differ from your projections? What differences (continuing for how long) will you consider serious?

Appendix B. Using Microcomputers in Your Small Business

GIGO: Garbage In, Garbage Out.

At the beginning of 1985, *Business Week* reported that almost 30 percent of all smaller companies were using microcomputers. Over the last five years, these micros have begun to take over many of the tedious functions involved in starting and running a business. They are particularly useful in performing repetitive tasks—doing payrolls, for example—and in keeping track of large numbers of things, as is necessary in inventory control.

For those of us who worked in computer-related fields in the mid-1960s, today's machines are truly mind-boggling. In the mid-sixties, a really large computer could store 190,000 (190K) units of information. And they were *giant.* Even those with less capacity took up entire rooms. They demanded raised flooring to handle all the special wiring. They required special air conditioning units. In the truest sense of the word, they were awesome.

Today, on a regular desk in my regular office sits a microcomputer with a storage capacity of 256K. No special anything. He is affectionately known as "Charlie." If I wanted to do so, I could make an addition that would let him handle more than 20 million units of information (20 megabytes or "megs"). Another addition would let him talk over regular telephone lines with his relatives—large or small—anywhere there was another phone hookup. He could still sit on my desk.

These microcomputers offer a manager like you the ability to extend your time and your abilities. They can be used to keep records, manipulate data, perform analyses, prepare reports, make projections, draw pictures. And they can do it faster and more accurately than you could on your own. In short, if you are willing to invest the money and the time to learn, you can use micros to help you with almost anything.

You can also manage to create utter confusion and egregious error in your operation. As the tag line goes, "To err is human, but to really mess up, you need a computer."

This appendix is not intended to turn you into a computer wizard. It is intended to introduce you to ways in which microcomputers might be of use in your company—and to some of the recognized problems they raise for companies. Brand names are not discussed, but general characteristics are. How computers work or how to program them are also not discussed. My sole purpose is to let you know what's out there (at least as of 1985) and how you might best take advantage of the availability.

This appendix also stresses that computers are wholly logical machines. No matter how much I personalize "Charlie," he will do only exactly what I tell him to do—nothing more, nothing less. If I tell him to do something wrong, but do-able, he will do it anyway. If I tell him in the wrong way, he will not do anything at all.

This is an extremely important point about computers because the tendency is to believe, almost without question, what a computer prints out or shows you on the screen. It is wise to remember, however, that what comes out is only as good as what went in (GIGO). If you feed it incorrect numbers or tell it to do the wrong things with those numbers, your "answers" could spell disaster. Thus, when you finally decide that a computer will be able to help you, always review the methods used to arrive at the answers you get and always test the answers for reasonableness.

SOFTWARE

Software is the item that gives instructions to your computer (specifically, to its operating system) about what to do with the data you feed it. If you wanted to, you could learn a programming language appropriate to your machine and build your own software. Most of us simply buy software packages, however—for two reasons. First, our objective is using the function, not programming computers. Second, for most purposes, other people have developed software that is more than adequate for our needs.

This section takes a look at the types of software readily available for the kinds of microcomputers generally used in small businesses. While beginning with the software rather than the hardware (the computer and peripheral equipment) itself may seem backwards, it really makes sense to do things in this order. No computer does all things equally well. No computer runs all the software that exists. In short, to a great extent, your choice of hardware should be dictated by the kinds of things you intend to do with it.

Software for most microcomputers comes on diskettes with extensive manuals explaining how to use the various functions provided. Two key items to consider when buying software are the actual functions and the ease of using those functions. While the sales staff of your local computer store may be helpful, the vast number of available products makes it impossible for them to know every product equally well. (Also, it is a better deal for them to sell the higher margin products.) Thus, in addition to talking with these salespeople, it is recommended that you find other users and talk with them about how they use the piece of software and how easy it is to use. We also recommend that you find a computer store that will let you try out a program you are seriously considering so that you can see for yourself how well it handles what you need it to do and how easy it is to operate.

There is some advantage to buying a package that has been used by numbers of people over a (relatively) long period of time. Most packages, particularly the more sophisticated ones, are difficult to develop and to operate. Choosing one that is "old" ensures that the "bugs" have already been worked out and that there are numbers of users around who can tell you about the package and help you with its application to your particular problems. While a new package may have a few additional bells and whistles, it may cause you a great deal of trouble.

I recall, particularly, a user who was seeking the absolutely perfect word processing software. She was a veteran of mainframe computers (the large kind that the big companies use), so she knew what she was doing. Through talking with salespeople, she found a program still in development for her system. It sounded perfect for her requirements. As soon as it began to be sold, she bought a copy and tried to work with it. It proved to be impossible. She spent hours on the phone with the software developers, trying to make it do what it had been intended to do. She lost data and text trying to use it. She finally gave it up entirely, having spent dollars and hours she did not have in the process. She then purchased a more standard package.

Software for microcomputers can be categorized into five main groups: special purpose programs, spreadsheets, word processors, databases, and integrated software. Each is described briefly below, along with notes about potential uses in your business.

Special Purpose Software

This group of programs includes those specially developed for smaller companies. They often include such applications as general ledger, accounts receivable and payable, payroll, inventory, and other functions that most smaller companies could computerize. Each is a separate software unit, but, if the pieces come from a single software maker, they are likely to be designed to work together. In fact, the existence of linkages among functions—particularly linkages into an accounting general ledger system—should be a key criterion of your search for your special purpose software.

If your business has or will have a fairly complicated inventory control problem or extensive receivables, a stand-alone software package to address that particular application might be appropriate for you. If you think that this is the way for you to go, check the packages you are considering for their fit with the methods you have already developed or are now using. Consider the difficulty of translating your current approach into the one(s) required by the packages. If your method has not yet been developed, consider how difficult it would be for you to build your methods to feed these packages the required data in the necessary ways.

The point here is that the requirements of packaged special purpose software may leave little room for flexibility in how you structure the corresponding function in your business. Thus, in addition to the standard questions about ease of use, you will also want to consider the relative ease of feeding any system you purchase. The flexibility of a given package may become a prime consideration for an owner who has not yet determined exactly what his or her company will need as it grows or changes.

In general, some of the issues you should consider in evaluating special purpose programs include:

- The number of items it will handle. How many inventory parts will an inventory control system handle, for example? How many employees will the payroll system cover? How many different accounts will a receivables package deal with?
- The number of ways it will produce information for you. Can you get receivables by age, for example? By dollar volume? By product? By purchaser? Will it let you examine all the aspects you may want to consider?
- Whether it will provide all the information you will want. Can you get the carrying costs for various inventory items, for example? Can the payroll system handle as many benefit options as you intend to have—not just today, but as your company grows?

As you can see, particularly for a company that is still defining itself and that is likely to grow, the flexibility of the software you purchase today may be critical to the value of the package to you in the future. Rather than changing software packages as you grow, a process that can involve considerable changeover time, effort, and money, you might want to purchase packages you can "grow into" or ones that are flexible enough to accommodate your growth.

Spreadsheets

A spreadsheet program looks very much like the buff or green accounting paper that auditors and other number-crunchers use with their pencils. The program creates a grid or matrix. Into each cell of the grid, you can place a number or a formula relating to some other cell(s) of the grid. The computer can be told to store your grid, and can recall and alter it whenever you need to do so. If you want to test an assumption or change a piece of data, the spreadsheet program will automatically recalculate all the other items that you have linked to it through the formulae.

Suppose, for example, you decided that you wanted to project an income statement for your company for the next five years. In very simple form, you expected your first year to look as follows.

	A	*B*	*C*
1		*Year 1*	*Year 2*
2	Sales	$100,000	
3	Cost-of-Goods-Sold	55,000	
4	Gross Margin	45,000	
5	Operating Expenses	40,000	
6	Net Income	5,000	

Now, suppose you expected your sales to grow at the rate of 10 percent per year, your COGS to grow at 12 percent per year, and your operating expenses to grow at only 8 percent per year. You could simply enter in column C the formula for figuring out the numbers—in this case, (cell) B2 times 1.10 for cell C2, B3 times 1.12 for cell C3, and B5 times 1.08 for C5. If you also set up Row 4 as Row 2 minus Row 3, and Row 6 as Row 4 minus Row 5, your second year would calculate itself as soon as you fed data into column B. The program would hold the formulae and would show you the number on the screen and/or in a printout (hard copy).

	A	*B*	*C*
1		*Year 1*	*Year 2*
2	Sales	$100,000	+B2 × 1.10
3	Cost-of-Goods-Sold	55,000	+B3 × 1.12
4	Gross Margin	45,000	+C2 − C3
5	Operating Expenses	40,000	+B5 × 1.08
6	Net Income	5,000	+C4 − C5

If you are working with only this very simple income statement, you may wonder why you should go to all this trouble when your handy little calculator will work just fine. And, in fact, if you are working only with items as simple as this, you probably do not need spreadsheet software to help you. But consider the benefit you would just have created had your statement been really complex. Suppose it becomes clear to you that your first year sales are not going to make the $100,000 you projected. Using the spreadsheet, and assuming that the relationships you expected still appear to be valid, all you would need to do is enter the new sales figure and the entire projection could be recalculated at the touch of a few computer keys. Alternatively, of course, you could retain the original numbers and alter the formulae representing the relationships.

An additional use of spreadsheets is to test the sensitivity of your projections. The speed and ease of recalculation, once you have structured the underlying formulae, make it easy to test a larger number of possibilities than you could reasonably do yourself by hand. Another use can be to perform comparisons between or among sets of data. You might, for example, compare your data against industry averages, build common size statements, do year-to-year comparisons of your own data. In short, you can use spreadsheet programs to assist you in your own financial analysis.

In addition to this rapid recalculation function, many spreadsheet programs also include the ability to create graphs from the data in the grids. Particularly if you are a person who finds it easier to see what is going on by looking at a graph than by scanning columns of numbers, this function of a spreadsheet program can be of significant value. It also may be important if you intend to use your data to make reports to others.

Databases

The joys of database programs lie in their ability to organize and store data and to retrieve the data by categories or groups. Many of them also perform counts of specific items and can be structured to perform various analyses of the data stored in them. Some can also match files and report on matches.

Consider a problem. You have a large sales staff, each member of which makes call reports on both successful and unsuccessful calls. You want to know which of your salespeople have been most productive, as measured by their "hit rates" over the last quarter. Assuming you have been entering their calls by salesperson, by date, and by result, you can tell your database to count calls by salesperson and by time period and to figure the ratio of "yes" responses to "no" responses. You can then let it rank order salespeople by hit rate. Had you also added size of order to your database, you would have a tool for analyzing whether large orders appear to take more calls than small ones or whether some salespeople have particularly high or low hit rates on large orders. Once you know these kinds of things, you can begin to restructure or change emphasis to help you get the kinds of sales you would prefer to service. Your database makes the collection and manipulation of the information almost effortless. (The conclusions and what needs to be done about them are still up to you.)

In addition to the analytic possibilities database managers offer, they are also particularly useful in maintaining continuing records. Given their ability to track specific kinds of information, database programs are often used as the basis for inventory control systems. You can use them to keep perpetual inventory records. You can set some of them up to alert you if inventory falls below some predetermined minimum. They are also often used to build payroll records and reporting systems, and to maintain personnel, manufacturing, and/or service records. In short, they can be helpful in any area of your company that requires you to maintain growing amounts of data—even if you do not wish to perform complex analyses using that data.

Depending on the particular software package, your database operations can be as sophisticated as you would care to make them. Some even offer very powerful and flexible programming functions for people who care to learn how to use and apply them.

Word Processors

Word processors turn your computer into a highly sophisticated typewriter with numerous editing capabilities. Most of the major word processing packages also include the ability to perform mailing list functions. Some include spelling checking functions or offer dictionary functions at a small additional cost.

Suppose you maintain a customer list and you want to send a personalized letter to each of your customers. With a good word processing program, there is no problem. You can develop your mailing piece, leaving appropriate codes in the places you wish personalization. You then simply tell your computer to match the letter with the list and you sit back and watch the "personal" letters roll off your printer. It will also print envelopes from your list. (Unfortunately, they have not yet figured out how to get a micro to fold and stuff envelopes.)

For many small small businesses, a word processor can eliminate the need for a full-time secretary. Drafts can be typed into the machine as easily as written down. Editing, even moving entire paragraphs, can be done quickly on screen. If you have a spelling checker, it will even pick out the typographical errors for you before you print (unless, of course, your typo happens to be a perfectly good word itself. Word processors do not read for context). The printer then produces clean copy faster and with fewer errors than any secretary known to man or woman.

Are you likely to be using a lot of "boilerplate"—paragraphs that you would normally use again and again in letters, proposals, or contracts? Most word processors can save you the bother of ever typing them again. They let you read material from an existing file into your present project. If you wanted to do so, you could create a number of stock paragraphs and create entire letters or proposals out of them. Alternatively, if you write letters in response to often-repeated questions, entire "canned" letters might be your answer. Rather than dictating or typing a new letter each time, you could simply call up Letter Number 3, add the new name and address, and ship it out.

As you can see, if you are going to use a computer for anything at all, a word processing package will probably be a useful addition.

Integrated Software

Integrated software packages generally combine the three generic types of software—spreadsheets, databases, and word processors—into one package that is intended to work together as a unit. At this time, integrated packages are still undergoing development and change. The industry is divided over whether the ease of moving data and items among the various functions is outweighed by the loss of flexibility in each piece that may be inherent in this kind of software.

Many of the stand-alone software programs permit some transferability of data with some other programs. The key is the underlying code in which the program stores its data. If it stores in ASCII, a standard code, and in appropriate formats, probably some transferability is possible. If it does not, there is no chance.

The advantage of transferability is that it allows you to incorporate data from, say, a spreadsheet directly into a report that you are developing on your word processing software. Or, you might want to create a report using your database and then incorporate it or part of it into the same report. While in some cases this can be done with stand-alone software packages, it is easy with an integrated package. In fact, they are designed to facilitate this process.

Integrated packages also generally offer the ability to "window" your computer screen. This means that you could actually look at a graph generated by your spreadsheet/graphics program at the same time you were writing about it using the word processing portion of the package. This feature is unavailable using stand-alone programs, even compatible ones.

General Tips on Evaluating Software

As you can see, consideration of the generic kinds of software packages available reveals numerous options and requires numerous choices on the part of a potential user. Here, as in other parts of your business planning, it is wise to have a good idea of what you want to do before you proceed to do it. In particular, you will want to pay attention to certain factors that can make your use of a specific package easier or more difficult. Some—flexibility, trans-ferability of data, and actual functions, for example—have already been mentioned. Others include:

- Size. A program takes up space in your computer's memory. The space taken up by the program cannot be used for your data or your text. Thus, you will need to pay careful attention to the specifications a software package gives regarding the capacities and peripheral equipment required of the computer intended to run it.
- Amount the software itself can handle. Some word processing software has limitations on the length of a single piece of text that it can work with, for example. You need to decide whether such limitations will cause you any difficulty given your intended use of the package. Other kinds of limitations may include the number of rows and/or columns a spreadsheet can work with or the numbers of fields a database manager can manage.

Since more sophisticated software packages tend to be the more expensive ones, figuring out in advance exactly what you are likely to need can save you money as well as difficulties.

HARDWARE

The item you purchase as "the computer" defines rather clearly the limits of what you will be able to do with it and what software it will be able to run. While most computers that could be used for small company applications are likely to be able to run software in each of the categories described, the features you expect to need in each should be your key criterion. In addition to being able to provide those key features, your hardware considerations should include at least the items discussed below.

Size

In computers, this generally refers to the storage capacity of the processing unit of the computer. As noted at the beginning of this appendix, it is usually stated in kilobytes (KB) or megabytes (megs). This matters in practice because storage capacity determines the amount of information that your computer will be able to work with at any given time. As implied earlier, many of the more sophisticated software packages require 192 or 256K of memory.

Most computers sold for business purposes today are at least 128K in capacity. Since 128K is not enough for many pieces of available software, you may want to add capacity to the base unit. Thus, whether the computer you are considering can be expanded to add memory may be a key factor. Most can accept expansion at relatively little cost and, if you are good at reading directions and wiring things, you can accomplish the expansion by yourself. (Be aware, however, that doing it yourself might void your warranty, a thing you definitely do not want to do. It could, therefore, be less expensive in the long run to let your authorized dealer do your expansions.)

Operating System

This is the internal programming that tells the computer how to handle instructions from your software or your programs. At present, there are two major operating systems in general use, MS-DOS and CP/M. While there is not complete compatibility across all versions of either system, there is *no* compatibility across systems. There are large numbers of software packages available to run on machines using either of these operating systems. New or other operating systems may limit your ability to run the applications you need.

Installed Base

The underlying issue here is continuing support for your computer and continuing development and support for the software you purchase or may want to purchase. As this very new field of microcomputers shakes itself out, many manufacturers will be forced to abandon the field. A number have already gotten out of certain segments of the computer market. Texas Instruments abandoned its low-end home computers. Coleco stopped making ADAM. Franklin is out of the field altogether. You do not want to have a machine whose manufacturer is no longer there to help you, to build expansions and/or extensions, and to encourage programmers to develop new applications software.

A large installed base signals that the manufacturer may be a winner in the computer market. More important from your perspective, however, is that a large installed base is likely to attract software manufacturers to your make and model of computer. It is also important that a large installed base means that there are lots of other users out there who will be able to help you if you have difficulties. There are probably established user groups, in fact, to which you can talk before you purchase and which you might join afterwards.

Beyond whether a particular computer will perform the applications you need, then, the key issue is its flexibility. The field of microcomputers is growing and changing so rapidly that it is unreasonable to say you will wait for the market to stabilize before you buy—assuming that you have decided that a computer could be of significant benefit to your business. Since that option is effectively closed, you want to be reasonably assured that what you buy today will be useful tomorrow, will be capable of some growth itself, and will have enough others who are concerned about it to make a difference.

SOME POTENTIAL DIFFICULTIES TO CONSIDER

Before you rush into automating your business, some planning is needed. To the extent that you are summarizing your records and committing them to the computer, your computer becomes a remarkably efficient vehicle for employee theft or disruption. If, for example, your inventory records and your payables records are on computer, it would be incredibly easy to simply alter a few numbers to increase them by corresponding amounts and have a check cut to a fictitious supplier. All your records would still agree among themselves. Your loss would probably not be caught until you did a physical inventory or you happened to look over a supplier list and notice this company you never heard of before. If your personnel records are on computer, adding a "new," nonexistent employee would be simple.

The point here is not that you should not automate, but rather that you should build in controls as you automate. Get an employee count every month, for example, and a listing of additions and deletions from staff. Couple that with a requirement that you personally sign an employee on or off payroll, and you will have gone a long way toward making it difficult to beat your payroll system. But understand that you are unlikely to be able to build a system that is impossible to beat. Major banks, credit agencies, government agencies, and universities have been unable to find an absolutely foolproof method of protecting against computer crime. The objective should be to make it difficult enough to discourage "casual" theft or manipulation of your data.

A second reason for discouraging free access to your company computer, and particularly to its data disks, is the disruption that could be caused by entering incorrect numbers, by altering existing numbers, or by deleting key items. None of this has to be done deliberately for the result to be highly disruptive. Consider the effect on our spreadsheet sample, for instance, if someone had inadvertently entered the growth rate for COGS as 9 percent instead of 12 percent. The bottom line would certainly look a great deal better. If you looked only at the projection for the fifth year (complete with compounded error), you might be overjoyed. If you based your expansion plans on the existence of a substantial profit, however, and if your original projection of 12 percent increase was correct, you would be riding for a major fall.

Here, too, there are ways to guard against, though not eliminate, this kind of problem. First, you might want to limit physical access to the computer. This may, however, be unrealistic for your operation. A second approach, and a practice that should be generally followed in any case, is to make backup copies of critical disks, keeping the copies updated and separate from the computer itself. Finally, whenever you are dealing with computer-generated reports, treat them as you would manual reports. Check the trends and the results for reasonableness. Try to build cross-checks into your systems so that errors are flagged. If something in a report seems unrealistic, unreasonable, or counterintuitive, check before you accept the conclusion. Someone (including yourself) may simply have mistyped a number or a direction to the computer.

SUMMARY

Microcomputers can be extremely useful in many smaller companies. They are not yet necessary to successful small company operations. If you are interested in automating parts of your operation, your first move should be to consider what functions you will want the computer to perform. Next, you should evaluate software packages available to perform the tasks you have outlined. Key considerations in this evaluation should include the flexibility and capabilities of the packages, the ease of use of the package in your operation, the specific features offered, and the previous record of the software package as described by actual users.

Only when you have seriously considered the software available to perform the functions you wish to automate should you begin to consider the specific make and model of computer and the peripheral equipment you will need. Key considerations in the hardware area, beyond the ability to run the software you want, should include the equipment's ability to accept expansions and additional peripherals should they be required later, and the installed base, indicating that there will be continuing interest in supporting and developing additional software for the machine.

As is true of any other business aspect, automating parts of your company requires planning. Centralized, automated records are easy and impersonal targets for theft and are subject to errors resulting in disruption and/or incorrect conclusions. Guarding against these potential problems consists of building computerized and manual checks into your monitoring and control systems, keeping current backup copies of key data disks separate from the computer area, and exercising good, old-fashioned common sense when evaluating data and conclusions.

INDEX

Notations following page numbers include *c* for case study; *f* for figure; and *t* for table.